Up Close and Personal in Third World Conflicts

by
Al J. Venter
and Friends

Protea Book House
Pretoria
2011

OTHER CONTRIBUTORS – IN ORDER OF APPEARANCE

AUBREY BROOKS AND GRAHAM LINSCOTT: Mike Hoare's Mercenary Invasion of the Seychelles; JIM MAGUIRE: Mission Impossible – On the Run across Southern Africa; PETER YOUNGHUSBAND: Zanzibar's Bloody Revolt; ROBERT DOSS: America's Secret Mission in Somalia; GRAHAM GILMORE: Angolan Skirmish with South Africa's 44 Parachute Brigade; PAUL ELS: SWAPO's First Attacks in South West Africa; MARK CORCORAN: Gunship for Hire; WILLEM STEENKAMP: Reporting on South Africa's Border War; HANNES WESSELS: "The Incredibles" – The Rhodesian Light Infantry; GREG LOVETT: An American Soldier of Fortune in Iraq and BRIAN ROBINSON: Rhodesia's Bush War with the SAS

For my lovely Caroline

Here's to again walking our beautiful Surrey Hills

BOOKS BY THE SAME AUTHOR INCLUDE:

Report on Portugal's War in Guiné-Bissau
Underwater Africa
Under the Indian Ocean
Africa At War
The Zambezi Salient
Coloured: Profile of Two Million South Africans
Africa Today
South African Handbook for Divers
Challenge: South Africa in the African Revolutionary Context
Underwater Mauritius
Where to Dive: In Southern Africa and Off the Islands
War in Angola
The Chopper Boys: Helicopter Warfare in Africa
The Iraqi War Debrief: Why Saddam Hussein Was Toppled
War Dog: Fighting Other Peoples' Wars
Iran's Nuclear Option
Allah's Bomb: The Islamic Quest for Nuclear Weapons
Cops: Cheating Death: How One Man Saved the Lives of 3,000 Americans
How South Africa Built Six Atom Bombs
Dive South Africa/Duik Suid Afrika
Barrel of a Gun: A War Correspondent's Misspent Moments in Combat

War Stories by Al J. Venter and Friends – Al J. Venter
First edition, first impression in 2011 by Protea Book House

PO Box 35110, Menlo Park, 0102
1067 Burnett Street, Hatfield, Pretoria
8 Minni Street, Clydesdale, Pretoria
protea@intekom.co.za
www.proteaboekhuis.com

Editor: Danél Hanekom
Cover design: Bruce Gonneau
Front and back cover images: Al J. Venter
Typography: Zapf Calligraphic, 10.5 pt by Bruce Gonneau
Printed and bound: Creda, Cape Town

© 2011 Al J. Venter
ISBN 978-1-86919-410-9

All rights reserved. No part of this book may be reproduced or transmitted in any form or by any electronic or mechanical means, including photocopying and recording, or by any other information storage or retrieval system, without written permission from the publisher.

CONTENTS

	PAGE
Foreword by James Penrith	1
Introduction – Back to Africa	14

CHAPTER

1	Into Angola With Charlie Company	29
2	Seychelles Mercenary Invasion: Mike Hoare and Associates	57
3	Operation Impossible – On the Run Across Southern Africa	75
4	Wartime Hunting in Africa	92
5	Africa's Backyard Firearms Factories	106
6	Zanzibar's Bloody Revolt	117
7	America's Secret Rescue Mission in Somalia	137
8	Somalia: Still burning	145
9	Angolan Skirmish with 44 Parachute Brigade	159
10	Ron Reid-Daly – A Tribute to the Man and his Scouts	179
11	Living on the Edge in Beirut	206
12	SWAPO'S First Attacks in South West Africa	221
13	Waiting in the Ground in Kosovo for the Deminers	241
14	Gunship for Hire: Sierra Leone (August 2000)	248
15	Portugal's Wars in Africa	258
16	Death of a Guerrilla Fighter	273
17	The War in Portuguese Guinea	282
18	Jungle Patrol	296
19	In the Heart of an African Military Struggle	312

CONTENTS contd.

20	Six Soviet Choppers Ambushed in Angola	326
21	Willem Steenkamp – Reporting on South Africa's Border Wars	339
22	"The Incredibles": The Rhodesian Light Infantry	360
23	Surviving Africa	381
24	An American Hostage of Hizbollah	402
25	Greg Lovett – An American Soldier of Fortune in Iraq	422
26	Freetown: Diamonds, a Civil War and Amputees	439
27	Into the Bush War with the Rhodesian SAS	457
28	Air Wing in Africa's Mountain Kingdom	479
Abbreviations		487
Acknowledgements		491
Index		494

Foreword by James Penrith
Author, travel writer and former Nairobi Bureau Chief, Argus Africa News Service

Wars are not what they used to be – well, certainly not in the geographical area once known as "The Dark Continent".

In my heyday as a foreign correspondent, newly independent countries in Africa were emerging virtually by the month, invariably followed by coups, rebellions and bloody conflagrations that all too often became full-blown wars. Even at that point in the 20th Century, a leading American news magazine was moved to note that one black state being profiled was "poised to leap into the Middle Ages".

Amazingly, most hacks drafted in to cover these troubles for their newspapers and magazines in Europe and the Americas during the decade that began in the mid-1960s with the implosion of the former Belgian Congo, emerged from their stints unscathed. In those far-off days – before the AK-47 had become the ubiquitous killing weapon of choice – many belligerents still believed that guns had to be fired into the air above the enemy so that bullets would rain down in an arc, like the more usual thrown spear. This might help to account for the fact that I can recall only three fatalities among the press corps during that era, two of them in the Congo and Priya Ramrakha in Biafra.

The rebels often relied on their own magical concoctions to protect themselves from harm in battle, sometimes by throwing small handfuls of dust in the air as they advanced into the fray. They believed the gesture would render them both invisible to the enemy and turn bullets to water.

Journalists arriving fresh were not much comforted by these stories from some of the older hands and in one memorable press briefing a nervous young greenhorn asked whether there was any danger of his being shot while out with a mercenary patrol.

"Only if your name is on the bullet", was the laconic assurance.

"What worries me," interjected a seasoned news-gatherer, "is the bullet that says: 'To Whom It May Concern'."

It was also an era when contingents of war correspondents were known as a "Flush of WCs", echoing the witty collective noun first coined by Ernest Hemingway during his European war years. Truth is, many of these ink-stained scribblers – usually from the red-tops

– were more at home covering local courts, chasing ambulances and doing police and fire station calls for their respective tabloid newspapers than dodging bullets, bad-tempered wildlife and voracious mosquitoes. They seemed to prefer filing colourful mailers in Rider Haggard mode, painting emergent Africa in lurid tones, which would have been more familiar to the readers of "penny dreadfuls" during Queen Victoria's reign. Lulls in activity at the Sharp End sometimes saw journalists honing pieces such as "I Escaped from the Valley of the Screaming Orchids", or "In the Clutches of the Cannibal King".

At a time when gambling on Britain's football pools was becoming popular in sub-Saharan Africa, one ingenious correspondent dreamt up a piece for his readers which began, "Under a dry, twisted mopani tree, I watched a gnarled old witchdoctor casting the bones that foretold the future and heard him chant: 'Manchester United three, Tottenham Hotspurs nil...'"

My own baptism of fire came in June 1960, when the Belgian Congo, abandoned as a totally unprepared, newly independent state by the hasty exodus of Belgium's *colons* took fire. It eventually became the blaze that still scorches much of Central Africa to this day.

Civilians lying dead in the streets of Stanleyville after the Simbas had rampaged the city. (Photo: Author's collection)

Forward
James Penrith

I spent my childhood in England during World War II and was accustomed to the sound of falling bombs and heavy anti-aircraft fire. But the slightly ridiculous popping sound of small-arms fire was a new experience as I stood on a dusty road in the southern Congo province of Katanga, watching what seemed to be a never-ending convoy of vehicles full of white refugees fleeing from the provincial capital Elizabethville (Lubumbashi today) for the safety of the Northern Rhodesian Copperbelt.

They had left a smouldering city and its environs in the grip of mayhem. The popping noises I heard, were riddling vehicles all along the line, leaving men, women and children dead or dying, with no hope of help.

From that momentous June day until the end of the decade, I was in and out of various regional trouble spots in the Congo to chronicle an appalling toll as tribes, political parties and factions sought to annihilate one another for the control of one of Africa's richest countries. They fought with the support and connivance of either the National Congolese Army (ANC) or a growing force of white mercenary soldiers, most of them from South Africa.

In-between these periodic visits, I made many similar excursions from my Nairobi bureau base to other turbulent states, my bailiwick being the whole of Black Africa from Egypt down to Zambia and all the way across to West Africa, all of which I covered for the Johannesburg-based Argus Africa News Service.

In November 1964 came an episode when the Western world was gripped by a drama unfolding in the north-eastern Congo, where Simba rebels had stormed through the region, murdering, raping and pillaging. Holed up in the provincial capital of Stanleyville (Kisangani), they held hundreds of Europeans captive. Among them was the American medical missionary Dr Paul Carlson.

Washington was intent on a rescue mission and joined forces with Belgium in a bid to mount it before it was too late. As soon as I heard through the grapevine that the date had been set for Belgian paratroopers to drop into Stanleyville and link up with two columns of mercenary-led forces racing there from the south, I chartered a small plane in Nairobi and headed for the beleaguered city. I touched down at Stanleyville airport while Belgian paratroopers were still shooting it out with Simba rebels around the runway and in the city. Bodies lay everywhere.

In the suburbs, ferocious emaciated dogs were already devouring the dead. Establishing that Dr Carlson and 30 or so other white captives were being held by the Simbas at the local Hotel Victoria,

I made a beeline for the place, but by the time I arrived, the rebels had gone.

In the courtyard lay a tangled sprawl of dead men, women and children. On top of the mound of bodies, barely recognisable, was the machine-gunned body of Dr Carlson. The massive air rescue mission had arrived too late. A local told me that even as the Paras were dropping on the city, rebel-controlled Radio Stanleyville was calling on "all true Congolese" to kill every white man, woman and child they could find.

Meantime, back at the airport, European soldiers and their mercenary compatriots were bent on vengeance. I watched as a small Congolese boy led a group of Belgian troops through a large hangar, crowded with suspected rebels. The boy would point at a sullen prisoner and say, "Simba" and the man would be dragged away and quickly executed outside with a bullet in the head after being taunted with the words, "Simba (lion) *non*, macaque (monkey) *oui*!"

When I remarked on the meting out of such summary justice to Colonel Robert Lamouline, the officer commanding one of the rescue columns from Kindu, he replied: "Do not waste your tears on these rebels. They are getting what they deserve." On their way here the Simba rebels have murdered and mutilated without mercy. They have killed many missionary priests and nuns, the very people here

While in Nairobi as Argus Africa News Service Bureau Chief, Jim Penrith was constantly involved with the Shifta problem in Kenya's Northern Frontier District. Here, just across the border in Somalia he jokes with a senior Somali politician and a bunch of Shiftas "who were not asupposed to be there", as Mogadishu constantly claimed. Not very much has changed in the past 40 years.
(Photo: James Penrith)

to help the Congolese. The priests were shot or hacked to death. The nuns they tied up and laid out like logs, before slowly beating them to death with beer bottles, the majority already raped and quite a few killed.

In some areas they lined up captured Europeans in public squares and carved off slices of flesh from them, which they then ate. According to the colonel, the rebels regarded the flesh cut from the inside of the upper arms and the inner thighs of their victims as the choicest bits.

Then, while I was in the town of Bukavu, in the Congo's Kivu Province, in August 1967, I had my own close call.

I was the only foreign correspondent there to watch from the banks of Lake Kivu's Rwanda shore as "Black Jack" Jeanne Schramme's mercenary flying column – under the fluttering old flag of secessionist Katanga – drove the ANC garrison out of Bukavu and took possession of the town. The ANC soldiers fled across the tiny border bridge into Shangugu, dumping their uniforms, helmets, weapons and insignia into the lake as they crossed into Rwanda. My account is all rather graphically described in Chapter 8 of Al Venter's *War Dog*, published some years ago[1].

I followed that gutsy bunch of mercenaries into town, which by then had become eerily quiet, and after interviewing the illustrious Schramme over a glass of looted *vin rouge*, I settled into a deserted premier-class hotel and hunkered down to await developments. While waiting, I opened up the kitchen and the wine cellars and whipped up a few delightful gourmet meals. Background music was the resounding crump of explosives announcing that mercenaries were making "withdrawals" from a local bank.

My lonely vigil was broken the following day when I was joined by an Italian cameraman. After sharing a satisfying *omelette aux fruits de mer* and a fortifying *marc*, I left him at the hotel while I nipped back across the border into Shangugu to ship my film back to the Fleet Street office of my news service. When I returned to the hotel a few hours later, I found the cameraman lying dead on the kitchen floor. He had been shot through the heart.

Driving through the wilds of Rwanda on my way back to Nairobi a few days later, I attempted to avoid military and rebel roadblocks along the way by opting to skirt the Congo. My plan was to take a little-used border road. Rounding a bend late that first afternoon, I was thrilled to see an enormous silverback gorilla high up in a roadside tree. As I jumped out of the car for a closer look at such a rare primate, this great, gentle beast crashed down through the branches and vanished into a thicket. I rather foolishly threw a rock into the bushes in the hope of startling the silverback so that I could get a closer look at him. I was not disappointed.

There was a dull thud as the missile hit the animal, which suddenly completely filled the frame of my Leica as it roared and charged up the incline towards me. I have never moved so fast in my life, either before or since. I was back in the car in a flash that Superman would have envied and left the gorilla in a cloud of dust.

My self-congratulation was short-lived. As I was admiring the sight of the sun setting over the endless forests of the Congo, a dreaded roadblock loomed in the road ahead. The position was manned by a rag-tag group of soldiers dressed in oddments of camouflage, and it was clear even before we stopped the car that they were all totally smashed. My heart sank as their leader, a huge man that reminded me strangely of my encounter with the silverback, poked his AK-47 through my window and said something in a language I didn't recognise.

I replied in Swahili and then in French. But his only response was to thrust the barrel of his weapon into my ribs, leaving an oily black mark on my bush jacket that remains to this day.

He then said something to his compatriots, which I gathered ran something along the lines of, "Leave this one to me. I'll speak to him in English." He removed the gun from my ribcage, stuck his enormous head through the window and with an equally enormous and engaging smile said to me: "Good evening darling."

After his *compadres* had applauded this linguistic triumph, they shepherded me to their bush camp and throughout the night, I discovered that the more the *pombe* flowed in industrial quantities, the more their formerly incomprehensible patois became comprehensible.

Closer to my Nairobi base during the 1960s, President Jomo *"Mzee"* Kenyatta's newly formed post-independence government was fighting its own relentless but little-publicised battle with the Somali Shifta, another group of rebels, like many Congolese malcontents, that simply refused to go away.

Then, as now, their cross-border incursions into neighbouring Kenya's arid Northern Frontier District (NFD) threatened to escalate into a war of secession.

This still undeclared conflict began shortly after Kenya gained its independence in December 1963, and went on for another five difficult years for the fledgling East African government. Although

Though very much in "Shifta territory" and not officially acknowledged by Mogadishu, it seemed odd to Penrith that the plane that brought the minister to the Kenya frontier area had Somali Police markings. (Photo: James Penrith)

Kenyatta downplayed the problem as simple brigandage, the Shifta, we were soon to discover, were actually members of the Somali government-backed NFD Liberation Movement. The majority comprised small groups of tough, Hamitic nomads who traditionally acted as militia in the otherwise lawless desert and mountain regions in the Horn of Africa, much of it lying beyond Mogadishu's direct control.

They were also politically motivated, remarkably well organised and dedicated to the geographical and ethnic reunion of the five constituent parts of a "Greater Somalia": this included the former British-controlled northern corner of the country, French Somalia (Djibouti today), great chunks of disputed territory in neighbouring Ethiopia (over which there has been at least one major war involving the Soviets), as well as Kenya's entire Northern Frontier District.

The Kenyan desert region fringes along almost its entire 800 kilometre frontier with Somalia and was the flashpoint in the struggle. Consequently, the Nairobi government enforced tight restrictions on travel to and within the NFD. I managed to circumvent these impediments by approaching the area through the Gedo region of Somalia, with the discreet blessing of the Somali authorities.

Mogadishu could not have been more helpful, so much so that in spite of constant official denials of any links with the Shifta, I was flown from the Somali capital in a police Cessna light aircraft to a large rebel encampment on the border that faced the NFD settlement of El Wak. After a gourd of millet porridge and a mug of camel milk, I was escorted to the frontier by a band of heavily armed Shifta and watched as they danced within sight of the Kenyan outpost and shouted: "Death to Kenyatta", all the while waving weapons recently brought into the country from the Soviet Union.

It was not until I left East Africa and the Argus Africa News Service that I discovered that while editorial colleagues had been tracking my movements and misadventures through some of the stories I filed through our Fleet Street office, the people who handled our accounts – in the jargon of us scribes, the "bean counters" – had likewise been following closely my peregrinations with a more jaundiced eye. They'd scrutinised every one of my expenses claims.

One cornered me at my farewell party to enquire how, for instance, my Leica came to be damaged by a spear and why I had been obliged to hire a war canoe on Lake Victoria.

Simple, I replied, refilling my glass from a nearby carafe. In May 1966, the Cambridge-educated Kabaka (King) of Buganda, the oldest, largest and richest of Uganda's five ancient kingdoms, fled from the smoking ruins of his royal palace on one of Kampala's seven hills after President Apollo Milton Obote unleashed his soldiers on the ruler and his subjects in what became known as "The Battle of Mengo Hill".

The army officer chosen by Obote to close his power struggle with the Kabaka was a certain Idi Amin, by then promoted from sergeant to general.

What most people in Africa, Europe and Africa did not realise was that the Buganda Kingdom encompassed a royal dynasty that went back to the 14th Century. It came to an abrupt and inglorious end when the man popularly known as "King Freddie" died.

I knew that earlier Kabakas had always sited their royal compounds close to Lake Victoria and it was done with a purpose: so that they could easily escape among the nearby islands in the event of rebellion or invasion. As Obote's thugs scoured the surrounding country for the missing King Freddie, it seemed logical to me that the Kabaka would probably emulate his ancestors and hide out on one of the islands. So I hired the war canoe that was to become the subject of an inquiry on the part of the Argus Company's accounts department.

My first objective was to search nearby Ssese Island, which I'd learned had once been used as a place of refuge by one of Freddie's earliest forebears, King Kato Kintu. He'd laid low there after a particularly ferocious internecine struggle. But if Freddie was out there on the lake, I never found him. Nor would the fiercely loyal Baganda divulge a clue as to his whereabouts.

Poor Freddie. He died three years later in suspicious circumstances, a lonely and penniless exile in a London council flat, just 45 years old.

The old kingdoms of Uganda have since been restored by President Yoweri Museveni and King Freddie's son, Ronald, became the 37th Kabaka of Buganda in 1993 to rule a people collectively called the Baganda (a single member of the tribe being called a Mugunda). The language they speak is Luganda, and they embrace a culture known as Kiganda. Uganda itself is Swahili for the "land of the Ganda".

Ah yes, the spear. During a visit to Uganda in 1965, I chanced to hear that another local Cambridge-educated royal, the lovely Princess Elizabeth of Toro was soon to celebrate her elevation to Princess Royal following the death of her father, King George Kamurasi. She would also possibly celebrate her 21st birthday, having no officially agreed birth date. The festivities took place at the palace in Kabalole, capital of the remote little kingdom of Toro, in Uganda's far and wild west.

Princess Elizabeth Bagaya Nyabongo was already a renowned beauty. Her mesmerising good looks would later see her gracing the covers of just about every international magazine of note, including *Life*, *Harper's Bazaar* and *Time*. At the same time she would be launched on a career as a film star, a supermodel, an actress and eventually, a diplomat.

Meanwhile, I quietly gate-crashed the royal celebrations in Toro. The press of jostling tribesmen and women in the tiny royal palace was overwhelming and just as the princess was graciously posing on the stairs for me, an overexcited retainer smacked my Leica camera with the haft of his spear. I wasn't aware of it at the time, but this sharp blow had knocked my focus mechanism out of kilter and consequently I had no worthwhile pictures of this historic occasion. Indeed, I wound up with a fairly hefty repair bill, the kind of expense that was almost certain to raise eyebrows back home.

As well as her subsequent fame as a model and actress in Europe and America, the illustrious Princess Elizabeth gained a measure of notoriety in 1974, and even succeeded in adding a satirical phrase to the journalistic lexicon while working as a Ugandan envoy.

During Idi Amin's unfortunate presidency, he was incensed by reports that the Princess had been discovered by the paparazzi *in flagrante* with an unknown man in a Paris toilet while in Europe on an official diplomatic mission. The British satirical magazine *Private Eye* gleefully seized on this royal peccadillo and coined the phrase "Ugandan Discussions" as a euphemism for anyone enjoying illicit sex while on official business.

SCUD B missile captured in Iraq and taken to the United States for examination. These weapons were decidedly primitive when compared to contemporary missiles, still reflecting World War II technical expertise. (Photo: Author)

An Angolan Air Force Mi-8 shot down by UNITA rebel forces with an American Stinger missile. (Photo: Author's collection)

Almost all the armour used by the South Lebanese Army against Islamic radicals came from Israel, including this APC used by mercenary troops around Marj'Ayoun. (Photo: Dave McGrady)

Business end of an American helicopter gunship deployed in Somalia during "Operation Restore Hope". (Photo: Author)

Royal Air Force Chinook helicopter air-lifting supplies into the jungles of Sierra Leone during the civil war. (Photo: Author's collection)

INTRODUCTION
Back to Africa

Working in Africa in those uncertain times after the chimerical independence of most of the black states was a lot less difficult than some journalists would have liked, or possibly would have their editors believe. For some it was rather a cushy number. I would come back to base after traipsing round West Africa, or having spent a week or two in Uganda and Tanzania, and my friends would be amazed at my recklessness. I rarely disabused them.

They thought it was all rather dangerous and exciting. "Just imagine it," they would say, "all those unwashed, uneducated, violent people... those unending revolutions. You'll catch it one of these days!" I would never contradict them, in part because I'd gained a marvellous measure of independence and the kind of confidence – both flamboyant and insouciant – that was all a part of it.

Although life in countries such as Liberia, Ghana, Rwanda and Libya could be rough, we generally did our thing and acted much as we might do elsewhere. Obviously there were moments when you could be at the wrong place at the wrong time, but that was a rare occurrence. We got our stories out and that was what really mattered. Also, the money was good.

Of course, Africa had some spectacular moments. After the first full-scale revolution in Togo on 13 January 1963 – when President Sylvanus Olympio was assassinated at the order of the *Osajyefo* Kwame Nkrumah – the event became something of a political template and many other black rulers were overthrown, often in rapid succession. Almost half a century later there are few countries in Africa where there had not been at least one revolt or *coup de main*, usually by the army and here South Africa and Botswana remain among the most remarkable exceptions.

Although there are a handful of other countries that have never experienced a military putsch, once an army takeover happens, more are certain to follow. Some countries, such as Sierra Leone, the Central African Republic, Uganda, the Sudan or Congo-Brazzaville, have had three, or four or eight or more. There were also some nasty civil wars and in a few of these states, carnage continues.

It was our business as foreign correspondents to report on all these insurgencies. Indeed, we sometimes did find ourselves in awkward situations, but not all that often. When we talked about it later, it was obviously with some retrospective pleasure that we managed to emerge intact.

There were several good reasons why I enjoyed working north of the Zambezi. I lived in Nigeria on and off for almost a year and cumulatively spent even longer in Nairobi, meandering along the Kenyan and Tanzanian coasts, usually with scuba gear in one of my bags.

First, there were few journalists doing such work. Second, I was getting paid for it. For me it had started without the benefit of even a month or two in the newsroom. I had to learn my job on the hoof, as it were. At the same time, I was lucky: I had some excellent people showing me the ropes, all journalists and writers who had been through the mill. Most were quite happy to let me get on with the dog work, as long as an acceptable and reasonably verifiable quantity of copy resulted. By then Peter Younghusband had added *Newsweek* to the London *Daily Mail* as part of his regular writing schedule and for a short while, I was the other half of his little team in Cape Town, which included writing for the *Sunday Express*.

African soldier deployed in the South Angolan bush. (Photo: Author)

"Fingers" van der Merwe was another remarkable character from that time. It was decades before cellphones and e-mails, the kind of progress that a handful of Americans were then only dreaming about. So we used the telex machine for our dispatches – except those that were phoned through direct – and "Fingers", bless his heart, had his telex office right next door. If we needed him at three in the morning, or all of a Saturday or a Sunday (or both) and sometimes without a break, "Fingers" would be there.

When Peter was somewhere in Africa, or perhaps covering Beirut or the war in Vietnam, I'd process copy to the ten or so newspapers and agencies that we covered or had strings for. That included London's *Daily Mail*, the BBC, *Newsweek*, UPI and a bunch of others. He'd do the same for me when I was out of town.

In *Banana Sunday*, Chris Munnion's remarkable book about reporting in Africa, he called many of the journalists who covered the continent in those turbulent days "Genuine Old Africa Hands", or as he liked to refer to the spunky little band of professionals, GOAHs. Indeed, our associates were a colourful bunch.

After I'd added the BBC string to my belt, I'd come to answer to Angus McDermid, a plump, carroty little Welshman who, among ourselves, we would call "Anguish". He was apt to get the vapours when things got tough, and in Africa that was often.

As Munnion would say, Angus had two vital qualities as a foreign correspondent: a sense of humour – which helped when you crossed borders manned by trigger-happy soldiers, usually drunk or doped or both – and the ability to tackle a problem head-on. McDermid was also blessed with the panache to tell a government functionary that he was talking crap in such a disarming way that the object of his vituperation actually believed he was being paid a compliment. We all tried it at some time or another, but few could succeed like Angus.

Don Wise, the eternally sanguine correspondent from the *Daily Mirror* possibly came closest to it: after listening to a Congolese general sprout drivel, he once suggested that somebody give the man a banana.

The military airport at the diamond city of Saurimo in Eastern Angola hosted various Angolan Air Force units, many of them flown by South African mercenary pilots working for Executive Outcomes. (Photo: Author)

In truth, those African governments with whom we were dealing – and frankly, not much has changed in the interim – were always doing their best to conceal, obfuscate or distort facts, or to see us tiresome busybodies off the premises, or preferably, right out of the country. To most of these sometimes lethal tin-pot despots, we were trouble.

An unflattering story in a British or American publication could make difficulties for power-hungry black demagogues, especially when they noted the disappearance of money from foreign "aid". Or some former crony's body was dragged out of the river. Amnesty International was not yet fully into its stride.

It was McDermid who convinced our old friend Chris Munnion, who died suddenly in 2010, that working in Africa could be a gas.

We all had our favourite stories, moments that sometimes seemed likely to be our last, when we'd double up in a strange mixture of horror and hilarity. In some respects, there was a "Boy's Own" heroics about it all.

Like the time, after having spent a week diving off Zanzibar island, when I tried to explain to a Tanzanian immigration officer at a remote crossing on the Zambian frontier that the scuba tank in my trunk wasn't a bomb. To the uninitiated, it probably looked like one; it was round, it was made of steel, it was elongated and all that. Who knew what it might have contained…? I was then obliged to go to great lengths to explain to this very sceptical officer with a pistol on his belt, that you strapped the device on your back in order to breathe underwater. His eyes rolled.

Scuba-diving in those faraway days was still a pretty novel affair, especially in Africa. To some primitives, it was regarded as something akin to moon probes … and as I was to discover for myself on a visit to Somalia shortly after Armstrong had taken his first giant step for mankind, there was some doubt about that as well. In Mogadishu, the Mullahs would argue with American Embassy staff that the pictures of the lunar surface could just as easily have been taken somewhere north of the Somali capital. It was a rather similar kind of terrain and, of course, they were right.

There were other experiences. I once tried to take explosives on board an Israeli passenger aircraft, which sounds a lot worse than it was, but I know of no other journalist to have actually succeeded. The event always made for some unusual post-prandial chatter.

One of my friends in Namibia, Colonel Des Radmore, collected the head-stamps of Soviet ammunition, particularly AK-47. It was an unusual interest and word had it that he possessed one of the biggest private Kalashnikov head-stamp collections in the world. He'd heard that I was going to Lebanon and asked that I get him a few "samples", specifically with Arabic markings.

I flew from Johannesburg to Israel and from there to Larnaca in Cyprus. Beirut, in those days, had already become the proverbial killing ground.

While in Lebanon, I acquired a dozen AK-47 rounds, some Syrian, others Iraqi and a few of obscure origin. It seemed that they were no different from run-of-the-mill Bulgarian, Russian or East German rounds that the South African forces in Angola were picking up, but Des believed otherwise.

In Beirut, I promptly shoved the ammunition into a side pocket of my overnight bag and went back to Cyprus by boat. Middle East Airlines in Lebanon had suspended all flights because of the civil war. Only after I'd been standing in line at Larnaca Airport on my way back to Tel Aviv did I see ahead of me two or three Israelis going through the process of thoroughly frisking passengers and their luggage. Cyprus airport had no X-ray equipment in those days.

There was no question that the security officials knew what they were looking for. Also, they were as meticulous as only Israeli airline personnel can be, because the danger of an Arab terrorist attack in those days was real. Not very long before, the Palestinian Al Fatah

Gunner's eye-view of the African jungle from a Russian-built Mi-8 helicopter. (Photo: Author)

The civil war in Lebanon offered military correspondents marvellous opportunities. Al Venter spent long stretches with elements of the South Lebanese Army in the south of the country. (Photo: Author)

movement had blown up three Western passenger aircraft on the ground at Dawson's Field in Jordan.

I am not altogether sure how, with a bag of live ammunition in my luggage, I managed to talk my way past those women, but I did. And having done so once, I did it again a week later when I boarded another El Al flight for home. I think what inspired me was the knowledge that if they found the ammunition, they'd arrest me and I would almost certainly miss my flight. But in the end, I just knew I'd be able to prove that I meant no harm. Besides, I was a military correspondent already very well known to the Israeli authorities since I'd worked with the IDF on several fronts, Beirut included.

I'd never try such stupidity today, certainly not with the level of international terrorism that we're all experiencing and the looming spectre of al-Qaeda just about everywhere. I'd probably do time if I was caught, though only a few years ago, in 2006, I did get hauled in by Homeland Security in the United States for "running guns" across the border from Canada to the Detroit side of the bridge. That took several hours and quite a few calls to Washington to sort out, but in the end I wasn't arrested or charged.

It was annoying that they confiscated both firearms – a Colt 45 ACP pistol and a 12-gauge Remington-870 pump shotgun – together with a hefty load of ammunition.

I think the most telling occasion was during the Angolan War when I was standing on top of an armoured personnel carrier, or in the lingo, an APC. It was Operation Daisy, and we were threading our way out of a minefield after five other vehicles around us, including a fuel tanker, had taken hits and detonated a series of Soviet TM-57 anti-tank mines. Mines seemed to have been laid everywhere by the guerrillas, including under my own APC – a command Ratel that was hurled a metre into the air by the blast. Just then, I had been standing on the turret and once the dust had settled, I found myself some distance away with a broken arm.

At the time I was making a TV documentary for the SABC on the "Border War" and in my next "piece to camera" I had my arm in plaster. The film was called *The Last Domino* and interestingly, it can still be viewed on *YouTube*.

Over the years there were several incidents involving landmines, some of them fatal.

At one stage, during that same Operation Daisy, I followed some crude steps cut into the entrance of an underground bunker in the enemy base that we'd taken after a three-day slog across South Angola: our armoured column was miles long. It was a stupid move going in there, if only because we'd been warned about booby traps. The youngster that followed me a minute or two after I'd emerged back into the sunlight, tripped a PMN anti-personnel mine. Since we had to bend down almost double to get inside, the young soldier took the blast full in the face and was killed.

More recently, in Croatia with Richard Davis, on whom I based my book *Cops: Cheating Death* (because Richard had originally invented concealable body armour which every law enforcer in the United States wears these days)[2], we found ourselves in the middle of a minefield with a bunch of mine-clearing engineers. Richard was looking at using the Kevlar that he employed in his "vests" to

South African soldier in one of the border camps during the war. (Photo: Author)

devise a new anti-blast system which ostensibly would avoid mine-clearers taking it in the face. None of it was dramatic, but that time, alongside the main rail link to the north, which had not yet been cleared, we both had to gingerly feel our way out of it because again, there were anti-tank mines peppered with APs all over the place.

Probably the most stupid incident involving landmines in which I was involved, took place while I was with the South African mercenary group Executive Outcomes on which the film *Blood Diamond* is based. We'd been checking some alluvial diggings along a remote, diamondiferous waterway near Saurimo, Angola's "diamond city" in the extreme east of the country.

Border war: South African troops prepare for an ambush adjacent to the cutline immediately south of Angola. (Photo: Author)

I'd wandered off to take some photos of a pontoon over a river: the only bridge for hundreds of kilometres. The next thing I knew was that the Angolan colonel leading our group rushed wide-eyed towards me and started screaming something about the bridge having been mined. It took a while, but I emerged from that predicament by jumping from one rock to another and reflected afterwards that it was perhaps a bit silly of me to go off on my own in an area where hostilities could sometimes be quite intense.

On a totally different tack, Paul Moorcraft, with a string of books to his name, also has a few stories to relate. Paul was one of the "faces" I sometimes used to present television documentaries that I'd been commissioned to produce in countries like Morocco, the Ivory Coast, Ghana and elsewhere.

The most significant of these episodes was probably the one-hour documentary I made on the war in Afghanistan: its purpose, completed under the auspices of the CIA, was to commemorate the fifth anniversary of Moscow's invasion of this vast Central Asian

Several units that served on the Angolan border fielded unusual weaponry, including bike-mounted FNs. These combat-ready motorcycles were able to extend the range of bush operations ten-fold under the right conditions. (Photo: Author)

country and something that I deal with more comprehensively in *Barrel of a Gun*[3].

Paul and the rest of the crew had several tight moments, but as he says, the closest he came to being fried was a helicopter gunship attack. He takes up the story:

> The mountains that encircled Kabul are savage, beautiful, and often treacherous – like the people who inhabit them. Death had stalked their valleys for five years in the form of Soviet Mi-24 helicopter gunships.
>
> Those flying tanks were exquisitely armed: a 12,7 mm cannon protruded from the nose, and the stub wings carried bombs and rockets. At first I wasn't too worried about them, as they had been swashbuckling across the clear Afghan skies for days, ignoring us as eagles scorn flies. The mountains seemed to provide protection: the guerrillas were blasé, and I too had become complacent.

Introduction
Back to Africa

That complacency was shattered early on the morning of 21 July 1984 when the gunships called. The Russians had launched a concerted offensive to clear the mujahideen rebels from their positions around the capital. I was dozing in a mud hut, along with the rest of our five-man film team, when someone shouted urgently "Choppers!"

Two sleek Mi-24 Hind helicopters were hovering above our position like expectant vultures. Our cameraman, Chris Everson, rushed to set up the equipment to film them. Our "Captain", a richly-moustachioed Afghan officer who had defected to the mujahideen screamed at us to take cover. He knew what was coming. We grabbed our heavy rucksacks together with some of the bulky film equipment. Doc, our translator shouted: "Put your equipment in the cave." We hastily shoved our kit away as the five-bladed helicopters drew closer.

"Take cover in there," Doc ordered nervously.

The tiny exposed cave was full of ammunition – it seemed suicidal to hide there if high-explosive bombs started to crash down on us, so Chris and I ran into a small gully. There was no other cover on the stark hillside except a few trees and three decrepit mud huts about 100 metres away. As the only buildings in the area, they would presumably be prime targets for the gunships' rockets. Crouching in the gully, we realised it was used as a latrine, but we didn't dare move. Better shit than shrapnel.

Worse, I had broken a golden rule about never sharing a foxhole with anyone braver than me. Chris had seen far more action than me during the Rhodesian war.

Four sleek MiG-23 aircraft arrived, performed a high-altitude turn above the valley and then swooped down and started to bomb the valley floor half a mile from where we were crouched. Then two more MiGs joined the party. Framed against the cloudless sky, their deadly grace was almost bewitching.

The helicopters dropped altitude and hovered just above us. A guerrilla opened up with a DshKa anti-aircraft gun. If by some miracle the Hinds hadn't seen us before, they could hardly ignore us now.

Pointlessly, I shouted, "Shut up!"

He was only 60 yards away but he couldn't have heard me above the gunfire, even if he had spoken English. In vain, I ransacked my severely limited Pushtu vocabulary for a translation.

The MiGs blasted away. As they came out of their bombing runs they sometimes shot out anti-heat-seeking missile flares, which left a mosaic of cloud patterns against the deep blue sky. Chris was cursing like a banshee. Action all around, and from our gully we could not film properly.

"Bend over," he shouted.

"Is this some last perverted wish, Chris?" I asked, with more bravado in my voice than I felt.

"No, you fool, I haven't got the tripod. Bend over and kiss your arse goodbye."

"You forget the tripod, I'm likely to have my face full of crap and my backside napalmed. Great holiday!"

Chris laughed. "If it was easy everybody would be doing it."

I bent over, nose into the shit, and Chris put the camera vertically on my back to film the gunships right above us. What a way to go, I thought, acting the human tripod as we filmed – in full colour – our own demise. Each long minute had an acute intensity, a strange purification. Despite the fear, a kind of unreality also intruded. I felt I was the subject, and also the observer, of a surreal Fellini movie. Above all, I pondered the psychological role reversal acted out by our film crew. We had seen lots of war recently in southern Africa. The other four members of the TV crew – including Tim Lambon, until recently deputy news editor with Channel Four in London – had all been soldiers before becoming film-makers, veterans of conflicts in Rhodesia, Angola, Namibia, and Mozambique. I had covered these wars as a journalist and had often flown in helicopters, chasing or filming black insurgents on the ground.

Right now, the tables were turned. We were indistinguishable from our scruffy companions. We, too, were dirty, smelly, frightened guerrillas, caught in the open by government gunships. After years of being on the "other side" – the mechanised, "death-from-the-air", safe side – the hunters had become the hunted. I understood a lot about Africa in those few Afghan minutes.

Mujahideen tracers flecked past the heavily armoured gunships as they dropped closer, seeming oblivious to the ground fire. Cowering in the gully I thought we might stand a chance if the aircraft bombed us, but the choppers' napalm would devastate the whole mountainside, and us with it.

Two MiGs flew low along the valley and turned in long, graceful arcs: real World War II stuff. With the heavy 16 mm Arriflex camera on my back, I craned my head around to stare straight up at the hovering Hinds. I could see their vast array of weaponry very clearly.

Chris muttered: "Right, they've finished bombing below us. It's our turn next."

"What the hell am I doing in Afghanistan?" I asked myself.

Back to Africa: Through it all, us scribes did a lot of crazy things. But there were few incidents as interesting as the one that took place during one of my journeys from Burundi to Kampala. It was a long haul, tedious too, through Rwanda and on into Uganda, all of it overland by truck or bush taxi.

On that trip I was keen to get from Lake Tanganyika to Entebbe as soon as possible, but I simply couldn't get onto a flight from Bujumbura.

So, what the hell, I hitchhiked!

It was hard going; the roads were bad and there were few vehicles, especially at night. Because there was so much military hardware around, bandits had become a problem. A truck dropped me by the side of the road about a kilometre from the main lodge at the Kagera National Park in Rwanda, south-east of the legendary Mountains of the Moon in neighbouring Uganda and it was quite dark when I got there, perhaps eight o'clock.

There was no moon, but I could clearly see the road leading up to the lodge where the lights were on. I shouldered my gear and set off at a good pace.

When I finally walked through the door into the reception building about 10 minutes later, a French tourist sitting with a small group looked up at me in disbelief and dropped her glass. For a few seconds they all gaped at me. Then one of the men came forward, a Belgian who was managing the camp. They didn't know I was coming, he told me.

"We didn't hear your car."
"I have no car."
"So how did you get here?"
"I walked. How else?"
"From the road? All the way?"
"Yes, of course."
Silence.

One of the women in the group suggested that I was kidding. "Look outside and see where his car is, Jean," she suggested. The Belgian did so and returned to the group.

"No car!" he said flatly. I asked what this was all about.

In the past week, he told me, a pride of lions had been terrorising the countryside around the lodge. Three of their staff had been eaten. Everybody in the area was terrified.

"Nobody even budges at night except in a vehicle. It's simply too dangerous," he told me.

"So why don't you shoot the brutes?" I asked, perturbed.

"Because we haven't got a permit. We've asked, but this is Africa …you know the scene."

I suppose I was just lucky that night. Or possibly the lions had already dined.

I want to end on a more reflective note about the continent of my birth, a place that nurtured my soul, my passions as well as my aspirations over many decades. Africa is a continent that has also given me much joy and sorrow and here I want to share something I culled from one of the American greats who emerged after Hitler's War, Martha Gellhorn, also in her own right an exceptional journalist and author.

Married briefly to Ernest Hemingway, she was a remarkably enterprising woman, never afraid to say what she felt about a situation or exactly what was on her mind.

She died in London in 1998 at the ripe old age of 90, and over many years managed to get to know Africa well enough to end up buying a house near Lake Naivasha in Kenya. No hidden agendas for Martha, she was the ultimate pragmatist. Though she became a close friend of the arch American liberal Eleanor Roosevelt, she was prepared to accept Africa for what it was, no holds barred. By her own admission, it actually wasn't all that much.

Martha Gellhorn wrote a lot about this vast continent in her letters home[4], having first visited West Africa in 1961 and later, east and southern Africa. In a missive to a friend in America, she complained that it was a great pity that she had "found Africa" so late in her career. She went on: "Those black people will make a sewer of Africa (from our point of view) in no time; they don't mind sewers. But though I think of them as largely half-witted, I'm on their side. The whites have become either too chummy with them or [they] get out; otherwise (as will happen in South Africa) they'll drown in blood. But no one learns from history; and common sense is the rare human attitude."

A few pages further, there is a letter to Adlai Stevenson, another prominent liberal who was also a democratic candidate for president (he lost twice to Eisenhower in 1952 and 1956). Again she bemoans Africa's fate. This time she suggests that it would take the blacks there "two centuries to get their house in order".

As for Africans trying to emulate Europeans, she adds: "What's so hot about white civilisation that they should aim for it? They may prefer the muddle and the mess, African style, to ours. From my travels, I think the least civilised (i.e. contaminated by whites) of the Africans, are not only the happiest but the best adjusted to life on that beautiful, murderous continent. They may, you know, work out something entirely their own. I bet it will be tough and bloody, but so is ours."

She continues: "The other point is this: we always talk of 'helping' them. Psychologically, this is all wrong. Children don't grow up by taking their parent's advice; but by disobeying and learning the hard way, through their own experience. I think they will have to do that. Individuals waste a lot of time that way; so do nations."

A perspicacious (and invariably controversial) observer of humanity that she was, Martha Gellhorn appears to have been right on the button, except that she left out the single most debilitating perversion of all: corruption.

1 Al J. Venter: *War Dog: Fighting Other Peoples Wars*, Casemate Publishers, Philadelphia (US)and Newbury (UK), 2006.
2 Al J. Venter: *Cops: Cheating Death – How One Man Saved the Lives of 3,000 Americans*, Lyons Press, New Haven, Connecticut 2007.
3 Al J. Venter: *Barrel of a Gun: A War Correspondent's Misspent Moments in Combat*, Casemate Publishers, 2010.
4 *The Letters of Martha Gellhorn*; selected and edited by Caroline Moorehead: Chatto & Windus, London, 2006, p 288.

Moscow supplied the Angolan Air Force with a range of modern jet fighter and bomber aircraft, as well as helicopter gunships. These included the Sukhoi, Mi-24 Hinds and these advanced MiG-23s which, in the later stages of the war (because of a United Nations arms embargo) were able to outgun, outperform and outrange aircraft fielded by the South African Air Force.
(Photo: Pierre Victor)

CHAPTER ONE

INTO ANGOLA WITH CHARLIE COMPANY

Theo Kluyts recalls that in all base attacks (in the war in Angola) there was always some form of rehearsal or retraining before an operation, especially if it was cross-border. At Cuamato there was simply no opportunity, so the Parabats had to rely on what they had learned months before. He refers specifically to routines such as fire-in-movement and trench-clearing drills that took place in the final stages of the attack, all of which, he declares, were brilliantly executed: "it was good that while there were several more casualties on that hectic second day, nobody else in our ranks was killed."

Kluyts went operational with Charlie Company in several Angolan strikes, and later served as a member of the operational HQ of 1 Parachute Battalion. He then reported directly to Commandant James Hills.

The stench that came up at us as we jumped from the choppers was unmistakable: a pungent odour of death that hung over the bush like a fetid premonition of what lay ahead. It was a remnant of the previous night's fire-fight, a battle that had claimed lives on both sides, two of them our own.

There was no conscious acknowledgement of any of it among the troops in the helicopter. Rather, it permeated a vast, sandy terrain dotted by stunted mopani trees with a presence that was foreboding. Being summer, the heat was intense, even that early in the day, and it hardly made things easier.

Small-arms fire crackled around the perimeter and there was no mistaking the heavier thuds of 12.7s and 14.5s. Soviet heavy machine guns have been used by one side or the other in hundreds of large and small wars on just about every continent over the past half-century, many of them in Africa. Their presence on the outskirts

Former British SAS-operative Peter McAleese – then serving with the SADF's 44 Parachute Battalion and who was dropped in with our group – having first disarmed the enemy soldier, pats him down. (Photo: Author)

of Cuamato – and in such numbers – surprised us because SWAPO didn't often use them. Nor could you miss the whack and whoosh of the occasional RPG-7.

We were lucky. The Puma that took us in dropped us on the periphery of the camp, well away from the main defences, and we were spared the big stuff. Still, we'd been warned, there was enemy just about everywhere and by the time it was over, there were perhaps a score or more dead in our quadrant, but they were all opposition.

In contrast, we were still very much alive. The majority of the young conscripts barely spared the bloody, blasted bodies a glance as we swiftly made our way through one trench line and bunker hole after another: most were littered with still more cadavers and the detritus of war. Except for one man. His image remains etched in my mind as if it had just happened.

I found him sprawled face down, the back of his head blown into unrecognisable pulp. He must have been the base commander because apart from the blood, the rest of his uniform was spotless and the pips on his shoulders were obvious. Nor could you miss the fact that it had been neatly ironed before having been donned, probably a short time before the fight started. Lying prostrate outside an improvised command post that had radio aerials protruding out the back, the officer still clutched a pair of binoculars in his left hand. His other arm extended grotesquely out from under him, as if, even in death, he was still directing his men in battle. He couldn't have been more than 25 years old.

We didn't bury the man, or any of the others sprawled about the battlefield. We left that to their *confreres*, who would arrive some time after the last South African Air Force helicopter had chattered back across no-man's-land into the sanctuary of what was then still South West Africa (Namibia). In the interim, Charlie Company, the unit to which I was attached, had two of its own dead to contend with, both still in their teens and as far as we were concerned, two too many.

For me, the loss had become personal: either could have been my son Johan. Attached to 61 Mech, he was to fight a succession of similar battles a year or so later in a long-range armoured penetration strike towards Cassinga, further to the north. When his vehicle was blown up by a boosted Soviet TM-57 anti-tank mine, he and others were hauled back to No. 1 Military Hospital in Pretoria, most of them on stretchers that slotted neatly into the fuselage of a C-130. Johan survived, but his two mates who had been standing on either side of him on the back of a mine-protected Buffel when it went up, weren't so fortunate ...

In many other respects, Cuamato was different, and for once, the fat lady smiled. On the day of the big battle, there were more than a dozen of us cramped in the back of the Puma helicopter after take-off from the tiny hamlet of Cuamato. The chopper threaded its way through the early morning mist to a spot on the map that had been arbitrarily chosen the night before by Commandant Deon Ferreira, his rank equivalent to that of a half-colonel in US Forces. With his counterpart from No. 1 Parachute Battalion – the Parabats – this bluff, burly, no-holds-barred field commander ran the show.

Heading out that morning, images of the previous night's engagement were still fresh in our minds. To everybody on board, the prospect of a contact was imminent ... dry-mouth real.

Most of the youngsters clustered shoulder-to-shoulder around me aboard the chopper were still in their teens, their tautly-drawn faces showing little emotion. Peter McAleese and I were the oldest, by a very long chalk. Formerly with Britain's Special Air Service, followed by a lengthy spell with the Rhodesian Light Infantry, McAleese had been detached from Colonel Jan Breytenbach's Pathfinder Company of the SADF's 44 Parachute Brigade and given charge of this squad. I could see that he was still tense after the previous evening's battle.

My presence was a bit more tenuous. As a scribe, I was the unknown factor in what lay ahead and these youngsters had no idea how I was likely to react under fire.

It mattered little to the young men going in that morning that the events ahead were the culmination of a succession of hot pursuit raids carried out in Angola over previous months. Envisaged targets included the western headquarters of SWAPO, the insurgent South West African People's Organisation.

The operation involving Cuamato in mid-January 1981 was initially aimed at the larger southern city of Xangongo, further towards the north. An untidy, sprawling, typically African conurbation, Xangongo lay on the northern shore of the Kunene River and featured often enough in the war in the past. With time, the city was to become a focal point of hostilities, though several spans of the great bridge along its southern approaches had already been destroyed by SAAF bombers. The word put out by Pretoria at the time was that it had been the work of the Recces, but that was all part of an elaborate disinformation charade that both sides played.

The plan to hit Xangongo had been prepared at Defence Headquarters a month or so before and provided for a joint attack by both the paratroopers and members of Commandant Ferreira's 32 Battalion. Ancillary support would come from 31 Battalion, a unit that comprised troops recruited within the Bushmen community of the Kalahari. Outstanding trackers in primitive terrain, these little San people had been persecuted by the Angolans for years, to the extent that, like vermin, they were often shot on sight whenever they were encountered by Angolan security forces.

Sensing an opportunity to counter the balance, Pretoria recruited a number of Bushmen to the SADF, and with solid skills taught by South African military instructors, 31 Battalion was moulded into an aggressive and competent fighting group. Linked to the "Border War" as it was called, these machinations were all part of white South Africa's bid to hold back the tide of communist-backed black rule sweeping across the continent.

The conflict ran from 1966 to 1989 and was viewed largely as a delaying action. Indeed, back in the late 1960s, a young South African Department of Information staffer – much later to become a distinguished ambassador under Nelson Mandela's ANC government – told James Mitchell, formerly with the Johannesburg newspaper *The Star*, that Pretoria needed to hold on only "until the fall of communism". Prescient indeed, recalls Mitchell today, because

Chapter 1
Into Angola with Charlie Company

it was to be some three decades before the reluctant opening of the Berlin Wall signalled the end of the perceived Soviet threat. The conflict along southern Africa's northern frontiers ended at roughly the same time, after 21 years of fighting.

For white South Africa, the former League of Nations mandated territory of South West Africa was a buffer zone, as much moral as physical, and SWAPO – although largely Ovambo tribally based – was the strongest guerrilla movement fighting to end South African rule. With bases for its military wing – the People's Liberation Army of Namibia (PLAN) – the movement was initially hosted in Zambia and then, with Lisbon's ignominious exit from the continent in 1975, it switched almost all its resources to neighbouring Angola.

Ultimately, South Africa's quasi-colonial military efforts featured many such battles, mostly directed towards preventing PLAN – and therefore SWAPO – from becoming a more significant presence in this vast disputed land. By attacking its camps and destabilising host countries, Pretoria hoped to buy time. Curiously, America at one stage believed they could do the same in Vietnam …

And as with previous "hot pursuit" raids into Angola – several taking place hundreds of kilometres into the interior – the South African authorities made it clear from the start that its argument was not with the people of the former Portuguese territory, but rather with the guerrilla group. Indeed, shortly before we lifted off to establish a forward position in Cuamato, a South African Air Force spotter aircraft dropped leaflets in the area that indicated as much.

As a result, the arrival of Pumas as well as Alouette helicopter gunships in South Angola on that muggy January afternoon in 1981 caused little surprise. Except for a few very old men and women, everybody else in Cuamato had fled, leaving strings of vehicle tracks across the dry terrain to testify to the recent departure of scores of military trucks. In retrospect, that alone should have alerted South

South African Air Force Pumas were the work horses of the operation, taking men in and returning to base with casualties, crew and others after the day's fighting. With the Alouette gunships, the air crews set up base in a large open area adjacent to Cuamato town. (Photo: Author)

African intelligence boffins that Cuamato was not the isolated settlement in the middle of nowhere that it was perceived to be.

Undeterred, the comparatively modest force of South African Airborne troops wasted no time in securing a perimeter defence around the town. Trenches were dug, patrols sent out and secure radio communications established with Sector One Zero, the regional South African Army headquarters at Oshakati. By noon on the first day, all the soldiers were in place and it was only flies and the occasional tsetse that bothered us. This winged pestilence seemed to be worse in Angola than anywhere else in Africa and settled on eyes and mouths and anything edible throughout the day. By evening – although we were miles from any kind of permanent water – mosquitoes arrived; trillions of them.

Meanwhile, senior officers pored over a series of charts that were spread out in the temporary command post, while reports of SWAPO activity elsewhere were being monitored. Commandant Deon Ferreira called his officers together for a late-afternoon Order Group.

The bulk of his force comprised white-officered 32 Battalion combatants, the majority of them formerly Angolan nationals. There was also a detachment from No. 1 Parachute Battalion, colloquially known as Parabats, or in the lingo, the "Bats". And, of course, the Bushmen unit. In total, Ferreira's force numbered perhaps 300 men, although at the end of the day it was the paratroopers that bore the brunt and suffered the most casualties.

There were problems, of course: in wartime there always are. For extensive operations involving choppers, Xangongo lies relatively distant from Ondangua, the main SAAF base in Ovamboland. That meant that a Helicopter Administrative Group – a HAG – needed to be established at a point roughly halfway to the target town of Xangongo, which would allow for these machines to refuel. Cuamato had been chosen for this purpose and the hamlet would also become the tactical headquarters for the coming fray.

It was all supposed to be fairly routine to start with, especially since intelligence sources had indicated no real Angolan Army presence in the area. There were elements of the paramilitary ODP (a variation of the civilian police) as well as TGFA (border guards) around, but they were hardly a threat. That was about it, the commandant was assured. There was certainly no mention of a major FAPLA base less than five kilometres from where we had landed.

Yet, looking over photos I took immediately after the battle, you could hardly miss several clearly discernable military strong points, as well as complex strings of zig zag trenchlines – very much in the Soviet mould and stretching off in all directions. Somebody in Pretoria had to be answerable for the oversight because it cost lives. More to the point, had the base remained undetected until the HAG was firmly in place and the Angolans had resorted to using their heavy weapons and mortars to bombard us newcomers – as undoubtedly they would have done, because they had the resources to do so – they could have caused havoc.

It is interesting that following the Cuamato debacle, the entire force was pulled back behind South African lines and the Xangongo attack left for another day.

The first suggestion that something was amiss at Cuamato came late that first afternoon of 15 January.

Several SAAF Aérospatiale SA 330 Puma and Alouette III helicopters had earlier flown the 100 kilometres from the main embarkation point at Ombalantu to Cuamato, just 35 clicks north of the Angolan border. The idea was that they would pave the way for Operation Vastrap 5, due to commence the next morning.

The Puma mission chief was Commandant H.A.P. Potgieter, who piloted one of the machines. The first pair of Alouette gunships, brought in to provide top cover for ground forces once the fighting had started, were piloted by a youthful Lieutenant Arthur Walker and Captain Mike McGee. Their mission chief was Captain Heinz Katzke, who arrived on board one of the larger helicopters.

Things were quiet at first, but not long after the aviators had settled in, the advance party was greeted by salvos of rocket and machine-gun fire from positions out east where some of the patrols had been heading. These were followed by the unmistakable thumps of 82 mm mortars. Then it dawned: the South Africans had a scrap on their hands.

What we didn't yet know was that the route taken by one of the patrols sent out by Charlie Company earlier, led directly towards a major military base that, until then, nobody knew anything about. The installation was huge, and manned not by SWAPO irregulars, but by a large number of well-drilled and well-equipped Angolan soldiers. More salient, they were regular Angolan Army and not the ill-trained, badly motivated bunch of local, souped-up conscript troops. Only much later was it established that the base was manned by a battalion or more of FAPLA soldiers, troops of the *Forças Armadas Populares de Libertação de Angola*, the People's Armed Forces for the Liberation of Angola.

Elements of 32 Battalion also took part in the Cuamato attack, but the main thrust of the onslaught, through a succession of trench lines, was left to the Parabats. (Photo: Author)

Mike Pearson, then a young Parabat lance-corporal has vivid recall of the events of that afternoon. As he remembers, the sections under Corporals Hennie Viljoen and Pepe Tommasi – accompanied by Lieutenant J.C. du Plessis and Sergeant 'Min Dae' Wessels – were sent out on a recce to check on enemy activity in the area, if any. Pearson reported as follows:

"In the late afternoon we came across a long, straight road heading north. We were standing among the bushes when, undetected, we suddenly saw a bunch of enemy soldiers cross the road about half-a-kilometre ahead of us. Apart from the lieutenant and 'Min Dae', there were also Doug Winning and Rob Anderson, and our group wasted no time going forward until we intersected with their tracks.

"This was obviously a serious business, so we crept forward on the spoor for another 200 metres until we heard voices ahead. Continuing quietly, we finally had a group of five of them visual sitting on a termite mound, which was when we went down low.

"The lieutenant and I crawled under a fallen tree with a clear view of the enemy group, waiting for Corporals Viljoen and Tommasi to join us; we had already informed them of the situation by radio. But then, unexpectedly, one of the gooks started walking straight towards us, stopped about 10 or 12 metres of our position and started to unzip his fly. The guy was taking a piss ...

"The problem just then was that with Viljoen and Tommasi coming up behind us, the man who had stopped to pee heard them approach. I already had a bead on him and as he turned to make a run for it, I nailed him. We managed to drop a couple more on the termite mound before the rest bolted back to their base.

"Undeterred, our group crept forward until we came to the edge of the tree line. There we discovered that all the foliage and shrubs had been cleared for about 70 metres immediately in front of us, and once the soldiers at the base opened fire, we had no option but to go down and take up defensive positions.

"The firing was intense. It was so bad that after a couple of minutes every one of us lying on the ground was covered in foliage as all the rounds aimed in our direction – especially the heavy stuff, the 14.5s and 12.7s – were going high and lopping off twigs, branches and sometimes the tops of the trees.

"Having called for reinforcements, it didn't take long for the helicopters to bring in more sections, including Sergeant Major Peter McAleese and a French guy whose name I can't remember. It was actually the sergeant major who, after jumping up, shouted that we couldn't lie there for the rest of the afternoon. He asked who was going to join him and make a dash for the trenches.

"Well, everyone did and we fired as we ran across a large open area. I recall emptying my magazine halfway across and stopped to insert a fresh one thinking that the bastards were going to nail me. But they didn't, even though I paused momentarily while doing it.

"Then, once we got abreast of the first line of trenches, the enemy seemed to take fright and they hopped out like jack rabbits to get away from us. Sergeant 'Min Dae' Wessels made the mistake of looking into a trench before hurling his grenade: he was shot through the head, neck and chest.

"Lieutenant Du Plessis was a hellova lot luckier. He took a round in his pack, but it was deflected upwards and ricocheted under the skin on his back and clipped the back of his head. De Bruyn, the radio operator was shot at about the same time."

There was high praise in the unit afterwards for the way that Danie Els provided covering fire with his LMG. Said one of his mates: " ... the guy was relentless ... he managed to keep a lot of enemy heads down."

It was Steven MacDougal who sent the original signal back on the A-53 radio he carried on his back to the nearby HAG that the unit was under attack. In terse language, he told headquarters that two members of his squad had been wounded and urgently requested casualty evacuation and back-up. Within the next half hour, another three platoons were hauled in by the Pumas.

MacDougal: "The new arrivals weren't much help either because as the fire intensified, they, like us, could do nothing but duck down low." More reinforcements were called for and flown in shortly afterwards, but again, the odds were overwhelming. To Commandant Ferreira, the situation had quickly become untenable. In his customary uncompromising manner, he told his commanders to get their act together and find out what the fuck was going on.

It was about then that "Chunky" Truter, one of the paratroop youngsters, took a shard of steel in the brain after an enemy mortar landed in the middle of his squad. He died shortly afterwards. It was a lucky shot for the enemy but did serious damage. I was there after he had been carried in by his mates and when – after a spell of going in and out of consciousness – "Chunky" breathed his last breath. I afterwards visited his mother in Cape Town to tell her that just before he died, he'd quietly called for her. I heard afterwards that she never got over his death.

As Charlie Company section leader Manie Troskie recalled afterwards, "Chunky's death had an effect on all the men. If any of our group had reservations about killing before, a kind of primitive hatred seemed to emerge from nowhere. Most of the guys were still in their teens, but overnight we became focused, our instincts atavistic, brutish and elemental and certainly beyond the comprehension of most ordinary folk."

But then, that's the way it is with all wars, which was why Charlie Company went in the next day and thought nothing about killing as many of the enemy as they encountered in an engagement that lasted several hours.

Meanwhile, the rest of us at Cuamato – only a short hike away across the sand – watched in awe as firepower poured out of the base in all directions. Had it all been concentrated where MacDougal and the rest of the group were cowering, they would almost certainly have been wiped out. To some of us, it might have been a film sequence out of Iraq.

Casualty details were vague at first and came in snatches ... "One of our boys dead ... Casevac required ... things are bad ... really bad!" By then another man had been wounded, which was when somebody asked whether it had become too risky to send in the choppers to haul them out.

Tasked to handle the situation by the commandant, Captain Heinz Katzke said that he was reluctant to send in his gunships. Support was needed for the Parabats who were under fire, he agreed, but it had suddenly become too risky, and for three reasons: the flak was too heavy, the bush too sparse, and pretty damn soon it would be dark. He suggested that there was no alternative but to wait for nightfall and for those caught in the mêlée, to walk out. And that is what finally happened, with the seriously wounded and the dead ultimately hauled to safety by their mates on improvised stretchers. Don recalls helping to carry his mates out on litters made from branches threaded through the sleeves of their bush jackets, "with a fireworks display of tracers around us".

Only then was it established that along one stretch of the base perimeter, large numbers of enemy troops were entrenched in a parallel set of trenches, in places only 30 metres from where the paratroopers had taken refuge. Both sides had kept firing at each other, though after things had kind of settled in, the two adversaries started hurling insults, the Angolans in Portuguese (which none of the South Africans understood) and the Parabats in Afrikaans, which to those listening on the other side, could just as easily have been in Mandarin.

To Rifleman George "Org" Hennig – he today owns and runs the famous Die Bos restaurant in Pretoria – it was the worst kind of contact imaginable: "The first we knew that there were enemy around was when the bush seemed to catch alight ... we were under attack and it was fucking heavy," said Hennig.

As MacDougal recalls, it didn't help that the entire region was pancake flat, the nearest row of hills was several days' march away and all the high points in enemy hands. These were defensive positions that had been carefully constructed by the enemy using bulldozers, and it was from there that the paratroopers took a pounding.

TRENCH-LINE AND BUNKER CLEARING

WITH CHARLIE COMPANY AT CUAMATO

Al Venter was close on the heels of Captain Johan Blaauw when this Parabat officer led an assault on an enemy bunker strongpoint. Having killed some of the occupants, the officer hurled a grenade into the opening, only to have it ignite several fuel drums which exploded. The captain was burned in the process and was airlifted to hospital at Ondangua shortly afterwards. Other images show conditions in and around the military base, including the town's water tower at Cuamato.
(Photos: Author)

"What was even more terrifying," he remembers, "was that we couldn't even pull back ... to do so would have meant us crossing a couple of hundred metres of open terrain with almost no tree cover ... we would have sustained terrible losses. So we did what was left to us and lay flat on our backs watching strings of tracers whistling past only centimetres over our heads. But that didn't stop most of the guys pulling out their cigarettes and lighting up...". It stayed that way until dark.

After the sun had set and the rest of the squad were back in Cuamato and the wounded treated, Commandant Ferreira pulled back all his non-essential troops. He told the officers that they would wait until dawn before again "getting down to business". I would go in with the first wave, he said when he pulled me aside, adding that it would be the first time a South African journalist had been allowed to accompany his men into combat, never mind that everything pointed to a fully conventional battle ahead.

"You sure you still want to go in – two of the men already dead and there could be more tomorrow?"

The prospect was sobering, but I'd come that far, I replied. There was simply no going back.

Night settled uneasily on both sides of the front. As the evening wore on, we could hear the occasional blast as approaching Angolan Army vehicles detonated anti-tank landmines that both the Recces and 32 Battalion reconnaissance elements had been laying under cover of darkness along the only approach road to the base. You can never miss the distinctive hollow thump of an anti-tank mine going up.

Questioned about vehicles using the roads, the Bushman leader of his fighting group said that the way he gauged the situation, the trucks arrived full and left empty. That meant that a steady stream of men and matériel kept arriving at the base, obviously bolstering FAPLA defences. Also, the blackness was irregularly punctuated by mortar and small-arms fire, but it was erratic and there was no damage.

The biggest problem facing Commandant Ferreira and his field commanders that evening (they had since been joined by Major General Jannie Geldenhuys, who was running this northern war out of Sector One Zero) was who would actually lead the attack on the base the following morning? And that was when the name of one of the young officers attached to the Parachute Battalion became prominent.

Captain Johan Blaauw was in command of the Parabat contingent at Cuamato and, unlike most of the officers, he was soft-spoken and unobtrusive: most of the time you didn't know he was there, until he offered a comment. Then everybody listened, which was unusual for a junior officer.

What mattered most in this youthful captain's mind was that his unit had already taken seven casualties – two dead and five wounded. He needed to even things up a little, he declared.

According to Blaauw's intelligence officer, an even younger Theo Kluyts, the captain had been severely affected by the events that had taken place earlier. Respectfully, but inordinately direct, Captain Blaauw told Commandant Ferreira that there was no question that the job was his. While 32 Battalion might have been blooded more often than Charlie Company, his men had a score to settle. He added that of all the officers in the Order Group, he was not only best suited for the task, but circumstances had also made him the most motivated. Moreover, he reminded the senior officers present, this would not be the first time he or his men had seen action. They had proved themselves in a series of heavy actions in Operation Smokeshell a short while before. There had been other battles before that, all of them successful. Consequently, he declared, his hands firmly on the map in front of him, he and his men knew exactly what was required of them.

Doubtful at first, the head of 32 Battalion looked around at the faces gathered in the temporary HAG. There was no dissent. Nor did General Geldenhuys object when apprised of the situation a short while later. That much decided, the Order Group turned to other matters.

It was decided that before Charlie Company went in, the base would be softened up at first light by a napalm and conventional bomb strike involving SAAF Impala jets. That would be followed by a pounding from 32 Battalion mortar units.

There were at least four of these Aeromacchi light ground-attack/fighter jets already waiting at the Ondangua Air Force Base about 130 kilometres to the south when orders were radioed through. Often used far beyond their advertised capabilities as ground-support aircraft in this Border War, the Impalas finally had to be withdrawn from the front line over Angola in the late 1980s.

The appointment of Captain Blaauw as strike leader was fortuitous, and for several reasons. Youthful, imaginative and aggressive, he invariably led from the front. At the same time, Cuamato was unique, not least of all that the placing of the FAPLA military base close to the town was an intelligence blunder of significant proportions. As a result, there was no knowledge of enemy numbers, their weaponry, base layout, defensive doctrines and so forth. Essentially, the men would be going in "blind". The fact that the attacking force were to take only two or three more wounded in an assault that lasted a good part of the following day, was remarkable.

There was no time for any kind of retraining or rehearsals of skills and techniques needed for the fight, both normally essential in order to succeed in combat. Nobody needed to tell the captain that he could not just storm a base and hope for success. Yet, this was what was achieved at Cuamato.

As the South Africans were to learn later, the layout of the base was very cleverly handled. There were trenches, fox holes and underground bunkers just about everywhere. Several of the officers declared that they had never come across an Angolan base as well designed as the one at Cuamato. What amazed Theo Kluyts was that even though the enemy had cleared an area around the base to a depth of about 200 metres (to improve fields of fire), the base itself was extremely well camouflaged both from the air and on the ground. In some places fresh branches and dead bushes were pulled haphazardly into position to avoid any suggestion of a human presence, very much as had been the case in Vietnam.

"That made it extremely difficult to determine where everything was," declared Kluyts. "To me, it was obvious that they'd made the base difficult for a ground attack, which was why I actually asked one of the pilots afterwards to take me up so that I could get a good view of the place. I did a sketch of the area and gave a copy to the 32 Battalion intelligence officer, which, I believe, resulted in them later building a scale model at the training area of No. 1 Parachute Battalion in Bloemfontein."

Having bedded down for the night in my army-issue sleeping bag with the rest of the men in one of the solid brick Portuguese colonial structures in Cuamato, everybody was wakened before dawn. We ate, but not heartily.

Tea was consumed by the mugful from our fire-buckets, warmed by solid fuel briquettes that came with our issued "ratpacks". That and liquid in cleverly contrived plastic sachets, which were filled at one end and could be sucked out at the other. Neat! Conflict has always initiated new ideas, even when it comes to feeding armies.

The call to move towards the chopper staging area followed shortly afterwards and we were told that the first two Parabat "sticks" would leave the ground within minutes: it would take us a couple of minutes more to reach contact point.

The orders issued by ground staff immediately before take-off was brief: we would have roughly eight to ten seconds to get onto the ground from a hover of anything between two and three metres. After that, the Pumas would pull away and head back to base to fetch the next batch.

Word had come from Commandant Ferreira about my clearance and that there was no problem with me accompanying the strike. But if I didn't jump together with my squad, he warned, there would be no going back. Also, he had no objection to me "carrying": especially since we'd be going into the kind of terrain where it was expected that there would be enemy all over the place. I was issued with a folding-stock AK and two magazines. I asked for a couple of grenades and got them.

It had become clear to everybody in Cuamato the previous night that the events of the previous day had left its mark on the youngsters who crowded into the Puma around me. There were no smiles and none of the banter usually encountered when training. Their eyes were set in fixed stares ahead and, clearly, there wasn't one among them who wasn't prepared to see it through.

Immediately before boarding, fire across the way picked up sharply and we had to accept the odds: this time we would be the attackers.

Our battle started as soon as the feet of the first members of our detachment touched the ground.

Crouched in the bush, perhaps 30 or 40 metres from our hovering Puma were two of the enemy, both clad in FAPLA cammo. One was armed with an RPG-7 rocket launcher and the other with an RPD machine gun. On reflection, they could probably have taken our chopper out in a flash, but curiously, in one of those quirky developments that characterise so many Third World confrontations, fate decreed otherwise. Instead of taking aim, both men simply dropped their weapons and raised their hands.

Having raced hard that first 100 metres to find cover, most of the guys were already breathing hard, in part, because fire had picked up along the line, which probably extended a good three or four hundred metres in all directions.

Peter McAleese was the first to reach the two Angolan soldiers and he wasted no time in cuffing them to ground, at the same time kicking their weapons away. He spent a short while going through their pockets and then, using the kind of universal sign language that everybody understands, ordered them onto their feet again. We took both men with us as we moved forward through this sparse bush country and when we were halted once more, they were bound and sent back to base on the next chopper for interrogation.

Asked later why they hadn't fired, one of the Angolan captives answered that it was pointless. "We shoot and shoot, but still more of these machines come." He suggested that his people were totally "outgunned".

Time and the sequence of events often have little relevance in battle and it was no different at Cuamato. Asked afterwards how long the onslaught lasted, I really had no idea. It could have been an hour, or possibly three. Images, sensations, feelings: all were compressed into the immediate. That and the elation of still being intact and having weathered the first two mortar and RPG barrages, together with the relief of seeing some of your own people walk out of an all-encompassing layer of smoke in a situation that looked hopeless moments before.

That flank probably felt the same about us when the situation was reversed, for this man-to-man contact is usually unspoken. You watched your flanks and your rear, not so much because the enemy might be lurking there, but rather to spot problems within your own lines. You were aware too, that you were the subject of scrutiny,

Charlie Company troops confront several enemy soldiers immediately after we were dropped into the action by the Pumas near the enemy base. They were armed with RPG-7s (which can be seen, centre left) but curiously, they didn't use them. (Photo: Author)

Chapter 1
Into Angola with Charlie Company

Sergeant Major Peter McAleese examines some of the documents taken off enemy soldiers who were on the ground when we arrived. (Photo: Author)

which was comforting: Peter McAleese kept his beady eyes on me throughout.

The routine was the same while the attack continued. Our unit would move ahead from one trench-line to another, consolidating as we moved. Fire was sporadic, with enemy mortars more troubling, for the gunships as well because they had to be wary of entering the potential trajectory arc of fired mortars.

We'd constantly encounter bunkers, all of which needed to be cleared. At one of these locations, a couple of squadies moved in, but in coming out of direct sunlight, they could discern nothing in the dark interiors of these primitive fortifications. Still, in one case, a soldier persisted and moved forward, until somebody at the far end opened fire and wounded him in the arm. He dropped to the ground and crawled out on his hands and knees: two of his mates silenced the attacker with grenades.

At another bunker filled to the rooftop with firewood, Manie Troskie and another member of the squad moved in, but movement within its narrow confines was limited and it was all fairly cursory. Sensing a presence in the darkness beyond, both men crept silently back towards the entrance, turned once more before exiting and emptied their magazines into the gloom. Two dead enemy soldiers were later found slumped at the far end of the bunker.

As Manie reflects today, "it could just as easily have been us …".

Then we almost lost the captain. I'd been on Blaauw's tail in the latter stages of the attack while he and several of his men were clearing trenches and at one set of fortifications that led directly to a bunker, he almost came unstuck. He had already killed one FAPLA soldier who had been waiting for him around a narrow bend, when he decided to throw a grenade into the adjacent bunker. If there was one enemy soldier in the area, the captain reasoned, there could be more.

"There was nothing planned about it," Captain Blaauw recalled afterwards. "The entrance to the bunker was immediately ahead, so I grabbed a grenade, drew myself up out of the trench, pulled the pin and hurled it into the entrance."

I was immediately behind the captain taking my pictures when it all happened. The grenade exploded in the bunker and with it, ignited several drums of fuel that had been stored there, creating a massive back-blast that all but enveloped the Parabat captain. Though he didn't actually catch alight, Blaauw was seriously burned, his hair and all exposed skin seared. In fact, his entire face was scorched black. The captain was taken to safety some distance behind our lines and flown out. Within hours he was in hospital in Oshakati.

Meantime, the rest of the unit took up positions adjacent to two Gaz ammunition trucks that were burning fiercely: the Soviet vehicles had probably been targeted in an earlier air strike. Although there was still some enemy action coming from more distant positions, the air around us was constantly being shattered by exploding rockets, mortars, grenades and small arms still left on the trucks. To my mind, we were a lot more at risk from the explosives on the trucks "cooking off" than from the enemy, which was when McAleese decided to take his unit forward. It was a sensible move.

Once through a second line of trenches, the camp was all but ours. There were still small clusters of the enemy about, but when detected they ran and our guys would pick them off. We were aware too, that there were other enemy troops still hiding underground, but all these bunkers and tunnels would eventually be systematically cleared.

Speaking about the Cuamato attack years later, Alouette gunship pilot Arthur Walker recalls that that very first afternoon, before all this had happened, things couldn't have been more settled.

"The Puma and Alouette guys were just parking off, all us pilots sitting under the trees and making coffee. We were actually preparing to spend the evening there," says Walker, who was to win his first gold Honoris Crux decoration at Cuamato.

Awarded for acts of conspicuous bravery, HC decorations came in three classifications: bronze, silver and gold, the last being South Africa's highest decoration for bravery and roughly equivalent to the Victoria Cross or the Congressional Medal of Honour. There were only six Honoris Crux decorations in gold awarded during the more than two decades of Border War and it says a lot that Arthur Walker got two of them.

What struck us as unusual at Cuamato, recalls Walker, was that apart from the operational head, Commandant Ferreira, an entire headquarters contingent descended on the HAG, almost as if everybody wanted to get in on the act. "It included air force and army commanders, the majority gathered around to fine-tune the next day's operation towards Xangongo and nobody having the faintest idea that a huge enemy force was only a rifle shot away."

As he remembers, this number included Air Force Commandant J.B. West (Military Air Operations Team – SAAF liaison officer) and the SAAF officer-in-charge of fighter backup, Brigadier Piet Bosman "Bossie" Huyser. Major General Jannie Geldenhuys came in from Oshakati soon afterwards.

Walker: "The contact call following the first shots exchanged near the as-yet-undetermined enemy base was soon followed by a report that two of our troops had been wounded. Not long afterwards, a helicopter extraction was asked for, which was when we were alerted.

"So Captain Mike McGee and I went off in our gunships to try and secure a landing zone. The idea was that a Puma would follow and pull the casualties out. To our surprise, Mike and I came under some really heavy anti-aircraft fire, with even RPG-7s headed in our direction. There were scores of them," recalls Arthur.

"The troops on the ground threw yellow smoke to mark their positions, which was when Mike and I went ahead with an attack in a bid to suppress the increased AA fire. We were trying hard to allow the Puma access, but because it was getting dark and the sky was illuminated by tracer bullets which was pretty dramatic, especially for those watching on the ground, it didn't take us long to realise that the enemy was powerfully equipped.

"We detected three emplaced 14.5 mm ZPU-2 twin-barrelled anti-aircraft guns firing an effective 300 rounds-a-minute, never mind who-knows-how-many 12.7 mms and the RPG-7s."

Against these, he explained, the gunships each had a single, laterally-mounted 20 mm cannon and these had to be fired from a low and relatively slow orbit for accuracy.

"We'd see the muzzle flashes when they were aiming at us and then the tracers. It all seemed to come at us in a kind of slow motion, just like in the movies: then suddenly this stuff was whooshing past your head. We'd fire back, of course, using their tracers to direct our fire to source ... but it wasn't something that would have worked in the daytime.

"My engineer/gunner was Sergeant Danie Brink and he took on the anti-aircraft guns until we ran out of ammunition, which wasn't much because the gunships normally carried only 150 rounds each.

"I broke off out of the orbit and called to Mike on the radio. I told him I was going to re-arm ... we certainly hadn't given up the battle yet," says Walker. "But that was when Mike suddenly called on the radio and shouted that he was coming under heavy fire. He thought he was going to crash."

Walker explained that the two gunships were flying about 500 feet above ground level while in orbit. If you came under fire under those conditions, he said, it was best to get down low and fast. "But in his rapid descent, McGee must have become disoriented, which is why he thought he was headed into the dirt.

"In the darkness I couldn't see him," said Arthur, "so I turned around in a bid to search for his chopper and even put on my navigation lights. I told him to fly towards me, but that caused more problems.

"We didn't expect to draw all the fire that we did, but that's exactly what happened, though it did give Mike the brief opportunity to recover."

Heinz Katzke, who was running the show from the ground, made the point that the area was already well lit up with all that flak flying about. In addition, there were the lights of Cuamato, which were clearly visible in the south. "It's also worth noting," he added, that the Alouettes were not equipped for night operations, though sometimes, needs must ..."

Using evasive manoeuvring to interfere with the aim of the enemy gunners, including sharp turns and height changes, Walker and McGee finally broke free.

"Mike followed me back to the base, where we landed and shut down to re-arm, refuel and reassess the situation," Walker elaborates, "but we realised that it was pointless going back. The position where the South African casualties were lying was just too close to the enemy, less than 200 metres from their lines."

While all this had been going on, recalls Walker, "we still hadn't assessed what exactly was down there. In fact, when we went up, we had no idea that this base even existed," Walker told Mitchell. "Obviously our intelligence was lacking."

Later that night, the command element gathered in Cuamato determined that the men would go in again at first light to what was then accepted as a significant enemy position. Ferreira warned that it would be a tough exchange. By then too, the Pumas had returned to Ombalantu across the border, with Walker and McGee as passengers. They'd left behind their gunships to be serviced for the second day's battle.

Four Pumas headed back north to Cuamato early the next morning, bringing Walker and McGee with them. The flight was accompanied by four extra Alouettes flown by Katzke (No. 1) and Willem Ras (No. 2) as the first pair, with Billy Port (No. 3) and "Klip" Reynolds (No. 4) to supplement firepower.

Judging by performances past, the enemy might confidently have been expected to have flitted during the night. Isolated, totally cut off and totally lacking in air cover, the Angolans must have realised that come first light, they would be under heavy attack from a well-armed, well-trained and motivated "First World" military force. Standard operating procedures for FAPLA might have been to "shoot and scoot", which had happened often enough in the past. But not at Cuamato.

By then the South Africans had to accept that the Angolans had established a full-on defended area. In open ground, with its sandy soil and light grass cover, was a huge military complex traversed by Soviet-style zig-zag trenches: "It was all straight out of Soviet manual stuff and included numerous firing emplacements and positions for 82 mm mortars," recalled one of the pilots afterwards.

"When we went out again," said Walker, "it was an altogether different game. "But even then we thought that the enemy might have pulled out and we didn't expect any real resistance. So when we moved off, we sent up four Alouette gunships, with two remaining behind to be serviced, the idea being to check out the situation from up close. And immediately a lot of heavy fire came our way.

"Much of it was 12.7 mm and 14.5 mm anti-aircraft guns, volleys of RPG-7s and even some SA-7 ground-to-air missiles … about five of them were fired at us. None of the Manpads[1] hit, but they came close … very close indeed."

Looking back, Walker reckons that the lack of success with SAM-7

Some of the Parabats wounded in the attack earlier in the afternoon had to wait until dark before they could extricate themselves from an extremely hostile situation and have their wounds dressed back at base. Most of the injured were airlifted to hospital the next morning. (Photo: Author)

ground-to-air missiles was because of the extremely low level at which the South Africans normally flew, sometimes just over the tops of the terrain's tree cover. He explained that, the Angolan troops operating the heat-seeking Manpads didn't have time to let their missiles engage before blasting them off.

"They were fired in haste before they could lock on … it needs a few seconds to do that," explained Arthur. In effect, they were dispatched ballistically and therefore no more accurate than the similarly unguided RPG-7s that FAPLA was using.

It may also have had to do with the K-Car gunship, as this Alouette configuration was termed. Hovering over the battle in a command and control capacity and fitted with heat shields to deflect exhaust gases up through the rotor and in this manner minimise the heat signature, it was a formidable combination in this primitive bush war.

"One of the funniest things I can remember from this campaign (Walker also saw service with the Rhodesian Air Force for what he called 'the best year of my life' with sometimes up to three contacts in a single day) was what happened with Kevin 'Klip' Reynolds and Billy Port over Cuamato.

"The gunships customarily flew in pairs," although on this day, commented Heinz Katzke later, "all the Alos worked in unison."

As Arthur Walker recalls, "Klip" was flying with Billy when he called: "Billy, Billy, I've been hit."

"Billy, with his dry sense of fun, called back: 'Klip, are you bleeding?' You could hear all the guys chuckling into their intercoms. It was the adrenaline of course … there, in the heat of battle, some of the aviators laughing out loud.

"So there we were, all of us in the air over an Angolan strongpoint, with all that shit coming in at us. It was obviously a dangerous, and to some of us, a pointless exercise, so in the end the ground commander ordered us to withdraw." Walker said that it was then time to bring in the Impalas, though he acknowledged that he was surprised they hadn't been called in sooner.

"Our tactic under those circumstances would normally be to use the Imps to create devastation on the ground with their rockets and bombs. Only then would we move in with the helicopters to clean up." So, some 20 minutes later, the jets headed in for their initial strikes, guided by a forward air controller sitting in a twin-seat Bosbok spotter plane high above the battle.

However, on their first run in, the Impalas encountered some really heavy flak, recalls Katzke. The pilots decided that they would go in at 20,000 feet, dive vertically down and release bombs and pull out at 15,000 feet. There was a French-speaking Impala pilot, who after a while said in English with a French accent: "Our weapons are ineffective for this target."

By then, said Walker, the Impalas had already streamed in: they were operating in echelon, two at a time. "There must have been at least eight such pairs of strikes," he recalls, after which the gunships went in again and more surprises followed.

"What we found amazing after all this, was that the anti-aircraft guns that should have been destroyed in the bombing runs were still firing," he ruminated. "As one group of Angolan gunners were killed – literally taken out by gunships and the ground troops – the defenders would simply call forward more men and put new teams onto the guns. Once again, we still couldn't understand why these guys still kept fighting as hard as they did."

That done, it was time for the planned full-on assault on the Angolan base and, as Walker concedes, there were to be no more half-measures once the Paratroopers went in. Captain Blaauw eventually ran it from an Alouette gunship, with Charlie Company's second-in-command Lieutenant Dawid Willemse overseeing things on the ground.

Visualising those dramatic events a quarter-century later, Arthur

Walker paused, and added thoughtfully: "They fought hard, fucking hard! It was a ding-dong of a battle."

Katzke agrees, "It was a tough fight ... once our boys took the initiative, they went into the trenches and cleaned up. Those FAPLA troops that had survived were fleeing helter-skelter towards the north and the base was taken."

Walker: "Then we withdrew, we all went back to Cuamato and so did our ground forces. Later that day, all the helicopters returned to Ombalantu and more assessment followed, more planning. But at least this time the South Africans would be mopping up after a beaten enemy."

The citation for Arthur Walker's Honoris Crux (Gold) noted that he had "displayed exceptional courage and bravery under fire by remaining on station and providing the close air support required by own ground forces."

Describing the manner in which he went to the assistance of Mike McGee, the citation continued: "His courageous act prevented the loss of an Alouette and its crew. Lieutenant Walker's actions were not only an outstanding display of professionalism, devotion to duty and courage, but also constituted exceptional deeds of bravery under enemy fire ..."

It was towards the end of the Cuamato attack, after I had been detached from Charlie Company, that another event took place which will always be memorable. Things could have turned out very differently for us had our gunner not been ultra-alert. Although I've told this story before in my book *Barrel of a Gun*, it's worth repeating here.

I went up with Heinz Katzke in his Alouette gunship shortly after the base had been taken. An easygoing professional, Heinz seemed to enjoy any challenge while at the controls. If he could manage it, I suggested, I'd like to get my hands on a bayonet, preferably for a Kalashnikov.

"No problem," was his insouciant reply. "Let's see if we can find you one," and off we went.

A short time later, we spotted the body of an Angolan soldier kind of half-secreted under a tree, his AK lying at an odd angle across his knees. We were aware that all these troops carried bayonets, although in Africa they were rarely attached to the barrel. Most were tied to their webbing and prominently displayed, almost like a badge of courage.

"Looks like he's not going to need his AK any time soon," said

Heinz half jokingly as he lost altitude and went into the hover. "Or his bayonet," the gunner behind us added with a chortle.

We were still at about 300 feet when Heinz decided to bring the chopper down onto an open clearing in the bush a short distance from our man. Over the mike – to which all three of us on board were connected – he told the gunner that he would land about 20 paces from the body. "I'm taking her down just south of that large tree to the south," he said pointing.

"Roger," was the reply. By then the gunner was already unstrapping himself. There was no question of telling headquarters what we were doing because it was illegal. Instead, Heinz just went in: it was that kind of war.

Once on the ground, the helicopter's gunner – a sergeant who was normally crouched across his 20 mm cannon protruding from the portside hatch – undid his last safety belt, took off his helmet, grabbed his issue carbine and sprinted towards the "gook".

Having lost two of their own in the attack, members of the Charlie Company took scant notice of dead enemy scattered about the camp, like this one, killed in a bunker. (Photo: Author)

He was perhaps two or three metres from the Angolan when the "dead man" suddenly sat up, took hold of his AK and lowered the barrel. But he wasn't quick enough; the gunner killed the combatant with a short burst of automatic fire. Wasting little time, he turned over the body, ran his hands over the now-dead man's uniform and, having found the blade, sprinted back towards the helicopter. Perhaps 30 seconds later, we were back in the air.

Nobody said a word while we soared back up to operational height and I was able to check my new-found trophy in its red-baked Bakelite sheath.

SWAPO guerrillas killed in an earlier attack on a nearby base: the bodies were gathered together for fingerprinting by the police. (Photo: Author)

About then the gunner came through on the mike. "He wasn't wounded, Captain ... very far from dead, in fact," he told his captain.

"How do you know?"

"Patted him down, Sir ... there were no other wounds on him. He was playing possum ... probably would have made a run for it as soon as the sky was clear."

A silence followed, none of us knowing what to say ...

"Well," said the captain after a little while, motioning with his left hand in my direction, "at least you got your bayonet ... and what's another dead fucker between friends?"

"But just don't tell the Colonel about it when we get back ..."

1 Man-portable air-defense systems (MANPADs or MPADs) are shoulder-launched, supersonic surface-to-air missiles (SAMs). They are typically guided weapons and in the past have included Soviet SAM-7s and SAM-14s, American-built Stingers and, more recently, Chinese and reverse-engineered Iranian versions. All are a threat to low-flying aircraft, especially helicopters.

CHAPTER TWO

SEYCHELLES MERCENARY INVASION WITH MIKE HOARE

Aubrey Brooks made his name fighting guerrillas in Rhodesia while serving with the Selous Scouts. Small wonder then, that the legendary Mike Hoare – of *Congo Mercenary* fame – offered him a job when he wanted to invade the Seychelles and overthrow the government. Aubrey tells us how it all unravelled …

It was like something out of a bad movie, recalls Aubrey. War is not supposed to be like this.

There was Roger, Charlie, Ken and myself going up to the guardroom of the barracks on Seychelles' main island of Mahé as if we were a bunch of rookies checking in after a weekend pass. Charlie held out his Kalashnikov to the Seychellois soldier on sentry duty, barrel pointed outwards. Then, barely audible, he asked: "Anyone lost this?"

It all seemed so casual, yet we were there to storm the place, or at least hold the armoury in a bid to stop elements of the Tanzanian Army – who were guarding the airport – from attacking our main invading force. They would need weapons to do that and our job was to stop them getting any. It was all so unreal, crazy in fact; just the four of us determined to stop a fairly substantial military force.

"Don't panic," said Charlie to the soldiers manning the armoury gate. "Just put your guns down and nobody will get hurt." I was still getting out of the car that had driven us there when this fellow in front of us simply emptied his magazine in our direction. He started firing blindly from his hip, typically Third World.

Charlie took a bullet in his left shoulder and another hit my right thigh, clipping the bone and obviously causing damage and pain. I went down immediately and rolled behind the vehicle for cover.

Although I suddenly found myself in a relatively secure position, I didn't hesitate before I began to return fire at the guardhouse with my own weapon, also an AK that had originally seen good service in some remote African conflict. We'd all been issued with them before leaving South Africa.

Momentarily I'd lost sight of Ken, but he was firing from somewhere close. Charlie had taken cover behind a bush away to the left, but Roger was standing right out in the open and exchanging shots with the Tanzanian from about 20 paces away. It was like the gunfight at the O.K. Corral.

"For God's sake take cover!" I yelled. That was when he ran across to a little house across the way that appeared to be perched on stilts and started shooting from there.

We were obviously in a pickle, but for the moment we kept on laying down suppressing fire, which I was able to do because I had good cover under a tree. I knew we'd have to move fast because at any moment a bunch of Tanzanian troops would be pouring out of there with only us between them and the main force at the airport.

By then our guys would be in control of the place, but with only AK-47s along with a few clips of ammunition with which they'd arrived, the odds weren't all that good.

Suddenly, a heavy 14.5 mm Soviet-built DshKa anti-aircraft gun opened up on us from somewhere within the barracks. At almost point-blank range my protective tree was being shredded. Whoever was manning the weapon knew what he was doing and with every loud explosion, more shrubbery would topple to the ground around me. Within moments, I was badly exposed.

Still, this was no time to hesitate and I did what I could to retaliate. I was determined to get the bastard who'd shot me. I could clearly see him there, crouched low behind a wall on the veranda just ahead of the guardroom, randomly firing bursts in my direction. It was one of these volleys, initially aimed at Roger, which had hit me.

Things were getting serious and I was becoming desperate for some kind of headway. Try as I may, I just couldn't score. My rounds would strike the roof over my attacker's head and the next burst would hit the ground in front of him, both times sending up puffs of dirt. Stripped-down Kalashnikovs are perfect for close-quarter combat, but seriously inadequate when it comes to accuracy.

We then crawled under the stilted house for better cover, but the anti-aircraft gun was no less of a menace. Fortunately, it jammed fairly regularly, which meant that the barrel had to be cleared every few shots and that gave us a bit of a breather. Then the heavy stuff

Mercenary soldiers and former Rhodesian Selous Scout Aubrey Brooks (left) together with his fellow conspirator Roger England being paraded before the world press after being captured on Mahe Island in the Seychelles following their aborted attempt at overthrowing the government.
(Photo: Aubrey Brooks)

would whine about our ears again. Still worse, time was running out, not to mention our ammo.

It was at about this point that we decided to try to move up the hillside and work out a way to get into the base and silence the gun. All we had to do, according to the original plan, was to seize that armoury, but suddenly everything seemed to have come very badly unstuck.

From our improvised vantage point we spotted movement towards the rear of the barracks, but at that distance, we couldn't be sure whether the troops were being issued with weapons or moving away. Also, I wasn't in good shape: my right leg felt numb and there was blood everywhere. Roger tried to assure me that it was just a flesh wound and during a lull he tied a tourniquet around the wound, using an improvised bandage torn from my shirt, but it didn't seem to be of much help, which was when the DshKa opened up again and started to track us up the hillside. At least we had decent cover in the bush, or so we thought. It was almost like the old days in Rhodesia.

Roger had just finished his first aid on me when on the road leading to the airport below, we spotted Colonel Hoare and Barney Carey. The colonel, still in his navy blue blazer, seemed unfazed by the battle going on around him, while Barney was busy with what appeared to be a radio. They were directing things, almost impervious to bullets ricocheting off the buildings around them.

We'd lost Ken somewhere in the bush. It was getting toward dusk and starting to drizzle and my leg was beginning to seriously play up. Worse, this was more than a flesh wound, and I was becoming a hindrance to the party, especially as the hill became steeper. We decided I should go down again in a bid to meet up with the main body.

I set off on my own down the hillside, getting cut to ribbons by the thorns, and then I blacked out, probably because of a loss of blood. I came to what must have been hours later, woken, I think, by the sound of a large jet coming in to land at the airport down below.

There was an absolute din of small-arms fire coming from the airport, as well as the lower slopes of the hill on which I'd found myself. But you couldn't tell which side was which. We were all using AKs, and it was not at all like it was in the Rhodesian bush where you could always pick out the R1s, R5s or SLRs being used by our own people. I realised then that there was no way that I would be able to get through that lot and reach the main force.

I decided to head higher up the hill again and see if I could make out the lights of the Reef Hotel, where some of us had been staying. I desperately needed to work out some way of getting there and possibly getting help: I was wounded and bleeding. But I guess I didn't think that far ahead, especially as to how you are likely to stagger unobserved into a holiday hotel with a gunshot wound, pick up your key at the desk and go upstairs to call room service for a doctor and a cold lager.

I was in a worse state than ever. Moments later I dropped to my knees and said the Lord's Prayer. I also prayed for some kind of deliverance from a situation that I'd helped create. Suddenly I felt calm and, strange to say, I believe that in spite of what still lay ahead, things began to change for me in the long run. It would be a very long run …

Just then a Seychellois youngster and his sister came up the footpath and almost tripped over me.

"Stop!" I shouted. Stand still and you won't get hurt!" But the woman started screaming, which was the last thing I needed. Her brother and I managed to quieten her down and they gave me a metal mug, a bottle of orange juice and a piece of cloth, which I used to form a more effective tourniquet.

The pair slipped away into the bush, eager to put distance between themselves and this crazy wounded guy with a gun because by now bullets and ricochets were beginning to ping through the trees all around us.

The juice the pair had given me was like nectar. I crawled a short distance up the hillside and found what I thought was a small indent in the hillside, a cave almost, and crawled in. I could still see the lights of the Reef Hotel – so near and yet so far – but the airport sector was a complete blackout. There was no missing the war raging there. Then the pain became intense.

I pulled my leg up onto the branch of a tree to try to stop the bleeding, I knew that with the possibility of shock setting in, I shouldn't fall asleep, but it wasn't too long before I dozed off.

I don't know how long I slept, but I was suddenly awoken by the sound of a large passenger jet taking off. The noise seemed to drown everything else and I was not to know that it had on board our main invasion party, all of them heading back to Durban, comparative safety and arrest. Nor was I to know that my buddy, Barney Carey, who I'd earlier spotted down on the road with Colonel Hoare, had refused to fly back with them and had come to search for me. In fact, he was on the same hill and not all that far from me. We were to share the hardship of the next three years in very close proximity.

What a guy! I reckon I wouldn't have made it without him.

How did I get involved in this escapade? There were several factors and almost all coincided at about the same time while living in Durban.

I was more or less at a loose end at the time I was approached to join an operation that, had it succeeded, would have replaced one government leader in the Seychelles with another. The incumbent when we made our move was a socialist who had developed strong ties with Moscow, Beijing, Pyongyang, Cuba and the rest. Our man was Jimmy Mancham, the anti-communist, blue-eyed boy with Washington and London.

By the time that I'd been approached to get involved in what was clearly an extremely risky venture, I was broke: I'd just been swindled out of just about all the money I could call my own. Like many whites in southern Africa at the time, I had observed the growing presence of both the Soviets and the Chinese in the Indian Ocean Basin. Tanzania had been a radical hot-spot for years, fomenting revolution

Mercenaries tell of brutal ordeal

By EUGENE HUGO, Seychelles

THE personal ordeals of four of "Mad Mike" Hoare's mercenaries are related in affidavits given to the Sunday Times this week.

Apparent from the affidavits is that the mercenary leader had no conception of what his men would go through when he left them behind to flee to South Africa aboard an Air India boeing.

Theirs is a tale of horror told while they sought to stay alive in the hands of military forces shortly after the bungled coup which plunged them into an experience they will never forget.

Bernard Carey's story starts the day after the attempted coup when he was spotted on a hill near the Seychelles airport after electing to stay behind to find his wounded colleague Aubrey Brooks.

Unarmed

The Seychelles army opened up with automatic fire before they physically caught him.

He was unarmed but they kicked and hit him with rifle butts, and then dragged, punched and bundled him into a military vehicle with legs bound and hands handcuffed behind his back.

Rifles were pointed at his head and two soldiers tramped on him alternatively. They kept kicking at a wound he had sustained.

He was beaten with rifle butts, kicked, punched and stripped of his clothing. "They threatened to cut off my testicles, take my eyes out and then they prepared to execute me."

Periodically Brooks was ordered to stand up and lie down quickly — if this was not done quickly enough his guards would come into the cell and punch and kick him.

Brooks received water for the first time two days after the attempted coup — and that evening a doctor came to see him.

"I lost complete us of my hands for about five weeks because of what the doctor called compaction," he said.

the Reef Hotel on November 27 — two days after the failed coup.

At Army HQ, he says, he was "locked in a box".

"I was in this box for two-and-a-half days being questioned daily ... during this time I was allowed no toilet facilities and had to complete them where I stood. I then had to try and sleep the night in it."

England said the handcuffs on him were so tight he could no longer feel his hands.

Cell

Robert Sims' story starts at the mercenary hideout at La Misere, high up in the hills above Victoria.

He says he was arrested and taken to the army barracks and put in a 3m square cell.

"I was told that I would be given food and water every second day and would be allowed to go to the toilet only then. I spent about five days there."

He said he was then taken by the army back to the same

Early newspaper report of the attempted invasion of the Seychelles by a group of mercenaries led by Colonel 'Mad' Mike Hoare.

in the Portuguese territories, Rhodesia and elsewhere; Madagascar had gone communist and by all accounts, the Seychelles Archipelago, a beautiful tropical paradise, appeared to be headed down the same road. Anything to reverse this trend simply had to be a good cause.

Four factors, all of them coinciding, got me into the venture. Apart from the cause, I sensed a good chance of success. Had I not done so, I probably would not have become involved.

Colonel Mike Hoare – some of his associates called him "Mad Mike" Hoare – I knew by repute. I'd met with him, heard him explain the operation and to my mind it sounded good. It was clearly dodgy, he warned, but as he suggested, this operation would be carefully planned. I banked on the extensive military experience of this veteran who had not only launched several operations in the Congo, but knew and understood the imponderables of the Third World, Africa and its islands in particular.

Mike Hoare's book on his Congolese exploits, *Congo Mercenary*, was first published almost half-a-century ago. The fact that it appeared again in print in Britain and America for the umpteenth time in 2008, tells you a lot.

And then, of course there was the money: I needed lots of it. On top of which, *I was available*. Had I still been running the printing business I'd bought after coming to South Africa from Rhodesia after the war, I would probably have given it a miss. But that, too, was history. Bottom line: I was eager to get into something that was both interesting and lucrative.

It was Ken who had originally approached me and while I said I was interested, I wanted to know a bit more about how things would happen. Logistics was only a part of it: the team with whom I'd be involved was the other half.

With the passage of time, the story seems somehow to have been spread about that the Seychelles operation was originally hatched across the bar counter in Durban's Riviera Hotel. That is simply not true.

Granted, the Riviera Hotel was the haunt of various former Rhodesians. We'd gather there after a day's work for a beer or two, in my case partly because it was just down the road from where I worked, but also because Ken Dalglish, the man who owned and ran the place was himself an ex-Rhodesian and, as one wag phrased it, our kind of expatriates like to hang out together.

That said, the hotel was simply not the sort of place where things happened. You couldn't get a crowd of fellows together in a public place to discuss something as sensitive as this. In any event, the Durban Press Club was on the floor above and what we did not need was for the media to get wind of it.

Ken was very well placed to contact a number of former Rhodesian Army veterans and he initially approached me in the pub. I expect it was the same with other former servicemen from north of the Limpopo who ended up joining forces with Mike Hoare. In the end, it was all quiet talk out on the veranda, never more than two or three people at a time, and when we eventually met the colonel for an initial briefing, I didn't recognise half the people there.

First impressions of Colonel Mike Hoare were memorable. For a start, I was surprised how small he was: I'd always imagined him as a fairly big fellow, but he was actually quite short and wiry.

Yet, when he addressed us that first time in Durban, I could see that there was a lot more to him than the component parts of the individual who greeted us at the door. This was a giant of a man, an officer and a gentleman,

His first briefing came across with total clarity and once over, you felt that he had a good command of the situation. In clipped, professional military lingo, he explained that we would be reinstalling a legitimately elected president who had been deposed by a bunch of Marxist revolutionaries – something that had taken place in June 1977. He went on to tell us that our basic strength lay not in the number of guns involved, but in the element of surprise.

He intimated that the opposition would be weak; that a majority of the citizens in the Seychelles were not only deeply concerned with the new leader's radical policies, but were unhappy that their children were subjected to compulsory youth camps where they were all but brainwashed. The youngsters were taught some skills, granted, but the focus was on basic military training. Colonel Hoare declared that there would be popular support for us on the islands and it would all be over in weeks.

When I emerged from that first meeting, I knew that this was something for me. When you've experienced as many military operations as I have – numerous with Ron Reid-Daly's Selous Scouts – you soon come to recognise quality. I'd spotted it in the manner that Colonel Hoare methodically ticked off item by item and dealt with every possibly option, including the strength and deployment of "enemy" forces. He'd obviously done his homework. I was also impressed by the way he kept cool about what was clearly a major operation. There was no question: the leadership element was sound.

By this stage, Colonel Hoare had not actually named our target country. Instead he dealt with generalities, talking about "some country up north". There was no mention of an Indian Ocean island, though obviously some of those involved were already aware of our ultimate destination.

Before he was prepared to identify our objective, Colonel Hoare told the gathering this was the time for anyone who had misgivings to withdraw. Only one man did, an officer with a local Citizen Force regiment. The man had spent some good time on the border, but said he couldn't make himself available for this kind of thing. But he thanked the colonel all the same for inviting him and withdrew.

At that, Colonel Hoare unrolled a map of the Seychelles. He explained to the uninitiated that it was a tropical island group in the Indian Ocean, populated mainly by Madagascans, Indians and Creoles, but that as everybody was aware, it was already a popular tourist destination. As he explained, the Seychelles had formerly been a French colonial possession – which is why so many of the locals remained Francophonic. It was annexed during the Napoleonic Wars by Britain, but as we have also seen in Mauritius – also previously French and called Bourbon – social traditions die hard. At this point he produced a detailed battle plan.

"Gentlemen," said the Colonel, "this is our objective." He disclosed that a safe house had already been established on Mahé, the main island. What emerged only after it was all over was that his brother-in-law Bobby Simms, together with Susan Ingle, had set it up a few months before. Already installed was a small stock of weapons, which had been smuggled through customs and immigration at the airport. Security, he added, was pretty lax.

An advance party of six, to which both Ken and I were designated, would arrive on the main island about a week before it was all due to happen. We would pass ourselves off as businessmen and tourists and our main job would be to reconnoitre and check intelligence already provided by an underground resistance movement known locally as the Movement for the Resistance, or *Mouvement Pour La Résistance*.

'Happy snap' taken by a member of the main mercenary group as it arrived at Mahe Airport.
(Photo: Aubrey Brooks' collection)

We would also be tasked to prepare for the arrival of the main group by air from southern Africa and armed, be waiting at the airport to greet them, in case anything went amiss. If necessary, we'd organise a diversionary attack, which is basically what we ended up doing. Others in the advance party would handle reconnaissance and prepare for the main attack: All in all, there would have been ten of us, but the colonel finally cut it down to six: anything bigger might become noticeable, he felt.

The main attack group – about 40 men in all – would come into the Seychelles on a charter flight from Swaziland, posing as members of the Ancient Order of Froth Blowers, a charity organisation, which combined good deeds with heavy partying. Ostensibly, they were there to play a game of rugby, get tanked up and distribute toys to orphanages. It seemed a fairly effective cover at the time.

Finally the big day arrived for our initial party and we headed out from Johannesburg on a commercial flight. It was sobering to accept that this was for real: we'd have to pass through customs at Mahé with our baggage with false bottoms that had been specially adapted to hold automatic weapons as well as ammunition. It was already dark when the intercom on board told us to buckle up and next thing our wheels touched down gently on Mahé island.

I'd been a little light-headed with in-flight drinks but, as I glanced at the lights along the runway whizzing past and which gradually slowed, I sobered up fast. Our objective was at hand and this was for real. There were the usual pleasantries with cabin crew staff as we left, but I was knotted up inside.

As I stepped out of the cabin onto the stairway, I was struck full in the face by a moist tropical night with just a hint of saltiness in it.

Ken and I stood in line in the arrival hall with just that little touch of apprehension to add to the tiredness and anticlimax that follows a tedious air flight. At the immigration desk, an officer helped Des Botes to fill in his form as he played to the full his role of a heartbroken inebriate. Ken and I went through without any hold-ups.

"Enjoy your stay Monsieur Brooks," the white-clad Creole official said with a broad smile as he stamped my passport and handed it back.

"I'm sure I will," I replied beaming.

Seychelles Customs and Excise followed, the moment of truth. The officers appeared to be examining luggage at random and just ahead in the queue was a minister of religion and his wife. We'd learned earlier on board the aircraft that they had just got married and were on their honeymoon. The couple had to open their bags and the customs officer rifled through them, which was when I felt my palms go clammy.

Then, to my surprise, I was waved through and before we knew it, Ken and I had our bags loaded on to a minibus by a hugely social Seychellois with an enormous smile who just threw them on the roof without a care: at least the AKs weren't loaded. Moments later we were bowling along a succession of narrow, twisting roads; our passage interrupted only by the occasional pothole.

Our route to the hotel took us across a mountain ridge and the speed was hair-raising. But I was pleased we'd come through and at last we were headed for a shower, a meal and bed. On reflection afterwards, I thought it had perhaps been a little too easy. To start with, Ken and I were booked into the beautiful Beau Vallon Bay Hotel, while Barney stayed at the Coral Strand. Roger England and Charlie Dukes, two other members of the advance party, were scheduled to arrive the next day and were scheduled to stay at the Reef Hotel.

The initial plan was for us to be located separately, so as not to raise any kind of suspicion that we might be connected, but some members of the advance party had already met on the plane and it was only natural that we should hang out together.

The next day we hired a car and started on the reconnaissance work, all the while carefully blending in with the usual sort of thing that tourists do. We met up with some of the folk we'd met on the flight and who had nothing to do with the mission and kept it sociable.

Principally, we were involved in verifying intelligence supplied by the Seychellois Resistance Movement with regard to troop numbers and deployment, the presence of foreign soldiers (including a Tanzanian Army unit and some Chinese) and the numbers of police normally in the capital and their location.

My key objective was to check out the country's radio and broadcast stations. Once the rest of the party had taken the barracks and captured the armoury, it would be our job to take over the radio station and play tapes that had been prepared in advance. These would announce that a countercoup had taken place and that President James Mancham was back in power. The people would be told that within an hour of a successful putsch, the new government would arrive by air from Kenya, and hopefully, welcomed by jubilant crowds in the streets.

Information supplied by the island resistance movement seemed reasonably accurate. There were two companies of Tanzanian troops on the islands – roughly 200 men. Most were billeted in the main barracks near the airport and, as the need might arise, would be supplied with weapons from the same armoury we attempted to capture. Essentially, it would be our job to stop that happening, which was why I found myself outside that building at the start of the insurrection.

The barracks were also supported by a couple of armoured cars and, as we were to discover, there certainly were Russians about, but they were mainly construction workers. It was the same with expatriate Chinese groups working in the Seychelles.

We carefully built up a picture over several days, combining these activities with some tourist stuff like snorkelling and swimming in the marvellously clear ocean while mingling with genuine tourists and partying with them. There were times when some of us would genuinely forget the task at hand and then we would pull ourselves together again.

At one stage we came across a topless bathing beach and this, too, was an experience for this former Rhodesian …

There is no doubt that as a holiday destination, the Seychelles is idyllic. There are palm-fringed beaches in every direction, interspersed by a patchwork of small farms that produce sugar, coffee and other crops. There's a theory around that the Seychelles was the original Garden of Eden and I wouldn't knock it.

We managed to complete much of our reconnaissance work within the first four or five days and on the face of it, everything seemed as it should be. We believed that taken by surprise, the army barracks at Pointe Larue – which housed the main concentration of Tanzanian troops near the airport – would be a pushover. Though there would be less than 50 of us, if we moved in quickly and decisively and followed the original plan – which included taking the armoury – everything would be over fairly quickly.

The idea was that the "Froth Blowers" would stick to their cover role as tourists until Zero Hour, which would be something like three or four days after they arrived.

The intention was to launch the main attack on a Saturday afternoon, while the majority of the army and a lot of the population were at a football match, always a popular pastime on the island. Once we had wrapped things up, Kenyan troops would arrive from the mainland to take over the principal administration role in the country and we would quietly disappear over the horizon.

Before any of that happened, we would linger unobtrusively at the airport with our weapons as the main group arrived. Our presence was regarded as essential in the event of something going wrong. If something were to take place that might jeopardise the mission, our job would be to create a diversion by firing a number of rounds off at the barracks, drive away, ditch our weapons in the sea and quietly merge back into our roles as bona fide tourists.

That kind of activity at the airport would be a signal for the aircraft to abort the landing and head back to South Africa.

Perhaps it was an unlucky omen, but the night before the main party was due to arrive on the island, Ken went down with a stomach bug that floored him. He ended up pale as a sheet, sweating and shaking between bouts of diarrhoea and vomiting. The next morning he was still sick and I told him to remain behind. By lunch he'd improved enough to feel competent to do his job and said he would come along.

Some of our party spent the morning snorkelling at a reef, after which we returned to the hotel and had a steak *braai* – the southern African term for a barbeque. We didn't know it at the time, but that was the last bit of red meat some of us were to enjoy for a very long time. After that we assembled our weapons in our hotel rooms and clipped in the ammo.

The AKs in their protective covering were placed in our car boot and covered with beach gear and we set out for the airport to meet the boys. The flight was due shortly after three in the afternoon.

When we arrived at the airport, Bobby Simms was already there. So was my ultimate nemesis, Martin Dolinchek.

Bobby had Dolinchek's AK in the boot of his car because this Yugoslav – being the self-centred cuss he is – had hired an open-sided "mini-moke" taxi which had no trunk. This was not the only anticlimax, because the flight was also delayed for two hours. As previously arranged, we dispersed and did a last-minute recce of the barracks and the radio station.

Instead of hanging about the airport and drawing attention to ourselves, Ken, Barney, Des and I went to the Reef Hotel for tea and buns; we even had a quick game of tennis, but by now the butterflies were doing overtime.

The inevitable questions were being asked: Had the boys been rumbled in Swaziland and their weapons discovered? We didn't like the delay but there was nothing we could do about it. Soon enough we were back at the airport doing final checks along the way. Everything seemed normal. Our group sat around drinking tea or beer in the cafeteria and at this point we were all fairly relaxed.

Aubrey Brooks (front left) with Bobby Simms on the way to stand trial in a Seychelles court.

The Swazi Air flight eventually arrived and it wasn't long before the "Froth Blowers" were filing through immigration. Our worries had evaporated and it seemed that the game was on. The plan had gone into action and our intensely focused minds took over.

I got up and strolled outside the airport terminal. Our "Froth Blowers" bags were already being piled on the buses – Kalashnikovs, ammo and all. I spotted a couple of guys that I'd spent time with in the Rhodesian war: we exchanged brief flashes of recognition and nothing more. It was good to see that the men were still professionals.

Barney and I waited at the door for Colonel Hoare to give him a lift to his hotel.

We had just asked him to give us a few moments while I told the fellows in the cafeteria to get back to their hotels, when there was commotion inside the main terminal building. I heard a woman yell something and then a shot rang out. She came running past us shouting: "He's got a gun ... *he's got a gun!*" At this point our plan unravelled.

It had actually begun to go sour when the plane put down at Moroni, capital of the island republic of the Comores, about 600 kilometres south of the Seychelles. Three passengers had arrived at Moroni Airport and asked whether there was space available on the aircraft to the Seychelles. Although our flight was a private charter, somebody felt that perhaps the three tourists would provide a little additional cover to the mission.

Sadly though, one of the French passengers had some litchis, a type of tropical fruit in his baggage and had ignored the in-flight warning of the stewardesses that it was illegal to take any kind of plant into the Seychelles. This was fate at its cruellest.

Additionally, one of the men from the Transvaal contingent disobeyed orders by assembling his AK and placing it in the normal luggage part of his bag. He believed it would be handy if things went wrong. We weren't to know it, but the trap was sprung and baited.

Meantime, Colonel Hoare and most of the main party had already passed through immigration and customs, and their bags loaded onto the hotel vehicles.

Their baggage had been randomly opened, with some of the customs officers amused by squeaky toys and things they found that were intended for the orphans. Colonel Hoare suggests in his book *The Seychelles Affair*[1], that his friends in the Resistance had organised for their supporters to be on duty in customs that day, and true or not, things went smoothly until one of the officers found the bunch of litchis in one of the passengers' luggage from the Comores.

A noisy altercation followed and the litchis were confiscated. Then a customs supervisor (not a Resistance supporter according to the Colonel's account) insisted that all the remaining bags be properly searched: they apparently take their fruit regulations seriously in the Seychelles. And as luck would have it, the next person in line was our man who had assembled his AK.

If the litchis caused a fuss, everything at the airport came to an abrupt halt once the automatic weapon emerged. Initially the customs officer mistook the carbine for an underwater spear gun, which is illegal in the Seychelles. He would have to confiscate it, he said. A receipt would be provided and he could pick it up again on his way out of the country, which was fair enough. But when he tried to confiscate it, a noisy tug-of-war followed.

The commotion caught the attention of a security officer, who picked up a telephone. It turned out that he was alerting the military barracks. With that things got totally out of control: a loose round was fired from the weapon and the security guard high-tailed it out of the building.

It was that single shot that alerted me to the problems we faced. Next, we saw that a member of our party was down. Johan Fritz, standing some distance from the tussle and already in the arrivals hall, was struck in the heart by the stray bullet. His life ebbed away and there was absolutely nothing anyone could do to help him. After that things got serious. Jerry Puren, one of the veterans from Durban who had been flying combat as a mercenary pilot in the Congo – and who was also a friend of Colonel Hoare – was on the roof of one of the buses. Sensing the inevitable, he flung down the bags and ordered the group to assemble their weapons.

The colonel moved briskly across to me, "Aubrey, get the rest of your guys together, hotfoot it to Point Laurie and delay any troops from leaving the barracks," were his words.

That was the last I saw of the engagement at the airport. I had to rely on what others, including Colonel Hoare, told me to sketch what happened next:

"Apparently, our people sent another group to attack the barracks but an armoured car blocked the gateway and turned them back. Our entire attacking force then threw a strong defensive position round the airport and somebody took the control tower without any problem. Apparently the air traffic controller took refuge in a dustbin.

"Several hundred civilians were herded into one of the airport halls for their own safety, followed shortly afterwards by three truckloads of Tanzanian troops that came hurtling down the runway, dismounted, and then advanced on foot. They were hardly effective: most of these African soldiers bolted when fired on and

Colonel Mike Hoare's welcome home party for Aubrey Brooks – left to right – unknown, Barney Carey, Colonel Hoare, Peter Duffy, Aubrey Brooks and Bobby Simms

were never seen again. However, one of the vehicles that had brought the Tanzanian troops was left abandoned on the runway, clearly a hazard to any aircraft that might land.

"It was dark by the time that two armoured cars moved onto the airport apron and started shelling the terminal buildings. One of the armoured vehicles was knocked out by our men and the other pulled back. Mortars were lobbed at the terminal by the defenders but with little accuracy.

"We had certainly achieved our cherished element of surprise but as Colonel Hoare maintains in his book, there was no reason at all why we should not have been able to take the barracks by daybreak and completed the mission."

However, things did not work out that way. There was an attempt to get the Air Swazi crew to come back to the airport from the Reef Hotel. They had already booked in and the idea was to get them to fly the party out again. Jerry Puren went across the road outside the airport to a small petrol station and telephoned the crew, but they opted out when they heard what was going on. In the end, their aircraft got hit in the ensuing shelling that came from some distance away and the plane was damaged. It was about then that an Air India Boeing 707 was approaching Mahé to land, a commercial flight from India with passengers on board.

There is some dispute as to what happened next. Colonel Hoare maintained that he ordered a former Rhodesian helicopter pilot to get himself into the control tower and take over the island's air traffic control function. The idea was to order the airliner to abort its landing and head elsewhere. Another source maintains that the colonel's order was countermanded. The Natal Supreme Court found differently in the subsequent hijacking trial of all the mercenaries who returned to South Africa, but I am inclined to believe the colonel because the position was by no means hopeless. According to some members of our group, the Tanzanian troops had no guts for a fight and our people could easily have taken the barracks.

All that is now for the record books. I wasn't at the airport; instead, I was in the bush somewhere overlooking the airport, believing that I was bleeding to death.

The colonel and the rest of his party eventually boarded the Air India jet and took off for Durban. That left behind Barney, a couple of others and myself – all of us stranded on the island we'd intended to conquer. I blame nobody, because quite simply, we had become casualties of war. Each one of us had been aware of the risks that we faced. But as I lay in the bush, badly wounded and listening to that

Air India passenger jet taking off in the dark, I wasn't yet aware that the rest of the gang had pulled out.

I actually had no idea quite how desperate our position had become, or what waited for us over the next three years of incarceration and trial, after which the death sentence was handed down, but all that is a story for another day …

1   Colonel Mike Hoare: *The Seychelles Affair*, Bantam Books, New York, 1986.

CHAPTER THREE

OPERATION IMPOSSIBLE – ON THE RUN ACROSS AFRICA

The first time I met Jim Maguire – he'd served in the Royal Marines and in Rhodesia's Special Air Service – it was at the behest of one of those shadowy characters that South Africa seems to produce in abundance. They're invariably charming, well-educated and erudite. Most times they are broke and flit about on the periphery of illegality.

The man who introduced me to Jim Maguire was one such a person. A former sergeant in the South African Army, he was so good at his ruse that while he'd never served in any of the country's elite combat units, he managed to get himself voted into the chair of the South African Special Forces League. How he did that is anybody's guess and some of the old fighters are still kicking themselves.

Then, while living in Constantia, arguably one of the plushest – and most expensive – suburbs in the southern hemisphere, he went on to ingratiate himself with Mark Thatcher and Simon Mann. That all happened under the auspices of South Africa's Military Intelligence while those two characters were living in Cape Town.

Thatcher, for those who aren't familiar with London's social scene, is the son of former British Prime Minister Margaret Thatcher. He evaded jail for his role in that sordid escapade by paying a fine of several millions and there are still questions being asked as to his actual role in the venture. For his part, Mann, a scion of the famous British brewing family who had earlier been linked to the South African mercenary organisation Executive Outcomes, wasn't as fortunate. He was caught, as the saying goes, on the job.

Mann was with dozens of others on board an aircraft that was transiting Harare while they were on their way to overthrow the government of Equatorial Guinea. As soon as the aircraft turned off its engines, Zimbabwean security forces arrested them all. Initially, those involved were told that they were en route to pick up all the weapons they would need for the "uprising", which begs the question: just how stupid can you get?

Who in his right mind would even consider touching base in what must arguably be the most paranoid country on the continent of Africa? Surely, one must ask, did the plotters really believe that Robert Mugabe was going to help a bunch of white freebooters overthrow the rule of an equally-demented black president? It all makes for a marvellous movie by some illustrious Hollywood film producer. John Milius, my old friend, are you listening?

The person at the core of this conspiracy must remain nameless, if only for the sake of his son who is stuck with a contemptible father, although everybody involved with him at the time will know who I'm talking about. I actually fingered him in an interview I did for CNN International the day that Mark Thatcher was released from jail. He threatened legal action, but nothing ever came of it.

At the end of it, just about all the South African veterans involved in that invidious African escapade ended up behind bars. They served time either in Zimbabwe or at Malabo's notorious Black Beach Prison, where some of those arrested have since died. Mann, following a spell in Chikurubi Prison in Harare, was extradited to Equatorial Guinea. In a blaze of publicity, he was brought to trial for trying to overthrow the government and then released after having served only a fraction of his sentence.

In the 1970s and 1980s, southern Africa's wars attracted a lot of these freebooters, almost all of them labelled soldiers of fortune. Among them were some Special Forces operators who had served either in British or American combat units.

These were people like Peter McAleese who went on to write his classic *No Mean Soldier* and American Vietnam veteran Chris Clay who eventually made a name for himself serving along the Angolan border as an officer with South Africa's crack 32 Battalion. Clay also spent time in Rhodesia's war, and the last time I spoke to him he was working in the Ivory Coast.

Their stories are riveting. Most were involved in shadowy cross-border strikes and there was intrigue by the bucketful, as well as the kind of duplicity that would please the likes of John le Carré. Betrayal sometimes featured prominently and there were those sucked into this military-politico maelstrom that would die.

Chapter 3
Operation Impossible – on the run across Africa

One such operation might easily have ended with the deaths of the two principal players. Launched from South Africa in 1988, it was handled by two British nationals, Sammy Beahan and Jim Maguire, both of whom had served in British Army Special Forces units and ended up fighting in Rhodesia's war. They went on to serve in the South African Defence Force in Angola, again in a succession of elite commandos.

While still in South Africa the two men got involved in one such escapade. It ended with one on the run and the other captured and tortured by Zimbabwe's North Korean-trained security goons. In their efforts to get away from their pursuers, they twice swam across the Zambezi at night. But more about that later ...

In the process, Sammy Beahan was arrested and served ten years in the same maximum security prison at Chikurubi where Simon Mann was briefly held some years later.

Jim Maguire originally told me the story, and the object of the exercise, he explained, was to find a way to rescue a bunch of former Rhodesian SAS operators held at Zimbabwe's maximum security prison. He wasn't specific about how that task might have been achieved, except that somebody back in Pretoria thought it was feasible to try. Whoever that was, reckoned Maguire, he had the presence of mind to label the task Operation Impossible, which just about says it all.

One of the men held in Chikurubi Prison at the time – and obviously somebody who they hoped to free – was Kevin Woods, the same person who had worked as a double agent for the South African apartheid government as well as for Mugabe's Central Intelligence Organisation or, more commonly, CIO. Somehow he'd let something critical slip and ended up 20 years behind bars, five of them on death row. Woods was released in 2006, after he received a presidential pardon and has since written a book about his experiences through those dreadful years.

Exactly how Maguire and Beahan intended to implement their plan remains vague, even today. There was talk among their colleagues of possibly storming the prison and flying in a clutch of helicopters to assist with the escape. What does become apparent, as they recount some of their unconventional exploits, is that both men were professionals who'd seen regular service in several wars on three or four continents. By the time they set out from Pretoria on what was regarded at the time as a low-key assignment, they'd made themselves thoroughly familiar with both the military and political parameters of all the countries in the region, Zimbabwe and Botswana included.

If successful, the South African military planners felt Operation Impossible might very well have a considerable impact on relations between South Africa and Zimbabwe. If not, their clandestine efforts could easily be disavowed. In the end, they were. Consequently, two highly experienced operators were compromised and hardly anybody was to lose any sleep following that misadventure.

Sammy Beahan, the team leader, had served for nine years in the British Parachute Regiment. During this time, he'd completed four tours in Northern Ireland, spent a couple of years in Berlin and another two conducting internal security tasks in Hong Kong on the Hong Kong-Chinese border. Beahan left the Parachute Regiment with an Exemplary Service Certificate. From there, he went to Rhodesia where he served a couple of years in the Rhodesian Light Infantry before transferring to Rhodesia's SAS. His tasks involved secret missions into the three neighbouring states of Botswana, Mozambique and Zambia.

For a while Beahan joined forces with another British national, Chief Superintendent "Mac" McGuiness of the Rhodesian Special Branch, who worked closely with Lt Col Ron Reid-Daly's Selous Scouts. McGuiness, an old hand at ferreting information from unlikely sources, was responsible for the Scouts' intelligence. He also ran various clandestine internal operations from his Bindura base in Rhodesia.

After Zimbabwe's independence, Beahan chose to head for South Africa rather than accept Mugabe's new political dispensation. He'd spent years trying to kill Mugabe and at that stage felt it made no sense working for him. Once ensconced in Pretoria, Beahan joined the SADF and was given the role in the offices of the Chief of Staff Intelligence (CSI).

Although he remains guarded about the outcome of the venture that he undertook with Maguire, what does become clear is that once Beahan arrived in South Africa, things didn't pan out as expected. It didn't surprise many of his colleagues that he returned to Zimbabwe to serve in the newly revamped Zimbabwe National Army. There are some who maintain he was an SADF plant. Whatever the truth, that didn't work out either, so it wasn't long before the always-cocky Beahan was back on South African soil.

Among his old "oppos" in the South African Army was Jim Maguire, somebody with whom he had worked closely for many years while in Rhodesia. The two men shared a host of common

Chapter 3
Operation Impossible – on the run across Africa

interests including drinking as much beer as possible as often as their women would allow.

Like Beahan, Maguire's track record is commendable. At last count he'd served for 20 years in nine different elite combat regiments in three countries. Since then, he has worked as a private military contractor east of Suez for many years, including lengthy spells in Iraq.

From 1972 onwards, James Maguire served in Britain's Royal Marine Commandos and completed three tours of duty in Northern Ireland. He also took part in the 1974 Cyprus conflict, besides completing the ultra-demanding Royal Marine Commando selection and training cycle as well as the British Paratroopers course.

But as Maguire tells it: "I went to Rhodesia in 1977, joined the Rhodesian Special Air Services, completed their selection training cycle as well as their jump course and spent time as an SAS operator. "From there I transferred to the Selous Scouts, completed their selection and training and worked mainly on border or cross-border operations. Afterwards I transferred back to "A" Troop, Special Forces – a specialised group conducting offensive operations."

Just about then, Rhodesia ceased to exist. Almost overnight Zimbabwe emerged from the shadows of conflict as the new national entity. Moreover it had Westminster's blessing and shortly afterwards became a member of the United Nations.

Maguire saw little hope in the long term for the fledgling African state and it wasn't long before he'd followed Beahan to Pretoria. Having also been inducted into the SADF, he too was posted to CSI for a period, together with several other colleagues from Rhodesia's Special Forces.

"From CSI," says Maguire, "I transferred to the Reconnaissance Wing of 32 Battalion and ended up in operations that sometimes took us deep into Angola." Among his contemporaries was Chris Clay, as well as Eeben Barlow, the man who went on to establish Executive Outcomes.

His next step, having successfully completed one of the most demanding selection courses in any man's army, was a move to 1 Reconnaissance Regiment – also known colloquially as the Recces – where he spent several years. By the end of 1987, he'd transferred to 5 Recce.

Fighting Angolans was interesting work, recalls Jim Maguire. Almost all of it, while attached to the Recces, took place behind enemy lines.

Most assignments involved gathering intelligence. Occasionally the unit was tasked to harass Angolan Army (FAPLA) lines of communication, planting mines or organising stand-off attacks that might involve bringing in an air strike or perhaps directing long-range artillery onto a specific target. He is of the opinion that while it took a while, the young soldiers who handled South Africa's G-5 155 mm long-range guns were good. They consistently proved their ability to home in on a target within about three or four shots, quite often assisted by a spotter perched nearby, usually up a tree with a view of the battlefield.

Like Beahan, Maguire was a major player in trying to dislodge a combined Angolan and Cuban force from Cuito Cuanavale. It was a massive semi-conventional effort and lasted for almost a year. Ultimately the Cuito Bridgehead became the focal point of war in the entire south-eastern Angolan region.

By early 1988, Maguire had been involved in conflict of one kind or another for 16 years, most of it on foreign soil. Another event that took place that year was the start of a series of combined efforts by South Africa, the Soviets, Moscow's Cuban cohorts as well as Portugal – the former colonial overlord – to make a determined effort to end the Angolan war. It had been tried often enough before, but even a Kremlin numbskull could see that this was a conflict that was going nowhere. It was then that a series of peace efforts on the part of the Americans produced dividends.

The Soviets had taken a mighty knock the year before, in what some historians like to refer to as "The Battle for Cuito" (where three Angolan brigades under Soviet, Cuban and East German leadership were routed during an eight-month campaign). Almost overnight, Moscow – still fettered and losing men and equipment at a dizzy pace in Afghanistan – seemed more amenable to bringing the campaign to a halt. Africa Watchers had been aware for some time that Angolan military issues had become problematic for Moscow's military planners: the war was going nowhere and it was costing the Soviets a lot of money. While Luanda got all the hardware it needed, it was nobody's secret that the Angolan Army couldn't fight a decent battle, never mind a war.

In the eyes of some of these East European strategists, Africa had suddenly become superfluous in the eyes of the Politburo, especially since Afghanistan had acquired a much higher profile. Therefore, with the Soviet economy in a tailspin, the Angolan effort had to go. Meantime, on the other side of the firing line, some Special Forces personnel – including Beahan and Maguire – were put on standby for other operations, including one that involved the possible snatch of former Rhodesian and South African soldiers from Zimbabwe prisons.

Initially, the idea was that Maguire and Beahan would go into Zimbabwe and pose as tourists. They'd avoid flying in directly and instead, take the circuitous route through Botswana, Zimbabwe's neighbour to the west. Once inside the country, they'd do reconnaissance for what was to follow.

Maguire and Beahan finally flew into Botswana's biggest airport at Gaborone. It had been arranged beforehand that a contact would be waiting for them outside the terminal building with a set of keys to a vehicle. That done, they'd head north towards the Zambezi River and Zimbabwe.

As Maguire remembers, on arrival in Botswana there was the customary tension associated with an initial phase of what was to become one of the hairiest clandestine operations on which he'd ever embarked. "What we didn't need, was to get into a situation where we'd have to talk to people who might question us, or worse, recognise us.

"Botswana – in terms of population – is a small country. But you never knew who you might run into: old friends from the Rhodesian days, or someone who knew you from home. A hint of suspicion, and it's over," he declared nonchalantly.

As planned, the two men spent the night at a hotel close to the Zimbabwe border and then waited until late afternoon the following day before proceeding.

"The idea was to reach the border post and cross just before last light. If there were problems, it'd be easier to set in motion our escape and evasion plan ... better in the dark than in daylight ...

"Then we ran into two Irish hitchhikers: they were actually at the customs post when we got there. One of the Botswana customs officials asked if we could give them a lift to the nearest hotel since we were all heading that way.

Sam and our two newfound Irish friends went through all the formalities and had no problems. But then the customs officer in charge of our entry discovered that he didn't have the necessary customs documents needed for vehicles.

No problem. One of the other officials suggested that I drive his colleague to the nearby border post to pick up the necessary forms and bring them back. We did this, me being aware that in the interest of good neighbourliness, we'd probably avoid having our vehicle searched," Maguire recalled.

"What I hadn't expected was to pass through a control point at the other border crossing where, to my horror, the policeman on duty at his desk had a full-face photograph and description of me before him. It was the first thing I spotted – I actually saw it lying almost discarded at his elbow: at that stage he hadn't yet clicked that it was a picture of me. I couldn't help thinking just then that it was an incredible stroke of bad luck. From where I stood in front of the officer's desk, I could see another page or two below my "wanted poster", still more documents that I surmised contained Beahan's details.

"For a moment I was too shocked to react. Clearly, we'd been shopped: those buggers had been waiting for us." By then, Maguire realised, the policeman had also clicked.

"Twice he looked at me and then glanced down at the poster on his desk before reacting. It was something almost instinctive. In a loud voice he called for the rest of his colleagues and told somebody to bring a gun."

Within seconds Maguire was completely surrounded by uniformed officials. By their immediate reaction, it was clear that the group was elated: they'd caught themselves a South African spy. The gathering became even more animated when the customs man told them that there was another man waiting to cross the border at the control point from which they had just arrived.

Maguire says that things then quickly developed in his mind. He could hear a police officer in the next room on his radio telling his Zimbabwe counterpart: "We've got them! We've got them! Come quickly!" There were several more messages going out, this time, to a Zimbabwe CIO team, obviously waiting for developments in Livingstone.

Meanwhile, a group of Botswana officials had gone back to the original border post to fetch Sam and the tourists. All four travellers were taken into custody and cramped into the back of the car that Maguire and Beahan had used to travel north. With a police vehicle in front and another bringing up the rear, the party was escorted to the local police base, followed by more radio calls to Zimbabwe.

"We could hear the Zimbabwe guys telling the Botswana Police that if we tried to make a run for it, they'd already deployed their people on the ground. About then the Botswana authorities started a search of our car and somebody noticed that there were items hidden inside the door panelling.

"About then, Sam and I were exchanging glances. We knew that hanging about there any longer would be suicide and since we were both familiar with the drill, I didn't have to tell Sam what to do. We'd revert to the Special Forces basic escape and evasion doctrine of not wasting time. We had to make our move.

"There were a lot of customs and police officials around us, and those in our immediate proximity weren't armed. Within moments, we'd knocked them down and made a run for a tall security fence that surrounded the base that we had a pretty good look at earlier. In the rush that followed, customs and police officers made a grab for our legs as we tried to scramble over the fence.

"But they couldn't stop us. We were in pretty good shape in those days and Sammy is as tough as old boots. Also, it's no secret that I can handle myself in a tight corner. We probably only avoided being shot because there were so many of their own people milling about. Once over the fence and into the bush on the other side where it was dark, we disappeared into the shadows and put some distance between us and them."

At this point Beahan turned to Maguire and said something about having hurt his ankle. It probably happened in the jump. The injury was serious, he said. "Either he'd broken a bone or had torn ligaments: which meant that he could hardly walk," reckoned Maguire.

With customs, the police and everybody else who could walk, run or crawl on their tracks, the two men made their way as best they could in the direction of the Zambezi River. Beahan limped badly all the way. It was only a few hundred metres, Maguire recalls, but it was a tough haul and he had to support him all the way.

Their hopes leapt as they emerged on the river bank and Maguire sprinted ahead towards a speedboat tethered to a makeshift jetty. Beahan arrived immediately afterwards, and having jumped on board what was clearly a customs patrol boat, they pushed off into the stream which was flowing at a rate of knots. While they had mobility, Maguire suddenly realised that there were no keys. The boat couldn't be started.

"So there we were, drifting downstream and just about everybody in town lining the river bank screaming at us, a wild, gesticulating mob that sensed blood. At that point the first of many shots pierced the gathering gloom.

"Obviously we couldn't stay where we were. Also, we couldn't get away any faster than the current allowed. Added to which, there was still enough light to silhouette us against the sky and give those taking pot shots at us a sense of direction. That was when we decided to swim for it.

"It was a momentuous decision. Bullets were plopping in the water all around the boat. If we stayed where we were, we'd probably be hit. Also, we'd already accepted the ramifications of the predicament we were in. We'd be facing the current of a fast-flowing river that was notorious for crocodiles and hippos. But we went ahead anyway and by the time we'd crossed and reached the Zambian bank of the river to the north, it was totally dark."

Maguire is uncertain about the time it took to swim across one of Africa's great waterways which, at that point, was easily a kilometre across, perhaps more. It was a hugely strenuous effort, but they got there in the end. For much of the time there were searchlights constantly scanning the river.

Maguire: "Once in Zambian territory, we had more problems, not least trying to move through an extremely dense and compacted reed bank that stretched out almost a hundred metres into the river. It would have been a cake walk with a panga (machete) but all we had was our hands. Also, we were up to our necks in mud in that final stage. That meant that to make any kind of progress, we had to force down the reeds in front of us to get some traction for our feet. We'd move forward a few inches, lift ourselves onto the embedded reeds and then repeat the process.

We didn't have time or the energy to give any of the creatures that might have been in the water around us more than a passing thought: this was damn hard work and it took a while. There were crocs there, we knew – there are crocs along the entire length of the river, some really big mothers – but they didn't bother us. Meanwhile, there had been a lot of activity on the opposite bank. People with torches were running along the water's edge, joined soon afterwards by some fast boats with spotlights. Everybody and his uncle were out looking for us.

"Finally we made it to hard ground and, for a little while, we rested. At least we'd made Zambia. I can tell you that we were mighty pleased to find nobody there waiting for us: communications between north and south just then was obviously not that hot.

"I took a few moments to look at Sam's ankle. It had taken a real beating moving through the reeds. But we couldn't stay there, right alongside the water because it was all pretty exposed. In any event, the Zimbabweans would have alerted Zambia's militia or army and they'd soon come looking for the two white bastards who'd given them the slip. In fact, it wasn't long before we saw some lights heading our way.

"Not long afterwards we spotted fires being lit along the river bank and could hear people moving around and shouting. This new group of searchers was getting closer. It was a progressive process, with the searchers carefully checking one area after the other and though it took some hours, they slowly edged closer. Since our options were limited, we decided that we couldn't do better than get back into the water."

As quickly as Beahan's ankle would allow, the two men moved some distance down the Zambian bank where they discovered a primitive wooden dug-out canoe hidden in the reeds, alongside what looked like a hippo path.

"We manoeuvred the makorro towards the stream and got in. Trouble was, it sank under us after about 10 metres, something we really hadn't bargained for. So we started swimming ... again." Quite a bit of time had elapsed by now, but there really was no opportunity to contemplate any kind of alternative," he said.

It was a long haul back to the Zimbabwe side of the river. As Maguire recalls, it seemed to take an eternity and by now they were aware of crocs and hippos because there was some movement in the water around them. Also, because there had been a huge amount of effort and the chase had been going on for hours, both men were near exhaustion. About all that was positive was that most of the search parties on the Botswana side of the river had moved further downstream.

"It was a long swim back across the Zambezi, and now we really were bushed. About all that kept us afloat was the thought that if we stayed in the river we'd either drown or be taken by the crocs. The current didn't help either, it was fast moving and constantly swirling around us.

"Finally we made it to dry ground. We got out of the water and made our way to a clump of bush, just as dawn was breaking."

Leaving Beahan behind to try to strap his ankle, Maguire set out to assess the situation before the world around them came alive. He needed to establish their position as quickly as possible, but found conditions confusing. What soon became apparent was that the current had swept the two men quite a long way downstream. Their immediate problem then was that they weren't quite sure whether they had drifted into Zimbabwe or were still in Botswana.

"By the time I got back to the hideout, Sam's ankle was worse. The ankle was swollen like a cricket ball and after all that exertion, he couldn't even stand on it.

"But what I'd found from my little sortie was that we'd actually made it back to the Botswana side of the river. In fact, we weren't all that far from the road that we'd intended travelling the previous evening. The way I worked it out, we must have been about eight or ten kilometres from the hotel where we'd spent the previous day.

"That meant still more decisions. Since Sam couldn't move, we decided that he'd stay in the hide where we'd holed up. I'd go back to the hotel and phone through to our contact that our operation had been blown. Obviously I'd do it innocuously enough and in code. Also, this would give me an opportunity to see what arrangements I could make to get us out of this mess … we had money, we had somebody that we could talk to and they hadn't caught us after an effort that probably involved hundreds of people. We'd become quite optimistic," recalls Maguire.

"Sam stayed in the hide while I walked through the bush to the hotel. Both he and I had an escape and evasion kit sewn into our belts, together with a couple of thousand British pounds between us. At the hotel, I made the call from the lobby phone to the appropriate person and gave him the emergency call-sign that indicated that the operation had been compromised. I had to do so in order that members of the team in other locations could be warned and take appropriate action. If I was blown, I reckoned, then so were they: as it turned out afterwards, I was right. I also told my contact that we were stuck and that Sam was injured badly. Discreetly, and with security utmost in my mind, I asked him what we should do and whether he was in a position to lend a hand considering that we were at the far end of Botswana from where he was. It was then that he told me, almost in as many words, that we were on our own.

"After I'd finished talking, I discreetly left the hotel. Meantime, I'd spent a bit of time trying to clean up as much as possible, especially since I'd arrived at the hotel in a filthy state from the mud, the reed beds and swimming the river. Though it was still early, I got quite a few quizzical glances from the staff.

"Just as I walked out of the front of the hotel, a guy who I recognised as one of the local game rangers we'd met a couple of nights before emerged from his game-viewing Land Rover. He saw me, did a double-take at my appalling condition and said hi. Which was when he jokingly added: 'Gee, you look like you've just swum the river.' Taking a chance, I replied that that was exactly what I'd done. I added that we'd been caught smuggling emeralds in Zambia and had been chased by the Zambian police. It was plausible and he smiled, adding that I was damn lucky to get away."

Chapter 3
Operation Impossible – on the run across Africa

Jim Maguire then asked the game ranger if he'd like to make a few quick bucks. He offered him 500 British pounds in cash if he'd drive him back to Sam and pick him up. The man didn't hesitate: the two of them got into his Land Rover and headed out.

Driving back towards the river, a convoy of Botswana Defence Force troops passed the Land Rover, heading in the opposite direction. The Zimbabweans had obviously alerted them and although Maguire said nothing to his new companion, it was clear that security forces throughout the area were mobilising. They'd shortly push out patrols, search parties and set up roadblocks. Fortunately, the two men weren't stopped because the hunter's Land Rover was well known to everybody in the area.

"So we drove along to the area where Sam was, and after checking that there was no roadblock or patrol nearby, I left the vehicle, fetched Sam, and helped him back to the road.

"At this stage, Sam and I'd managed to share a few thoughts while walking. We were aware that with new security measures that would shortly be put in place, we'd probably not be able to cross into South West Africa because of the Botswana Defence Force alert. All we could hope for would be to try to get as far away from the immediate area as quickly as possible. If we didn't manage that, we'd be picked up for sure. Even going back to the hotel would have been dodgy: they'd watch all the tourist haunts and probably distribute copies of the same photos we'd seen in the border post the evening before.

"We had weapons stashed in the car, but they had been seized by the police the night before. Also, things might have been different had Sam not been injured. Had he not hurt his ankle, we'd probably have tried heading out overland. Unarmed, both of us totally debilitated – and in daylight in an alien environment – it was hardly a sensible risk.

"The only option left was our newfound ranger friend, but even there time had become a factor. Sometime soon, with all the sudden military activity, he'd realise that there was something going on. Which was why I asked him whether there was an aircraft company in the area where we could perhaps charter a plane. We had to get away from the area, I explained, adding that the Zambians would be putting the word out about us.

"His reply astonished us. Yes, he said, he had a friend at a nearby farm who owned a light plane. If the price was right, he'd probably be happy to fly us to Gaborone. We drove to his friend's farm, had a brief discussion and for 1,000 pounds Sterling, he promised to get us to the Botswana capital before nightfall.

"In Gaborone, we walked directly from the aircraft through the terminal building without glancing either right or left. The first taxi we saw took us to a hotel on the edge of town where we took two rooms. Sam in the meantime busied himself with making a few calls. We needed to know how bad our situation was and whether there were any instructions from headquarters.

"The reaction from the military bosses in Pretoria was explicit. Things were bad, Sam was told. We could either remain in situ and keep a low profile at the hotel until things cooled, or possibly try to reach the South African border. The choice, he was peremptorily told, was ours. Also, there was no question of anybody coming to fetch us. When Sam and I spoke about the situation a little later, it was obvious that we were in Shit Street. Also, I had lost my passport in the Zambezi and was in Botswana with no valid documentation. Nor did it help that we'd used almost all our evasion and escape funds to get to the Botswana capital.

"There we were, we agreed, in serious trouble. We had no vehicle, no clothes, no money with which to hire a car and possibly only enough cash for two or three nights' stay at a hotel. More importantly, the Botswana police had my photograph. That would now go out nationwide and it was only a question of time before someone came knocking at the hotel and ask whether they'd seen these two Englishmen ..."

The two escapees finally decided that the risk was too great to stay put at the hotel and lie low. They'd make a break for the South African border, but it would be on foot and well away from the main trunk road.

They estimated that the trudge would be something like 30 kilometres. While they'd use the road as their reference point, they'd walk way out in the bush and only approach close enough to ensure that they were on track, after which they'd veer back into the scrub. It was a pattern the two men soon got used to.

They did quite well for about half the journey, but it was a slow process because of Sam's ankle. Maguire could see from the start that his buddy was in serious pain. Moving across irregular terrain in the bush, crossing fences, working their way through culverts and thickets only made it worse. At one stage he thought the ankle had swollen up like a small football.

Finally, at about the halfway point, Beahan said he couldn't go on. "Normally he's tough as they come, the guy simply had had enough," Maguire explained.

Chapter 3
Operation Impossible – on the run across Africa

The two men stopped a while to consider their options when his partner said it had become physically impossible for him to continue. A short while later Beahan suggested that perhaps if he stuck to the more level terrain alongside the road, things might go a bit better. If he heard a car, he said, he'd duck into the bush.

"I didn't like the idea and I said so. I was worried about roadblocks, I told Sammy."

During their flight from Northern Botswana to Gaborone, Beahan had asked the pilot and the ranger – who'd come along for the flight – whether they were aware of roadblocks on the main road between Gaborone and South Africa. They stuck to their emerald smuggling story and said that because the Zambians and Botswana people worked hand-in-glove, they could still be searching for them, even this far south. The pilot and his pal were optimistic, assuring them that from past experience along that route – they did the trip fairly often – there were no roadblocks. But as Maguire commented afterwards, he still didn't want to take any chances.

"At this point, Sam and I had a disagreement. He said that it was physically impossible for him to continue in the bush. He'd walk on the side of the road. I told him flat that the choice was his, but that I was sticking to the bush.

"That's when we split up. Sam moved across to the road and I started back into the bush. And what was really sad was that he hadn't gone 100 yards from that point when he walked straight into a BDF roadblock. Three guards stepped out of the bush at the side of the road and pointed their FN rifles at him and when this happened, he shouted to me for help. I did what I thought was right and ran straight out onto the road to help him.

"Sam was there with a trio of Botswana troops pointing their rifles at him. One of the guards came right up to me and stuck his FN up my nose.

"The first question was who we were and what we were doing there. We told them that we were British tourists and that our car had broken down a few kilometres up the road. We were on our way on foot to look for help. We also said that we were quite pleased that we'd run into them.

"However, their commander looked us up and down for a few moments and said, just like the Zimbabwean border policeman, that we were South African spies. 'You are under arrest' he told us. Then, surprisingly, two of the Botswana soldiers walked off towards the main roadblock position, apparently to radio in that we'd been caught. That left only one of them to guard the two of us.

"We looked at each other, which was when I muttered quietly under my breath that we should make a run for it. We should get back into the bush, I reckoned, but Sam didn't answer."

Just then a car drove up and slowed. Maguire thought it would stop, but it didn't. As it came alongside, he quickly moved around its front towards the other side of the car. The vehicle then was between him and the soldier. But Beahan didn't follow and the car moved off again. He'd already told his partner that when he shouted "run", that Beahan should try to get away as he could.

Maguire: "That's when I hollered at Sam, and I pushed off smartly into the bush, but heading in the other direction. I can't remember whether the soldier fired at me or not as I was running for everything I was worth. All I can recall is that Sam stayed put and was taken into custody."

Jim Maguire continued with his efforts at evasion and escape, successfully as it turned out, and finally crossed the border into South Africa. His has since spent a lot of time working security as a private military operative east of Suez and elsewhere.

Sam Beahan was formally arrested and peremptorily handed over to the Zimbabwe authorities. What Maguire and others learnt afterwards was that the first thing that they asked him was what he'd done with his beard. Then they told him to roll up his shirt sleeves and show them his tattoos.

Maguire: "Sam had never worn a beard. But I'd always done so. Also Sam was never tattooed, but I have large tattoos, one on each forearm.

"Obviously it was me that they were looking for. In fact they thought it was me that had been caught at the roadblock. Not only had the person who'd betrayed us passed on photos and a detailed description of me, a lot of personal information was also transmitted.

"I only discovered afterwards that the Botswana authorities had arrested two men the day before we infiltrated the country. They were accused of being South African soldiers. Meantime, the Botswana Defence Force and all internal authorities were put on a high state of alert.

"Under normal circumstances, being aware of all these developments beforehand, we should have aborted the operation. But the key personnel of our team in Pretoria met to discuss the situation and the consensus was that we wouldn't get another opportunity for the rescue. So we agreed: we'd go ahead and take the risk, we told them. We had friends and colleagues in Chikurubi Prison, all of them former operators who desperately needed help.

"The fact that we were betrayed from within our own ranks makes it a bitter pill to swallow. What only emerged much later was that Sammy, once in custody in Zimbabwe, was badly tortured and that punishment went on for an inordinately long time. More important, it was meted out by a combined team comprised of Botswana security people and a Zimbabwean CIO group who were already waiting for us to arrive.

"One of the Zimbabwean intelligence people involved in the torture had actually been staying in the same hotel in Gaborone where Sam and I had spent the night before we intended infiltrating Zimbabwe. In fact, the Gaborone government had decided to kill Sam – they were going to use the waterboarding treatment with hessian sacks, which was when Harare instructed their operatives to keep him alive for further questioning.

"Despite beatings and torture, Sammy kept his mouth shut. He never compromised his friends and those colleagues in Zimbabwe that he knew about. He could easily have done so because he knew everyone's names, their locations, the various rendezvous points, future plans, transport arrangements and the rest. He allowed them all good time to escape.

"He then spent ten years in a maximum security prison with hard labour. He got extra time coupled to an extra-severe sentence, precisely because he refused to provide the information that Harare was looking for."

Jim Maguire's evasion and escape is listed as the longest ever to take place in the history of the South African Defence Force. The person that "shopped" the operation – the mole at the heart of it all – will, for the sake of his family, remain unidentified, except for his initials: GB was killed a while later working security in Iraq. The consensus among his former colleagues was that his actions were based solely on greed. Worse, they cost several operatives their lives and quite a few more decades behind bars in Chikurubi. Those taken into custody by Mugabe's security detachments as a consequence of GB's subterfuge were cruelly tortured ...

CHAPTER FOUR

WARTIME HUNTING IN AFRICA

Conflict in a region does not always deter those eager to acquire a trophy set of horns. Almost until the end of the Rhodesian war, professional hunters in this embattled land were taking their clients into the bush. It was the same in Mozambique and Angola early on, but finally things became simply too dangerous. It was impossible to actually hunt in some areas, though that never deterred us from going in there.

I'd first met Giorgio Grasselli in Mozambique while travelling in convoy with the Portuguese Army northwards out of Tete, a sprawling town on the Zambezi. We were among the few white civilians on a journey that took a couple of days and I suppose it was natural that we'd gravitate and end up sharing a few cookouts under the stars. These were always under the watchful eyes of the sentries after our column halted for the night: you never knew who else was out there watching us *wazungus*.

The Italian was in his Land Rover and I in mine, and between us, with good lashings of fine Chianti – together with an always excellent KWV brandy – it became a brief but memorable little sojourn.

Africa was like that in the old days. No matter that we were sniped at, or that there might have been a landmine or three and that some of the vehicles ended as scrap after being blown up, we eventually all got to the Malawi border intact. Grasselli tells it the way it was in his excellent memoire *African Sunsets*[1].

When I met Giorgio on that first visit, he was actually on what he referred to as his "Journey of Discovery". He'd come from the Cameroons – the "Armpit of Africa", he'd call it – on the west coast of Africa and like me, was transiting Mozambique, then already in its fifth or six year of hostilities. Dissatisfied with an encroaching African political structure in West Africa that had become harsh towards people of the wrong colour who were working there, he'd listened attentively when some of his European clients told him about the remarkable plethora of wildlife in the southern half of the continent. Parts of it were still under white rule, they told him and the wildlife was plentiful: just the way he liked it.

They'd mentioned several countries, including Botswana and Rhodesia, both of which were still comparatively undeveloped. Also, they said, they had a lot to offer somebody in the professional hunting game, which was why he decided to head south and take a look for himself.

Giorgio Grasselli found what he was looking for at *Rushoek*, an isolated, somewhat dilapidated farm near Matetsi. It was just a short drive from the great Wankie Game Park and about 60 kilometres south of Victoria Falls, from where he would collect his clients after they had flown through from Salisbury or Johannesburg.

He did a deal with the original owners, knocked down their old shack and its surrounding outbuildings, all of which had probably stood on that stretch of turf for half-a-century, and built a most beautiful safari lodge. With a fine thatched roof, it was one of the best hunting camps in southern Africa; I was to get to know it well over the next few years.

Italian professional hunter Giorgio Grasselli at his boma in the Central African Republic. The CAR army had just mutinied and he was taking no chances – hence the AK on his lap. (Photo: Giorgio Grasselli)

The Italian didn't waste any time in choosing a well-watered area near the main residence to plant rows of maize, millet and sorghum. Specifically, his idea was to attract the animals and it wasn't long before the area had resident herds of antelope – as well as a good number of baboons. At dusk we would sit under one of the colourful old fever trees and, sundowners in hand, watch the animals cavort, though more than once a prowling lion or leopard would send us scurrying.

From *Rushoek*, I went on many hunts with this exuberant Italian national. We'd search for lion, sometimes adjacent to Wankie and at other times in the Zambezi Valley. We'd also look for sable, kudu, waterbuck, wildebeest, leopard, and, on one memorable dawn run-in in a heavily wooded stretch along the river north of the Falls, we were surrounded for an hour by what must have been a herd of about a thousand Cape buffalo. They thundered up and down the river bank while we took cover behind some hefty trees, but since most were all either females or immature males, there was no hunting that day. The larger, more mature "trophy" males – the ones with the big horns and much sought after by the hunting fraternity – had already mated and gone off into remoter bush country on their own, which was the way it would remain until the next mating season.

Another memorable event evolved after a group of Matabele tribal elders from a local village arrived at *Rushoek*. They were a pretty distressed group and obviously desperate.

In his own language, the leader complained that a pride of eight or nine lions had been indiscriminately killing their cattle. The predators wouldn't hunt down just one animal and devour it; they would sometimes kill three or four of the poor beasts in a night, much of the flesh going to waste. And since cattle have always been a measure of status within rural African societies, they urgently needed Giorgio to do something about it. "Protection", they called it, using the English word.

With much emotion, the spokesman for these Africans explained that if things went on like that for much longer, all their cattle, their only real assets, would soon be gone and being a temperamental sort, Grasselli couldn't resist the challenge.

The next afternoon, with his client and me in tow, we set up a hide near the previous evening's slaughter, using one of the quarter-eaten carcasses strung up at bait in a mopani tree. Just as the sun was about to disappear over the horizon, the pride returned. In about 40 seconds we'd shot dead five of the eight lions that had been terrorizing the area and none too soon either; within minutes it was

Chapter 4
Wartime hunting in Africa

dark. The three surviving members of the pride, all mature females, steered well clear of the area thereafter ...

The trouble was that years later, when I showed my daughter Leighla the photo of the three of us standing over the carcasses, hunting rifles in hand, her immediate reaction was that it was "disgusting"! It took a while for her to accept that what we'd done was essential, and that such things happened in the African bush. Even so, she wasn't totally convinced.

In time, I was to discover for myself that lions in that corner of north-west Rhodesia, which adjoins north-east Botswana, were an unusually aggressive breed of the big cats. In fact, attacks on locals were commonplace. On the hunt, it would sometimes take a shot in the air to stop them stalking us, which was awkward because it also frightened away other animals, and, more often than not, the potential trophies we were stalking. These predators seemed to be perpetually on the hunt.

Grasselli himself narrowly escaped being taken by a large black-maned male while we were out scouting near the Botswana border one sunny afternoon. He'd got out of his Land Rover for a pee, and in deference to his clients, did his thing a few metres to the rear of the vehicle. Without even a warning growl, a huge lion shot out of the bush about 50 metres away and headed straight at him. Swift, silent and deadly, these creatures are able to move at incredible speed.

Because the Italian didn't take his rifle with him – and firing it at such a short distance might have proved problematical anyway – he giant-strided it back to the Land Rover, opened the door and jumped in. The impact of the animal slamming into the side of the vehicle closed it for him.

Lucky man ...

It was the war in Rhodesia that gradually gathered its own momentum and ultimately affected everybody, the Grasselli family included.

Hostilities might have been expected to flow southwards from Zambia into the Victoria Falls and Wankie areas known tactically as Op Tangent, and eventually Grasselli and all other active men living in the area ended up serving in one of the security units. These were interim but fairly effective measures that were established specifically to counter the kind of insurgency then blighting the nation.

After a short spell of military training in the Matopo Hills near Bulawayo, Grasselli found himself attached to the Police Anti-Terrorist Unit (PATU), a wartime element of Rhodesia's British South Africa Police. Like other hunters, game conservationists and farmers,

The first time Leighla, my daughter, saw this photo all she could exclaim was "Disgusting"! (Photo: Author's collection)

he was handed an R1 rifle in NATO 7.62 mm calibre, given some basic training in enemy methodology as well as the use of explosives. On tracking in the bush, his personal metier, he was able to show his instructors a thing or two.

With the war, much else changed in Rhodesia, including the constant threat of landmines on unsurfaced roads. Giorgio and family liked to spend the occasional evening in Victoria Falls, but that became an increasingly rare event as travelling in remote areas after dark soon became too risky.

In his book Grasselli explained how the gun culture gradually took hold. When he and his wife Liliana did go to the Falls for the day, they obviously couldn't leave their weapons in their car unattended. As he recounts, "the inconvenience of this was not the handguns, which we kept well hidden under our jackets in holsters specially designed to conceal them, but the long weapons like assault rifles and our sub-machine guns. The country got itself organised for this contingency too.

"As soon as you stepped inside the hotel, you were in what might be called a cloakroom in a European hotel. And instead of handing over your coat, you left your FN and received a receipt with a number on it, just like you get in a theatre cloakroom. This took place once you'd taken out the magazine and shown the attendant that there were no cartridges in the chamber. When more than one customer came into the cloakroom at the same time, you could hear the jolly rattling of bolts that gave a tone of virility to the whole environment, as happens whenever there are groups of armed men about."

Each time I visited the Grassellis at *Rushoek*, I'd take along a few of the things that Rhodesia, then seriously under siege, was short of. Good quality pâté was unobtainable locally and instead of paying for my stay, I'd take him a carton of the best quality stuff in cans, as well as a case of vintage Bordeaux which wasn't nearly as expensive then as it is today: it was something he liked to serve his clients after a hard day in the bush.

I was covering South Africa's border wars at the time, and would sometimes even smuggle out a bunch of grenades and occasionally a claymore mine or two and take that lot along to Rhodesia as well. These were the kind of things with which local reservists were not supplied by the local security forces and for Giorgio and family, they became a useful adjunct to their home defence.

In smuggling military hardware across the border by car at Beit Bridge, I'd usually secrete it all under the hood as our trunks were invariably searched by customs inspectors. But they never once peered into our engine compartment. Then, a mile or two up the road, I'd move the stuff again before the ammunition became too hot, although I'd always keep a couple of grenades on the seat next to me in case we were ambushed along a sometimes lonely road that took a long day's travel northwards from the Limpopo.

My wife Madelon did the trip with me several times and we were never attacked, although a lot of other people were and quite a few lives were lost during the course of the war.

I'd been staying with Giorgio and his family a few days before the man we'd been hunting with on an adjoining farm was murdered. The victim was Arthur Cumming, a dapper, brave individualist and a veteran of that protracted bush war. Arthur had long before been dubbed "Gentleman Jim" by some of the members of his unit, the Rhodesian Light Infantry. Whether in civvies or in the distinctive mottled green cammo gear worn by Ian Smith's "rebel" army, he was always, as they say, bespoke.

First details of his having been killed were sparse. But since, we'd got to know the Cumming family quite well – I'd been there with a group that included Bob Brown, owner and editor of *Soldier of Fortune* magazine as well as its demolitions editor, John Donovan. We'd been hosted by Arthur and his wife Sandy in their home in a region that we knew had had its share of violence in the ongoing guerrilla struggle and we were consequently able to relate to what little we'd been told. Bob had even bagged a decent-sized kudu bull and a sable while out there.

The routine at the ranch was the same for each of the five or six mornings that we hunted. We'd go out in Arthur's Land Rover before dawn each day and though we'd have to use dirt roads to get to our destination, which was troubling, we weren't really deterred. We probably should have been because there had been landmines detonated under vehicles in much of the area during the previous two or three years – most of them civilian cars or trucks – but so far, none on the huge ranch owned by the Cumming family.

We were also aware that a few weeks before we'd arrived, an insurgent group active in the region had used a couple of TM-57s to boost an explosive charge that dropped one of the bridge spans across the nearby Matetsi River.

Our tracker on this leg of our Rhodesian adventure was Tickey, a black man from the local Tonga tribe, who had been with the Cumming family for more than 30 years. Small, with a pinched face and wiry physique, he could read the bush like you or I scan a newspaper. Tickey would follow a trail through this fairly overgrown scrub country and be able to tell you how many animals had used it, what they were, how they were moving – in haste or passively – and when last they'd passed. He could even spot a lioness in the long grass before she knew he was watching her. As Arthur said, Tickey was the best in his league and he was justifiably proud of his ability. Also, he was "part of the family", he told us.

When asked about his loyalties, considering that so many of the other tribal people around had been subverted by the insurgents, Arthur was unequivocal: "I've grown up among his people, so did my dad and his dad. Consequently *his* people are *my* people … what more need I say?" He went on to mention something about a bond of understanding between the people on his ranch that he'd seen demonstrated over and over again. In fact, the family was on such good terms with its staff, that Arthur actually declined a government offer to erect a security fence around the farmhouse.

So who were we to argue when Tickey rode shotgun on board our four-by-four while we hunted the big stuff? What we didn't know – and which only emerged afterwards – was that that same trusted tracker ended up murdering his boss, Arthur Cumming. Long before the homestead was attacked, he was already a fully paid-up member of the guerrilla force active in the region. Had he been a bit smarter,

Chapter 4
Wartime hunting in Africa

Poaching of elephant for their tusks has created a series of virtual war zones in some parts of Africa. This was a scene captured in Kenya some years ago. (Photo: Mohammed Amin)

he could probably have led our group of visitors into an ambush and then the guerrillas might have scored a major publicity coup by bagging themselves a prominent pair of Americans as well as a journalist then working for Britain's Jane's Information Group. I was listed on the masthead of *Jane's International Defence Review* as its Middle East and Africa correspondent.

He could certainly have done so had he wished, because subsequent reports spoke of a squad of Zimbabwe People's Revolutionary Army (ZIPRA) guerrillas some 30 or 40 strong having entered across the Zambezi River from Zambia. Further, they were armed with some of the best squad weapons in the Soviet armoury including the usual infantry squad weapons as well as RPG-7s.

In the end, Tickey waited until we'd gone home before he led his group of terrorists into the Cumming home, and that happened shortly after Arthur's brother Lawrence had left for Bulawayo earlier in the day.

Giorgio Grasselli takes up the story in *African Sunsets*[2]:

> In Matetsi disaster struck suddenly one night in November. As we did every evening, we switched on our Agric-Alert two-way receiver at 7 o'clock and were waiting for our turn to check in. Our code was 'Whisky-30', the last of a long list, which meant that there were another 29 isolated households that had to call the army base before us, one after the other. We were only allowed to jump the queue and call in ahead if we had

an emergency. Every report was important, from the sighting of people (who almost always turned out to be harmless) to firearms discharged (which had to be reported as soon as possible after the event if they were due to hunting, and before, if it was shooting practice), as well as anything else considered suspect.

That night everything seemed quiet and within just 10 minutes, all calls ended with a 'Good night, over and out'. There followed the usual routine of checking outside and locking up. The dogs followed me, wagging their tails and the horses in the stables gave no sign of being nervous.

I went indoors and checked the state of the battery charge on the radio receiver, knowing that in case of an emergency our lives might depend on it. We had supper at eight and usually went to bed at half-past, but that evening we stayed up for an hour longer. I turned off the gas lamps and checked again that all the doors were locked, then perceived, rather than heard a feeble, anguished woman's voice repeating 'Help, help!' I turned up the volume but the tone seemed even lower, then I heard nothing more. I got down on the floor next to the radio and sat there with my wife, ears glued to it, both of us horror stricken. Who could it be?

Suddenly a professional-sounding, low-toned man's voice broke the silence and asked who was calling, repeating the question at short intervals. It was the security forces headquarters and a few minutes later a woman's voice, still very low and interrupted by sobs, said, 'Help, this is Sandy Cumming … we have terrorists here. They've shot Arthur and they're looking for me.' Then another long, anguished, never-ending silence. We sat there listening to the drama, unable to do anything about it. After what seemed an eternity, during which we were sure she had been killed as well, we heard her voice again: 'Arthur is dead, maybe they've gone, please come and help me!' It was heart-rending. We were 40 kilometres away, but could do nothing.

Only afterwards did we hear that on that night, Arthur Cumming had got up to lock the outside doors. Moments later, his wife Sandy found that three black men wearing the uniforms of the Rhodesian

I took Colonel Robert K. Brown, owner and publisher of *Soldier of Fortune* magazine (right) to hunt in Giorgio Grasselli's concession in Rhodesia and he shot this fine kudu bull. With him is John Donovan who regularly hunted in the operational areas. (Photo: Author)

Grasselli had to do his stint with the Rhodesian Army while the war went on. He is seen here with some of his army pals against the backdrop of a mine-protected vehicle near Victoria Falls. (Photo: Giorgio Grasselli)

Army – complete with camouflage cloth caps – had entered the room from the kitchen. Her first words were "Arthur, what's the army doing in the house?"

All that Arthur could do was shout: "Run Sandy! Run for your life!" Then all three intruders opened up on him and he crumpled in a heap on the cement floor. Sandy, by then almost nine months pregnant, had slipped out into the garden through one of the side doors. Roughly 30 seconds later she heard more shots, some of them ricocheting off the concrete. The terrorists, she knew, had delivered the *coup de grâce*.

By slipping into a low clump of foliage outside, Sandy Cumming managed to survive the onslaught, even though her husband's killers spent a while searching for her. Finally she was able to sneak back into the house and activate the Agric-Alert alarm system that had only recently been installed. And though she played hide-and-seek with these killers a while longer, a nearby army patrol hastened to her rescue.

But even that took time because the favourite insurgent ploy in that war prior to an attack on a farmhouse, as with Malaya, was sometimes to lay a pattern of mines in the approach road – usually a single anti-tank mine surrounded by a cluster of APs. If nobody checked, one or more of these would be detonated by those rushing forward to help.

What was particularly sad about the attack was that Arthur Cumming, although critically wounded, did not die immediately. Also, because the entire farming community of the north-west – for a radius of more almost 150 kilometres – was connected to the same radio-based security system they, like the Grassellis, were able to follow the terrible drama at first hand. Reports that filtered through from Rhodesia afterwards indicated that Tickey, the trusted family tracker – who had often carried young Arthur on his back as a child – had been arrested. He was tried in court and executed by the authorities a short while later.

Giorgio told me afterwards that only two homesteads – that of Arthur and Sandy Cumming and his own – were the only farm residences in the region that did not have security fences.

"In my case," wrote Grasselli, "the decision was mostly to do with aesthetic reasons: I found it awkward for a safari camp to be fenced, thinking it would make my clients feel imprisoned. There was also the fact that large animals, including a few elephant, used to roam around our *rondavels* at night and I thought it a real pity to deprive ourselves of that pleasure. But in the end, I decided I had to accept that it wasn't worth risking our lives for this and put up the fence around *Rushoek*.

"Arthur's reasons for not wanting the fence were of a completely different nature. He told us that he was born on the farm, like the generations of Cummings before him, and knowing all his workers so well, the majority of whom he had grown up with, he was sure that none of them would try to hurt his family. He took it for granted that there was a lot of mutual trust and a special understanding between them all. If ever any terrorists came into the area, he told us, one of his workers was sure to warn him straightaway.

"Many years before, they had built a small school on the farm where Sandy used to teach the children of his employees."

It was not long afterwards that Giorgio and Liliana, as well as their daughters Luisa and Gabriella (who had been educated at one of the best schools in Rhodesia at Bulawayo) had to give way. The writing had been on the wall for a while and I wasn't surprised when I got a call from my old pal. Would I meet him the next day at Beit Bridge? It all happened very quickly. He and Liliana had packed up everything, the girls had already left for Italy and after his wife had spent a few days with us in Johannesburg, I was to drive his Land Rover to Durban and arrange to have it freighted to Europe.

Giorgio continued working in other parts of Africa and finally settled in a series of concessions known as Community Hunting Zones, or *Zones Cynégétiques Villageoises* along the Bangoran River in the Central African Republic (CAR). He remained there for ten good years.

The system, funded by the EU, worked very well and for a long while it was run by two expatriate Portuguese nationals from Mozambique, José Lobáo Tello and Tereza d'Espiney. José had originally been in charge of the Gorongosa National Park north of the Zambezi River and, for a while after *uhuru*, founder-director of Emofauna, the Mozambique state company set up to deal with wildlife management.

But being Africa, things there started to go seriously wrong as well. One ambitious army officer after the other launched a series of coups détat that finally crippled the nation. A lot of the unrest had to do with the corruption, directly linked to the CAR's rich natural resources, diamonds especially, all of which leaves one with a very distinct sense of déjà vu when you look at recent events in the Congo, Liberia and Sierra Leone.

Giorgio recalls one of the first serious army mutinies in the Central African Republic, which took place while he was on safari in a remote fly camp with a client, far from his home base. For security reasons all foreigners were being airlifted out of the country and he managed to get his man onto the last aircraft out. It would be a while before the French Foreign Legion moved in to settle matters in their customary way, something they had done with considerable success elsewhere on the continent, including in the mining town of Kolwezi in the southern Congo a short while before, where they'd killed hundreds of dissident Katangese soldiers who had invaded the region from Angola in a bid to overthrow the government.

In the subsequent rebellion in the Central African Republic, Grasselli was aware that the rebels were moving from Birao in the north towards Bangui, the capital further to the south. In so doing, they would have to pass quite close to his own base, which meant that the Italian hunter made a few plans of his own.

"Although the likelihood of an attack was remote, we were very well armed: our hunting rifles were supplemented by Kalashnikovs and what's more, we knew how to use them," he will tell you today. The mutineers eventually passed them by without causing trouble, but things remained tentative for weeks as those who remained awaited developments. "There were quite a few clashes in Bangui and the city was left quite battered, mostly as a result of the endless looting," he recalls.

This was the second military rebellion in a relatively short time. When the situation eventually normalised, Bangui was completely changed. It would never be the same again, reckoned Grasselli at the time. "Bullets had left most buildings pock-marked and the people who had been robbed of all their belongings, the majority of them white residents, were gone, most never to return.

"It wasn't long before many of the hunting concessions were being plundered, for ivory in particular, with many of those responsible armed with automatic weapons. They travelled long distances on camels from the Sudan to slaughter herds of these beautiful creatures," recalls Grasselli.

A rout developed into a massacre and although both José and Tereza did what they could, 15 difficult years of work backed by the European Community failed to save most of the Central African Republic's elephant population.

1 Giorgio Grasselli: *African Sunsets: The Story of an Adventurous Life*, Rowland Ward Publications, Johannesburg and Spotsylvania, Pennsylvania: Italian edition 2005, English edition 2007 p.178. See also "Tete Convoy" (Chapter 30) in Al J. Venter's *Barrel of a Gun – Misspent Moments in Combat*, Casemate Publishers, Philadelphia and London, 2010
2 Ibid, Grasselli, pp. 180–183.

CHAPTER FIVE

AFRICA'S BACKYARD FIREARM FACTORIES

> South Africa's former Anglican Archbishop Desmond Tutu has described the small arms trade in Africa as "the modern-day slave trade which is out of control". It continues unabated, largely because of corruption and the complicity of most governments in sub-Saharan Africa, he maintains, "including, I am sad to say, my own beloved country, which turns a blind eye to the appalling suffering associated with the proliferation of these weapons".

South Africa's much-depleted security services are fighting a low-intensity struggle in the lush farmlands of KwaZulu-Natal. The numbers of victims are relatively modest: two dead in a village today and another somewhere else the day before, but as in Northern Ireland in years past, some of the issues were intense enough not very long ago to have involved the South African Army. For many of those involved in the killings, it was payback time.

Those not hacked to death in these ongoing vendettas are shot with a variety of firearms, many of them home-made. And since some of these guns can be put together in any backyard, it's important to take a close look at them. All are lethal and many are adaptations of the ubiquitous "Saturday Night Special", the weapon-of-choice of many American youth gangs.

The majority are cheeky adaptations of 12-bore shotguns. It is most popular in less-developed regions because of the spread of its lead pellets and the impact. The rationale among those who use shotshell is that there are no tell-tale ballistic "fingerprints" for forensics to work with afterwards. Other firearms range from primitive adaptations of the Kalashnikov to drilling through the barrel of a starter's pistol so that it will chamber a .38 calibre cartridge. In the long term it probably cannot be used very often, but by then it will have adequately served its purpose.

Curiously, there are an astonishing number of military carbines about – AK-47s, .556 mm South African Army R-4s (the South African hybrid of the Israeli Galil), an occasional FN 7.62 mm or a former Portuguese Army G3 brought across the border from Mozambique. As police operations begin to take effect, it is hoped that this illegal arsenal is thinning.

Most of the people living in the embattled zone will disagree. Barely a week goes by when farmers and, increasingly, their families aren't killed or wounded in road ambushes or onslaughts on isolated homesteads in attacks that are taking place throughout the country. Since the ANC came to power in the early 1990s, more than 3,000 members of the white farming community have been murdered. Many of those involved maintain that as the attacks increase – with scores of farmers killed each year – that it's little more than a concerted effort to drive them off their properties. They point to the fact that along the Tugela, and further south, in the foothills of the Drakensberg Mountains, Mpumalanga (formerly Eastern Transvaal) and elsewhere, some farms have already been abandoned. During visits to KwaZulu-Natal in 2007 and 2010, I was to see evidence of this trend for myself.

Farm killings are only part of it: there are more people dying violently in South Africa today than any other country in the world outside a war zone, with the single exception of Mexico.

Despite an increased security presence in much of South Africa, criminals have become more active. And as long as these dissident elements are hunted by the SAPS, they are obliged to turn to their own resources to acquire weapons. Apart from those stolen, there have been some remarkable adaptations.

Technical expertise, I found, while basic, was largely Heath-Robinson and very rarely involved machines. In the countryside, where many of these "workshops" are situated, there is often no electricity. The tools can be as basic as a hammer, a hacksaw and a file, together with an *umfaan* who will provide muscle to drive a set of cowhide bellows over a charcoal fire.

I was shown a starting pistol that had been made into an effective single-shot weapon. It was a .22 long-rifle calibre and had been used in a political assassination that had been big news at the time. A prominent Inkatha political figure of Zulu ancestry had been shot behind the ear from a range of centimetres. The man died instantly.

A SELECTION OF HANDMADE GUNS CAPTURED BY POLICE IN RAIDS IN KWAZULU-NATAL

A selection of 'home-made' firearms, all lethal, taken during several raids on rural firearm factories in KwaZulu-Natal. The device resembling a 'submachine-gun' was made from industrial farm parts; the barrel on the rifle came from water piping and several of the guns depicted are capable of firing 12-gauge ammunition. (Photos: Author)

Chapter 5
Africa's backyard firearm factories

A few more of the weapons that I handled were nothing short of dangerous. One or two had fairly large gaps between the receiver and the barrel (which, when on the move, are usually carried separately). Or the cartridges were so loose-fitting that the gun emitted a sheet of flame from the breech.

"Often, if the piping is too big for the cartridge, a short length of wire is wound around the base of the brass to keep it in position" a police officer familiar with the illegal trade in firearms told me. "This is often the case with the 9 mm Parabellum pistol."

The most basic system, he reckoned, was to improvise and have two lengths of ordinary metal piping; the one fitting neatly into the other. A small, sharp piece of steel – the firing pin – would be soldered to one end. With the cartridge in place, you literally banged one section of the "gun" hard against the other. Obviously, you need to take great care where it is pointing just then.

"Tricky, but it works, although not always if you've been drinking, which is often the case," said Mike P, another policeman who did not want to be identified because he is still involved in ballistics work. "Also", he added, "you have to know how to hold it … fingers have been severed in the past."

A new development, he declared, had been to take toy pistols or revolvers – the kind that kids use to play cowboys and crooks – drill out the barrels for use in bank hold-ups, for which South Africa is now a world leader. If, for instance, an AK is not available, the 9 mm Para is still the preferred calibre. Another armourer said that these improvised firearms worked very well for five or six rounds, after which the barrel tended to split.

About half the weapons brought in while I spent time with the South African police were 12-gauge calibre shotguns, factory manufactured or improvised. Ammunition, an officer pointed out, was plentiful: just about every farmhouse has a box or two of shells. More significant, in close quarters, it is difficult to miss your target whether you've had a few beers or not. Quite a few members of the police with whom I worked out of Margate Airport had taken fire from these improvised weapons: several had ended up in hospital with serious wounds.

One had taken the full impact of a Remington 870, 12-gauge shotgun in the chest. Even though he was wearing body armour, the blast knocked him down, half concussed. Apart from a bruise the size of a plate that stayed with him for months, he wasn't badly hurt. Just 10 or 12 centimetres higher, he reckoned, and he would have taken it full in the face.

The best home-made weapons, it is generally accepted in Natal, were for a long time made by a fugitive known to the police as "Dum-Dum" Dumisane. He was appropriately named: having eluded the police for years, he taught his associates how to nip off the tip of a bullet that always results in the victim being seriously wounded. It says much that the inappropriately named "Dum-Dum" bullet was banned generations ago by the Geneva Convention.

Dumisane is also a bit of shotgun boffin. One of his creations was recovered while I was there. It was a 12-gauge and could be fired as a handgun. Those who have tried it say you need strong wrists ...

Meanwhile, according to South Africa's Institute for Security Studies, it is estimated that 100 million small arms exist in Africa, especially around the Horn, including Somalia, Ethiopia, southern Sudan, the violent belt of Central Africa and many areas of West Africa.

Accurate figures, it declares, are hard to obtain and Africa has many illegal weapons manufacturers as well as illicit sales. Egypt, Ethiopia, South Africa and Zimbabwe all have manufacturing and distribution factories and illegal sales networks. AK-47s can be bought in some countries on the open market for as little as the price of a sack of flour or a chicken. Those intent on acquiring a handgun for overnight use in cities like Johannesburg or Durban, can hire an automatic pistol or a large-calibre revolver for as little as R300, with ammunition costing extra.

Matt Schroeder, who manages the Arms Sales Monitoring Project at the Federation of American Scientists in Washington, and who worked with Guy Lamb of South Africa's Institute for Security Studies, has his own take on these developments.

In a report labelled "The Illicit Arms Trade in Africa" Schroeder and Lamb maintained that in Africa, the illicit trade in small arms and light weapons is opaque, amorphous and dynamic. "It is ... a global enterprise, with illicit weapons across Africa coming from virtually every major arms producing country in the world." Only a handful of African countries have the capacity to legally manufacture arms and ammunition and South Africa tops the list, they state. The small arms component of the South African industry comprises less than ten manufacturers and their output is insignificant in terms of the global small-arms trade.

Much of the illegal arms traffic that reaches Africa is either a remnant of large-scale weapons' shipments to rebel movements (like Angola's UNITA guerrilla movement or RENAMO in Mozambique, when civil war still raged in Angola and Mozambique) or are more

Chapter 5
Africa's backyard firearm factories

A soldier with an improvised 12-gauge shotgun used in several robberies in and around Durban. (Photo: Author)

recent supplies from massive, sanctions-busting shipments organised by the so-called "Merchants of Death". These often involve globe-trotting arms brokers like the Russian Viktor Bout, who, for decades, specialised in the clandestine delivery of weapons to war zones and dictators. Bout, to the consternation of Moscow (because of his links to senior members of the former Soviet political establishment) has since been arrested and is awaiting trial in the United States.

"Representative of these transfers is a 68-ton shipment that was flown into Burkina Faso in March 1999 and later shipped to Liberia and Sierra Leone's Revolutionary United Front (RUF). UN investigators, who summarised their findings in a July 2000 report, reviewed the shipment and found 715 boxes containing 3,000 assault rifles, 25 rocket-propelled grenades, 50 machine guns, and several guided anti-tank and anti-aircraft missiles."

They reported that UN experts investigating arms embargo violations in Somalia regularly documented the delivery of weapons to Somali warlords and militias by Ethiopian truck convoys. Similarly, when Liberia's Charles Taylor was still in power (he has since stood trial in the International Court of Justice in The Hague for crimes against humanity) he was instrumental in transporting many of the weapons provided to Sierra Leone's rebel RUF. Much of this hardware was moved across the border in trucks.

Rogue soldiers, rebels, refugees and others, the report points out, also walk across borders with one or two small arms at a time.

Sophisticated methods are used to track criminals who tout home-made weapons, including this South African-built "drone", being launched here from Margate Airport on the South Coast. (Photo: Author)

Still more traffickers smuggle small arms along Africa's rivers and coasts. Researchers from the Small Arms Survey claim that weapons' smugglers in Mali pack small arms into waterproof sacks, attach them to the bottom of boats, and run them up the Niger River.

In the Horn of Africa along the Red Sea, smugglers that ply the Gulf of Aden often use dhows – large, wooden-hulled vessels with distinctive triangular sails – to deliver quantities of small arms from Yemen to Somali warlords. Not that long ago, the dhow *Alshadax* delivered nearly 500 assault rifles, grenade launchers and machine guns to a Somali faction leader.

Finally, the unauthorised craft production of firearms by local gunsmiths is a significant source of illicit small arms in some areas.

"A recent study of this kind of illegal activity in Ghana by Emmanuel Kwesi Aning found that the country's unlicensed gunsmiths have the collective capacity to produce up to 200,000 firearms a year, some of which are reportedly 'of a quality comparable with industrially produced guns'. Governments and armed groups in neighbouring states are also significant sources of illicit small arms.

"Many civil conflicts in Africa quickly transform into regional wars as neighbouring governments provide material support to one or more of the parties to the conflict. This support often includes large numbers of small arms, many of which are transferred illicitly.

"*Small Arms Survey* claims that Liberian rebels have reportedly crossed the poorly secured Ivorian border to trade their weapons for motorcycles. Similarly, anecdotal evidence suggests that members of *Forces Nouvelles*, an Ivorian rebel group, have smuggled weapons into Mali and Ghana, trading them for food and other consumer goods. Arms traffickers on other continents also fly or ship weapons illicitly into Africa."

Schroeder and Lamb go on to say that in the few African countries where reliable data is available, small arms are a leading cause of unnatural deaths. For example, in South Africa, small arms are the principal cause of unnatural deaths (close to 30 per cent of the total) – quite significantly more than road accident fatalities.

"The availability of small arms combined with the experience of protracted armed conflict has resulted in the emergence of a 'gun culture' in certain African countries.

"It entails a socio-legal system of norms and values where gun ownership is highly valued and is linked to identity and status. In some societies, gun culture may even result in the perception of armed violence (or the threat of armed violence) as an acceptable and legitimate means of social interaction between people. This is particularly the case in areas where the state is weak, or absent, such as the eastern provinces of the Democratic Republic of Congo (DRC) and Somalia.

"Illicit small arms have also led to the violent intensification of intercommunity tensions and conflicts over scarce resources. For instance, low-scale cattle rustling has been a feature of rural life in

A primitive home-made rifle that was used in an attempted murder. (Photo: Author)

Air Force Oryx helicopter crew fuel-up one of their choppers in the field (Photo: Author)

eastern Africa for centuries, particularly in the border areas of Kenya and Uganda. However, approximately 20 years ago, cattle rustlers began to acquire small arms illicitly. The nature of the conflict has since changed because of the availability of small arms.

"Hundreds of people have been killed and numerous communities displaced, with the Karamojong and the Pokot nomadic cattle herders believed to be the principal perpetrators. In April 2003, more than 2000 Pokot cattle rustlers from Kenya killed 28 people and displaced thousands in eastern Uganda in raids using illicit firearms.

"Small arms have also been used to engage in poaching activities in poverty-stricken areas near wildlife parks and sanctuaries. For example, nature conservationists estimate that between 1977 and 1997 the elephant population in Africa halved in size, largely due to poaching.

"According to the United Kingdom Parliamentary Office on Science and Technology, the combination of the lucrative 'bushmeat' trade – which supplies the meat of wild animals – and ineffective governance in many central African areas, has encouraged the formation of well-armed paramilitary poaching groups whose actions have decimated endangered wildlife populations.

"Similarly, military cargo planes often play important roles in the large, intercontinental illicit transfers arranged by international

South African Army troops being airlifted in an Oryx helicopter during a drug and weapons raid on the KwaZulu-Natal South Coast (Photo: Author)

brokers. These transfers are often dizzyingly complex, consisting of front companies, false paperwork, and a loose collection of brokers, financiers and corrupt officials operating out of several different countries. A good example is the July 2000 shipment of Ukrainian small-arms ammunition to the Ivory Coast, which was investigated by a UN panel of experts.

"Initially, the shipment of five million 7.62 mm cartridges appeared legitimate. The broker, a Moscow-based company named Aviatrend, provided the Ukrainian government with a signed and authenticated Ivorian End-User Certificate and allowed a Ukrainian military officer to fly with ammunition to Abidjan to make sure it was not diverted en route. As planned, the plane arrived in the Ivory Coast, and its contents were unloaded. However, shortly thereafter, boxes of the ammunition were loaded onto a plane owned by a company that UN officials claim was 'set up for … smuggling operations only' and flown to Liberia, where it was delivered to Charles Taylor's embargoed regime.

"The deal, which was partially organised by the Ukrainian arms dealer Leonid Minin, was apparently one of several illicit arms transfers scheduled for that summer. Minin's plans fell apart when he was arrested in Italy on drug and prostitution charges. In his hotel room, Italian police reportedly found forged copies of the original (authentic) Ivorian End-User Certificate, documents linking Minin to the Ukrainian ammunition deal and the Aviatrend representative who had helped arrange it, and plans for additional illicit arms transfers to Liberia."

One of the astonishing conclusions reached in a study conducted by *Small Arms Survey* **is that small arms have resulted in hundreds of thousands of deaths and millions of injuries each year. They are further responsible for between 60 and 90 per cent of total conflict deaths.**

CHAPTER SIX

ZANZIBAR'S BLOODY REVOLT

It is not that long ago that Cape Town's Peter Younghusband was one of the top foreign correspondents in Africa. He started working for the London Daily Mail *in his twenties and ended his illustrious career with* Newsweek. *The revolution in Zanzibar in the early 1960s featured prominently among some of his earlier exploits and he tells us of one of his adventures.*

For me, the Zanzibar revolution was a story that began badly and ended well. So well, in fact, that at some universities and colleges where journalism is taught, the story is mentioned occasionally as an example of how good fortune can turn a doomed foreign assignment into a success. I suspect it also provides some light relief for the students.

It certainly underlines something anyone contemplating a career in journalism should know: that luck plays a major role in the success of a reporting assignment, but you have to go and find it. There is a motto on the crest of the badge of that famous fighting unit of the British army, the Special Air Service, that puts it so well: WHO DARES WINS. It could be phrased even better: WHO DARES MORE WINS MOST.

The retelling of my Zanzibar story gives me an opportunity to reveal a secret I have kept ever since the event and, to some extent, has troubled my conscience. So let me expunge myself of this guilt in the following pages.

The revolution that turned Zanzibar into a blood bath in January 1964 took everyone by surprise. One moment it was a peaceful island in the Indian Ocean, fragrant with the scent of its clove plantations, steeped in the centuries of colourful history and romantic in its palm-fringed beaches and the fascinating Arab-style architecture of its ancient town. The next moment it was a battleground upon which most gruesome atrocities were taking place.

Yes, there had been race riots at various times in the years preceding the independence from its status as a British protectorate a month earlier. But they had been of no great significance. Ethnic rioting is a standard feature of African life. The point was that there had been nothing so unusual as to indicate that a major uprising was around the corner.

Zanzibar lies 35 kilometres off the coast of East Africa, northeast of Dar es Salaam, main seaport and capital of what was then called Tanganyika, later to become Tanzania. For hundreds of years, Zanzibar was an island ruled and populated by Arabs who founded its spice plantations and used it as a staging post for their African slave trade. The slavers would set off from the island on their expeditions into the African mainland and return to Zanzibar with captured slaves to market them on the original site that still exists to this day. The famous explorers Burton, Speke and Stanley all used Zanzibar as a starting base for their ventures into the interior. Britain acquired Zanzibar as a protectorate in 1890, but allowed Arab rule to continue under a sultanate.

When independence came in December 1963, there were about 40,000 Arabs living on the island. They owned most of the land and dominated trade and commerce. There were 300,000 Africans, mostly plantation workers, manual labourers and fishermen. The Sultan of Zanzibar had a palace, a private yacht and a red Rolls Royce, and lived stylishly. It certainly was not a situation that could continue indefinitely.

I was in Nairobi when the first BBC report of the morning carried

The Tanzanian capital of Dar es Salaam has not changed much in its half-century of independence. The clock tower still stands near the centre of the city. (Photo: Author)

a flash by Reuters that serious fighting had broken out in Zanzibar. The local time was 09h15 and there was no time for discussion with London. I knew there was a flight leaving Nairobi for Dar es Salaam within the hour, so I flung some essential things into a bag and telephoned the bank, where I made a pit stop to pick up a wad of American dollars and East African currency. I knew already it was going to be that kind of story. Everything would be shot to hell or closed, including banks. Cash would be king.

I was in Dar es Salaam four hours later, as were several other colleagues. We fought to get on a flight to the island, but all scheduled flights had been cancelled. We hastened to the offices of the two air-charter companies that operated out of Dar es Salaam, only to find the management crouched over radio broadcasts saying that rebels were in control of the Zanzibar airport and had warned that any approaching aircraft would be shot down. So no go there either.

We raced to the harbour in search of seacraft. A fast motor launch was capable of reaching the island in under three hours, but we found that the Tanganyikan government had ordered a ban on all departures to Zanzibar. The growing number of press correspondents in Dar es Salaam – being supplemented by the hour by further arrivals from Nairobi, Johannesburg, London, Rome and elsewhere – were milling around in frustration. Zanzibar was only a short distance away and we couldn't get there!

The few telephone calls from residents on the island indicated there was mayhem, but accounts were confused. Ominously, telephone contact with the mainland went dead after a few more hours, and our only link thereafter was via a radio ham until that too came to an abrupt end. The British Embassy in Dar es Salaam seemed to have intermittent contact, but was as uncooperative as usual in releasing information. ("Sorry old chap but everything has to go through London.") Then their link faded as well.

By late afternoon we had bits and pieces to file plus the latest news that a British warship was on its way to the island to protect the 300 British residents there, of whom little had been heard. But all news was second-hand out of Dar es Salaam. No one had yet managed to reach the island.

What was emerging now was the classic anatomy of a foreign correspondent's nightmare: to have the world's most important story of the moment blasting away just over the horizon and no way of getting there. To be holed up with colleagues – all of us well-trained and piranha-honed in the art of ruthlessly scooping one another – and not knowing who would get there first.

I happened to remember that about 70 kilometres north of Dar es Salaam was Bagamoyo, the ancient and derelict port through which the old Arab slavers used to ship their miserable human cargos by dhow from the African mainland to the slave marketplace in Zanzibar. Bagamoyo was now a fishing harbour and although dhows still operated there, they did little else than bring in the daily catch. The point was that Bagamoyo was even nearer to Zanzibar than Dar es Salaam, if only by a mile or two. Surely a fishing dhow could sail the distance in a few hours?

One of the Arab dhows that routinely ply their trade along the east coast of Africa; this one is almost identical to the one "bought' by Younghusband and Monks to take them from Tanganyika to Zanzibar. (Photo: Author)

I set off by taxi to Bagamoyo in the late afternoon and by evening I was trudging the beach, even wading into the shallow surf, to plead with fishermen landing their catches, offering amounts of money that would have made the *Daily Mail* accountants shudder, to set sail for Zanzibar immediately. No one seemed interested. Some seemed to think I was mad.

It was dark before I got lucky. I was taken by a fisherman to a group of people in a mud hut in a foul alley some distance behind the harbour where we did business by the light of a kerosene lamp, watched, from the shadows, by various family members including an old crone who smoked a pipe and irritated everyone by offering advice in a cracked voice.

The fisherman who had guided me had disappeared and I was grateful for the presence of my taxi driver, who had stayed, mainly because I had not paid him yet. My own Swahili was not up to the occasion and I needed him as an interpreter. At one point he drew me aside and warned: "These people are not fishermen. They are smugglers and could be dangerous." I agreed they could be dangerous, but where else to go?

The key negotiator in the group was the boat owner and talking to him was disconcerting because he had no nose and a terribly scarred mouth, all of it possibly caused by one slash of a machete. The disfiguration impeded his speech, which didn't help the negotiations because he became vexed when misunderstood.

He wished to know what would happen if the expedition to Zanzibar resulted in the seizure or loss of his craft. I readily offered to buy the boat. After nearly an hour of wrangling we agreed on a price of $800, which was a sizeable chunk out of the money I had on me. They wanted the money immediately but I refused and finally they agreed to accept half upfront and the balance on arrival in Zanzibar. We shook hands on the deal. His grasp was limp and brief. I felt I was saying goodbye to 400 dollars.

I was told to go and wait on the beach and my taxi driver, after taking me there and getting paid, fled gratefully into the night. I sat down wearily on the sand. It was not the best night of my life.

I had filed a second-hand story from Dar es Salaam and achieved nothing else except to buy the *Daily Mail* a dhow. There would probably be trouble about that and I shuddered as it occurred to me that I had forgotten to ask for a receipt.

I looked about me but there was no electricity in Bagamoyo and the populace had long since gone to sleep. The village had disappeared into the night. All about me was pitch-darkness.

The night wind that comes off the sea on the East African coast had risen. The surf was crashing, the wind was moaning, the sand was shifting and the sand-fleas were beginning to bite. The tropical warmth of the day had receded and it was cold. Fatigue began to set in but there was no question of sleeping. What if Scarface and his men came to rob me of the rest of the money they knew I had?

More to the point, what if in the morning they did not come at all and I had no one to sail my dhow? What if the boys back in Dar es Salaam had found a plane or a fast boat by now and were on their way to Zanzibar? I spent the night worrying about whether I was going to be robbed, killed or scooped. I ate the remains of a chocolate bar and finished what was left of a bottle of soda water.

Dawn came and the dhows anchored beyond the surf took shape in the gathering light. I shuffled up and down the beach wondering which one was mine and where the hell my crew was. Just as I was beginning to believe that I had been well and truly conned, they hove into sight, trudging through the sand, carrying oars, boat hooks, buckets and other tools of their trade. If anything, they looked worse by daylight than they had looked by lamplight, but I loved the sight of them and my relief at their appearance was great.

We waded out into the surf to the most decrepit of the dhows, an open craft about 10 metres long, and clambered aboard. The first thing we had to do was bale it out. Nevertheless, I had a dhow and a crew and we were off to Zanzibar, the story adrenalin was beginning to flow again and I felt good.

But now a serious crisis arose. There was a faint cry from the shore and there, to my astonishment, stood John Monks of the London *Daily Express*. "Piggy" Monks, as he was affectionately known in the business, was an Australian, and his words, in the jagged vowels of that nation, carried clearly across the sound of the surf. I couldn't pretend not to hear them.

"Any chance of a lift, mate?"

He was standing in the surf, an airline bag and cameras slung about his neck, typewriter in one hand and his shoes in the other. His trousers were rolled up above his pudgy knees. That's what irritated me more than his sudden appearance. He had taken his shoes off and rolled up his pants as though he took it for granted that I would invite him aboard.

Let me explain the situation to those unfamiliar with the great rivalries of Fleet Street. The *Daily Mail* and the *Daily Express* were – especially in the era of which I write – the fiercest competitors in the British newspaper industry. They fought for scoops on an eye-for-an-eye, a tooth-for-a-tooth basis. They strove to outbid each other in paying vast sums of money for world exclusives. Their reporters and foreign correspondents were expected to go to extraordinary lengths and do all that was necessary short of actually physically knifing each other in the back to get ahead on a story.

How, in these circumstances, could I now offer the *Daily Express* a ride in the *Daily Mail* dhow?

For years Monks and I had raced each other up and down the African continent and performed Machiavellian feats in our attempts to outdo each other on stories. Sometimes I scooped him and sometimes he scooped me.

On one assignment in the Congo we hired separate twin-engined Cessnas to race each other in the afternoons across Lake Tanganyika to file our stories from a tiny lakeside village in Tanganyika where the proprietor of the trade store, who was also the postmaster, operated a Morse key. Monks had come to know Africa, its mysteries and byways, almost as well as I had, which was how, when all other hopes faded, he had also remembered Bagamoyo.

What now to do? Fleet Street rules were that I should refuse to allow him aboard and leave him to his fate.

But perhaps a surprising result of the years of our fierce competition and professional throat-slashing and eye-gouging had been the emergence of a great friendship between us. And we had already experienced one or two occasions where logistics or the sheer pressure of events had forced us into cooperation. I was not sure that the present situation justified a shared expedition. His presence on the beach indicated that alternative ways to Zanzibar had not yet been found and I felt I was a nose ahead. But the sight of him stranded in the surf rang the bell of a kind of comradeship that in certain circumstances obliges one to say screw the grand traditions of Fleet Street and all its editors.

So I decided to take him aboard.

But there remained an important consideration. "I had to buy this fucking tub. Will you pay half the cost?" I shouted.

He didn't even ask what it had cost. "Is the Pope a Catholic?" he yelled back (a convoluted Australian form of assent, fashionably in use at the time). He waded out towards us, holding his typewriter and cameras above the waves.

"Good on yer, mate," he grunted as we hauled him over the gunwale. Scarface and his men raised the tattered sail and we set off, creaking and leaking, for Zanzibar. The sun was a red orb above the horizon and by midday we were cursing it.

Scarface had four men to help him sail the dhow and while this might sound a little overcrewed for a 10-metre craft, a dhow is a cumbersome thing that hasn't changed in shape or style since the 12th Century. It takes muscle to manage its heavy boom and clumsy sail.

There was no shade on the craft. Monks's hat, a silly straw thing that looked like fugitive headgear from a girls' high school, was blown overboard by a gust of wind and the crew understandably were disinclined to stop to fish for it. I had foolishly forgotten to bring a hat. I wrapped an old T-shirt about my head. Monks replaced his hat with a pair of used underpants. We looked a right pair of pricks.

I had also been thoughtless about provisions. John had two bottles of Coca-Cola with him and generously gave me one. The hot Coke made us thirstier than ever.

The crew offered us water from a battered old ferry can and I took a grateful swig from it. But Piggy declined. He had seen Scarface drink from it and was convinced that his ghastly facial scar involving the loss of his nose and upper lip was the result of syphilis, and he thought he might catch it. I tried to persuade him there was only one way to contract syphilis and that it was safe to drink from the can. But he steadfastly refused.

By noon the sun was hellish. John's very fair complexion was taking a beating. His face was breaking up like a road map before my very eyes.

The wind was against us as we tacked laboriously back and forth and it was clear that the trip was taking longer than expected. There was a small triangle of shade on board formed by the shape of the bow and we took turns lying full length with our heads in it. The crew regarded our plight contemptuously and cursed as they stumbled over us to swing the boom and, at other times, to bail out the boat, using a large old Pyotts biscuit tin.

A new problem had arisen. Scarface had a small transistor radio on board and had begun to pick up broadcasts from Zanzibar where the rebels had seized the radio station. The hysterical outbursts came across in a mixture of English and Swahili, and a picture began to emerge. Someone, previously unheard of, called "Field Marshal" Okello was leading the revolution and repeated warnings were issued in his name that any aircraft or ship that approached the island would be fired on.

Each time this threat was broadcast Scarface ordered our sail to be lowered and demanded an extra fee before progressing because, he said, we were sailing into a life-threatening situation. When he did this a second time we argued furiously and he actually began to turn back in the direction of the mainland until I conceded and paid another ransom.

I then, casually, offered to buy his radio. He seized on this gladly as another moneymaking opportunity and demanded an outrageous price for it, which I paid. As soon as he handed me the radio I threw it overboard. Monks said it was a stupid thing to do and he was probably right. But it did put an end to Scarface's blackmailing.

However, the tensions between us were still rising, Scarface and his crew were muttering among themselves and we were nervously wondering what they were going to do with us. For a while we had been conscious of the scent of cloves and to our relief, the low profile of the island began to take shape ahead of us.

But suddenly there was pandemonium among our crew. A motor launch was approaching us from the direction of the island and it was coming fast. It circled us and finally cruised up alongside. It was filled with an ungodly-looking bunch of ruffians armed with a variety of weapons ranging from machetes and shotguns and pistols to AK-47s. All the firearms were levelled at us.

A man wearing blue jeans, a camouflage jacket and a dirty turban and holding a sub-machine gun, who seemed to be their commander, yelled something in Swahili. Scarface replied pointing an accusatory finger at us. Whatever he was telling them, the message seemed to be that it was all our fault.

"Who are you?" demanded the commander, pointing his weapon at us.

I launched into a formal explanation but was interrupted by Monks. With the inspirational bullshit that seems to come to the aid of Australians at times like these he said: "We are British reporters who have been sent for by Field Marshall Okello to tell the world about this revolution."

The launch commander conferred with some of his mob. Then he ordered: "Lower your sail!" and I think we all feared the worst. But they merely threw us a line and took us in tow. The old dhow plunged along in the wake of the launch at a rate of knots that threatened to tear it apart. In less than an hour we were in Zanzibar harbour.

"You wait here!" shouted the launch commander. Obediently Scarface and his men dropped anchor and there we rocked, about 300 metres from the shore. We saw the launch tie up alongside the quay and its crew go ashore and disappear among the harbour buildings. A lone sentry, a rifle slung over his shoulder, paced up and down the quay, watching us. There was no one else in sight.

There was no doubt the revolution was still in full swing. The sound of small-arms fire interspersed with the thud of heavier weaponry and the thump of explosions could be clearly heard. We could see a pall of smoke above the inner reaches of the town.

We waited one hour, two hours. The sun set and we knew dusk was less than an hour away. Nothing happened. The sentry on the quay paced up and down. It began to dawn on me that no one was coming to get us. In the town the fighting rattled and boomed on.

I ordered Scarface to up anchor and dock alongside the quay. He refused and we argued in our usual tangled and broken mixture of Swahili and English. He drew a finger across his throat to emphasise that we would be killed if we did not obey orders and stay where we were.

But I was worried about John, who was seriously sunburned, feverish and beginning to look ill. I was also worried about what the consequences might be of doing nothing. We were exhausted, had no food and hardly any water and our crew were likely to rob us, maybe even murder us, if we slept. There was also the important fact that, although we had reached the story, we were still half a mile away from the action.

I began to take my clothes off.

"What are you doing, sport?" asked John, anxiously.

"I'm going to swim ashore to get some help." I stood on the side of the dhow in my underpants.

"You're crazy, mate. That bugger on the quay will shoot you!"

"Let's hope not. And if you think about it carefully, we've got no option. We certainly can't spend the night here doing nothing."

"And what am I supposed to do with these sods?" He indicated the crew.

"Try and keep them amused until I get back." To avoid further discussion I quickly dived overboard and began to swim to the quay.

I nearly drowned because of two serious oversights. The first was that the tide was going out, so I was swimming against a current. The second was that I had underestimated my exhaustion. I had not slept for two nights, I had eaten very little and the day's exposure beneath a tropical sun in an open boat had taken its toll.

I had estimated the distance to the quay at about 300 yards and reckoned I was a strong enough swimmer to make it. But before I got halfway I was in trouble. The fatigue that seized me was frightening. It was as if a paralysis was setting in. I had come quite close to another craft and I changed my direction to reach it. I managed to grab hold of its anchor chain and hung there to rest. I looked back at our dhow. Monks was watching me anxiously. The crew seemed indifferent. One of them had hung his backside over the stern to take a crap.

I looked at the quay. The sentry had stopped pacing and was watching me. Ominously, he had unslung his rifle from his shoulder and was holding it in the crook of his arm.

I started to swim again. I concentrated on keeping the strokes even and coordinating my kicking and breathing. I counted the strokes and I think that helped. But eventually I lost count and, without doubt, if the quay had been another ten yards away I would not have made it. As it was I floundered through the last few yards and went under a couple of times.

Once I'd reached the quay I hooked my arm through a motorcar tyre that hung from a rope. Another tyre hung a few feet above it. They were buffers for vessels when they tied up alongside. I could not move for several minutes. I was actually sobbing with exhaustion and relief.

Eventually, painfully, I began to climb up the quayside, tyre by tyre. Monks told me later that the sentry lit a cigarette and smoked it while he watched me. He didn't bother to tell me that there was a flight of steps a few yards to one side. There were barnacles on the quayside and I cut and scratched myself on the way up.

Finally I made it and rolled onto the quay in my Y-fronts, sodden and bleeding. The sentry put the muzzle of his rifle against my head and said: "You're under arrest." Fuck it, I thought. Shoot me if you like. I tried to say it, but didn't have the strength to speak.

Actually he was quite kindly at first. He allowed me to lie on the quayside for several minutes while he finished his cigarette. Then he kicked me in the ribs, not ungently, and told me to get up. I couldn't manage it at first, so he helped me up. He then pointed at a small building nearby and nudged me towards it with the barrel of his rifle.

When we got to it, he opened a door and shoved me inside, slammed the door shut and locked it. He peered at me through the window and grinned at me. I was his prisoner and he was beginning to like it. He strolled back to his position on the quay. I was in a room with a desk and a chair behind it and I immediately flopped into the chair. I looked around me and at the books and documents on the desk. I seemed to be in a customs or harbour administration office.

I began to shiver. It was a warm tropical evening and the sea had not been cold. But I was wearing only a pair of wet underpants and sunburn, exposure, fatigue and reaction were beginning to set in.

Suddenly my attention became riveted. My God, I was looking at a telephone. To arrest a newspaperman and lock him in a room with a telephone was either a monstrous oversight or some kind of trap. I got up and looked out the window. In the fading light I could make out the sentry standing at his post.

I went back to the desk and looked at the phone again and thought about it. No, dammit, it couldn't be a trap. How could they have known I was coming to Zanzibar and how could they have known I would swim ashore? The dickhead on the quay simply hadn't thought about the telephone. Wow!

Gingerly I picked up the receiver and dialled zero. There was an immediate response. A frightened voice said in unmistakable Asian accents: "Who is that please, I am asking you kindly?" He repeated the question in Swahili. I hesitated, and he said: "Jambo?"

"I am from the London *Daily Mail*", I said.

"But you are phoning from the harbour!"

"Yes, I have just arrived. Am I talking to the central exchange?"

"Yes, yes. I am being trapped in here since the fighting began during my shift. Without having food, you understand? I am having water. I am making tea. But I am having no food for two days. It is too dangerous to go outside. Can you help me?" He sounded deranged.

"I think you had better stay where you are and I will see if someone can get food to you. Meantime can you help me? Can you get me a line to London?"

"London impossible, sir. But I am now managing to make contact with Nairobi."

I felt dizzy with excitement. I gave him the number of the *Daily Nation* in Nairobi and in less than a minute I was speaking to its editor, John Bierman.

Good professional that he was, John wasted no time on preliminaries.

"Nice work, you're the first one in. Have you got a story?"

"Yes, can you take a dictate and pass it on to the *Mail*?"

"Sure – and can I use it for the *Daily Nation*?"

"Yes. Are you ready?"

"Yep. Go-go-go …"

I dictated six paragraphs, sitting there in my wet underpants, mopping at my cuts and scratches with bits of blotting paper that I tore from the pad on the desk. I kept it short, knowing that in

London they would be close to the first-edition deadline and that all they would want at this stage would be to lead joyfully with the fact that their correspondent had reached Zanzibar first. They would tag on whatever other bits and pieces they had from the news agencies.

Some time after I put the telephone down I thought of more to say and telephoned John Bierman again with another dictation. He had already passed on my first take and spoken to the *Daily Mail*.

"They're ecstatic," he reported. "They're jumping over the moon. You're Fleet Street's hero tomorrow!"

Youths with automatic weapons were commonplace in Africa following the Uhuru (Freedom) era. It was no different on Zanzibar island during the rebellion in which thousands of Arab residents were murdered. (Photo: Author)

"Yeah, just for the day, of course."

"True. But make the most of it. Hit 'em for a raise." I made a mental note of the advice.

I had hardly put the phone down when there was an uproar outside. The door was unlocked and flung open and John Monks was propelled into the room by the quayside sentry who was shouting at him in Swahili. Monks, carrying my personal effects as well as his own, was in a foul temper and looked terrible. His face, scorched crimson and blotched by the day's exposure to the elements, looked like an Aztec sun worshipper's dream.

He flung our possessions on the floor and said: "Tell this bastard to stop prodding me with his fucking gun!" I tried to remonstrate with the guard in my limited Swahili and took the opportunity to demand our release.

"*Wapi Bwana Makuba Field Marshall Okello?*" I asked in the best Swahili I could muster, hoping he'd understand I was asking for the highest authority. But he sneered at me and walked out. In doing so, he slammed and locked the door.

I got dressed, wincing at the touch of the clothing on my sunburn and cuts, while John told me of the miracle of his own arrival. The outgoing tide had swung the dhow and another similar craft nearby around until they were bows onto each other, and good old Piggy, noticing that the other craft had a dinghy attached to it, had flung our possessions from the one dhow to the other and jumped across, and then transferred to the dinghy.

There was a hullabaloo from the Scarface mob that feared the consequences of what he was doing. "One of them followed me onto the other boat and grabbed hold of the dinghy as I was pushing off," said Piggy. "I had to clobber him with an oar."

There was now another hullabaloo – this time from outside our prison, and the door was again unlocked and flung open in anger.

This time it was the launch commander who stormed in, waving his sub-machine gun and, boy, was he pissed off. "I ordered you to stay where you were! You have entered the People's Republic of Zanzibar illegally. You are spies! You will now be taken to Field Marshal Okello!" It sounded ominous. We were being taken to the head honcho, and maybe not, after all, for a friendly interview.

We were bundled out of the harbour office and onto the back of a truck, hemmed about by armed men, and driven through the town. In the headlights we could see bodies lying in the streets, and the smell of death, which pervades so swiftly in tropical places, was already fouling the air.

Chapter 6
Zanzibar's bloody revolt

The rebel forces had made the radio-station building and its environments their military headquarters. The scenes in the courtyard were horrific. Prisoners were being interrogated, beaten, tortured and executed in one of the most gruesome excesses in savagery Monks and I had ever witnessed. Their screams rent the air and made normal conversation impossible. The sight of two white men, even though obviously under guard, gave some of those being held the impression that foreign intervention of some sort was at hand and people clutched at us as we passed, imploring help, until beaten back by guards.

Even wounded rebels were in despair. They lay in rows on the ground, crying for help, in some cases bleeding to death. There seemed to be no medical facilities or assistance for them.

Piles of loot, presumably from the shops and the homes of Arabs, lay strewn about the courtyard, ranging from household utensils to hi-fi and TV sets and, as Monks remarked later, "anything shiny".

Now thoroughly unnerved and fearing the worst, Monks and I waited, crammed at the head of a flight of stairs, stifled and sweating while our guards, dangerously excited by the tempo around them, pressed their guns into our ribs.

Finally the door before us was opened and we were pushed through into what had once been the office of the head of broadcasting. The launch commander and two of his henchmen came in with us. What we saw was not encouraging.

There sat one of the blackest Africans I had ever seen, made sinister by the fact that he was wearing a black military uniform with silver insignia. He sat with his black-booted feet on the table. This was Field Marshal Okello.

There was no paperwork on the field marshal's desk and no sign of maps or battle plans on the walls. He was clearly conducting the war off the cuff, so to speak. All that was on the desk was a half-eaten banana, an ashtray filled with cigarette butts, numerous empty beer bottles, a pack of Lucky Strike cigarettes with a backup carton close to hand, and a telephone.

The field marshal, clearly a chain-smoker, lit up another Lucky Strike while he listened to the launch commander's list of our sins. At the end of it he barked: "Search them!"

"Sir, we have already."

"Search them again!"

They began with a body search as the field marshal smoked and looked on. There was a squawk from Monks.

"Don't touch me there!" He turned to me and implored: "Tell

this bastard to stop feeling my balls, mate." I sighed. Monks had a tendency to speak at times when silence would be the better alternative. "Shush," I said.

I thought I detected a slight flicker of amusement in the eyes of the field marshal. Perhaps this wasn't going to end too badly.

Then all hell broke loose. Examining our personal effects, they found in Monks's bag a Zanzibar telephone directory. It was the one I had used in the harbour office and John, always an alert operator, had chucked it into his bag in case it became useful later on.

But now it was held up as dramatic evidence that we were spies. Why else would we be carrying a Zanzibar telephone directory but to make secret contact with subversive and reactionary elements on the island?

The launch commander was putting his case against us like a barrister in open court when the telephone rang. Whatever business came over the line seemed to capture all the field marshal's attention. When he put the phone down he stared at us as if surprised we were still there.

"Get them out of here," he said irritably, making shooing motions with his hands.

"But, sir ..."

"Get them out of here!" screamed the field marshal with such loudness that we were pushed out of the office at a speed that gave the guards waiting outside the impression we were trying to escape and they pushed us back into the office. But another yell from the field marshal, who was turning out to be a real yeller, drove us all back out and we were hustled downstairs, past the mayhem in the courtyard and back onto the truck.

The launch commander, visibly discomfited, was now anxious to be rid of us. "You are under house arrest!" he said. "You will be held at the English Club!"

We couldn't believe our luck. There was air-conditioning at the English Club. There was a bar and good food and, although the sleeping quarters below always smelt like a public swimming pool, the rooms were comfortable and there were clean sheets.

But when we were offloaded there, it was to find that things were not as usual. About 200 of Zanzibar's 300 British residents had taken refuge in or had been banished to the English Club. It was packed with elderly folk (who had come to Zanzibar for peaceful retirement, only to see their homes burnt down or looted in the past 48 hours) and various matrons and young wives whose husbands were diplomats or civil servants or commercial representatives. And of course there were children of various ages, either screaming or running around wild. There was no electric power, which meant the air-conditioning was off too. The toilets were not working either.

There was controlled pandemonium. A large-breasted lady was walking around saying: "Don't panic! Remember we're British!" The club secretary, an elderly man retired from the old Tanganyika King's African Rifles who had lost an ear, lopped off with a spear in a skirmish with "natives", was heard to tell her testily that no one was panicking. But he himself panicked when he saw us. He distrusted journalists, believing they always stirred up trouble, and wasn't there enough already?

We soothed him and he very kindly took John Monks to his own quarters to provide salve for his sunburn.

I took the opportunity to seek out the telephone in his office. There was now substantial news to report and I dialled the central exchange. The same Indian operator answered. "I am still having no food," he said. I reassured him I would get him help by morning and he put me through to John Bierman again.

I now had the corpses in the streets, the appalling scenes at the radio station, the meeting with Okello and the scenes in the English Club to tell about, and I dictated three wholesome purple pages of events and colour. The first edition, leading with my arrival, was already on the streets, but the new stuff would build up the story for the next four editions. The *Daily Mail* had a fat and complete story. Now I could sleep.

I figured it was time to tell Piggy that the telephone was working to Nairobi and that John Bierman, kindly staying late at his office, was standing by to take his story. He was understandably angry that I had not told him earlier, but was forgiving, as I would have been. He was still in time for the final editions of his newspaper.

We spent the night sleeping on the floor in the crowded club. We were so exhausted that it was more like going into a coma and we were unconscious until midday the following day, reviving to find that a lot was going on, for example, that refugees were leaving the club, stepping over our recumbent bodies. The frigate, *HMS Owen*, and an American warship, the *USS Manley*, had arrived to evacuate citizens of their respective nations.

The Sultan of Zanzibar and his family, who had fled in his private yacht, were picked up by *HMS Owen* at sea, and the frigate then took British evacuees aboard in Zanzibar harbour. The English Club returned to something like normal and we were able to get beds.

A departing British resident kindly gave us the keys of his car

After the uprising on Zanzibar, President Julius Nyerere of the newly created Tanzanian Republic (an amalgamation of Tanganyika and Zanzibar) took a much more forceful role with his military because he was also almost unseated by his troops in a mutiny that spread to the African Mainland. (Photo: Author)

and we cruised about the town. We saw a wild gang of armed revolutionaries driving around in the sultan's red Rolls-Royce.

But an important promise had to be kept. We scrounged some stale rolls and a slab of cheese from the English Club and delivered it to the telephone operator at the central telephone exchange. He was so grateful that he wept on Piggy Monks's shoulder. He was a thin, middle-aged and bespectacled Zanzibari of Indian origin who dared not risk his life by venturing outside. We promised to bring him more food the following morning. Compassion and gratitude aside, it was important to keep him fed. He was our only line of communication to the outside world. He allowed us to file that day's dispatches from his office.

On the way back from that mercy mission, we almost collided with the truck that had driven us to the revolutionary headquarters the night before and we were reminded that we were under arrest. We were chased back to the English Club and threatened with execution if we ventured out again. At the club we found that Major Walters, the one-eared club secretary had found food and a way of preparing it and we sat down blissfully and gratefully to a supper of bacon and eggs and fruit salad.

Meanwhile the news of our arrival by dhow had hit the wires

and awakened the rest of the international press to the existence of Bagamoyo. They converged on the little old seaport like locusts, buying and hiring dhows wherever they could find them, giving the little seaport the best boost of prosperity since the days of the slave trade.

Dennis Neeld of Associated Press and Mohammed Amin, his photographer, were the first of the new arrivals, having found a dhow equipped with a motor. They were seized immediately on landing and placed under house arrest in the Zanzibar Hotel.

Jack Nugent of *Newsweek* arrived after a 20-hour trip almost as harrowing as ours and was seriously beaten up by revolutionaries when they searched him and found his American Express credit card, which they said proved he was a CIA spy. He was hauled off to be executed but was saved by the intervention of Fritz Picard, the American Consul, who had stoically remained at his post on the island.

Other foreign correspondents who arrived included Richard Beeston of the London *Daily Telegraph*, Clyde Sanger of the *Guardian*, Bill Smith of *Time Magazine*, Robert Miller of the *Toronto Globe Mail*, Bob Conley of the *New York Times* and Peter Rand of the *New York Herald Tribune*.

American correspondents were hated on sight, very badly knocked around at times and virtually imprisoned in the Zanzibar Hotel. British and other correspondents were more leniently treated and allowed to file stories via the local cable and wireless office that had reopened for business. But all dispatches had to be censored by – guess who? Our old friend the launch commander who appeared to be one of the few members of the new People's Republic of Zanzibar administration who could read. He used a loaded pistol as a paperweight and we had to place our dispatches under it gingerly when he raised it. He read each dispatch laboriously with a furrowed brow and crossed out everything he did not like as well as everything he failed to understand, which left very little of the stories intact.

Piggy Monks and I filed copy through the censor for appearances' sake, but filed our real dispatches at night through our friend at the central telephone exchange who we kept carefully nourished with daily deliveries of food.

The fighting in the town had died down but slaughter continued in other parts of the island where young communist revolutionaries murdered, maimed, tortured and looted at will. More than 5,000 Arabs were killed in the purge.

Meanwhile, something resembling a political picture began to take shape. Field Marshal Okello disappeared as mysteriously as he had appeared on the scene. A semi-literate brawling ex-seaman called Abeid Karume, who called himself a sheikh – which he was not – proclaimed himself chairman of the Revolutionary Council of the People's Republic of Zanzibar.

Tanganyikan troops arrived from the mainland to "stabilise" the situation and Zanzibar was, in due course, enjoined with Tanganyika to form the new state of Tanzania under President Julius Nyerere.

It appeared that the revolution had, from the beginning, been planned and directed from the mainland.

On the third day after our arrival, I had occasion to return to the wharf where I had originally swum ashore. My epic swim had received a great deal of publicity (not least of all from the satirical magazine *Private Eye*, which treated it with the usual irreverence) and is part of Fleet Street history.

It was again late evening but, as I looked out into the harbour, assessing where I had dived from the dhow, something seemed wrong.

The tide had again ebbed. I studied the scene in some puzzlement, seeing that some of the craft in the harbour had tilted onto their sides and that the water close to the quayside was so shallow that outcrops of coral were showing above the surface.

It was then that I realised what I have guiltily kept secret for all these years and what I feel I must now reveal to cleanse my soul. Although it had probably been necessary to swim the first 100 yards, for the rest, I could have waded ashore. If I'd drowned, it would have been in a metre of water …

CHAPTER SEVEN

AMERICA'S SECRET RESCUE MISSION IN SOMALIA

American Forces were busily engaged in the military build-up prior to Iraq's Operation Desert Storm when Washington was suddenly faced with an emergency in a country that few Americans had even heard of: Somalia. In spite of the imminence of conflict in the Gulf, a carrier force was detached to deal with a critical problem. It was a huge gamble, but the Americans pulled it off ... only just.

Long before names like General Farrah Aideed or Mogadishu started making news, a drama began to unfold in this troubled East African country where violence seems to have been the norm for centuries. It happened at roughly the same time that American and Coalition Forces were gathering strength to invade Saddam Hussein's Iraq for the first time in what became known as Gulf War 1. Robert Doss, then a captain in the United States Marines, a mission planner and a CH-46E Sea Knight helicopter pilot during Operation Eastern Exit – for that is what the rescue mission was called – takes up the story[1]:

Shortly before Gulf War 1 kicked off, a United States Naval task force, Amphibious Group Two and the 4th Marine Expeditionary Brigade wrapped up their fourth month in the Middle East. The aircraft carrier *USS Guam* with Marine Medium Helicopter Squadrons (HMM)-263 and -365 onboard, together with other Marine Corps elements – left the Persian Gulf to conduct night-vision goggle (NVG) training and support operations in the North Arabian Sea.

A detachment of HMM-263 helicopters on board the *USS Trenton* had shortly before intercepted two defiant Iraqi vessels, the *Ibn Khaldoon* and the *Ain Zalah*, for a UN-sanctioned boarding and inspection by an embarked naval raid force.

President George Bush's mid-January deadline for the Iraqi withdrawal from Kuwait loomed. At that stage we were uncertain when the Gulf War would begin, even though we continued to prepare for it. There were also numerous contradictions. Our force had been issued with arctic gear for a NATO deployment one August day, and then we had to replace it with desert camouflage the next. We departed for the Middle East a short while later.

For the Marines in the Brigade responding to these rapidly changing events, the words "every clime and place" from the Marines' Hymn rang true.

Rumours always find a home on board ship, and, as day turned into night on 2 January, a new bit of what US Forces like to refer to as "scuttlebutt" was doing the rounds about some serious trouble developing in Somalia. We were aware that the country was being torn apart by a brutal civil war that ravaged the capital city of Mogadishu and that was about it.

Things started to develop once it emerged that the American Embassy there was under heavy pressure while rebels and government forces roamed the streets outside. These lawless groups left in their wake indiscriminate death and violence. They were, in effect, terrorists, although nobody dared call them that. Not yet, anyway.

Then, quite suddenly, after our aircraft had been recalled to the ship one evening, we learned that we were headed to Somalia to conduct what was termed a "non-combatant evacuation operation" to rescue Americans and foreign nationals from the US Embassy compound. It lay to the immediate north of Mogadishu International Airport, was the report. There was also news about several other navies, air forces, and commercial carriers attempting evacuations of their own, but at that stage, ongoing violence had driven them away.

As the aircraft carrier *Guam* and the amphibious transport dock *Trenton* started south, information about the threat, evacuees, and landing zones had not yet begun to arrive; no one knew the exact location of the embassy compound and, of course, there were no adequate maps.

The first word we received from the US ambassador in Somalia, James Bishop, detailed a desperate situation. Each message provided a small piece of the planning puzzle, but it still kept us wondering if we were doing enough. More important, were we doing it in time?

Mission-planning cells worked feverishly to construct a programme for the evacuation. Fortunately, problems with communication and coordination never materialised; aviation, ground and Navy units on the *Guam* had developed a rapport in the preceding months that supported close cooperation.

Incoming communication from the US Embassy gave some of us the distinct impression that they were being written from cover, probably from under a desk as a fire-fight raged nearby: one message reported that a rocket-propelled grenade had slammed into the compound; others described automatic weapons fire and armed aggressors being repulsed as they attempted to scale the walls of the compound. The ships were making best speed southwards out of the Persian Gulf, but despite the intensity with which we planned, we could not forestall those who threatened our embassy and diplomats.

Meantime, our course paralleled the coast of Somalia, a lengthy stretch of shoreline just north of Kenya that leads to Mogadishu.

In the very early hours of 5 January, following another frantic call from Ambassador Bishop, we moved to within the range of our CH-53E Sea Stallion helicopters, with their aerial refuelling capability. The most recent messages from the embassy indicated that the compound was in real and imminent danger of being overrun – with the logical implication to all of us that the evacuation effort would be lost as well.

Two Sea Stallions from one of the Marine Heavy Helicopter Squadrons on board *Trenton* were loaded with troops and sent on an almost 800 kilometre overwater night flight to reinforce the compound and assist with the evacuation: Operation Eastern Exit had begun.

This flight was not without event. During the first effort at re-fuelling, a pressure seal on the second CH-53E failed. High octane apparently sprayed into the cabin but the leak was quickly fixed by the crew chief and refuelling continued. Also, because the helicopters' Omega Navigation Systems were not functioning properly, pilots had to rely on the refuelling C-130s as well as directional control from the ships.

After two en-route aerial refuellings by Marine KC-130 air tankers operating out of the Persian Gulf, the helicopters arrived at the compound just as dawn broke over the north-west Indian Ocean.

In total, a 60-man Marine evacuation force, including a nine-man SEAL team were landed in the embassy compound, supplementing the five Marine security guards who had been "holding the fort" until then. They were a welcome addition to the team.

Their "run-in" was not without event. Because of the lack of

United States Marines CH-46E 'Sea Knights' prepare to launch on an extended cross-water operation that necessitated several air-to-air refuelling sessions. (Photo: Jerome Conley)

adequate maps, the CH-53Es spent 20 minutes over Mogadishu looking for the embassy compound. They found it eventually, but it was a close call.

The first of the evacuees were gathered and carried to the safety of the *Guam*, still more than 300 miles and another aerial refuelling away. Italian C-130s started another evacuation effort at the airport, but increasingly, bitter fighting kept them from returning to Mogadishu that day.

Mission planning on board the aircraft carrier continued. The timing of the main evacuation was a key concern: as the team considered a daylight mission, it also developed a night alternative.

Daylight would afford us the opportunity for an evenly paced hands-above-the-table evacuation. If we could be recognised as a neutral third party attempting an overt evacuation of innocents, we might proceed unmolested. The likelihood of locating the US Embassy in the daylight was also considerably better than trying to spot it in the dark; particularly since pilots had only recently obtained a few black-and-white photographs and 1:50 000 scale maps of area for navigation purposes.

If we flew into Mogadishu after sunset, we could do so under the cover of darkness. But, there was also a risk that a night mission – if compromised – might be construed as a sneak attack on behalf of one or other of the civil war adversaries. Night-vision goggles would permit us to see in the dark, and we could turn off all of our aircraft lights and become "invisible" to those on the ground, depriving hostile forces of much of their precision. Nevertheless, any

Chapter 7
America's secret rescue mission in Somalia

advantage gained by flying in the dark would be lost by meandering flights searching for a darkened landing zone over extremely hostile positions with unlimited supplies of ammunition.

To make matters worse, the landing zone (LZ) had been described to us as "extremely sandy and filled with unspecified obstacles". Even in the daylight, trying to land five helicopters in such a confined area would be a serious challenge.

More messages continued to arrive on board that described further mayhem and conflict around the perimeter of the embassy compound. The erratic nature of these attacks convinced us that our helicopters would almost certainly be targeted if spotted. With the report that the fighting appeared to decrease at night, the decision was made: we would go in under cover of darkness.

It is axiomatic that a night operation poses more dangers than any daytime mission. But these were problems over which pilots could exercise control. That was another factor: at this point, our night option made better tactical sense, simply because we were a force that presumed a capability to strike at night against Iraq. Consequently, there was no reason to balk at a night strike into Somalia.

Shortly before midnight on 5 January, the first of our two waves of five armed CH-46s – led by aviation mission commander Lieutenant Colonel R.J. Wallace – prepared to launch from 50 kilometres out to sea. We were that close to the Somali capital.

Once in the air, you couldn't miss the lights of Mogadishu in the distance. The sky in this tropical region was clear, though the city itself was overcast. A pall of smoke drifted towards the sea. What did come as a surprise was that the almost totally dysfunctional Mogadishu still had electrical power. Occasionally we could see flashes of battle and now and again long lines of tracers, but very little more. It was all pretty ominous.

The Initial Point (IP) – the point at which the flight was intended to cross the coast – would not be easy to find, but the importance of flying over it on the first crossing had been stressed during our planning and briefing sessions. We were aware that an error of a thousand metres to the right would take the flight directly over known surface-to-air missile (SAM) and anti-aircraft artillery (AAA) sites and, presumably, troop concentrations. A thousand metres to the left would head us off the edge of our maps. These were the only ones we had, so the initial effort was crucial to the success of the whole operation.

When it finally happened, the flight crossed the IP as planned and descended to 100 feet. We slowed down to about 80 knots. Lt Col

Wallace spotted the embassy compound's infrared strobe light that marked our intended LZ and he transitioned to land.

The decision to put a little distance between the aircraft during this final transition proved critical. The LZ was more confined than anticipated and each helicopter "browned-out" in the whirling sand and debris swept up by the rotors immediately before touchdown. Without caution, things could have gone badly wrong.

Once the dust had settled, we were offered a view through our NVGs of what it was all about. We could see groups of civilians huddled near an embassy building. The evacuees moved quickly in organised batches of 15 to get on board. Once they were seated, the aircraft launched and signalled the second wave of five aircraft to begin the ingress.

Like ships almost, our aircraft passed one another in the night – five Thunder aircraft from HMM-263 returning to the ship and five Rugby aircraft from HMM-365 inbound to Mogadishu. Continuing the process, Rugby departed from the embassy with evacuees and Thunder prepared to launch from the ship and return to the city.

Suddenly, the silence of the radios was broken by a call from the ambassador's office saying we'd been ordered to cease the evacuation immediately. We were told to leave Somalia or be shot down. Some of us were surprised it had taken the Somalis so long to react.

Since we had begun our operation – with the understanding that the environment was hostile – the threat had no effect on our mission. Crews did double-check their body armour, and there were some hasty discussions reiterating procedures for the transfer of flight controls between pilots if one of them took a hit. There were also rules of engagement passed on to the gunners.

Moments after the Thunder departure from the ship, the overhead Air Force AC-130 reported that his radar warning receiver had detected an active SAM system towards the west. The message was noted by all the aviators. We continued inwards towards the embassy, fully aware that the situation could only get worse if we delayed any longer. Approaching the LZ, this time, we received SAM radar-search indications from the east, but by flying low and keeping our airspeeds high, we prevented acquisition and lock-on possibility.

The evacuations continued. One more load for Thunder and another for Rugby.

As the number of evacuees dwindled, the security force began to pull inward into a tighter security perimeter in the embassy compound. At this point, as reported by Adam Siegel in *Proceedings:*

Chapter 7
America's secret rescue mission in Somalia

A cluster of CH-53s on the flight deck of an American helicopter carrier at sea. These choppers played a significant role in subsequent land operations in Somalia, the majority based at the Baledogle air base in the interior, once a pivotal Soviet airport during the Cold War. (Photo :Jerome Conley)

US Naval Institute, there were some curious developments. As he recalled, a more serious threat emerged as the second wave arrived:

"A Somali major approached the gate with two truckloads of troops and threatened to shoot down the helicopters if the 'illegal operation' did not cease immediately. With the concurrence of the US Ambassador, the operation continued unimpeded as Ambassador Bishop negotiated with the major. Because the ambassador, his immediate staff as well as the Marine security guards had been scheduled to go on the third wave, it took off for the *Guam* with only a portion of the planned evacuees (and only four helicopters instead of five). Before the arrival of the final wave, the Somali major withdrew his opposition in exchange for several thousand dollars in cash and the keys to the ambassador's car. The last wave, therefore, had six helicopters."

Final head counts were taken and the last helicopter prepared to leave the LZ. Masses of armed Somalis were gathered at the embassy gate and our gunners were prepared to repel and attack, but none materialised. When we were certain no evacuees remained, the last aircraft left Mogadishu, but not before the two-man Marine communications team was almost left behind because of a misunderstanding. They were not aware that this was the final wave.

The State Department later reported that the embassy was blown up, its doors blasted with grenades immediately after the evacuation had been completed. Two days later, Italian C-130s and a French

American warship *USS Ogden*, sister-ship of the *USS Trenton* that was a mainstay in the rescue of American and other foreign nationals from the US diplomatic compound in Mogadishu. (Photo: Jerome Conley)

warship evacuated more foreign citizens. Heavy fighting kept the Italian C-130s from returning until 12 January, when they managed to complete their evacuation and that was barely a year before the United States sent its troops into Somalia as part of the United Nations Operation Restore Hope.

Each aircraft passenger manifest told a story. One listed the names of Kuwaiti and Soviet diplomats; there were 39 Soviet nationals in the group. Another roster contained the name of a woman who had been shot. One more named the Sudanese ambassador's wife, who was about to give birth – which she did shortly afterwards – and still another included a woman who boarded a helicopter with a parachute draped around her – the only personal belonging that she had managed to salvage from her home.

Altogether 281 men, women and children from 30 nations moved to the aircraft elevator on board the *Guam*. The ship looked like an international bazaar, with a curious assortment of apparel from various cultures and countries. At three in the morning, after a final accounting of evacuees and troops, the last two helicopters landed and Operation Eastern Exit was over.

The ships turned north and headed out of Somali waters, back to the Persian Gulf, towards that other "clime and place" where, days later, another mission was about to begin: we were on the cusp of Operation Desert Storm and the beginning of the end for Saddam Hussein.

1 Extracts from this chapter were taken from Al J. Venter's *The Chopper Boys*, published in 1994 by Stackpole Books in the US and Greenhill Books in London.

CHAPTER EIGHT

SOMALIA: STILL BURNING

> Following the American-led UN Operation Restore Hope in Somalia of the early 1990s, the country remained quietly under the radar for a few years. Then Washington was made aware that some of the bombers who destroyed two American embassies – in Nairobi, Kenya and Dar es Salaam, Tanzania – had powerful Somali links. Meanwhile, the country had become ungovernable. Al-Qaeda has moved into the Horn of Africa in force and interestingly, some American Special Forces have already gone in to have a look ...

The word is out in Mogadishu: some of al-Qaeda's Somali fighters who were involved in the war in Iraq have returned home. Still more have moved on to Afghanistan. Others from the United States – mostly young people and quite a few students among them – have replaced them. All undergo rigorous training to answer what local Imams refer to as "The Call". If you were to get anywhere near that country and start to ask questions about these people, it would almost guarantee a bullet.

It's a mean place, Mogadishu, made worse because unlike Baghdad or Tehran, the country doesn't have a government. Instead, it is run by a hodge-podge bunch of crazies that make Iran's mullahs look quite civilised by comparison. In the contemporary argot, these people are termed Jihadis and they belong to fundamentalist organisations like al-Shabaab or any one of a dozen other fanatical Muslim groups. One and all, these are religious zealots and in their own words, they are in the service of Allah until death smiles.

It is a violent country, Somalia. In Mogadishu, its so-called capital, you can die because of a whim. It might be something as simple as somebody not liking your face. Or perhaps he covets your *Nike* running shoes. Worse, there's nobody willing or able to stop this anarchy. There is, or by the time you read this, there was an interim government of sorts in place, but its role was recently compared to that of a Boy Scouts troop trying to bring order to a race riot at Attica.

If you want to know what Somalia is like today, Mark Bowan's book *Black Hawk Down* presents a pretty accurate picture of the country as it was in 1993. Since then, conditions have deteriorated still further and as anybody who has visited the place recently will affirm, the shooting can start at any time.

Conditions for most of us hacks who spent time in Mogadishu in the early 1990s were tough. They were dangerous enough to get several members of the press corps murdered. For the majority of journalists who didn't have the advantage of sleeping on one of the American military bases – I ended up staying at an American air base at Baledogle about 120 kilometres north of Mogadishu for a week – it was always a matter of watching your back, or paying somebody else good money to do so.

That said, it wasn't an inordinately difficult task. Somalis – or "Skinnies" as some of us would deprecatingly refer to them – were never first in line in any kind of bravery stakes. Most would wait until dark before attempting to harm you. Face-to-face confrontations were usually limited to when there was a crowd and perhaps only a handful of *farangi* (foreigners). Tanked up with drugs, it is another matter: then the bastards suddenly have courage in abundance.

Interestingly, before the war started, I'd visited Mogadishu with my wife. Madelon and I went there on a week-long excursion from Nairobi and it was an unusual experience even then. There was no war, but the place was tense. Staying in one of the run-down local hotels, we at least had clean sheets. That was the same old Olympia Hotel, originally built by Italian colonials who ran the country for decades and which features prominently in the film.

With the emergence of half-a-dozen warlords that were as demented as they were callous, conditions deteriorated pretty quickly afterwards. These psychotics didn't need an excuse to kill anybody: they just went ahead and ordered it done. By the time US Forces arrived, you were taking your life in your hands just getting off the plane at Mogadishu International Airport. With successive droughts, ongoing hostilities in a never-ending civil war and a lunatic fringe that is constantly trying to wrest control, the number of people who have ended up dead has been conservatively estimated at about a million, give or take a few hundred thousand ...

What began to emerge in the 1990s was that US administration officials realised that Africa had become a potential breeding ground for terrorism. Indeed, by the early 2000s, Washington was aware that Africa was both an important staging area and training centre for al-Qaeda cadres. Somalia, in particular, had become the place either to target American interests or to plan for such operations somewhere else. The attack on the United States' guided missile destroyer *USS Cole* in the Yemeni port of Aden on 9 June 2009, in which 16 American sailors were killed and scores wounded was one such an event. Several of the planners and the person responsible for logistics and finance in the terror attack were all Somalis.

But the real meat and potatoes of an al-Qaeda terrorist attack had already taken place the previous year. Midmorning explosions demolished the United States Embassy in Nairobi, Kenya and ended up killing 213 people, twelve of whom were American citizens. That attack took place on 7 August 1998; another eleven people died when the US embassy in Tanzania was bombed a little later that day. Before that, in June 1995, members of what called itself The Islamic Group – a Cairo-based extremist faction – tried to assassinate former Egyptian President Hosni Mubarak while on a state visit to Addis Ababa, the Ethiopian capital[1].

All these efforts – and others still to come – demonstrated solid Somali terror involvement, though anybody with any sense had fled the country, which, in turn, made it increasingly difficult for Western nations to monitor developments in the Horn of Africa. Most educated Somali nationals had already gone elsewhere.

A visit to Mogadishu, the Somali capital – "The Dish" as US forces liked to call it – was essential in the old days in order to understand the complexity of that country's political struggles and the violence that it spawned. Somalia's revolution, like a miasmic virus, infected an entire region that stretches from the Sudan and Eritrea in the north, to Kenya, Tanzania, Mozambique and all their approaches to the south.

These days, with the Americans tending to other priorities, the Ethiopians are trying to restore a semblance of stability. Their military has been at it for several years now and while their main force has withdrawn, Addis Ababa continues to plug away at the rebel periphery.

Getting to grips with terror in Somalia is always going to be a difficult task. Mogadishu, for instance, sprawls. Approaching the city from the sea and during the monsoon it is an awesome mishmash of muddy pools, piles of garbage, open sewers and everywhere,

Final approach to Mogadishu Airport, which has the distinction of having the most number of derelict or damaged military aircraft in the world. Some of these abandoned hulks can be spotted centre, foreground. There are still more to the left. (Photo: Author)

the turmoil of acres of screaming, dysfunctional pullulating crowds. This conglomeration on any day of the week stretches as far as you can see: in sheer size alone, the numbers of people are powerfully intimidating. As one correspondent commented in the British *Spectator*, the place makes Kabul look like Manhattan by comparison.

The Mogadishu International Airport, even then, was no better, with clusters of smashed and mortared buildings and more wrecked military aircraft lying about than any other terminal in the world. When I last visited the place, there wasn't a single glass pane left intact, though since then, things appear to have been patched up a bit, at least until the next bomb attack.

The last time I did the trip by vehicle into town from the airport – shortly before the Americans pulled out – I was instructed to "hunker well down; don't expose yourself because they sometimes snipe at us". The sergeant who issued instructions was explicit: "If your vehicle stops and one of them tries to climb on board, hold on tight to your bags, your wallet, your eye glasses and the rest. If it isn't bolted down," he joked, "they will snatch it." The man was serious. Then we were off, a column of five United Nations vehicles headed into the fiery cauldron that became known around the world as the Mogadishu Hell Hole.

We were escorted by French-built APCs with their hatches shut and that wasn't exactly a hopeful sign. Meanwhile I'd shifted forward

Chapter 8
Somalia: still burning

and taken up position behind a couple of Omani soldiers manning a .50 Browning. The rest of the escort sat facing out, their weapons cocked. Nobody had forgotten the massacre of a squad of Pakistani troops by a hoard of Somali militants.

Our convoy headed north-east past the old Russian compound. The drivers turned left before we reached the *Villagio Quattro Chilometri* when, quite suddenly, we were in an environment more alien than anything I had ever experienced before, although not for lack of experience. I'd spent time at Ba'abda, the Beirut suburb during the 1982 Israeli invasion of Lebanon and that was relatively tame by comparison. At least that civil war had some kind of disjointed shape to it; dangerous but not mindlessly frenzied like this. Also, for all its excesses, abductions, internecine rivalry and the rest, conflict in Lebanon was a more disciplined kind of war. Mogadishu, in contrast, was a jumble of sometimes terrifying confusion, violence and bloodshed amid the dross of conflict.

From where I could observe what was going on around us as our convoy headed into town, every building had been blasted. The wrecks of cars and trucks blown apart by rockets and mortars lined the route. A burnt-out Humvee suggested some of the events that had gone before. There was a time when any American military vehicle was fair game for Mohammed Aideed's rag-tag fanatics, the majority with their heads in clouds of dope. Our escorts had several hefty clubs or shillelaghs, or what the Zulus like to call *knobkieries*, and they didn't mind using them on the heads of those who tried to clamber on board. Nor was there any clear line of demarcation between the warring factions that we passed on the way into the city.

Every male – quite a few of them not yet into their teens – carried a weapon, usually the requisite AK, although there were a lot of RPGs around. The rest of the population – which included women, children, the aged and the maimed – milled about aimlessly on the road and off it, in and out of narrow alleys. There were hundreds of paths and improvised foxholes between the buildings and each one of them appeared to have its purpose.

When we reached the market – it lies just beyond 27th October Square – the throng overflowed onto the road and our convoy slowed to a crawl. It was as if the place had suddenly become a Middle Eastern *souk*. People were shouting, gesticulating at us, at each other, arms flailing, faces contorted and spittle, unguided and generous, flying everywhere.

Many of the eyes of those on the road around us were glazed.

Others were bloodshot; the effects of *Qat*, the amphetamine leaf that is universally chewed in this part of Africa, and across the water in Yemen. That means that if you're going to do anything at all, get it finished in the morning because everybody's whacked out on the drug by the time lunchtime comes around.

It's the same today. If you're not smuggling *Qat* or are a member of an international aid team crazy enough to risk your life by volunteering to work there – or possibly on your way to see one of the demagogues about weapons – you're likely to have some serious problems.

For a start, it'll seriously limit your ability to move about. Nobody goes anywhere in Somalia today without an armed escort and to get one, you need to have a very good reason indeed. Fail that test and in the eyes of the average Somalia, you're an American spy. Or worse, an Israeli, especially now that al-Qaeda has close ties with those nominally in control.

It was al-Qaeda, coincidentally, that supplied the bulk of the RPG-7s that were used against US forces in 1993. Indeed, there are some who maintain that it was Bin Laden's activists that originally primed Mogadishu mobs in preparation for the confrontation that featured in *Black Hawk Down*.

These days all security is supposed to be in the hands of an African military force that is dangerously under-resourced and calls itself AMISOM, the African Union Mission in Somalia. What makes it distinctive is that its vehicle of preference is the old South African Defence Force Casspir, which underscores the quality of the hardware we used in our own Border War. A quarter-century later Casspirs are still going strong in Somalia, even if most of them were sold to India after Nelson Mandela came into power.

As for Osama bin Laden's combatants, many of whom have returned to Somalia from other wars, a source in Nairobi with close ties to Kenya's coastal Islamic community reckoned that most of these fugitives escaped through Pakistan. From there, they were routed back to Africa either by boat or on commercial airline flights in and out of the Gulf.

He disclosed, too, that a group of more than a dozen Somalis, posing as crew, shipped out of Mombasa for Mogadishu in an Omani-owned dhow shortly before the US surge in Afghanistan. This was not an unusual event: those motorised sailing boats are a colourful feature along the East African coast for many months of the year and Somalis are regarded to be among the most peripatetic of Africa's

Chapter 8
Somalia: still burning

travellers. What is more, the old sailing craft are in ready demand among Arab boat owners, a tradition that goes back a millennia or more.

Discreet enquiries in Mogadishu yielded nothing about the returnees, except that Somali police announced shortly afterwards that it had arrested four Iraqi Kurds and a Palestinian who were thought to have links to the al-Qaeda leader. Or more likely, to his Egyptian deputy, a former gynaecologist by the name of Ayman al-Zahawiri, who has sported a $25 million bounty on his head for more than a decade, even when he spent some of that time moving about in South Africa.

For the rest, Mogadishu's so-called interim government denies that its nationals have been involved in conflicts, in Afghanistan, Iraq or anywhere else. Or even that al-Qaeda has a presence in the country. Washington believes otherwise, underscored by thousands of posters depicting Osama bin Laden as the ultimate Islamic hero. These flyers appeared overnight throughout the country after September 11 and are regularly replaced.

Meanwhile, there is considerable pressure in the United States to expand the search for members of Bin Laden's recruits to Africa's Horn, which is one of the reasons why there are now four or five

Italian Air Force helicopter gunship attached to the original United Nations Operation Restore Hope, which was abandoned soon after the United States lost almost 20 of its soldiers in an aborted raid on the headquarters of one of the Somali warlords. (Photo: Author)

Mogadishu harbour when things still worked in the country: the ship alongside was bringing emergency food for the country's starving millions, almost all of which was "appropriated" by strong-arm militia bands. Today the port is a hive of illegal activity and piracy. (Photo: Author)

American surveillance over-flights conducted across Somalia each week, most of them launched from the former French colony of Djibouti, further up the Red Sea coast.

In the American view, there is a compelling argument for doing so. Following the discovery of caches of al-Qaeda documents in Afghanistan, Kenya and elsewhere, several Somali sites – including bases at Las Anod in the north and in the countryside around El Wak near the Kenyan and Ethiopian frontiers – have been pinpointed as two of the most important al-Qaeda training bases in Africa.

It has been common knowledge in Nairobi for a while now that another al-Qaeda staging post was south of the port of Kismayu, not far from the Kenyan border. This was the same facility that was originally implicated in the terrorist bombing of the two American embassies: explosives used in both attacks came from there before they were sent by road to Kenya and Tanzania. Each time, we've been told in evidence, there were Somalis either in control or otherwise involved.

A Washington source also disclosed that outside the Sudan, several Somali terrorist bases were among the first to have been established abroad by Osama bin Laden in the mid-1990s. Other terrorist training camps mentioned in a preliminary report include Boosaaso in the north-east of this desperately impoverished country, as well as on Ras Kamboni island off the country's southern coast. In addition, there is a substantial body of evidence that implicates fundamentalists from all of these training bases – as well as several others whose names remain classified, pending military action – having been active militarily in several other regional wars, including Chechnya and Kashmir.

And we now have the spectre of international piracy affecting vast reaches of the Indian Ocean. Somali ports play host to the largest group of pirates operating in any ocean for the past three or four centuries and they are allowed to do almost as they please, for a piece of the take, of course. Right now nobody – not even the United States – knows how to tackle this problem that appears to be getting worse and costs the international maritime community more than $100 million a year.

Short of a full-scale invasion, this is something that is going to be with us for a while ...

Meantime, the ungoverned and ungovernable Somalia plays an uncertain role in African politics in the north-eastern quadrant of the African continent. Conditions in the country fluctuate almost day by day and the entire international community accepts that it could get worse. Last heard, there were warships from about 20 countries patrolling adjacent seas in a bid to end piracy, but even that threat is not being afforded the full attention that it deserves: the Indian Ocean is just too vast and Somali privateers have been operating in much of it.

Washington's Jamestown Foundation has issued several reports about the various roles of the country's warlords, including the effects of weapons and drug running, piracy and whatever else al-Qaeda might be doing today in this former Italian colony. One of these is titled "Weapons for War Lords: Arms Trafficking in the Gulf of Aden", published in June, 2009. It presents a sobering panoply[2]:

"In the Hobbesian anarchy that has been the norm in Somalia since the late 1980s," says the report, "the proliferation of weapons has been associated not only with the pursuit of political power, but also with international terrorism and the protection and furtherance of economic objectives in the region.

"Somalia lies at the heart of regional arms trafficking networks that include governments and private traders in East Africa and the Arabian Peninsula. Developed over many years, this market relies on traditional trade routes, military supply lines and corruptible government actors to provide material support to clansmen, warlords, and militants who purchase or barter for small arms, such as Kalashnikov rifles, rocket-propelled grenades (RPGs) and larger weapons systems, such as anti-aircraft guns and 'technicals' (armoured pick-up trucks with weapons mounted on the back). Currently, sustained and developed primarily by a mix of opportunistic businessmen and foreign governments who are strengthening local proxies, the arms trade in and around Somalia serves as a reliable, highly adaptable, and readily accessible wellspring of the kind of armaments that feeds regional conflicts."

Another influx of armaments occurred in the 1990s as governments and private vendors supplied the Ethiopian and Eritrean militaries in their terrible war against one another that left hundreds of thousands of people killed[3].

All sorts of ploys are used to get weapons to North East Africa. A Warsaw newspaper reported that Centrex, a Polish company, exported arms to Latvia, which were then passed on to Croatia and Somalia, two countries under United Nations arms embargos at the time.

The report goes on[4]: "European businesses also supplied weapons to Somali clansmen and warlords as a means of obtaining permission for various activities such as illegal fishing or toxic waste disposal. One example involved an Italian firm that dumped toxic waste in Somalia after providing weapons and ammunition to powerful Somali clansmen.

"Included in this network was Giancarlo Marocchino, a well-known Italian shipping businessman based in the port city of Karaan, who was arrested by UN troops in Mogadishu in 1993 for his suspected involvement in arms trafficking. Deals arranged by this Italian network and other brokers included arms shipments from Ravenna, La Spezia, and Leghorn in Italy, and the involvement of Italian Mafia, particularly the Calabrians. Other publicised trafficking routes from this era includes one running from Ireland to Somalia, via Cyprus and Lebanon[5]".

Andrew Black also reports that the government of Eritrea has been singled out as having provided significant weapon and financial support to a variety of Islamist groups.

In late July 2006, he states, "two cargo shipments that landed at Mogadishu International Airport were suspected of bringing arms to the Islamic Courts Union (ICU). Though bearing Kazakh markings and rumoured to be owned by or affiliated with Russian arms dealer Viktor Bout (now arrested and awaiting trial in the United States). The shipment is widely suspected to have been provided by Eritrea, but may have originated in Yemen or Libya, according to a Western diplomat stationed in the region at the time." More recently, Omar Hashi Aden, the Security Minister of the TFG Transitional

Chapter 8
Somalia: still burning

Government, claimed that three aircraft landed at an airstrip outside Mogadishu loaded with arms from Eritrea for Islamist insurgents.

Transport routes for arms entering Somalia are fluid and varied, following traditional trade routes across the Gulf of Aden and responding rapidly to new markets and government countermeasures. For example, an investigation by the Stockholm International Peace Research Institute (SIPRI) reported that aircraft used to transport humanitarian aid and peacekeeping support had also been used in transporting arms[6]:

"Weapons trading from Yemeni dhows through remote natural ports are a part of the wider general trade (fuel, plastic-ware, cement, food, etc.) aimed at avoiding customs duties. Usually, several weapons traders arrange for their respective consignments to be transported on the same dhow to share transport costs ... Kismayu [south of Mogadishu] has been a common port for arms from the Arabian Peninsula and East African sources ..."

More disturbing are consistent reports of UN and other forces involved in illegal arms trading. Indeed, says Black, several militant leaders have noted the corruptible role of government forces in the Somali arms markets[7]. This is nothing new: Nigerian troops – and in particular, Nigerian Army officers – were heavily involved in the illegal diamond dealings while deployed on peacekeeping missions during the civil war in Sierra Leone. They also meddled in illicit tropical hardwood shipments out of the region, specifically from Liberia.

With regard to Somalia, Sheikh Mukhtar Robow Abu Mansur, a former spokesman for al-Shabaab (with close al-Qaeda links),

Coalition Force Chinook helicopters drawn up in echelon at Mogadishu Internationl Airport. (Photo: Author)

addressed the issue of TFG troops returning to southern Somalia after training in Ethiopia by declaring, "We say to these troops: do not imperil your lives, but rather abandon your duties ... if you come to us, we will buy your arms and save your lives." A year earlier, the rebel chairman denied that his organisation was receiving support from Eritrea. Instead, he admitted they were acquiring weapons in Somalia from sources that included the Ethiopian military[8].

Traditionally, the principal access point to the Somali arms market was through the Bakaara Market in Mogadishu. However, since 2006, the market has devolved into a network of smaller markets due to pressure from the ICU and increasing insecurity in the traditional Bakaara Market area of Mogadishu. The UN reports that a somewhat coordinated network of markets has emerged in and immediately surrounding Mogadishu, centered around sub-clan areas and buyers and located at Suuq Ba'ad, Karaan, Huriwa, Elasha, Medina and Arjantin.

Using revenues from smuggling, remittances from the Diaspora, piracy revenues, and even funding from the Eritrean government, al-Shabaab and similar groups are able to readily obtain a broad array of weaponry, according to the UN. The typical kind of hardware available through these markets are small arms and crew-served infantry weapons, including Kalashnikov assault rifles, RPGs, mortars, anti-tank weapons as well as surface-to-air missiles like SAM-7 or SAM-16 Manpads."

From the sea, Mogadishu looks almost picturesque. All the modern buildings (on the right) have since been destroyed in the quarter-century of bloodshed that followed America's rescue efforts.
(Photo: Author)

Chapter 8
Somalia: still burning

Obviously the West, and in particular Washington, needs to get to grips with what is viewed as an escalating security in a region half the size of Western Europe. All the issues mentioned have made Somalia the sun-kissed destination of choice for even more Jihadi fundamentalists who were unable to make the grade in either Iraq or Afghanistan.

The piracy issue continues unabated and there have been merchant ships hijacked in areas deep into the Indian Ocean. Apart from the Seychelles Archipelago and off the Tanzanian coast, there have been cargo ships taken by Somalis off Madagascar, a couple of thousand kilometres south of the country.

Quietly and unheralded, the United States military is making some discreet inroads of its own, including the occasional abduction of the occasional radical religious leader who, after being put on trial, will be provided with all the facilities he might need to turn to Mecca five times a day within the comfort of is own remote cell, though probably not at Guantanamo.

Somali recruits are being trained by American instructors and the "legal" provisional government in Mogadishu does get a supply of weapons, though these are carefully monitored to prevent them from being sold on the black market to al-Shabaab, a relative newcomer to the fray that today controls much of southern Somalia.

There is good evidence of clandestine US involvement. Recent returnees from the Horn talk of mysterious "surveillance aircraft" that appear to hover over Mogadishu. These are unmanned drones, in all probability launched from United States warships and their purpose is to track rebel movements. Asked about them by an American reporter, General Mohamed Gelle Kahiye – the chief of Somalia's military – conceded that his people were indeed getting some support from Washington. He was not prepared to comment on whether US Special Forces had recently launched raids in the country to capture some of the opposition leaders who were causing trouble, though it is clear that al-Qaeda has fostered links between Somalia and Yemen in what one Somali watcher in Nairobi referred to as an "al-Qaeda exchange programme".

Countering Western efforts throughout is al-Shabaab, also believed to have strong Iranian links. Its fortunes are nominally led by Sheikh Mohamed Mukhtar Abdirahman (or Abu Zubeyr, his *nom de guerre*).

Estimated to number several thousand fighters, the movement is well-equipped and motivated. There are numerous foreigners in its ranks, including combatants from Chechnya, Saudi Arabia, Egypt and even South Africa. Not averse to suicide bombings, al-Shabaab has all the hallmarks of an al-Qaeda group, with a central group of clerics guiding its actions.

One source maintained that the group had been able to expand its footprint in Somalia with relatively small numbers for two reasons: there has been no central government in Somalia for two decades and many of the warlords that have filled the power vacuum have shown themselves willing to cooperate with these Jihadis, if only to save their own skins.

For this, and other reasons, they tend to turn a blind eye towards the kind of forced recruitment currently being practised by al-Shabaab militants in Somalia.

1 *Africa and the War on Terrorism*: A CRS Report for Congress: Ted Dagne, Specialist in International Relations, Foreign Affairs, Defense and Trade Division, Washington DC: 17 January 2002.
2 Andrew Black *Weapons for War Lords: Arms Trafficking in the Gulf of Aden*, Jamestown Foundation, *Terrorism Monitor*, Volume 7, Issue 17: 18 June 2009.
3 *Yemen Times*, 15 March 1999; 21 March 1999.
4 *Famiglia Cristiana*, Milan, 1 October 2000.
5 *La Republica*, Rome, 3 June 1996.
6 Hugh Griffiths and Mark Bromley: *Air Transport and Destabilizing Commodity Flows*: SIPRI *Policy Paper:* 24 May 2009.
7 For a complete list of the reports of the UN Monitoring Group on Somalia, refer to: www.un.org/sc/committees/751/mongroup.shtml.
8 *Voice of America News*, 25 April 2007.

CHAPTER NINE

ANGOLAN SKIRMISH WITH 44 PARACHUTE BRIGADE

It was the classic attack: Task Force Alpha would drive north so that they would be in position by noon to attack Xangongo, a fairly big town that sits astride the great Kunene River in southern Angola. The operation was code-named "Target Yankee" and Pathfinder Company of 44 Parachute Brigade would be in it from the start. The unit was originally formed by Colonel Jan Breytenbach from members of the old Rhodesian Army and would lead the way. Graham Gilmore who wrote *Pathfinder Company: 44 Parachute Brigade – "The Philistines"* was there and he tells us about it[1].

With Colonel Jan "Bruin Man" Breytenbach in charge of the Para Brigade, and a South African Army officer, Captain Veldhuizen commanding our group – all other personnel being *uitlanders* (foreigners) – the attack promised results.

Headquarters at Sector 10 in Oshakati further to the south, had long been aware that the town was the base of an Angolan armoured brigade. The word was that if we took Xangongo and the great bridge across the river – or what was left of it after it had been blasted by the South African Air Force – our forces would be home and dry. In theory, we could end up dominating a huge part of southern Angola.

First though, it would be the job of the Pathfinders – 44 Parachute Brigade – to quietly bypass the town and, if possible, attack from the north where its defences were expected to be weak since they faced friendly forces in the interior. It was a tough call, problematic as well.

The Angolan Army, officially known as FAPLA, the acronym for *Forças Armadas Populares de Libertação de Angola* – was made up of a hodgepodge of local troops reinforced by a strong Cuban veteran

When 44 Parachute Battalion went across the border into Angola, they took everything bar the kitchen sink with them because re-supply was not always ensured. That invariably included heavy automatic and AAA guns. (Photo: Author)

element as well as a sprinkling of Soviets in command. These people had been in this game as long as we had, and none of us was under any illusion that the task ahead would be easy. As the colonel told his men, it was a gamble we simply had to take and so we did.

Mid-year temperatures in the southern African midwinter are often extreme – even by African standards. It can be boiling hot in the day, with the barometer sometimes dropping to almost freezing after dark and then it sometimes takes until mid-morning to warm up.

But this was Africa and the creatures of the bush added their own symphony of sound to the procedures: bullfrogs croaking, insects buzzing and the crickets making their customary chirrups within an arm's length of where you've got your head down: which more often than not means a restless night.

It was after midnight that some of the men woke from their slumber. A number were disturbed by what the day ahead would hold and for several, it was unsettling. Nobody said anything though, but they were aware that only several hundred metres to their immediate north lay the cut-line that marked the international boundary with Angola. Beyond lay Injun country, the region they were about to invade.

About an hour before dawn, the men started getting ready. Scores

Chapter 9
Angolan skirmish with 44 Parachute Brigade

of trucks started their engines, creating a discordant rhythm that roared across the open savannah. Line upon line of brown South African Army troop-carrying Buffels and Ratel armoured personnel carriers were being prepared for what lay ahead and even with all that noise, the men tended to keep their voices low. Meantime, as had been arranged the night before, officers and NCOs got their men together and onto the vehicles.

It had taken weeks of preparation to get this far: the massive onslaught, codenamed Operation Protea, was about to get a kick-start.

Apart from Afrikaans as the lingua franca, a lot of Portuguese could be heard among some of the combatants, especially those attached to the three 32 Battalion companies on our flank as they got ready for the move. Those veteran black soldiers with their white officers and NCOs would see a lot of action in the hours ahead, and at the end of it, some would not survive. It was that kind of war.

Those troops were not the most unusual element of Task Force Alpha. The rearmost unit of the invading force consisted of light fighting vehicles, each of them painted in the kind of distinctive camouflage routinely used by FAPLA. And that wasn't the only difference. Called Sabres and built onto the chassis of improvised Land Rover and Unimog four-by-four trucks – with heavy machine guns mounted on the cab – the trucks would be used in a dual deception and attack mode on a series of long-range penetrations behind enemy lines.

David Stirling, the founder of the original British Special Air Service, devised the system in the North African desert against Rommel's Desert Rats with remarkable success. As the men knew, if the ploy didn't work, the results could be disastrous.

Also, in this unit, English alone – in its various guises – was spoken. The men had accents that reflected British, Canadian, Australian, American and a few other former colonial heritages. There was also a sizeable bunch of Rhodesians among them, some having served in the Rhodesian Light Infantry, others in the Rhodesian SAS, Selous Scouts or Grey Scouts.

What Pretoria made perfectly clear early on – both regionally and through various diplomatic channels abroad – was that the strike was not specifically aimed at Angola. This was to be a settling of scores with SWAPO, the South West African People's Organisation, and its military wing PLAN (People's Liberation Army of Namibia). Nor was it a secret that PLAN – headed by an Ovambo politician by the name of Sam Nujoma – had as its main objective to gain control of South West Africa (later Namibia). In "exile", all its operational bases were in Angola, as was SWAPO's military headquarters and principal training establishments.

It was common knowledge that the Angolan government supported SWAPO. It had actually incorporated some of Nujoma's cadres within FAPLA and others had been sent abroad with Angolan elements for training in Russia, Cuba, Libya, Tanzania, China and elsewhere. Luanda cooperated completely with this insurgent force, and it was no surprise that the South Africans reacted accordingly. The Angolan Army had long ago become a legitimate military target, which was why Operation Protea was aimed specifically at taking Xangongo: it was the regional FAPLA headquarters.

The way the general officer commanding South African forces explained it in his build-up, all SWAPO camps in the region – together with all FAPLA armoured forces – had to be neutralised. There was simply no other way, he declared.

Finally it was time to move. Colonel Breytenbach and his men enjoyed their last hot drink, aware that there would be no stopping until the strategic city along the Kunene had been taken. The first vehicle in a column that moved off, slowly and tentatively stretched back kilometres as it moved off into the unknown.

The Pathfinders were still waiting for their turn to start when an explosion ahead sounded the first casualty of the operation. There was no mistaking the blast from an anti-tank mine – probably a TM-57 – and it wasn't long before word was passed down the line that a multiple-barrelled rocket launcher mounted on a Mercedes Unimog had taken a hit.

Finally it was the turn of 44 Brigade. With the Colonel's command Sabre leading the way, the tiny column set off at a heady pace. Only breakdown vehicles and supply trucks that included fuel and water bowsers remained behind.

As the sun began to rise, so did the temperature. But it brought no comfort to the Pathfinders who by then were eating dust and bouncing along in the heavily rutted tracks left by the dozens of trucks ahead. With the route sometimes blocked by broken-down vehicles, Colonel Breytenbach directed Lang, his American driver, to move towards the right and take a parallel course. In doing so, they were able to gradually move their position up the line.

Lang, like the other members of this crew, had spent time in Rhodesia fighting in the RLI. Another American was Dave, who manned twin .50 calibre machine guns on board one of the Sabres. He had served in the US Marines in Vietnam and as a paratrooper in the Israeli Defence Force, one of the few Christians to do so in the Jewish State.

The forth crewmember was Gilly, the company signals sergeant who had been a Grenadier Guardsman in the British Army before joining the RLI. These foreigners were a diverse lot: all had thrown in their lot into what was clearly a southern African war that played a role of its own in the Cold War.

Their story had begun little more than a year before. In acceding to international pressure, underwritten by both Britain and the United States, the old Rhodesia had embraced Marxism by electing Robert Mugabe in April 1980. Almost overnight the country's name was changed to Zimbabwe, and members of the Rhodesian Army were free to leave the country. In the end, almost all of them did.

Regular Rhodesian forces had included a large number of foreigners who had volunteered to join the anti-terrorist struggle, and Colonel Jan Breytenbach had recruited many of these soldiers into his newly-formed Pathfinder Company.

A well-known and outspoken character in the South West African operational area, Colonel Breytenbach had originally formed 32 Battalion, composed largely of troops from the pro-Western FNLA movement who opposed Marxist rule and, indirectly, Cuban domination from Luanda.

South African troops, most of them conscripts still in their teens, were sometimes called upon to fill numerous roles in the cross-border war, including handling captured enemy AAA guns. (Photo: Pierre Victor)

He was also involved in establishing South Africa's crack Special Forces regiment, the Reconnaissance Commandos, or in the lingo, the Recces.

Having been offered the command of 44 Parachute Brigade, one of his first tasks was planning and leading the daring 1978 airborne assault on Cassinga, ostensibly a refugee camp. Instead, it turned out to be the core of SWAPO's command structure with enough Soviet military hardware lying around – including SAM-7s – to start a revolution.

Although that operation was hugely successful – even if SWAPO claimed afterwards that only civilian targets were hit – the strike highlighted the need for a specially trained combat unit that could handle the kind of unconventional warfare then developing in Southern Africa. With the demise of the Salisbury regime and the recruitment of many experienced Rhodesian veterans, the colonel suddenly had the means with which to form such a military unit.

Among early recruits were former British paratrooper and mercenary Peter McAleese. Appointed company sergeant major under Colonel Breytenbach, he used a wealth of knowledge gained during his service in the British and Rhodesian SAS to establish a rigorous selection regimen that only the most dedicated soldiers would be able to complete. In a sense, it was an extension of what Recce aspirants were subjected to.

Recruits came from all over. In the ranks were Americans, a preponderance of Rhodesians, former British vets as well as those from other Commonwealth countries who put themselves through what was clearly a gruelling routine. Some of the more mature troops were into their second, third or even fourth periods of army service, their determination the only factor that got them through in the end.

Not everybody made it. Less-committed candidates gave way under the series of strenuous sessions that pitted mind against body, until only the best remained. It was these men who ultimately deployed to South West Africa where they mounted operations into Angola. At the end of it, they were in peak physical shape, well motivated, and adequately primed for combat.

While the Sabre was Colonel Breytenbach's patrol vehicle of choice and his favoured means of operation, it did not supplant foot patrols, the *sine qua non* of this kind of warfare in the African bush.

Elements from the unit would routinely deploy on long-term patrols and investigate villages, constantly on the lookout for evidence of a SWAPO presence. Essentially, the objective was to locate enemy camps and hit them hard in a bid to halt insurgent infiltration into South West Africa.

While some of these efforts were successful, it was left to Sabre patrols to make the difference. They had both the range and the mobility and when required to do so, could cause serious damage. Once an enemy base was pin-pointed, the Sabres would move forward in concerted group attacks: most of the time they would provide heavy machine-gun cover for 32 Battalion's ground assault troops.

A clear difference of attitudes became apparent between the South African hierarchy and this unusual bunch of foreigners.

The Pathfinders had their own way of fighting and Colonel Breytenbach, within reason, let them get on with the job. The men on the ground were accustomed to both hardship and combat and they tended to use opportunities as and when they arose. There would be no quarter given and none asked for, and to the average South African officer, this unconventional approach sometimes caused offence. To some of the South Africans, 44 Parachute Brigade was little more than a bunch of renegades on the rampage. Others, further up the chain of command believed they were capable of achieving results and that was what mattered most: this diverse bunch of troops were fighting a war, not a political crusade.

Gradually the word "Philistines" crept into the lexicon when it was used to describe the unit, and while initially intended as an insult, it was soon adopted by the men as a badge of honour, much as "The Incredibles" had been by the RLI in Rhodesia.

After months of ground and vehicle patrols, the Pathfinders were soon moulded into a skilled and confident fighting element in this new environment, which, apart from the flat, sandy terrain, was a little different from their experiences in the Rhodesian bush war.

Before Operation Protea had been launched in August 1981, the majority of those involved were flown to Sector 10 Operational Area. They landed either at the main South African Air Force base at Ondangua, or further south at Grootfontein. A succession of combat groups and task forces were established around 61 Mechanised Brigade. For two weeks the units were rigorously put through their paces in their envisaged battlefield roles. Colonel Breytenbach and his Pathfinders arrived with the intent of being associated with whoever would lead the way.

The company was finally attached to Battle Group 40 and given the ignominious role of "tank hunters". They were issued with

French 89 mm rocket launchers to replace the less effective Soviet RPG-7 rocket launchers with which they were customarily equipped. Familiarisation training with the new weapon followed. Company Sergeant Major Peter McAleese had in the meantime been detached from the unit to run the unit's training team.

In his place, another former Rhodesian career soldier Dennis Croukamp was brought in. Formerly the company sergeant major of the RLI's Support Commando, he took up the same challenge with the parachute brigade. No slouch when it came to mixing it with the gooks, Croukamp was awarded the Bronze Cross of Rhodesia for gallantry, having also spent time in the Selous Scouts. He excelled in small-team reconnaissance units behind enemy lines and his excellent book *Bush War in Rhodesia* covers much of that period[2].

Preparations before the cross-border raid, the biggest yet to enter Angola, were thorough. Once a refuelling exercise had been completed, the invasion force moved forward on 23 August to a point just below the cut-line as the official frontier was designated: it was actually a long, unbroken line that stretched almost from the Atlantic to the Zambezi and the Zambian border.

After a major refuelling exercise had been carried out, all the vehicles involved in the attack lined up in readiness for the move north.

One of the specially adapted Sabre vehicles used by Special Forces – including 44 Parachute Brigade – in their Angolan operations. (Photo: Pierre Victor)

Chapter 9
Angolan skirmish with 44 Parachute Brigade

Colonel Breytenbach had a single priority to start with. As soon as the column crossed onto Angolan soil, his intention was to move out and ahead of the main group and as he would so often phrase it, "look for trouble". For that his Sabre-equipped group needed to have the freedom of movement on the battlefield, something not always appreciated by those officers further up the ladder of command. One immediate consequence was that he was often at loggerheads with his generals, not all of whom would appreciate that since he was on the ground and in the middle of the war, he had a more complete picture of developments than they. To some of these stuffed shirts, Colonel Breytenbach was considered a maverick, but he perfectly fitted the role of a modern-day buccaneer and in the end, achieved good results. The trouble was that if something was wrong or it simply didn't fit, he wasn't afraid to speak his mind, which was hardly a recipe for promotion – this might be one of the reasons why he never progressed beyond the rank of colonel.

The men under him reflected this ethos. They were all tough and well trained. The majority had good experience in fighting an unconventional war and were prepared for the harsh conditions to which they were exposed on extended bush operations. In keeping with the demands of the job, they carried only a modicum of personal kit, and only enough clothes to keep warm during those sometimes bitterly cold winter nights: all that was supplemented by heavy loads of extra weapons and munitions.

As well as their R4 assault rifles, the troops were equipped with rocket launchers, GPMGs, M-79 grenade launchers, individual pistols and grenades well in excess of standard issue. Other priorities included water, radios, batteries, claymores and medical packs – overall, enough to sometimes bend the frames on the ruck-sacks the unit used for foot patrols.

Numerous contacts with SWAPO had created a wariness of the enemy. They had seen often enough in the past that guerrilla groups would bitterly defend their ground, even if it meant taking heavy losses. While earlier SWAPO groups preferred to put space between themselves and the South Africans, these latecomers were the results of many years of hard fighting and they could often give as good as they got.

It was lost on none of them that through guerrilla efforts – with powerful foreign backing, they had driven Portugal out of Africa. Now they were ready for a new kind of conventional warfare, instilled by their Russian advisers and supported by many of the 50,000 Cuban troops in Angola.

By noon on the first day of the attack, the company with its bevy of four-by-fours found itself in position just north of the riverside town of Xangongo and stopped their machines in whatever shade they could find in the bush. Being a temporary halt, they didn't post sentries or set up camouflage nets.

Throughout, the men remained vigilant: they waited for an air attack which they had been warned would almost certainly follow: the Angolan Air Force was equipped with Soviet MiG-23s, French-built Mirage strike fighters as well as Sukhoi fighter-bombers. The South African Air Force still had their much-vaunted air superiority over the Angolans, but because of United Nations sanctions, they couldn't compete with the kind of sophisticated aircraft that Moscow was pumping into the region.

As intended, 32 Battalion would take the lead in an assault on the town. The Pathfinders would follow up and provide support. Apart from rapid reaction, their job was also to deal with FAPLA battle tanks that included T-54/55s as well as a smattering of T-62s – which, Pretoria warned, were deployed in depth throughout the region. But first they stood and watched as South African jets briefly pounded the town's defences.

While retaliation wasn't as furious as might have been expected, it wasn't exactly a one-way street. Anti-aircraft defences on the outskirts of Xangongo retaliated from several positions along the river and then stopped firing. On the ground, once the order to advance had been given, 32 Battalion advanced on foot while South African artillery to the rear – most of it 155 mm G-5s – pounded positions ahead.

Although the level of retaliatory fire was light, it was a slow process. Soon enough though, some of the Pathfinders came under attack from some distant fire, but that turned out to be from a 32 Battalion patrol that had been confused by the Sabre camouflage markings. A radio call soon put that right. At the same time enemy fire remained desultory, slowly giving way in the face of a resolute advance.

Steadily 32 Battalion and the Pathfinders pushed their way towards the centre of town, when a message over the radio indicated that a house used by the Russian advisers had been taken. A grid reference was provided and the colonel ordered Lang to take him there.

On arrival, it quickly became apparent that South African forces dominated the area and that if there had been an enemy military presence, most of it had disappeared. While there was still the occasional skirmish, the bulk of those FAPLA and SWAPO troops who had originally occupied Xangongo appeared to have fled north.

Apart from a large number of vintage DC-3 Dakotas that served with the SAAF in the war, there was also a handful of four-engined DC-4s, some of which were converted into communications aircraft, or rather basic versions of AWAC aircraft. They served a useful role over Angolan air space for the duration of hostilities. (Photo: Pierre Victor)

Curious about the recently departed Soviet presence, Colonel Breytenbach and his crew were at first a bit tentative about entering the house, but they were bolder when it became clear that the place was more residential than military. Going by what had been left behind, the Russians had obviously had their wives with them, but they must have left when word arrived that the South Africans were on their way. It couldn't have been that long before either, because one of these women was killed in a contact when her husband, an adviser to the Angolan Army, was taken captive.

By early evening the town was in South African hands. The Pathfinders drove into Fort Roçadas, the main military base south of the ancient Portuguese citadel. It stood on a high point that dominated the town and overlooked the huge multi-spanned bridge across the Kunene River, which not long afterwards was destroyed in a South African Air Force bombing strike. If there was to have been a counter-attack, it would almost certainly have come from there, but nothing happened.

Eager to investigate Fort Roçadas, the men were ordered to stand down. Word had spread that the place had been booby-trapped, underscored by the death of a South African soldier who had gone in without checking. That didn't prevent some of the Pathfinders searching for FAPLA uniforms which they would use in future clandestine operations.

Once the area had been cleared, the men started their search in earnest. Huge stocks of food and charity gifts from Oxfam as well as a variety of Scandinavian governments were found in storehouses in the *Quartel*. Intended for the civilian population, everything had been appropriated by the military.

As the international community was to discover for itself not long afterwards, this was to become standard procedure in Africa. Grain and other commodities intended for the starving millions in Ethiopia, Somalia, Eritrea, the Congo, the Sudan and elsewhere soon found itself on sale in the open market, supply and demand in the hands of warlords. Angola was no different.

The same holds for Nigeria today: the ruling elite has total control of the nation's oil revenues, with the result that there are almost no public clinics. Very few schools have adequate everyday needs such as blackboards, pencils and even paper for the children on which to write. But then that's Africa, well into the New Millennium.

The same was to happen in Angola, but meantime Luanda had a war on its hands and a powerful invasion force from the south threatening to destabilise the nation. And for those troops involved with the Pathfinders, the majority was finding their way about in one of the largest towns in the south.

By the time it got dark, the men had already prepared their vehicles and personal kit for any eventuality after dark: the unit had taken up positions on the edge of town. Those who were not on sentry duty sought cover in the event of an artillery or mortar attack, a wise move, because around midnight, sounds of a fierce engagement emerged from the town: the chattering of heavy machine guns accentuated by streams of green tracer. By now everybody was awake and the men were told to stand by their vehicles: preplanning had the Pathfinders move into positions to engage anything coming over the bridge.

Meanwhile, CSM Dennis Croukamp had some of his men set up their 60 mm mortars, while Gordon, a British volunteer, fired illumination flares over the town. It hardly helped that their exposed position was being continually raked by enemy fire until, suddenly, the shooting stopped. Other South African forces in the town had apparently overwhelmed an Angolan Army unit that was attempting a break out. With the excitement over, the men remained in their stand-to positions a short while before getting their heads down again.

At first light a clearance patrol was sent out to check the perimeter, another standard procedure on cross-border operations. They had hardly left the temporary base when there was an explosion along another nearby unit. A call came for help and Peter, an RLI-trained medic already on the clearance patrol, rushed forward to help.

He was met by a grisly scene. A young South African national serviceman had entered a building where the door had been booby-trapped with a grenade. The explosion ripped off his lower arm and shrapnel shards peppered his entire chest area. Still conscious, he was sinking fast. The former RLI troopie struggled to find a vein, eventually getting a saline drip into his ankle, but within minutes the man was dead.

Later that morning the vanguard of 61 Mechanised Brigade arrived in Xangongo and took control of the town. In doing so, they effectively freed the three 32 Battalion companies as well as the Pathfinders from holding duties. Colonel Breytenbach took time off and visited his tactical headquarters and requested a new tasking for his men.

Major General "Witkop" Badenhorst responded immediately. The Pathfinders were to accompany Battle Group 30, about to cross the river and advance on the town of Cahama, known to headquarter at least one Cuban division in the region. Their job would be to stop any kind of enemy advance on Xangongo from the north or from the west.

As with the road leading towards the Kunene River from the south, the major "highway" between Xangongo and Cahama was tarred, which meant that the battle group made good progress. Ratel infantry fighting vehicles led the advance, with Pathfinder Sabres following up close. At one stage Colonel Breytenbach ordered his unit to check out a hospital run by the Catholic Church. As the Sabres cruised up and down the tended lawns, white uniformed nurses and patients in pyjamas observed the goings-on from verandas and from behind shuttered windows. Most of the patients were FAPLA battle casualties, but the colonel just then had another mission on his mind. After a short stop, the mobile company moved on, leaving the hospital undisturbed.

What was striking about the entire south Angolan region was that it was astonishingly sparsely populated. Most of the locals had left their rural villages and gravitated towards the towns, a problem shared by many African states these days.

Some distance short of Cahama, the unit spotted a tall iron tower whose girders supported an aerial, all part of a complex radio transmission system that beamed SWAPO propaganda into South West Africa. Reportedly the highest single structure of its kind in Angola, the tower had been targeted before in an operation launched by the Recces – but they were unsuccessful because the entire area was defended by both troops and minefields.

With the arrival of Colonel Breytenbach's Pathfinders, all enemy troops had fled: the place was totally deserted. Having established radio communications with Oshakati to advise that he was going to

Almost every time the Angolan Army crossed swords with South African forces, they were obliged to leave behind huge quantities of war material on the battlefield. Much of this was recycled and passed on to Dr Jonas Savimbi's UNITA. (Photo: Pierre Victor)

destroy the tower, he was ordered not to do so. No reason was given, nor has anybody subsequently been able to explain why.

It was almost dark when the colonel ordered his battle group to disperse into the bush, leaving behind a company of Ratel IFVs to hold the road against any kind of enemy approach. The Pathfinders circled their vehicles in a defensive laager about a click from the Ratels, ate a cold meal and settled down for the night.

Customarily, the unit operated in two-vehicle sections so that at least one member of the eight men in any section would be on guard during the dark hours. Their job essentially was to maintain a watch over a defensive arc while the remainder slept alongside their vehicles. An hour later, the sentry would wake up his relief, and so it would go on until about a half an hour before dawn when the entire camp would quietly move to stand-to positions, a precaution against enemy attack. With the sun up, the men would revert to daytime routine.

But then everything suddenly changed at about two hours before midnight. With Dave on guard duty in the colonel's section, he was alerted when a convoy of trucks swung distantly into view. Puzzled that it was heading towards Cahama – the same direction from which the battle group had arrived a few hours before – Dave also noted that while all South African vehicles except the Sabres were diesel, the newcomers all had petrol engines.

He woke his partner Gilly, but by that time the convoy – obviously Angolan Army – had run into the South African stopper group a short distance away and was already exchanging fire. Wide awake by now, the entire group of Pathfinders moved closer to their vehicles and heavier stuff.

The battle, almost within sight of where the Sabres were parked, went on for about ten minutes. Then, as suddenly as it had begun, it ended, with the new arrivals pulling back smartly down the road along which they had arrived. Without further ado, they halted alongside the Pathfinders' overnight position, totally unaware of this second South African combat-ready presence.

As Colonel Breytenbach recounted years later, it was a God-given opportunity. Quietly and effectively, he prepared his men, having already sent some of his troops across the highway with rifles and M-79 Bloopers to provide lateral support. Moments later an illumination flare fired from one of the 60 mm mortars by CSM Croukamp, turned night into day and the Pathfinders opened up at almost point-blank range on what was found the following day to have been an enemy reconnaissance unit.

As a general rule, a Western tracer is red while that of Soviet-backed forces is green, but on this occasion enemy 23 mm anti-aircraft machine guns being used by the Angolan soldiers to return fire was red. It was mixed conglomeration of colour with volleys of green small-arms fire.

Retaliating with a Russian 14.5 mm captured earlier, the Canadian Sean provided a pyrotechnic display of his own. That, coupled to a bunch of standard South African Army issue .50s, and the volume of fire was intense. The Angolans, while not taken completely by surprise, suffered a pounding.

To their credit, most of the FAPLA troops caught out in the open, stood their ground and maintained a steady rate of return fire. But by now their efforts were withering, further dissipated by mortar bombs fired from the rear of the company sergeant-major's Unimog. Handling the mortar was Gordon, the most effective mortar-man in the region, and although he was targeted several times by the twin-barrelled 23 mm heavy weapon on the back of one of the Russian trucks, one of his shells finally silenced the heavy weapon.

Although there were several South African artillery units that had taken up position some distance south of the contact area, Colonel Breytenbach didn't call on them to provide any fire support. So lacking clear target orders, their commander fired only illumination rounds in the direction of where most of the action was taking place.

These almost fluorescent lights slowly arched across the sky, casting a ghostly grey light over the scene. Finally, enemy fire slackened and then ceased altogether.

The Pathfinders stopped shooting as well and for the time, did some serious listening. Previous engagements with SWAPO had long ago taught them the basic Soviet tactic of retreat: that was to use mortars to mask a withdrawal and as a consequence, quite a few of the men suffered shrapnel wounds to remind them. This bunch of Angolan troops was certainly not running away: instead, they appeared to be preparing for a withdrawal with honour, which meant more action.

As one of the men said later, there was also a very real danger of them being mortared again. On the far side of the road, some of the Pathfinders could distinctly hear sounds of vehicle engines being started, coupled to commands shouted in Portuguese. Colonel Breytenbach's men quickly reorganised.

So far they had suffered no casualties and ammunition was plentiful: the unit was consequently in high spirits. It was time to take the war to the enemy.

Captain Veldhuizen quickly formed a ten-man patrol armed with the 89 mm anti-tank rocket launchers. Leading from the front, he took them single file into the darkness, guided solely by the voices of the enemy ahead. Once they reached the road – banked up at a slight incline above the surrounding countryside – they moved with added caution. Had they been spotted then, serious casualties might have resulted because they were moving through a part of this bush country where they would have been unavoidably exposed.

But no shots or challenges followed. Instead, the group progressed, stumbling in turn into scrub bushes or getting snagged on thorns. Gradually the men were able to move closer to the enemy, still undetected.

By now, some of the enemy vehicles were clearly visible in the gloom. Before moving any further, Captain Veldhuizen took stock.

In an area ahead that appeared almost clear of any kind of bush overhang, a group of FAPLA troops was frenziedly preparing for something in the vicinity of a pair of trucks. It didn't take the South African officer long to realise that the Angolans were setting up mortars. Several mortar tubes were already in position and still more troops were hauling forward boxes of ammunition.

Totally preoccupied with the task at hand, the Angolans made no effort to work quietly. Instead there were orders loudly passed down the line from their officers. There was clearly a sense of urgency

The Soviets gave Angola hundreds of their vaunted BM-21 vehicle-mounted, 40-tube multiple launcher systems which could fire 122 mm rockets 20 kilometres. These weapons were used against South African forces by FAPLA in the Xangongo battle. (Photo: Pierre Victor)

about what was taking place.

Stopping only metres from the enemy Captain Veldhuizen ordered his men to halt. His patrol – spread out to his right – formed a firing line where each of the men had a clear sight of the enemy. On his knees, the captain observed these goings-on ahead for a little longer and then he turned towards Jim, the man at his side. A Scot and a veteran of both the British Army and the Rhodesian Light Infantry couldn't miss the order whispered loud and clear: "OK, Jim, let's mix it!"

The Scot rose to one knee with the rocket launcher already on his shoulder. Taking aim at the first of the trucks, he said afterwards, "I really couldn't miss."

He didn't. The vehicle, perhaps 100 metres ahead, disintegrated in a massive explosion coupled to a flash of light that lit up the entire area. Another member of the Pathfinder Company hit a second truck with a rocket, which was when everyone opened up with small arms and blooper rounds.

Recovering momentarily, some of the FAPLA troops took cover in a desperate effort to retaliate. They had to have been aware that they were caught on the hop: it would have been impossible for their group to recover from such a vigorous onslaught and, judging by some of the cries, their men were taking hits.

Moments later the shooting slackened, which was about as much

Because there was a real possibility of the Angolans and their Cuban and Soviet allies giving air support to their ground forces, Pretoria kept good numbers of its own air force on standby either at Ondangua air base in Ovamboland, or at Grootfontein further to the south in present-day Namibia, (Photo: Pierre Victor)

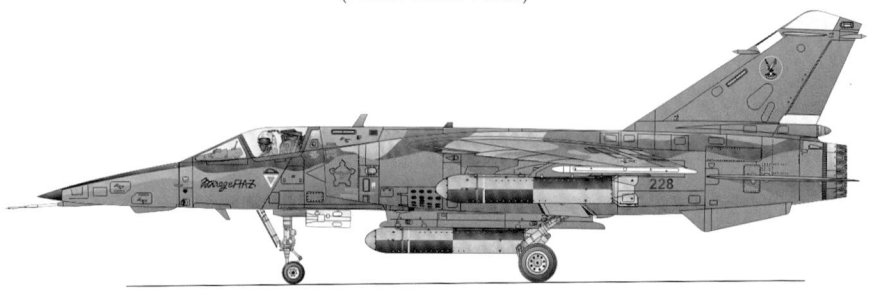

South African Air Force Mirage III. (Illustration: Pierre Victor)

as Captain Veldhuizen was able to discern in the shadows, by then only half-lit by the two burning trucks. It seemed that some of the enemy soldiers had already begun to slip away into the shadows beyond. A minute or two later, everything went quiet: even their wounded had stopped screaming.

"It was fucking eerie," one of the men recalled afterwards.

One member of the Pathfinder team had a disappointing time of it. Dave, a member of the colonel's crew, had earlier not been able to bring his beloved twin-50 calibre machine guns into action because his pair of Sabres were on the far side of the laager. Undeterred, and with his blooper in hand, he ran across to assist and dropped a number of 40 mm grenades on target. Once the enemy started pulling back, he raised his trajectory and dropped a few grenades onto their line of flight.

With the enemy gone, the Pathfinders stopped for a while and watched for any kind of development. Normal procedures after daytime engagements were customarily to sweep the contact area and collect weapons and where possible, search the dead and wounded for intelligence material. But this was too dangerous a proposition in the dark, so the men stayed put: the sweep would be carried out at first light. The captain gathered his men and went back to their original position.

Back in camp the crews returned to their Sabres to prepare their weapons for the possibility of another attack. Colonel Breytenbach reported that his unit had suffered neither casualties nor damage to their vehicles. With the excitement over, sentries were posted and the rest of the group returned to their sleeping bags, but any kind of real sleeping was impossible because of ammunition on the burning trucks constantly popping off.

By morning, everybody was eager to see the results of the previous night's fire-fight. Having followed normal morning procedures, including stand-to, breakfast and loading up, they started their engines and with the colonel in his command Sabre in the lead, the column snaked its way back onto the road.

A remarkable sight greeted the men. The entire FAPLA convoy stood on the road totally abandoned. It was almost as if it had arrived an hour before. Apart from the two burnt-out trucks, the rest of the convoy were more or less intact, though there were holes everywhere. And then it dawned: there were no bodies: not a single dead or wounded, even though there were blood spoors everywhere.

The direction of the enemy's retreat indicated numerous drag marks, which meant that even with the thumping that they took, these Angolan troops retained enough discipline under fire to escape in good order: they had taken their dead and wounded with them. This was clearly a well-disciplined unit, probably an Angolan version of Special Forces.

The area where the fighting had taken place was in disarray: kit, empty magazines, discarded broken weapons and even a few bloodied battle dressings lay about everywhere. All the webbing packs were checked and many were found to have spanking new uniforms in distinctive Angolan Army camouflage. Their labels proclaimed proudly, in English, "Made in Cuba": these they also gathered for future use.

Towards the rear of the column was a fully equipped radio jeep: all its code books, signals, orders as well as instructional documentation had been removed. Also taken by the South African force were four BM-21s, better known as "Stalin's Organs". These multiple-rocket launchers were in use by just about all the revolutionary armies of the world at the time, the same weapon which had swung scores of battles for the Soviets during World War II.

Four more trucks, all GAZ heavy vehicles with twin 23 mm anti-aircraft guns mounted on their cabs were also recovered and would eventually be handed over to Savimbi's UNITA movement.

Dave, who wasn't able to use his own heavy weapons the previous night, requested permission to test his twin .50s on one of the two BTR armoured personnel carriers that had been left standing by the enemy. The colonel agreed, so after telling everybody to stand clear, he let rip with a mix of linked ammunition that included ball, armour-piercing and incendiary tracers.

It was interesting that while both the ball and tracer rounds penetrated only one side of the armoured BTR, the AP rounds went all the way through. It was an impressive display of fire power.

Having done the job they came for, and leaving much of the enemy convoy still intact to be recovered by other units, Colonel Breytenbach and his Pathfinders were ordered back to Xangongo. But he wasn't quite done just yet. Buoyed by the success of his unit, he directed Lang to head back towards the radio transmitter mast. Arriving at the giant tower, the colonel didn't waste time. He ordered the demo guys to take her down, which they did in short shrift.

Arriving back at base a day or two later, there wasn't a word about the success of the operation. Nor any comment about the radio tower. It was enough that the "Philistines" had accomplished their mission.

It would have been nice to have somebody at headquarters say "Well done!", but it never happened …

1 Graham Gillmore: *Pathfinder Company: 44 Parachute Brigade "The Philistines"*, 30 Degrees South, Johannesburg, 2010.
2 Dennis Croukamp, *Bush War in Rhodesia: The Extraordinary Combat Memories of a Rhodesian Reconnaissance Specialist*, Paladin Press, 2007.

CHAPTER TEN

RON REID-DALY – A TRIBUTE TO THE MAN AND HIS SCOUTS

> There was something about the way that Lieutenant Colonel Reid-Daly interacted with people that made an immediate impression on first acquaintance. It was his eyes, some said, both piercing and intimidating. Also, when he had something to say, people listened …

Like few other military men who achieved prominence on the battlefield, you sensed a very distinct presence when you first met the man. Ron Reid-Daly was one of those individuals who knew exactly what he wanted and by sheer force of character he achieved results, sometimes against impossible odds. Which was one of the reasons why, in an impecunious Rhodesia that fielded a largely under-funded and under-manned army, this rather unconventional officer was able to create one of the finest counter-insurgency units in modern times. It was perhaps inevitable that he would make enemies in the process.

Of all the military commanders that I have met in a lifetime of covering conflicts, Ronald Frances Reid-Daly – or just plain Uncle Ron to his friends – established a niche well above many of his contemporaries. Among his equally distinguished peers of the period, I would rate him with General Sir David Richards, the British Chief of the Defence Staff who, while in command of a UK Joint Task Force in Sierra Leone during the year 2000, turned around the biggest rebel insurrection that West Africa had experienced since the end of World War II.

Interestingly, putting down the rebels wasn't the brief he'd initially been given by his superiors. His stated role was to evacuate all Westerners who were threatened by the approaching rebels, but instead, he used what resources were available and turned the civil

RSM Ron Reid-Daly. (Photo: Courtesy of Hannes Wessels)

war on its head. He finally vanquished the barbarians, who had promised to turn the clock back in all of Africa.

During this time, I was able to observe the – then Brigadier Richards from up close at his improvised Freetown headquarters and I was among many who were impressed by his style of command. It was both forceful and surprisingly low key. With a few quiet words he would almost always achieve good results. I commented as much in one of my reports to *Jane's Defence Weekly* at the time, saying

Chapter 10
Ron Reid-Daly – A tribute to the man and his scouts

An RLI "stick" goes into action following a sighting of an insurgent group by a pair of Selous Scouts who had been observing their camp from a high point for some days. (Photo: Author's collection)

something about this officer "shooting from the lip". As it happened, that quote wasn't used. But I recall that his actions were decisive, and terminal for former Sierra Leone Army Sergeant Foday Sankoh's Revolutionary United Front.

There was no question in the minds of anybody who was able to observe this senior British officer in action that Richards would go far, and so he has. By July 2006, command of the International Security Assistance Force in southern Afghanistan was passed to NATO forces under his command, but not before he had been promoted to the acting rank of a four-star general. In this capacity, Lieutenant General Richards was the first British senior officer to command American forces since the end of World War II.

I had quite a bit to say about General Sir David in *War Dog*, published five years after the Sierra Leone debacle ended and I quote[1]:

"The brigadier's comments [about using the Sierra Leone Air Wing, which was staffed solely by mercenaries and headed by Neall Ellis] were especially noteworthy, coming as they did from an officer everyone acknowledged wasn't afraid to say what he thought, and in an establishment rarely known for its candour. Sierra Leone was a sensitive operation that involved the potential race card, as well as a dozen other imbroglios. With time, it got so bad that word-games – semantics really – became the norm with any statement issued by the High Commission in Freetown.

"... in this regard, Richards was refreshingly different. As the front man for a rescue mission that could have gone horrifyingly wrong, he wasn't afraid to react when the situation demanded firm action, a character trait that hardly endeared him to many of the stuffed shirts back home. This youthful senior officer who, in his previous deployment, had commanded the British contingent in East Timor, must have learned very early on that style confessed grace. So, too, when briefing a bunch of hacks.

"Every question, no matter how astute or absurd was answered in full and usually with a smile that belied the gravity of what he knew was taking place in the country."

As British journalist Allan Little recalled long afterwards, "it was an astonishing thing to witness: the fortunes of a whole country transformed in the space of a few days by a single, decisive intervention. A total of 800 British paratroopers landed at Freetown airport just as the city was about to slip into the terrifying chaos of a rebel invasion and suddenly, unexpectedly, the shape of Sierra Leone's decade-long civil war was altered. Or so it seemed to me at the time. It was, in fact, a little more haphazard than that."

What had happened was that Whitehall had originally sent its army, backed by a substantial naval force that included two carriers to West Africa as a precautionary measure in a bid to carry out a limited operation, ostensibly geared to evacuate Western nationals.

It was planned that the Paras would secure the airport and the initial idea was that the operation would take seven to ten days, after which time the British troops would leave Sierra Leone to its fate. Freetown, we all knew, was paralysed with fear.

General Sir David told Allan Little that after familiarising himself with the situation: "I could see that with a little robustness, we could make a difference … if it had gone wrong, they'd have cut me off at the knees."

With that he went off to see Ahmed Tejan Kabbah, the Sierra Leone president who had already ordered his personal helicopter to park alongside State House and was preparing to flee the country with the requisite four or five bags of diamonds. Richards told him: "You won't be needing that, I promise you."

Allan Little records that at that meeting, held within hours of the British landing in Sierra Leone, the president was promised by Richards that Britain would supply arms and ammunition to government forces and that British helicopters would be made available to move men and matériel around the battlefield. Moreover, backed by a small team of British staff officers, the brigadier assured the president that he would take personal command of the war and seek to end it by defeating the rebel forces. In other words, suggests Little, Richards was committing Britain to taking sides in an African civil war.

"However, there was one important difficulty. The general's political bosses in London had sent him to carry out a quick evacuation and then leave. "So," I asked him ten years on, "you were promising the president all this before you had the political authority from London to do so?"

"Er, yes," he said, "I'm afraid I was, yes," was his reply.

For a few more days Richards endured the pressure from the Ministry of Defence to carry out his evacuation and then depart from West Africa. But the problem just then was that the British people who were in Freetown suddenly felt quite safe and most foreigners simply did not want to be evacuated.

The rest is history. In relatively short shrift, the rebels were beaten back, taking serious casualties in the process. Many of their leaders were captured and the rest fled to neighbouring Liberia, from where Foday Sankoh, the rebel leader of the RUF, had originally launched his insurrection.

I mention all this because it has significance to the memory of Uncle Ron. Like Lt Col Reid-Daly, the Brigadier Richards that I met in Sierra Leone was very different from other run-of-the-mill British officers we were accustomed to confronting in trouble spots. Also, he was not afraid to make radical change if the opportunity warranted it and he believed it might produce good results.

At the same time, there were several marked differences between the basic approach of the two men, the first being that the commander of the Selous Scouts wasn't afraid to stand on protruding toes to achieve results. The other was that, with very few exceptions, Uncle Ron despised journalists. For his part, General Sir David appreciated the value of a good press, which was why he didn't hesitate to speak to the media and, as a consequence, us hacks reciprocated accordingly.

The other military man whom I regard as being up there with the best of them in the post World War II period was General Bethencourt Rodrigues, the Portuguese commander who turned the decade-long African insurgency in Angola around. This was an almost-impossible task at the time because it involved what was arguably the poorest nation in Western Europe.

Like Reid-Daly, Bethencourt Rodrigues proved himself one of the best counter-insurgency specialists in any man's army, a remarkable attribute when you consider that Lisbon fought twice as long in Africa as the Americans were in Vietnam and, in proportion to their respective populations, Portugal suffered more casualties. There were roughly nine million people in Portugal in the 1970s; in the United States there were about 220 million by the time that hostilities in Southeast Asia became an everyday media event.

General Bethencourt Rodrigues, in contrast – very much like the founder-commander of the Selous Scouts when you look at results – was a very different kind of military individual when compared to his Lusitanian contemporaries.

An aristocrat by birth and scholar-turned-tactician, he was a rare creature in Lisbon's hidebound political and military bureaucracy. As somebody said at the time, if the Metropolis had just one more Bethencourt Rodrigues – who might have won the war in Mozambique – things might have turned out very differently for Portugal. But it was not to be.

I first met the man when he was still a colonel, serving as military attaché at the Portuguese Embassy in London in the mid-1960s. We'd had several meetings after I'd disclosed the presence of a large Soviet detachment operating within a rifle-shot of the border of Portuguese Guinea, and while he was eager to do something about it, his superiors back home were not.

Some years later he was dispatched to Angola in an effort to limit the escalating insurrection that nobody believed any colonial power would win. As it was, they didn't, but within two years, his leadership coupled to his sheer force of personality and the genius to counter a stifling metropolitan officialdom, General Bethencourt Rodrigues became the man who, like General Sir David Richards, managed to turn his war around.

It was subversive politics within his own ranks that ultimately caused Lisbon to pull out of Africa, at a time when not many people were aware that Portugal had been entrenched on the continent as a major colonial power for over five centuries.

Back to Uncle Ron. The career of this Rhodesian officer was never without its moments, quite a few of them controversial.

We were drinking with friends in a somewhat elegant club in Rivonia in Johannesburg a few years after he'd settled permanently in Johannesburg's northern suburbs when one of the men at the bar – a total stranger – started boasting about his experiences with the Selous Scouts. Of course, this drew a response from Uncle Ron: his first question was to ask the man for the name of his senior NCO.

Having established that the man was a "wannabee", he laid into him verbally with a passion that I only observed once during the course of our quarter-century friendship. The "intruder" had just bought us all a round, but about a minute later, he was out the front door, his own drink untouched.

Another time, according to Ron himself, he and his boys would decamp to the Long Bar at Meikles on Friday afternoons for a few toots. It was a tradition that went way back and was customarily intended to herald the weekend. That was when one of his NCOs approached him and in a soft voice, he enquired of his commanding officer whether he would like to join his group at the far end of the room?

"And why would you want me to do that?" the colonel asked with a smile.

"To come and meet yourself, Sir."

It was all pretty direct and Uncle Ron didn't need a second bidding. Nor did it take long to establish the facts and for a couple of his men to usher the idiot out of the hotel.

These events were fairly commonplace a few years ago, almost part of the mystique of being a Selous Scout, like there are thousands of people in Britain today who maintain that they served with the SAS. Were all these claims true, there would have been enough of these people around in the UK alone to allow for a full division at Hereford.

It's the same with the SEALS and Delta Force in the United States, only more so …

After he'd left Rhodesia in the early 1980s and spent a few years as the commanding general of the Transkei, a so-called "independent" Bantustan, Ron Reid-Daly tackled two concurrent issues simultaneously.

The first was his ability to effectively manage one of the biggest security companies in the southern hemisphere. Second came the much more intrusive task of battling cancer, something that he faced longer than any other person I know. He would get over one series of debilitating bouts and the disease would strike elsewhere in his body. In the end, it was melanoma that defeated him.

In-between, following Gulf War I, we flew to Britain to present a case to the British Ministry of Defence that we possibly had the answer to many of the minefields that the Iraqis had left behind after they had been driven out of Kuwait. The plan that we put on the table was the availability of scores of former SADF and Rhodesian

Army mine warfare specialists who were willing to drop everything to lift mines in a vast swathe of desert to the east of Suez, for a commensurate fee, of course.

The colonel did all the talking and he made a series of forceful presentations. He was so persuasive that we were assured that we had the job, but then the apartheid stigma kicked in shortly afterwards and the contract went elsewhere, at three or four times the price we were offering the Brits.

I was flush with cash in those days – having just completed a contract for Langley in Afghanistan – and the idea was to use some of it to set up a company in the UK. Ron and I even tried to buy a security firm in London, but while we sounded out several firms, we couldn't find a seller.

Having returned to Johannesburg, Ron applied himself to local interests, and because security in South Africa had deteriorated markedly in South Africa after the ANC took over, he found himself with an escalating market. Also, it was not surprising that Ron himself eventually became a target. One evening, on coming home from work, a bunch of armed thugs tried to tackle him as he was about to open his garden gate. Though he took a bullet in the leg, Reid-Daly reacted promptly with the 9 mm pistol that he always carried in his belt and dropped two of his attackers. The rest of the gang fled empty-handed.

These were not amateurs that accosted him. Before their leader was killed by a police task force a short while later, they had gunned

A Rhodesian Special Forces squad takes the long road home from Chimoio in Mozambique after a successful attack. (Photo: Author's collection)

CLOCKWISE FROM TOP LEFT: Into action at Cuamato from a South African Air Force Puma helicopter with Charlie Company (See Chapter 1): it was a tenuous start, with enemy everywhere, many of them armed with RPG-7s. • Some members of the white-officered Ovambo 101 Battalion were also present, but hardly inspired us with confidence. • SAAF Puma over South Angolan mopani country. • Al Venter went from South Angola to cover the Lords Resistance Army rebellion in Northern Uganda – he is seen here with some of the irregular troops encountered along the way. (Photos: Author)

CLOCKWISE FROM TOP: The South Lebanese Shi'ite and Hizbollah stronghold of Tyre (named Sur, in Arabic). Aerial photos were forbidden, but sometimes, we do what we have to. • Lebanese Force Command (Christian) soldiers on patrol along the Green Line in Beirut. • Chopper-pilot's view of an isolated United Nations strongpoint in South Lebanon. • United Nations position with ice-clad Mount Hebron's foothills stretching towards the Golan Heights in the background. (Photos: Author)

CLOCKWISE FROM TOP LEFt: Parts of Southern Lebanon are totally uninhabited and routinely used by Hizbollah cadres to infiltrate towards the Israeli border: It is difficult for the UN to police such actions. • Lonely mosque in a battle-scarred village in the south. • South Lebanese look-out post before the Israelis withdrew behind their own borders – many of these Christian soldiers were liquidated by Hizbollah. • While hostilities in South Lebanon went on, hospitals in the region were hard-pressed to cope with casualties and linking corridors served as wards. • Israel supplied the South Lebanese Army with much of its hardware, including these American-build APCs. (Photos Author)

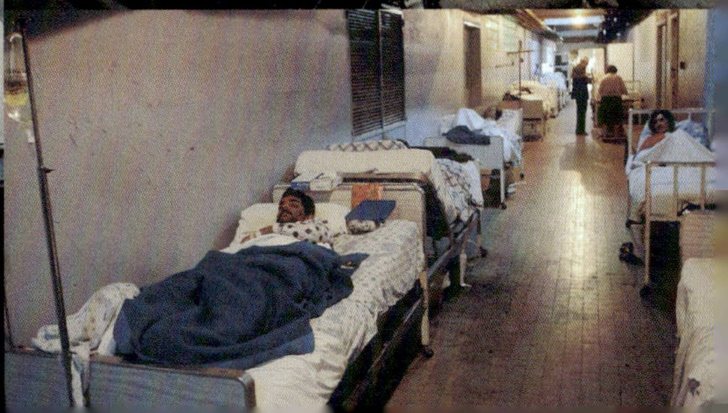

A WEST AFRICAN SELECTION OF PHOTOS (Clockwise from top): Helicopter pilot and former South African Air Force Colonel Neall Ellis in the cockpit of his Sierra Leone Mi-24 gunship. • It was British ground forces under the command of the then Brigadier David Richards – today, Chief of the Defence Staff in Britain – that quickly routed the rebels. • Summary open-air executions by firing squad in neighbouring Liberia – the public was welcome to watch and take pictures. (Photo: Craige Grice) • Preparing one of the Sierra Leone Air Wing's two gunships for a sortie at Aberdeen Barracks near Freetown. (Photos: Author)

CLOCKWISE FROM TOP: Mi-24 helicopter gunship with Neall Ellis in command comes in to land at Freetown after a sortie in the interior. • The rebels managed to trash just about every institution linked to the Sierra Leone government – and police stations became prime targets. • French helicopters deployed in Chad during factional disturbances in that troubled land. (Photo: Sirpa/ECPA France) • A C-130 transport plane approaches the runway at Mogadishu Airport during the UN's 'Operation Just Cause'. (Photos: Author)

CLOCKWISE FROM TOP: Rhodesian Air Force helicopter emerges from contact after dropping Fire Force in the Mtoko area. (Photo: Author's collection) • BSAP officer examines village dead left behind after a terrorist attack. (Photo: Author) • Tribal villagers brutally murdered by one of Robert Mugabe's guerrilla gangs. (Photo: Hannes Wessels) • RLI 'troopies' do a routine area patrol after a contact in the east. • Civil Affairs 'Keep' in the interior. (Photo: Author's collection)

CLOCKWISE FROM TOP: Improvised Israeli Defence Force mine-clearing tank doing the necessary along the Lebanese frontier. (Photo: Author) • South African Air Force Impala jet trainer/fighters, like those secretly deployed to knock out six Angolan Air Force Mi-17 and Mi-24 helicopters: See Chapter 20. (Photos courtesy of the late Herman Potgieter)

These photos show a series of events coupled to the search for illegal weapons along the KwaZulu-Natal South Coast. Raiding squads – both army and police – operated out of a temporary headquarters base at Margate with SAAF Oryx helicopters providing air-lift capability. The troops were dropped into pre-selected target areas. (top) • An army officer displays a selection of firearms recovered, many of them home-made but including a selection of AK-47, Kalashnikovs and SADF carbines as well as other automatic weapons and (below left) a police *Taakmag* unit breaks down a door in a remote village in a bid to find more weapons. (Photos: Author)

down a restaurant owner almost within shouting distance of Ron's home and had brutalised numerous families while breaking into their houses.

For all that, Ron Reid-Daly was a marvellous host. While Jean, his wife was alive, they would always have people around for a dinner or a braai, invariably over weekends. And as my wife Madelon always noted, he was the last of yesterday's consummate gentlemen: Ron would always stand up when a lady entered the room and when they left, he would escort his guests to the gate, sometimes all the way to their cars.

Like another of his acquaintances, the French mercenary commander Bob Denard (who twice successfully invaded the Comores Archipelago), Ron Reid-Daly was a military historian of note. He wrote several books and read prodigiously. Moreover, he liked to keep himself in good physical shape, something that went on well into his seventies, even when undergoing treatment. Rare was the day that Uncle Ron wouldn't complete his requisite early morning half-hour workout.

That was another of the reasons why Uncle Ron was still dating beautiful long-haired young women half his age until a few years before he died.

Lieutenant Colonel Ron Reid-Daly's military career was as illustrious as the man himself. He first became a soldier in 1951, when he volunteered to fight with "C" (Rhodesia) Squadron of the newly reformed British SAS to combat communist insurgency in Malaya, in part, he admitted often enough afterwards, because so many of his mates had volunteered. He just thought it the right thing to do, he would say. For that effort, chasing Chinese communist guerrillas in the Southeast Asian jungle with fairly good results and battling recurring bouts of malaria, he was awarded an MBE by the Queen.

Afterwards, he worked his way upwards through the ranks in the Rhodesian Army from trooper to become the regimental sergeant major of the Rhodesian Light Infantry, until he was commissioned as captain. He resigned his commission in 1973 to retire on pension, prematurely as it turned out, because there was a war about to happen.

Later that same year, he was persuaded by his old friend and fellow SAS inductee, the late Lieutenant General Peter Walls – by then the Rhodesian military Supremo – to return to active duty to form the Selous Scouts, an elite Special Forces unit to combat the growing threat posed by nationalist guerrillas.

Drawing on his Malayan experiences and by now holding the rank of a lieutenant colonel, Reid-Daly built up a skilled and highly professional regiment virtually from scratch. But though the Scouts achieved many of their military objectives, their unorthodox methods ended up creating a measure of tension within the military hierarchy and the commander had several brushes with his superiors.

In an African context, it was in the RLI that Reid-Daly was originally blooded, though he'd been active throughout the transitional Federation period and afterwards, when three African nations emerged from the breakdown: Zambia, formerly Northern Rhodesia, Malawi (Nyasaland) and Rhodesia itself, formerly Southern Rhodesia. It was also in the 1st Battalion, the Rhodesian Light Infantry, that a much younger Reid-Daly first made a name for himself on home ground. The unit had evolved into a regular airborne commando regiment and became a parachute battalion in 1977.

Regarded in its day as one of the world's foremost proponents of counter-insurgency warfare, its regular duties included both internal operations and external pre-emptive strikes against guerrillas based in the neighbouring territories of Mozambique and Zambia. Organised into four company-sized sub-units called commandos, average fighting strength was about 70 men, their characteristic deployment being the Fire Force, a reaction operation called out by radio whenever enemy units were spotted, usually in remote locations in the bush.

RLI "troopies" soon became the country's most effective rapid-deployment helicopter shock force. Small combat elements would consist of four men per "stick", each consisting of an NCO stick leader, a machine gunner, a trooper, as well as combatant-medic. Basic weapons were the 7.62 mm FN rifle and belt-fed MAGs.

Ron Reid-Daly had his quota of experiences while with the RLI. His first position as a commissioned officer in the 1st Battalion was training officer of the battalion.

"Occasionally I was required to deputise for commando commanders who were on leave, or on course at the School of Infantry," he recalled.

During their absence he would sometimes command the men on border control operations and it was during one of these stints that he had an experience which remained indelibly imprinted on his mind. As he explained, it was vital for troops operating in remote parts to be trained in bush survival, for the simple reason that their

Chapter 10
Ron Reid-Daly – A tribute to the man and his scouts

RSM Ron Reid-Daly and CSM Robin Tarl in front of the RLI colours. (Photo: Courtesy Hannes Wessels)

lives might ultimately depend on it. He takes up the story:

"It was November 1967, and I had been ordered to command the battalion's Support Group for a six-week border stint at the most northerly part of the country where Rhodesia, Zambia and Mozambique conjoined at the junction of the Luangwa and the Zambezi rivers. A temporary military base large enough to house a full company of men had been built behind the Kanyemba police post. Though set in picturesque surroundings on the bank of the

Zambezi, whoever had originally sited it obviously had its natural beauty in mind. Tactically, in the very likely event of an attack, it was a potential death-trap.

"The Rhodesian insurgency war was in its infancy and regular military forces were used to patrol those vast, uninhabited border regions of the country, always in search of signs of guerrilla infiltrations. I carried out the customary handover/takeover procedures which included a brief on the local operational situation with the outgoing company commander and sat down in the operations room with a large tin mug of tea to plan my own patrol programme.

"At this period all troop deployments were carried out by vehicles along atrocious tracks, or by boat along the Zambezi River."

As he recalled, the Mpata Gorge which formed his north-western boundary was considered "uncrossable" because the mighty Zambezi River, constricted into this steep-sided gorge, speeds up considerably, making any kind of traverse hazardous. Below the gorge, the river spreads out once again, the flow slowing down in the process. Also, the width of the Zambezi in this region is considerable and the Rhodesian military, taking cognisance of the insurgent inexperience in watermanship, considered it unlikely that this stretch of water would be selected for getting across. About 15 kilometres west of Kanyemba the river narrows once again, as it passes between two high promontories which thrust out towards one another from Zambia and Rhodesia. Not surprisingly, these were known as "The Gates".

The river narrows to about 200 metres at this point and because it is merely constricted here and opens out immediately as it passes through this natural obstacle, it does not pick up speed as it does in the Mpata Gorge. This, we felt was the most likely insurgent crossing point and for this reason the brigade responsible for the region ordered that the Rhodesian side of "The Gates" set up a permanent observation post.

He continues: "I went up to this point by boat, landed and looked around. I wasn't impressed with what I saw; the promontory was littered with junk dug up by wild animals from the rubbish pits of previous patrols. Numerous remains of large fires gave a clear indication that some of these patrols had carried out their duties unprofessionally. They'd been using fires at night either for warmth, or more likely, to keep prowling animals at bay.

"I didn't see much point in travelling up the Zambezi River in full view of the Zambian bank to take up what should have been a clandestine position of importance. On my return to camp I studied the 1:50 000 scale map pinned across a wall of the operations room, looking for a land route to 'The Gates'. There were no properly surveyed maps of this corner of the Zambezi Valley at the time and troops had to make do with white sheets of paper covered with an improvised military grid system. The rough outlines of the rivers were marked in blue and crosses with a figure pointed next to them gave the approximate altitude. Vague form lines here and there were designed to give the map reader an indication of high ground, but there were no contour lines so that one couldn't visualise the ground one was going to traverse with any accuracy.

"To compound problems, there were large bare blotches splattered across the map, where cloud cover had hidden the ground from the aircraft cameras. However, the cartographer was kind enough to print 'cloud cover' in each blotch.

"I now understand why the previous commanders had used boats to position patrols at 'The Gates'; but I was determined to find a way to insert a patrol into the area without the whole of Zambia being made aware of it."

A careful study of the map told Reid-Daly that the nearest accurate jump-off point for the patrol to enter "The Gates" area was the western corner of a bush airstrip which lay to the southeast and served the Kanyemba outpost. Meantime, he had worked out a compass bearing to the top of a high range of hills known as Kapsuku. If the patrol's map-reading was accurate, he reckoned, they would find themselves at the headwaters of the Euguta River and all they had to do was follow the river down through the hills either to "The Gates" or the Zambezi River.

"The total length of the patrol was 17 map kilometres, a distance which could be easily covered in about 12 hours. However, I took account of the fact that this was one of the hottest months of the year with temperatures running at 90 degrees Fahrenheit (about 32 degrees Celsius) when the sun is at its peak. In addition each man had to lug a heavy pack, which weighed almost 30 kilograms. All this, coupled with rough terrain which included steep hills, made me accept that the patrol might have to sleep out one night and reach 'The Gates' only the following morning."

Orders were given for the task. At dawn the patrol debussed at the airstrip in preparation for an early start so that as much ground as possible could be covered in the relatively cool part of the day. He checked the patrol commander's compass bearing and pointed out the clearly visible gap in the mountains that formed the headwaters

The pilot of a Rhodesian Air Force Alouette helicopter gunship banks sharply after reports of movement of a suspected guerrilla group on the ground. (Photo: Author)

of the river. That would lead them to "The Gates", he said. The patrol set off on its mission and Reid-Daly returned to his operations room to monitor other patrols on the valley floor.

He distinctly recalls that all troops going into that area were required to adhere to a strict radio schedule. They would call their control station (headquarters) at 07h00 every day with a situation report or sitrep. But he'd heard nothing from this patrol throughout the day and by last light he was starting to feel a little uneasy. Failure to observe radio schedules did happen, but it was an occasional thing. There were many reasons which might affect comms, from mechanical failure to a faulty radio or a possible screening by mountains. While the Matusadona Range might have had an effect, Reid-Daly admitted to a nagging sense that all was not well. Before going to bed, he advised Brigade Headquarters that he might need a helicopter for a casualty evacuation the next day.

"The following morning's radio schedule still showed no sign of the patrol, so I summoned the boat crew and proceeded upriver, stopping along the banks of the Zambezi to try to call them up by radio. It just so happened that one of our Canberra bombers on a cross-country map-reading exercise passed overhead and I gave him the approximate map coordinates and asked if he could deviate slightly from his course and give 'The Gates' patrol a radio call. He returned a few minutes later to report nothing heard or seen.

"By now I knew that this had become serious. I returned to Kanyemba base, called up Brigade Headquarters and requested the immediate use of a chopper. But it wasn't quite so easy: to enlist the services of a helicopter in those early days of border control was a major exercise and God help any army commander who called for a chopper only to discover that there was no emergency. But I got the machine I asked for in the end.

"Flying time to Kanyemba by chopper was about three hours and at 15h00 an Alouette arrived. I gave the pilot a hasty briefing while his technician refuelled and loaded as many water bags as could be found in the camp. Then, with my medic, we headed out to try to locate the missing men.

"We reached the area which the troops should have passed through and the pilot circled for several minutes: there was no sign of them. He then flew over the next range of hills, which was where he suddenly exclaimed loudly and banked sharply. With that, we were presented with an astonishing sight: running around in the bush below were seven stark-naked soldiers.

"With that we landed and actually had to fight the men off as they desperately tried to get to the water bags."

Although it was late afternoon, the sun still radiated intense heat and while there were many trees in the area, it was November and they had no leaves. Consequently, as he saw things, the parched soldiers had almost no shade to shield themselves from what was clearly a blistering sun. It was also obvious that most members of the patrol had reached their limits of endurance. Had the helicopter not arrived that afternoon, some of these young men would almost certainly have been dead by morning.

"I flew them back to camp in relays, where they rushed to stand or lie down under the cold showers. It was astonishing to see how quickly they recovered as they lay under the streams of water, mouths agape and drinking as much as they could."

In the subsequent debrief, it appeared they had missed the gap. But instead of pushing on north towards the Zambezi River, they wasted precious time trying to find the Euguta River in a bid to follow down to "The Gates". Climbing up and down steep hills, with the sun beating down was exhausting; even worse it had brought on a terrible thirst. They made good time on the first day and had their map-reading been more precise, they would have reached the Zambezi River that evening. But then, the colonel explained, an element of panic crept in when some of the soldiers thought they were lost. "They discovered they couldn't make radio contact with headquarters and those of us who have been placed in such circumstances know the feeling."

Anxiety and fear can make a man sweat profusely and with these fellows, it was no different. All this, plus heavy physical exertion while the patrol cross-grained exceptionally difficult terrain in fierce heat soon exhausted their two standard water bottles. Dehydration set in rapidly.

"I asked them why they had taken off their clothes and their reply was interesting. They found that dehydration had made their skins become paper dry: they simply couldn't stand the sensation of their uniforms rubbing against their skin. The only relief was to remove everything. In utter desperation, some of the men even tried to drink their urine, disguising the taste by mixing it with coffee powder.

"I also noticed that the younger soldiers had been the worst affected. It became obvious that the older men had a tougher mental outlook and were much better able to cope with stress. Bushcraft had only just begun to be taught within the Rhodesian Army and this particular group had not been through any of the drills.

"While flying to recover the group, we passed over an astonishing range of wildlife. In fact, a herd of elephants and large clusters of impala were almost constantly in sight, as they would have been while these soldiers were on patrol. Had the men been trained to deal with such an emergency, their problems would have been over because the average impala will provide about two litres of potable liquid from its stomach: an elephant holds something like 36 litres."

Consequently, during 1973, when the Rhodesian bush war began in earnest, Ron Reid-Daly was given the task of establishing and training a special multiracial unit which he named the Selous Scouts, the idea being to establish a new kind of counter-insurgency element that could deal with exactly this kind of problem. Bush survival and tracking formed an important segment of the operational training of these men, he said: it gave them a good measure of self-confidence in their abilities to survive and live comfortably in the African bush. Indeed, their self-assurance was such that they found nothing unusual in carrying out long-range two-man reconnaissance patrols, sometimes over distances of hundreds of kilometres deep behind enemy lines.

Comprising a black and a white soldier, the two-man "stick" would be dropped by parachute (HI-LO, or high altitude-low opening) often 200 kilometres from the Rhodesian border where they would operate for up to six weeks at a time. He suggested that it was a

Chapter 10
Ron Reid-Daly – A tribute to the man and his scouts

tribute to their training that during the course of these operations, they never once ran into bush survival problems.

The role of the Selous Scouts throughout the Rhodesian War was one of combat reconnaissance. Its mission, according to the unit's website – which remains active and which I quote below – was to infiltrate those areas where insurgents were active. They were to pinpoint rebel groups and relay vital information back to conventional forces which, often enough, would result in the RLI and its Fire Force being dispatched to score kills[2].

As Colonel Reid-Daly explained, his scouts were trained to operate in small undercover teams, mostly behind enemy lines and more often than not, right among them. Numbers were always flexible. There could sometimes be teams of four, but more often than not, two men operated alone. In earlier days, Chris Schulenburg – one of the most outstanding operators of his generation and later promoted to captain – preferred to work solo.

The men proved capable of operating independently in the bush for weeks on end, quite often taking the role of "Pseudo Terrorists"

Much controversy surrounded the activities of the Selous Scouts while they were operational in disputed areas. The insurgents liked to pin the deaths of many of their victims on these Special Forces elements. Here the BSAP remove the dead after a night attack in a remote area.
(Photo: Author)

and passing themselves off as rebels. That sometimes involved the scouts making direct contact with enemy groups, living and working with them for a period of time.

Significantly, the Selous Scouts was a strictly volunteer force: only highly motivated men of all races and of the highest calibre could fulfil the tasks they needed to undertake. On one selection course only 14 out of 126 candidates managed to complete the process: a mere 15 per cent finally emerged from the tough training programme with the right to wear the unit's distinctive brown beret. The selection process was conducted at camp Wafa Wafa, on the shores of Lake Kariba in the north of the country.

At its peak in 1977, the strength of the unit touched the 1,000-mark, though the Selous Scouts, on average, ranged around 700 members and more than four-fifths of its members were black, which was why members were required to be fluent in at least one of the country's African languages or dialects.

Their numbers were recruited from volunteers between the ages of 24 and 32. Without displaying the highest levels of motivation, toughness, guts, loyalty and a deep and significant professionalism, the aspirant scout would not make the grade: maturity and intelligence were integral to the mix.

As Colonel Reid-Daly observed, "a thorough understanding of the meaning of responsibility was as important as self-discipline. Being a loner and able to survive the rigours of the African bush, and at the other extreme, the ability to function as a team player, were criteria that removed the rest from the best."

By his own admission, Reid-Daly admitted that his selection process came largely from the training he had personally undergone as a British SAS operator. "Only I took it several steps further, because this was Africa and not Malaya," he told me.

No provisions were issued for the first five days of the course. The recruits had to live off the land. Then, on the fifth day, they were given a baboon or other carcass that had been left to rot in the sun for three days. Recruits had to prepare the meat – riddled with maggots – and eat it. For the remaining 13 days, they had rations that consisted of only one-sixth of a man's customary daily intake, the idea being to force hopefuls to make the bush their own habitat. Eating all kinds of animals was the norm, as was, in severe circumstances, drinking the liquid from the stomachs of dead animals, simply to stay alive.

In later stages, the men had to learn to act and talk like the enemy. In fact, the Wafa Wafa base was built and set out as an authentic rebel camp and instructors were on hand to turn the recruits into fully fledged members of the enemy. In this phase recruits were taught to break with habits such as shaving, rising at regular times, smoking and drinking and to adopt a guerrilla lifestyle. Effectively, the scouts became "Pseudo Operators", working well within the insurgent domain, very much as the British had done in Kenya against the mainly Kikuyu-oriented Mau Mau. The recruits ultimately became remarkably adept at it, so much so that it was eventually estimated that almost three-quarters of all enemy kills in the Rhodesian War resulted from these appropriately named Pseudo Operations.

The Selous Scouts barracks at Inkomo, near Salisbury, was named after another founder member of the Unit, Sergeant André Rabie, an outstanding soldier and in his day, a particularly skilled tracker. Killed while on operational duty, Rabie pioneered many of the techniques the unit employed while on the hunt for insurgents.

The regimental colours were green and brown which, as those in the know will tell you, are the dominant colours of the Rhodesian bush. The unit badge was a stylised Osprey, a noted bird of prey that is both swift and courageous. The unit's motto was Pamwe Chete, the Shona term for "all together".

It was also the title of Colonel Ron Reid-Daly's book on the Selous Scouts[3].

While still with the Rhodesian Light Infantry, Ron Reid-Daly played a significant role in evolving the Fire Force concept to the successful entity it eventually became. In his view, without it, the war would have ended much sooner, and in defeat.

As he has declared in his book, Fire Force was the single most successful offensive tactic used against the enemy during the Rhodesian war. However, it was his view that having developed this remarkable concept, his military counterparts viewed it in too narrow a perspective, with the result that for the greater part of the war, Fire Force was not utilised to its full potential.

Discussing this shortcoming, he would suggest that a similar situation developed with the British who, having invented the tank, failed to exploit its true value on the battlefield. "The British frittered away a unique battle-winning concept that enjoyed enormous battlefield advantages by using their tanks in a supportive role broken down into fragmented 'penny packets'."

In an Appendix to a book written by Richard Wood and published after the war[4] and which deals with an overview of the Fire Force ideal, we are told: The German Army, by contrast, understood very clearly that the value of the tank lay in its inherent ability to

A brief halt during an external raid into Mozambique following good work done by Colonel Reid-Daly's scounts in pin-pointing a rebel gathering point. Note the 81mm mortar on the back of the truck. (Photo: Author's collection)

provide mobility, shock action and firepower. They also realised that armour on its own was not enough and "married" it to supporting arms – principally motorised infantry, engineers, anti-tank guns and artillery. The result was the revolutionary and highly successful "Panzer Group".

The Fire Force concept, in contrast, enabled the Rhodesian security forces to bring to their bush battlefield the same characteristics as the tank: firepower, mobility and shock action – albeit on a much smaller scale. The advent of deploying small-unit Fire Forces allowed the security forces to neutralise to a large degree the advantage the insurgent normally has over security forces: the ability to elude their attention by using the local population as a screen. But for the Fire Force to operate effectively, a number of conditions had to be met, and principal among these, was the location of targets. This required good intelligence, which gave ground or air reconnaissance a solid platform from which to pinpoint enemy concentrations or camps for the Fire Force.

Speed and accuracy were vital and enabled maximum shock in the initial onslaught. This was normally achieved by a specially trained soldier on the ground, somebody who had the target visual from a distance (often a Selous Scout, who had radioed in the initial report), or possibly a reconnaissance aircraft flying at high altitude.

Therefore, the ground reconnaissance soldier was most times seminal to the deployment of a Fire Force action and his function was twofold. The first was to locate and pinpoint a target and pass back sufficient data to enable the Fire Force Commander to plan an assault. His other function was literally, to "talk" the Fire Force onto target, a procedure that required skill and expertise and was often the single most critical element in a successful Fire Force action.

Many good targets were lost because inexperienced or arrogant Fire Force commanders ignored the ground reconnaissance soldiers' in-flight briefing. There were many times when these men were berated by Fire Force commanders who, having disregarded the ground reconnaissance soldiers' briefing panicked when they weren't able to locate the designated target. One very well-known RLI officer who gained an excellent reputation as a Fire Force commander, never tired of relating how embarrassed he was after one such call-out by a bunch of scouts.

As he recalled, two black Selous Scouts had ingratiated themselves with a guerrilla group in the Mtoko area. One of them had established himself with a radio in an OP position on a kopje overlooking the enemy camp. The other scout entered the hideout and, having gathered the intelligence needed to make a Fire Force call-out, rejoined his comrade on the hill.

When the RLI Fire Force arrived, its commander, not able to see the camp because of dense forest foliage, expressed doubts to the two men in the OP whether the camp they had reported actually existed. To which the scout, with some acerbity replied: "Of course, I'm sure there is a camp. I have just come out of the fucking place!" Somewhat shocked at the retort, the commander hastily deployed his troops as suggested by the scout and in a hard-fought action that lasted three hours, eight of a dozen insurgents in the camp were killed.

In Lt Col Reid-Daly's view, it is also true that many so-called "lemons" were due to the inefficiency of the Fire Force and not his ground reconnaissance troops, who exposed themselves at considerable risk in order to locate targets. Spending on average six weeks in the bush and operating in small groups, scouts would take exception to inept performances by Fire Force commanders and they would not be shy to express resentment if things did not pan out quite as intended.

Colonel Reid-Daly himself had to make a "regimental" apology to the Rhodesian Air Force (who were usually remarkably efficient) after a particularly dismal performance by a Fire Force element. At the conclusion of an abortive attack, one of the scouts on the ground asked on the radio whether they were dealing with "Mugabe's Air Force".

There was also a marked reluctance on the part of some Fire Force commanders to accept targets at last light. This could result in an attack taking place without helicopter support, coupled to the need to possibly overnight in a target area.

As Colonel Reid-Daly would point out, ground reconnaissance troops spent many weeks moving day and night within a population group that was both hostile and belligerent. Their peregrinations often took them in among the enemy themselves, where they faced the constant threat of exposure. It was axiomatic, he would explain, that their fuses were short.

Like the Selous Scouts, the RLI faced numerous ancillary problems, including trying to spread their limited helicopter efforts to all the operational areas in the country, which, considering the size of the country and the numbers of troops available, was impossible. The result was what Reid-Daly called "penny packets", which could simply not put enough troops on the ground to seal off target areas. The consequences were inevitable: insufficient forces on the ground – with inadequate stop groups – which more often than not allowed the enemy to escape.

As the war dragged on, it was also Colonel Reid-Daly who voiced the view that command of a Fire Force deployment required skill, experience and expertise and should have resulted in special courses being run by the School of Infantry. While the Fire Force concept and its tactics were integral to combat team and company commander courses, only three days would be set aside for them. However, there were no special tactical wing courses: succeeding company commanders in the field were simply briefed by the outgoing senior officer and left to their own devices.

The same applied to the men. The paucity of choppers meant that only a small number of troops – normally three "sticks" of four men – could be dropped onto a specific target. This made it impossible for the soldiers to contain the insurgent element within the confines of the target area while a second wave of troops was brought in. It was then that the enemy would make their escape.

Helicopter pilots tried to remedy this deficiency by carrying out a series of dummy drops, but this usually resulted in the arrival of the second lift being delayed. In an attempt to remedy this, the dropping of RLI troopies in by parachuting – usually the jealously guarded reserve of Special Forces units – was instituted. Regular infantry units, notably the RLI and the Rhodesian African Rifles, were soon trained for airborne duties and a Dakota DC-3 aircraft – named a "Paradak" (because it was configured for paratrooping and was capable of dropping 16 paratroopers into the target area) – would supplement the usual chopper component.

In theory, each Fire Force could now deliver 28 soldiers into a contact area, a tremendous improvement from previous capability. Practically, however, the delivery of this number of men was not always possible: there were only so many members of the RLI available at any one time and far too many targets of opportunity that needed attention.

Weather, wind and suitable dropping zones free of obstructions were additional inhibiting factors, so that many Fire Force call-outs were still only attended to by three troop-carrying helicopters plus a K-Car.

As an acting captain with the Rhodesian Light Infantry, Ron Reid-Daly was the first Rhodesian officer to be attached to Portuguese forces then operating in neighbouring Mozambique. Some Rhodesian SAS specialists were seconded to this East African colony from time to time, but it was not a regular occurrence and their comments about the way in which the Portuguese fought their war in Mozambique (and, ultimately, why they eventually lost it) are illuminating.

From Reid-Daly's experience in Malaya, it was soon made clear to his superiors in Salisbury that the top Portuguese brass in Mozambique had no clear understanding either of the nature of guerrilla warfare or of the enemy they were encountering in increasing numbers in this vast country with a coastline that stretched northwards for more than 1,600 kilometres. They were certainly far behind anything that the British had seen in Borneo, Malaya or even Kenya during the Mau Mau emergency and that was surprising, suggests Reid-Daly, because many Portuguese Army commanders had already had good service in Lisbon's two other African wars in Angola and Portuguese Guinea.

The counter-insurgency pattern was the same each time. Some intelligence of insurgent activity would come in and the local garrison commander would spend a day or two getting together a force of several hundred men. This force, often 500-strong, would then make a massive cross-country sweep with all the noise and hoopla that such an effort entailed.

"They would never act immediately on a tip-off, with the result that when an operation was finally launched, the birds had flown," Reid-Daly recounted after spending lengthy periods with the Portuguese Army.

"During bush operations, everything in their path would be

destroyed; livestock slaughtered, crops and villages burnt, the local people rounded up for questioning and anyone acting in a suspicious manner arrested and hauled back to base. Tribesmen who attempted to escape this treatment were regarded as 'fleeing terrorists', and shot and these deaths listed as terrorist kills.

"If they managed to escape into the bush, all well and good; there was no question of sending in troops in some kind of a follow-up operation. By nightfall the entire unit would be back at base, congratulating itself on a job well done. Naturally, any one of the local people who had experienced one of these Portuguese 'search and destroy' missions was by then a firm supporter of FRELIMO; the business of 'hearts and minds' came only much later. In that way many neutral tribesmen soon became insurgent sympathisers."

Although the colonel was considered by his peers to be critical of the Portuguese war effort in Africa, and specifically what was going on in Mozambique, his views were essentially empirically based. He would say: "I was there. I saw it for myself. I went to war with these people, so I am in a very good position to assess both the insurgent threat as it develops and the people who are supposed to be doing the defending, and that is the Portuguese fighting man. I was impressed with neither."

He also had a measured opinion about Lisbon's *Aldeamentos* programme of resettling rural communities in organised camps, something that was already in full swing in all three of Portugal's African provinces and which was very much in line with what the British had achieved in Malaya in their protected villages programme. The idea, basically, both to the British and the Portuguese was to separate the civilian population from the terrorists. Consequently, large sections of the populace were moved *en bloc* into areas where they would be under government control and, in theory, out of reach of the guerrillas.

Ostensibly, the justification for this policy was that it denied the guerrillas the ability to wage war because there "would be no popular indigenous support and no food, which was supposed to be essential for survival in the bush". It was all part of the Mao dictum for the guerrillas to become "like fish in the water" among the civilian population.

"In reality," recounts Reid-Daly, "although a million people, or roughly 15 per cent of the population in Mozambique were resettled, it not only failed, the programme failed utterly." One American observer made the point that much of the food grown by people living in the *Aldeamentos* went straight to the guerrillas.

Chapter 10
Ron Reid-Daly – A tribute to the man and his scouts

Guerrilla leader Robert Mugabe was welcomed by the international community following his becoming president of the newly independent Republic of Zimbabwe. They were not to know that this crazed demagogue would almost totally destroy the country's infrastructure by seizing almost all the farms owned by white people and cause a million of his own people to flee, many to South Africa. Here, very early on, he is welcomed to Washington by President Ronald Reagan. (Photo: Author's collection)

For all that, the bulk of the war – apart from what was going on in Tete Province – was confined largely to the northern regions of Mozambique. Lourenço Marques, the capital (Maputo today), with its tourists and bright lights and from where almost all of us journalists operated, might have been in another country.

What became clear when speaking with Colonel Reid-Daly was that in actual combat, the South Africans and the Rhodesians regarded the Portuguese as both clumsy and inept.

There were some notable exceptions – like Oscar Cardoza, an unconventional counter-insurgency specialist who carved a swathe through guerrilla elements operating in South Angola. Generally, Portuguese army patrols in Mozambique were just too large and disjointed: marching columns sometimes stretching for hundreds of metres along isolated bush paths. As Reid-Daily pointed out in one of his reports, something like 30 or 40 men would go into the bush, and this at a time when his own people had become accustomed to four-man "sticks" and achieving good results.

The Rhodesians believed, correctly it transpired, that most Portuguese tactical failures resulted from a distinct lack of regular professional troops and the fact that most of these young boys from the metropolis neither understood Africa nor wished to be on what they referred to as "this horrific tropical hell hole". Their letters home were full of such comments and worse.

Even more disconcerting, as hostilities in Mozambique's war continued, the traditional trust between officers and the men under them started to wear thin. In a sense, it was almost a repeat of the Vietnamese syndrome, although as far as is known, there was never anything as dramatic as "fragging". There were many reasons for this imbroglio and Ron Reid-Daly listed some of them.

For a start, he suggested, radio communications were poor, which was one of the reasons why the troops in the field tended to work in large numbers. They were terrified of being overrun, which, he suggested might be expected of unprofessional troops.

"Their radio sets were unwieldy American instruments, originally designed for vehicles and not for hauling on the backs of soldiers in the debilitating African bush. Also, a few probably dated from the Korean War period. As a result, communications with the base was a long, complicated and often tedious business."

At one main base that he visited, the Portuguese were actually using oversized German sets from World War II.

Many of Reid-Daly's observations were insightful. During all the operations in which the Rhodesians took part in the Tete Panhandle, he recalled, the Portuguese were found to be completely base-bound. They fought much as the Americans had fought in Vietnam and are operating today in parts of Afghanistan.

The upper command was perfectly happy to let the insurgents control the bush while the Portuguese held on to the towns as well as communications links and certain strategic strongpoints, like the Cahora Bassa hydroelectric dam, then under construction.

Reid-Daly explained that in Tete, patrols lasting from four to six weeks should have been the norm: military units in the field could easily have been supplied by air. When he first propounded it, the idea was regarded as preposterous and Lisbon's upper command said so. At that time, the Portuguese would never consider spending anything beyond three days in the bush, with proper camps and attendant facilities for the officers each night. For their part, the Rhodesians, already regarded as masters of counter-insurgency warfare, always emphasised the need to dominate the bush by night as well as by day, and while most Portuguese officers tended to agree, they rarely did anything about it.

The ability of FRELIMO to move freely during the dark hours was clearly illustrated by the number of mines – both anti-tank and anti-personnel – that they were able to lay almost at will. This freedom extended all the way from the Ruvuma along the border with Tanzania to Tete in the distant central region of the country. Moreover, the guerrillas had been reasonably trained and were active. During one morning's operation in the Mueda area, Portuguese sappers cleared 189 mines along an 11-kilometre track, about a third of them Soviet TM-46s (anti-tank). The rest were anti-personnel mines. I was to see a bit of this for myself in the three-day safari that I completed from

Tete to the Malawi border in 1971, where dozens of mines were laid along the route we traversed[5].

There were other problems, recalled Reid-Daly. Physically, the Rhodesians regarded the average Portuguese conscript as "a poor physical specimen".

They couldn't march any distance without frequent rests. Most of these young men had come from poor backgrounds, and though they were put through their first physical training session on the day they joined the army, there were many that were barely strong enough initially to meet the fairly rigorous demands of their officers. Again, there were some notable exceptions and most of these European conscripts quickly adapted to the harsh demands of everyday life in primitive Africa.

There were limits, of course. One of their worst mistakes on the march was that the column was both noisy and straggling. They would talk loudly instead of maintaining silence, which even FRELIMO knew was one of the first principles of counter-insurgency warfare.

Reid-Daly found that once an ambush had been established, Portuguese soldiers would often cough and fidget. "It was as if they were trying to warn the enemy to keep clear, so that they would not be compelled to fight."

Clearly, he said at the time, this was an impossible situation: "For the Portuguese, Mozambique was a war waiting to be lost ..."

1 Al J. Venter: *War Dog: Fighting Other Peoples Wars*, Casemate Publications, US and UK, 2006, pp. 88 et seq.
2 http://selousscouts.tripod.com; accessed 18 June, 2010.
3 Ron Reid-Daly: *Pamwe Chete; The Legend of the Selous Scouts*, Covos Day, South Africa, 2000.
4 Richard Wood: *The War Diaries of André Dennison*, Ashanti Publishing, Rivonia, South Africa, 1992.
5 Al J. Venter: *Barrel of a Gun: A War Correspondent's Misspent Moments in Combat*, Chapter 24 – "Tete Convoy in Mozambique" pp. 415 – 438, Casemate, 2010.

CHAPTER ELEVEN

LIVING ON THE EDGE IN BEIRUT

Long after the civil war ended, Beirut remained somewhat at odds with its original self. Then, as today, the city epitomises just about everything for which the Levant has always been acknowledged. It remains the proverbial melting pot of cultures and an often-confused potpourri of traditions and religions – all 19 of them. Inevitably, these divergences are coupled to enough "attitude" to sometimes cause shoot-outs at traffic stops. But a lot has changed: you can come and go as you please, the hotels are thriving and tourists are welcome, though with the occasional car bomb exploding in the more affluent Christian areas, foreign visitors are not scurrying to get there.

Someone from the Lebanese Army was supposed to meet me on arrival at Beirut Airport, probably the only international air terminal that reminds me of an Arab *souk*. There were army and security people everywhere, but either my man wasn't in uniform or my plane arrived before he did. So what's new in the Middle East?

I latched onto a couple of crazy Irishmen posted to the UN contingent manning the Israeli border and they took me to their favourite watering hole, the appropriately-named Wild Geese Club in what was once the Christian sector of the city. The name says it all: part Irish, part Lebanese, rebellious and well-stocked with Kilkenny and Guinness draught. It was pleasant enough, but hardly the sort of dive you'd find either in Cape Town or San Francisco.

Some kids were there celebrating someone's birthday; seniors in their final year of school. The band was wild, the booze flowed and halfway through a youngster – obviously smashed – caused a commotion. In a tick the guns came out. Imagine it: a bunch of juvenile revellers enjoying a party, cake and all and some mother's son suddenly becomes a target. There were no shots fired that time, though the fight did end up in the street. And as somebody commented, it was close. More to the point, all this took place years after civil hostilities had ended.

Welcome to Beirut!

For some, getting to the Lebanese capital for the first time in the old days might have been likened to be stepping off the planet into a void.

It was real enough, like the Holiday Inn which the warring combatants had transformed into a high-rise chunk of Emmentaler. All of 20-something floors tall and dominating much of West Beirut, it took a while to patch the holes and today the hotel is one of the best on the Med.

Nor did it help to see Joseph Sullivan, chairman and the American representative of the Joint (ceasefire) Monitoring Committee being driven about the city, sirens wailing. He moved about in a seven-vehicle entourage with machine guns mounted fore and aft. When he stepped out, as I watched him do during a visit to the Lebanese Army Headquarters at Yarze, he was surrounded by a bunch of heavies. They had all the hardware they required and the guys obviously meant business.

But that was then and things have improved, although in recent years, unfortunately, the Lebanese capital has conjured up all sorts of images. It continues to do so.

What you couldn't escape, even quite recently, were the few remaining shell-blasted, skeletal ruins (some with people still living in them) that poked up untidily in the dust in some of the outlying areas where the Green Line used to run. It meandered, almost like an oversized bunker, throughout the length of the city. That, despite

After the civil war, Lebanon quickly picked up the pieces and began to put its society in order again. The United States came forward with much material help, including a squadron of these helicopters for the Lebanese Air Force. (Photo: Author)

one of the world's largest urban renewal programmes, which the Israelis managed to effectively disrupt in their furious onslaught on Beirut in the summer of 2006.

The scale of the attack was immense and lasted almost two weeks. In a preposterous and concerted effort, the Jewish State used preponderant air power to destroy huge swathes of Shi'ite (and Hizbollah) in South Beirut.

Visions of AK-toting warlords, even today, are a succession of nightmares that sometimes recur; only these zealots belong to the Party of God. Who can forget the 99 independent militias in the Balkanised cluster of enclaves that evolved during the course of the war? With the exception of Hizbollah, Amal and some Palestinian units still active in the south, all are long gone.

So has the destruction that enveloped the Places des Martyrs at el Bourj in the heart of the city. The statue that commemorates the murder of Lebanese dissidents by Turkish troops in 1915 still stands, complete with bullet and shrapnel holes from more recent battles. The adjacent area has been beautifully rebuilt and one of the most striking structures in the city overlooks the area, the Mohammad al-Amin Mosque with its distinctive four spire-like minarets.

While Lebanon's war has been relegated to the history books, memory can be fickle. Not everyone recalls that until fairly recently, Beirut was a crucible of war where Western journalists and clerics

Once Israel believed it was taking too many casualties from an extremely determined, belligerent and competent Hizbollah, it drew back behind its own borders leaving Christian towns like Marj'Ayoun in the south to fend for themselves. These tiny communities were soon overrun by Islamic zealots and thousands of Christians either fled or were murdered. (Photo: Author)

Chapter 11
Living on the edge in Beirut

were either kidnapped or murdered and simmering national, tribal, ethnic, religious and civil differences exploded into a bloody conflict that lasted 16 years.

Although the war ended in the early 1990s, one's senses are sharpened by the sort of routine military patrols in the streets of Beirut that you find just about everywhere in the Middle East. Until fairly recently, there was also a Syrian army of occupation, but they've now gone, thanks be to Allah. It's an interesting paradox that there are more guns fielded by Israeli soldiers and patrols in the streets of Haifa, Jerusalem and Tel Aviv today than in any comparably sized Lebanese city.

The presence of the Syrians – when they were still around – would jar. They were a brutal, almost mindless bunch of thugs: armed enforcers one and all. There wasn't anybody I met while in Lebanon that didn't despise the bastards. Syrian soldiers would strut about Beirut as if they owned the place, yet no one had the chutzpah to ask them to leave. If they did, we were warned at the time, the fighting might start again.

In those still fairly recent times, if there was a Syrian secret police roadblock up ahead, logic would dictate that you sought an alternate route, simply because they would arrest whomever they pleased. And when they did so, there was nothing that anyone could do about it.

Nor did they let you forget that it was a Syrian secret agent that assassinated Maronite President Bashir Gemayel in 1982. Five years before that, Assad had the tribal Druze leader, Kamal Jumblat, killed for daring to cross him in public. Kamal, it will be recalled, was the father of the present-day Druze leader Walid Jumblat.

These days it is common knowledge that Syrians murdered one of the most beloved of Lebanon's sons, Prime Minister Hariri, and they did so with an astonishing insouciance. The bomb that killed him was estimated to contain a ton of dynamite, buried in the road that his murderers knew he routinely travelled.

In his inimitable manner, British writer Robert Fisk described the murder in a piece for London's *Independent* on 15 February 2005. The article was headed: "The killing of 'Mr. Lebanon': Rafiq Hariri Assassinated in Beirut Bomb Blast". I quote:

> I saw the blast wave coming down the Corniche. My home is only a few hundred meters from the detonation and my first instinct was to look up, to search for the high-altitude Israeli planes that regularly break the sound barrier over Beirut. There were customers coming

bloodied from their broken-windowed restaurants and the great cancerous stain of smoke rising from the road outside the St George Hotel.

Beirut is my home-from-home, home from the dangers of Baghdad, and now here was Baghdad in Lebanon, a St Valentine's Day massacre in the streets of one of the Middle East's safest cities. I ran down the Corniche, everyone else fleeing in the opposite direction, and walked into a mass of rubble and flaming cars. There was a man, a big, plump man lying on the pavement opposite the still-derelict, war-damaged hotel, a sack, it seemed, except for the skull, the top missing. And there was a woman's hand in the road, still in a glove. There were bodies burning in a car, flaming away, a terrible hand hanging outside a motorist's window.

The event was both horrendous and historic. It told the Lebanese people that there were still those out there who wished them ill, specifically the Syrians.

Meantime, barely a month goes by without another report of an assassination or a car bombing, although this was one of the worst to strike this graceful, delightful city since the end of the Civil War. For those of us who had been in Lebanon then, it was impossible not to link some of the present-day images to what went on in the mid-1980s.

Olivia Nasr, until recently CNN's senior editor for Arab Affairs, added a whimsical note when she did a piece in November 2007 about how little had changed in Lebanon's hierarchy since the 1980s.

"Now I watch from another continent, but I find those same emotions resurfacing. The conspiracies, the car bombs, the threatening rhetoric and political deadlock are all eerily familiar. The actors are like shadows from a long gone past. They are more grey perhaps – those who have avoided assassination. But the cast in Lebanon's tragedy has changed little in two decades. Then, as now, a presidential election is the setting, and the struggle where religion and clan play the main roles threatens to set Lebanon back 20 years."

Looking at the bigger canvas, just about everyone accepts that there is both diversity and mendacity to certain aspects of Lebanese political life. The threat of more Israeli air attacks is a constant worry.

One must also accept that if not properly channelled, the system does tend towards violence, if only because of an unfortunate Lebanese propensity for vengeance: it can sometimes be feudal in its intensity. For instance, during one of my visits, there were shootouts between irate drivers on Lebanon's public roads. Most were caused by real or imagined slights.

It is easy to die while driving in Beirut. Apart from the fact that most Lebanese weave through the traffic like demons possessed, mayhem on the roads is of an Arab intensity. Beirut makes the streets of modern-day Rome appear quite docile. Add to that potentially explosive mix about four million people (with another million or so living in exile) and you get the picture.

There are Christians of half a dozen sects – some, when war raged, as bitterly opposed to each other as they were to those of the Islamic faith. Then there is the tough and uncompromising Druze community that has always made a place for its people in the Shouff, a society that does not like, or get on with Christians or other Muslims, be they Sunni or Shi'ite. In fact, said one of my associates, they hate the Christians more, if only because there are so many Druze people living on Israeli soil. There are quite a number of Druze soldiers serving in the Israeli Defence Force, some of them commissioned officers.

There are Muslims, too, who despise the Druze, and of course, hostilities between the Sunnis and Shi'ites go way back. From the time of the "Twelvers", they have never had much time for each other[1].

Add to that ethnic hodgepodge the occasional Turk and Pakistani hash dealer together with the odd Armenian and Kurdish refugee as well as French, Greek, Russian, Cypriot, Indian, Egyptian, Saudi, Philipino, American, British, South African, Irish and other expats and you might have one of the most cosmopolitan societies on earth.

Beirut today has about a dozen daily papers as well as two in English. Not a day goes by without each one of them providing comprehensive Israeli-wide coverage. Also, Beirut's American University has maintained excellent standards over the years (in spite of there being so few Yanks on the staff) that there are nationals from every Arab country clamouring to get through its portals.

They even opened a Beiruti version of the Hard Rock Cafe. It stands on the Corniche where half of the city seems to gather after work each evening: local folk like to watch the sun dip slowly towards the west and it's all rather amiable and different now compared to when people were trying to slaughter each other with great enthusiasm.

Memories of the civil war die hard, but somehow this Arab nation comprising mainly Muslims and Christians have put such operations along Beirut's Green Line behind them. (Photo: Author)

It was a time, some of us like to recall, when anyone strolling along the Corniche was automatically targeted by Christian snipers across the way.

Still, a car bomb blew a building apart while I was there. While the army thought it was someone settling a personal score, the media reported Israeli saboteurs. In fact it was neither. The police said afterwards that two men had almost come to blows and one of the malcontents had solved the problem his way. What a way to go: you differ with your neighbour and he wipes out the clan.

Just about everyone living in Beirut today is clustered together in an indeterminate hodgepodge of suburbs, villages and settlements wedged between the mountains and the sea. Coming in to land at night, there are strings of fairytale lights that stretch up and down the coast as far as you can see. It looks as enchanting as Disneyland, but the shadows hide a lot.

Garbage is a perennial problem; there is a lot of it and the Lebanese have their own solution. There is an unwritten law in the land that you are allowed to dump garbage in only two places in the country: on the left-hand side and the right-hand side of the road. Take one of the side roads off the highway leading south out of the city and you'll quickly see what I mean. It is unconscionable, but nobody seems to bother.

Then you have what was, until recently, the stiflingly overcrowded, fundamentalist suburbs to the south, at least until several were razed by the Israeli Air Force bombardments in the summer of 2006. It is here, too, that any stranger invariably gets a lot of attention. You don't rate in these impoverished, squalid streets if you are not of the faith; arguably, for good reason because this is the domain of the mullah. It struck me, when viewing the antics of some of these Imams on Lebanese television – or on the Hizbollah broadcast station *Al Manaar* – that each one of them seemed to be as intemperate and uncompromising as those in Tehran.

These days there are as many billboards featuring the bearded scowl of the Ayatollah Khomeini in Beirut as there are of "Sayyed" Hassan Nasrallah, general secretary of the Party of God. Just don't try to take any photos because you could end up answering questions.

The result was that the few times that I drove to Harek Horeik (where Hizbollah has its headquarters) I felt distinctly plummy, Western and exposed. And if you aren't sure where or where not to go in Beirut, the issue is possibly exemplified by Louis Armstrong's retort to a fan's request for a definition of jazz: "Man, if you gotta ask, you'll never know."

For all that, Beirut has a captivating charm, nurtured largely by enormous residual wealth. About 30 years ago it was one of the financial capitals of the world. Much of the money, then and now, came from Arab oil.

In truth, Lebanon's history goes back further, long before a succession of internecine wars ripped the nation apart. These people were civilised when our forefathers were trying to master the wheel. One also needs to be reminded that before Greece became famous for its philosophers and Rome for its Legions, the Phoenicians had already created the greatest trading nation in what was then the civilised world. These were the people who taught the founders of Athens to read.

In its recent prime, as the travel posters very appropriately phrase it – Beirut really might have been the Jewel of the Med. Those who visited the place in the old days recall an opulent, voguish conurbation. Not for nothing did sybarites refer to it as the Paris of the Mediterranean. Cannes and Nice and Saint Tropez simply didn't rate by comparison because they were too "provincial".

Depending on your perspective, the good news is that most Western countries have lifted a long-standing travel ban to Lebanon, although not all tourists are prepared to take the chance, especially since foreigners are still prohibited from travel in the south. And if you do make any sort of contact with the Party of God or the Islamic Jihad – organisations listed under the label of "terrorist organisations" by the State Department – somebody in Washington will most probably open a file with your name on it.

Just don't make light of any of it. Until recently there was a real war in the south and in any event, little happens in isolation in the Middle East.

There are a slew of anecdotes from the region. While the South Lebanese Army (SLA) was still around – they received the bulk of their support from the Israelis – one of their detachments picked up an American hitchhiker at a roadblock. A teenager, he had been steadily making his way through the region, having entered from Syria. The youngster actually passed through innumerable Lebanese Army, Amal and Hizbollah military checkpoints and was never stopped. Someone had originally told him to head south "where all the action is". That's exactly what he was doing.

There were problems, of course. He'd never obtained a Lebanese visa. Nor had he bothered to remove the eight-inch-high American flag that he had sewn onto his shoulder bag; none of this was picked up at any border post or anywhere else. He might have become a target had some zealot found him first and in a state of apoplexy, the SLA grabbed him and without formality, shuffled him smartly across the border into Israel. From there he was allowed to continue on his way, a bit older and possibly a little wiser. Lucky fellow!

For all this, Beirut, and most of the other big cities – such as Sidon in the south, Tripoli to the north of Beirut and even Baalbek in the Beka'a Valley in the east – seemed to have returned to normalcy, although in the summer of 2008 there were more car bombs both in the Christian areas around Jounieh and also in largely Sunni Tripoli.

If you are flying into the country, you need to get your act together before you enter Beirut's main terminal on arrival from out West.

No visa, no entry, and don't even try it. Several on my flight did. One obstreperous hopeful attempted to stretch his credibility. He flashed dollars and claimed presidential privileges, but there was no arguing with a gun in his face and he went straight back to Cyprus on the return flight.

Then, once through the barriers comes the awesome spectacle of a thousand sweaty, garrulous bodies and hands that create a throng that even the army sometimes can't control. It was the original

Chapter 11
Living on the edge in Beirut

Along the southern border with Israel, hostilities continue sporadically. The occasional artillery barrage out of the Jewish State still takes place and people are still killed, as were almost 100 civilians when IDF artillery shells poured down on the Shi'ite town of Qana. All the victims were buried with promises of bitter retribution. (Photo: Author)

seamless web of chaos; fingers would appear from nowhere to embrace me and, I suspect, my wallet. It took muscle to hold on to everything in that last desperate push for the gate.

"Taxi?" called a man, all teeth. Like most Beirut taxi drivers, he was a predator.

I made the mistake of catching his eye. I knew then that I was his, the infidel incarnate and a captive fare into town at six or eight times the going rate.

Anywhere else in the world I would have told him to move. Not in Lebanon. He could be anyone; not impossibly a cop who might have been tipped off that I had arrived fresh from Tel Aviv.

Hizbollah, I'd already been warned, are known to keep track of new arrivals in the country, especially those with American stamps in their passports, of which I had a few. What did worry me was that only two days before, I had been quoted in London on Iran's potential for building nuclear weapons. And since it is Tehran's Revolutionary Guards that bankroll Hizbollah's revolution, I smiled gracefully and started bargaining. By then Ahmed had a grip on my bag.

It stayed that way until my Irish buddies rescued me. They knew enough Arabic to cause a lot of scurrilous talk regarding somebody's genealogy before we sped off to the Wild Geese Club.

They have their own view of the world in Jounieh, the up-market Christian enclave to the north of the main city. It's the sort of place that wouldn't be out of place in one of Paris's better-heeled *arrondissements*. It is in Jounieh that they categorise an optimist as the man who builds a glass-fronted building, and back again on my first morning in the country, I was greeted by acres of it.

For all that Lebanon has been through, it seems improbable that anyone would wish to tempt fate by spending millions on a facade that would cost a Rajah's ransom fortune to fix if a single Israeli jet fighter broke the sound barrier over the port. Curiously, there are more glass and marble high-rise buildings in Beirut than any other city in the Near East, Haifa, Tel Aviv, Damascus and Cairo included, all of them sparkling new.

Jounieh has other attributes. It boasts several private clubs on the waterfront, and those that frequent them – including some of the best looking doe-eyed women in the world, with figures to match and bikinis that leave little to the imagination – seem to be among the most prosperous residents in the region.

There is also scuba diving. I took a group of South Africans into Beirut during the war, including some senior intelligence people and several Special Force characters that were eager to assimilate the basics of what they termed "Urban Guerrilla Warfare". Prior to Nelson Mandela's release from prison, South Africa was on the brink of it, and Pretoria thought a little practical experience might be needed to cope with the escalating threat. Essentially, it was to have been something of an exchange with Pretoria, in turn, offering the Christian forces training facilities and advanced weapons systems.

The commander of the Christian military was delighted with the newcomers and since I had orchestrated the visit, he asked what I'd like to do while the other members of the team were "talking business".

Being an avid diver, I suggested that it might be a good idea to try a dive in the waters off Jounieh. At which he retorted: "Are you mad?" There was a war on, he countered incredulously. Shelling was an everyday business, he added. "And you want to get into the water here?"

I answered yes, and for all his protestations about scuba diving in a war zone, I finally did exactly that. I spent an hour underwater off the port in what can best be described as a sub-sea desert. I don't recall spotting a single fish bigger than my hand. And while I was allowed my whim, I wasn't permitted to go into the water alone, which meant that I had two escorts, both military men, who dutifully swam on either side, but slightly towards my rear. Each was appropriately armed – with spear guns, of course …

There were no explanations forthcoming, but I did end up with a beautiful fifth- or sixth-century Byzantine bronze cross that had almost certainly been worn around the neck of some long-forgotten Christian proselytizer and who probably died when his boat went

Chapter 11
Living on the edge in Beirut

Flashback to the Israeli occupation of South Lebanon: Local Christian militia used Israeli-issued weapons almost exclusively, like this American-built armoured personnel carrier. (Photo: Author)

down in a storm. I've had it mounted and the tiny cross faces me today in my study, a legacy perhaps of something that should never have happened.

These are some curious anomalies in what is otherwise a strictly Arab environment. It is true that the two other major concentrations of expatriate Lebanese are in France and the United States and that a fair proportion move constantly between the two cultures. A lot of the money originally came from Africa, from the gold and diamond mines of Angola and Sierra Leone.

The clubs were beyond my financial bracket, but being with the Lebanese Army, we did eat at various officers' clubs and there was no question that the one at Jounieh was the best. Also, it was cheap; a four-course meal cost about $5 a head. But as I told somebody else who was going there, don't touch the wine because a glass of inferior plonk there costs half as much again, which is a pity because some of the Beka'a labels are excellent. It's a tad ironic that Lebanon's largest vineyards are within sight and sound of Hizbollah training grounds in the valley, one of the most rigid Islamic militant groups anywhere.

For all that, the local Almaza beer is great. If I didn't know better, with its similar flavour, colour and texture, I could have sworn it was the same Gold Star brew that I regularly enjoy in one of my regular hang-outs on Dizengoff Street in Tel Aviv.

Just about everything that is worth experiencing in Lebanon happens along the coast. Beka'a is interesting too, but it has never been healthy to linger there if you didn't have good reason to do so. And meantime, a lot has changed there too. Shortly before I arrived, Russian cellist Mstislav Rostropovich played to a huge gathering among the ruins of the ancient city of Baalbek.

On the negative side, there are Lebanon's dangerous roads. A dangerous, quarter-finished, double-lane highway fringes the sea from Tyre in the south (or Sur, in the lingo of the locals, just north of where the UN has its headquarters at Naqoura) to El Aabboudiye on the Syrian frontier in the north and you are lucky to reach your destination without a scrape. There are also snow-topped mountains an hour's drive from the shoreline where it is possible to ski for much of the year, but again, some of the drivers along these narrow byways are like lunatics behind the wheel. Parts of that area are prohibited to travellers because of political uncertainties; Nabatiya, a Shi'ite stronghold, especially.

I was scheduled to visit a forward Lebanese Army position in Nabatiya on the morning that the town was strafed by Israeli jets. A week or so before, Hizbollah had apparently used the place as a staging point for a raid.

So, instead, we sat and waited for the dust to clear at a well-guarded intersection at El Maamariye. I didn't regard that move as particularly clever because just behind us was the biggest oil refinery in the area. It had just gone on stream again after having been destroyed in an IDF strike six months before. Interestingly, this was the same area where an Israeli Special Forces group that had entered Lebanon on a night raid from the sea was almost wiped out by a combined Hizbollah/Amal/Lebanese Army reception committee two or three nights later.

Then, when more Israeli planes knocked out several strings of electricity pylons along the road we had travelled earlier – almost within sight of southern Beirut – my escort, Lieutenant Hussein Ghaddar thought that perhaps we should go home. But not before we were sidetracked and hosted at one of the finest little restaurants in the Near East. It sits adjacent to Sidon's ancient Crusader Castle in one of the oldest ports in the world, with small groups of aging guerrilla commanders at tables dutifully smoking their hubbly-bubblies. I didn't ask whether they were Hizbollah or Amal and they

Chapter 11
Living on the edge in Beirut

didn't say. In fact, they barely glanced at us.

We spent time in Tyre and Sidon and both cities reflect the after-effects of war as well as the occasional Israeli incursion, neither of which helps the economy. I then asked permission to visit one of the Palestinian refugee camps because there are several in the area, but my army hosts didn't think it wise. In any event Lebanon hardly needs to publicise the plight of hundreds of thousands of neglected and misplaced souls living under conditions that, anywhere else in the world, would have long ago been condemned.

The entrance to every Palestinian camp was, as the saying goes, bristling with heavy weapons and there wasn't a vehicle that entered the camp that wasn't thoroughly searched. Or perhaps the military was a little more tetchy than usual that day because of inordinate Israeli Air Force activity.

Tyre, the last place you reach before the barriers go up, has one of the most unusual markets in the world. Only recently they were still selling cars on the quay in the harbour as they are rolled off the ship. If you struck a deal you paid your money and you drove away: there were no documents, no insurance, in fact, no paper trail.

The majority were *almost*-new luxury German, Swedish or British sedans with the occasional Alfa Romeo or Masserati thrown in for choice. Each one still had its European licence plates and all were stolen, driven to some port on the Adriatic from where they were shipped to the Middle East, obviously with the collusion of local authorities. This sort of contraband has been going on for so long that the Italians must have wind of it by now. Certainly the insurance people do.

The bottom line is that for a fraction of the real value, it was possible to buy a neat little three- or seven-series BMW, or a Mercedes 190 or 500 and do with it what you please. Only, you couldn't even think about taking it home because international border controls prevent such things happening just about everywhere in the civilised world, except Lebanon, of course. Convertibles cost a good deal more and such is the demand that it takes a couple of months to fill an order.

The vendors will do everything to get you the Rolls-Royce of your colour and choice, but even in Lebanon that's big bucks. And again, it takes a while. The word has to go out and part of the expense, I'm told, was getting it across the channel. Fascinating subject for a documentary, especially since just about every other car in the country was German.

Like hard drugs, for which Lebanon has become something of an unofficial entrepôt, living on the edge will always be a feature of life in the Eastern Mediterranean. So, it seems, will conflict.

That there will be another war in the Levant in the foreseeable future is as predictable as somebody from the Hizbollah hierarchy becoming the next president of Lebanon …

1 A detailed analysis of differences between Shi'ites and Sunni Muslims appears in *Iran's Nuclear Option* by Al J. Venter. It was published by Casemate Publishers of Philadelphia in the United States and Newbury in Britain in 2005.

CHAPTER TWELVE

SWAPO'S FIRST ATTACKS IN SOUTH WEST AFRICA

The first phase of South Africa's Border War may be said to have begun late in 1965, when six insurgents who had sworn allegiance to the Peoples Liberation Army of Namibia (PLAN) infiltrated Ovamboland – that area adjacent to Angola in the northern reaches of South West Africa (Namibia today). That was the time when small groups of armed dissidents began the usual round of political activation. Hostilities followed soon afterwards and lasted 21 years …

South African military historian and author Paul Els, who wrote the book *Ongulumbashe – Where the Bush War Began*, takes up the story[1]:

During the course of South Africa's 24-year Border War, SWAPO – the South West African People's Organisation – managed to establish only one permanent training base on home soil. That was in mid-1966, in a remote, sparsely populated part of west Ovamboland. The camp itself, eventually to become a touchstone of SWAPO leader Sam Nujoma's liberation folklore, was in a lonely corner of this remote and desolate wilderness that was called Ongulumbashe.

The operation launched to destroy it, was comprised mainly of members of the South African Police, with a small army detachment, together with elements from the South African Air Force. The initial operation became known in southern African military lore as Operation Blouwildebees.

By modern standards, the strike was little more than a token effort. It was launched from what was then still an isolated northern outpost at Ruacana, a small town that straddled the great Kunene River with headwaters to the north in Angola. Had it taken place in later years, Ongulumbashe would probably have warranted little more than a footnote.

The main force comprised three police officers, a member of the Security Police (SP), and four police non-commissioned officers together with 37 other ranks. There were also four army officers, of which one was a doctor, and seven NCOs. Nine officers made up the SAAF contribution, almost all of them pilots. For the sake of weight, the eight Alouettes involved in the operation went in without their usual complement of flight techs and were able to carry five troops each.

The onslaught itself was fraught. The first of the rotors to reach the base actually flew over the camp in daylight, warning the insurgents of what lay ahead. And while the actual fire-fight lasted perhaps half-an-hour, mopping-up and subsequent ground searches for the dead, wounded as well as weapons caches took the rest of the day.

Looking back, most observers would agree that in the broader context of counter-insurgency, this effort represented one detachment of novices ranged against another. Many mistakes were made: defensive and offensive tactics were flawed, security was lax and battle plans were handled ad hoc. More significantly, the ability to take enemy fire and retaliate accordingly raised many questions back at headquarters. It was almost a case of the blind leading the blind, which was why casualty figures were so dismally low.

Take the instance of the helicopter pilot, having heard his craft take hits from enemy fire, immediately surmised that he was going to crash. He promptly sounded a mayday distress signal until one of his buddies shut him up. That was followed by Agape Ipangelwa, one of the SWAPO "veterans" – he had been trained in Russia – targeting the circling choppers with his PPsH sub-machine gun. He must have had a stoppage because at one stage he threw down his weapon in disgust and grabbed a bow and arrow. It was later found that the arrow heads were poisoned. Ipangelwa was killed soon afterwards by a single salvo.

Another time, a serious problem emerged when the helicopters returned to Ruacana to refuel. Getting back to base was easy enough, but when they tried to return to the scene of the action in the heart of Ovamboland's bush and mopani terrain, broken only very occasionally by a lonely makalani palm, they had great difficulty in locating the base again. At one stage of the search they believed they might have to abort.

It was what the attackers found in the camp itself that gave the South Africans something of an insight to the problems that the country was to face as the guerrilla war gathered pace.

Chapter 12
SWAPO's first attacks in South West Africa

It didn't take the SADF long to quickly get into stride after the first SWAPO attacks. More onslaughts followed soon afterwards in Caprivi where this photo was taken. The original caption read: "Darling, how often must I tell you not to call me at the office." (Photo: Author)

Ongulumbashe was no simple Ovambo bush village. Instead, it had all the hallmarks of the kind of influences then dominant within the SWAPO leadership and which were to constantly reappear during the rest of the war.

In his subsequent assessment of the campaign, Paul Els, author and former member of the Reconnaissance Regiment, quotes liberally from the inquiry that followed: "The camp was very carefully laid out in the classic insurgency pattern dictated by Mao Tse-tung and Che Guevara. There was even a copy of Mao's *Selected Military Writings* among some of the documents uncovered at the base," he records.

"Constructed as a standard defensive position, the camp was reinforced by trenches and firing points along the perimeters, all focused around a centrally located command position. There was even a large grass-covered hole in the ground in the middle where the unit commander, Comrade Johannes Otto Nankudhu, and his second in charge slept. The rest of the guerrillas were expected to make do in trenches.

"The camp office – or in the peculiar guerrilla argot of the time, the 'makeshift' – was constructed of grass and twigs, though the immediate area had been cleared, probably to allow for a clear field of fire. Here most of the insurgents' weapons, documents, travelling bags, sacks as well as several bicycles were stacked. There were also 34 carved pieces of wood that were made to resemble AKs and apparently used for square-bashing. A flagpole overlooked the parade ground."

Els tells us that in spite of lapses, security seemed to be significant. There was an area specifically set aside for the interrogation of suspects: a hollowed-out stump of what had once been a forest giant was used for this purpose. Water, always a consideration in this semi-arid terrain, was a pit dug into the ground about 100 metres from the main base and only reached with the help of an improvised ladder.

A puzzling discovery made fairly early on (and reported by the air wing, since it could only be seen from aloft), was a large white cross laid out in a cleared section of bush that conformed exactly to the four points of the compass. Questioned afterwards, survivors said that they prayed there, though that was hardly logical since maize, or mealie meal (at that stage hardly in plentiful supply in the middle of winter in a comparatively remote Ovamboland) was used to highlight it. More likely, Pretoria decided, it was here that troops or supplies from a foreign country would be dropped by air once the guerrillas had taken the northern part of the country by force (as the guerrilla force had intended to do in short shrift).

Perhaps the most significant haul of the day was uncovered in a well-camouflaged cave that lay about a kilometre from the main base and could only be reached through a concealed tunnel. Protected by a line of trenches and strongpoints, it was constructed as a weapons cache for supplies expected from Zambia and Tanzania.

Altogether a dozen firearms were recovered from Ongulumbashe, including two AKs together with ten pistols and ammunition. More than a thousand rounds of AK-47 ammunition was also taken. There were several police stations listed as targets on a document found in the cave, including the main ones at Grootfontein and Tsumeb. In addition, there were three large bush knives, five *assegais* (spears), three bows with numerous steel-tipped poisoned arrows. Comrade Nankudhu's typewriter was found later in the day: ditched in the bush, in his haste to escape. Apart from numerous blankets and eating utensils, a trunk-load of documentation also came to light, most of it East European propaganda.

Two notable insights into the attack emerged. The first was that while resistance was fierce, despite the limited armoury, helicopter pilots reported afterwards that most of the guerrillas tended to fire not at their machines, but some distance ahead of them. This was fine while on the move for the aviators, but apparently nobody had told the guerrillas about the ability of helicopters to hover. This was underscored during subsequent interrogation sessions when it emerged that the enemy was confident that any attack would have to come overland.

As one of the insurgents put it, "there was no other way since there was nowhere in that thick bush that an aircraft could land."

Following Pretoria's de facto military takeover of what had formerly been known as *Deutsche Südwest-Afrika* in the World War I, the South Africans – like the Imperial Germans before them – had always found the people of the northernmost Ovambo tribe a difficult and recalcitrant community. Although peaceable by nature among themselves, the Ovambos were fiercely proud and bitterly resented the intrusion of the white man, whatever his origin. In time and through their own efforts, the Ovambo nation at one stage controlled an area on both sides of the Angolan and South West African frontiers that was almost half the size of Britain.

While primitive by European norms, the average Ovambo has always been regarded (even by the Germans, who originally colonised the region) as a tough and shrewd operator who – as the South African Defence Force was to find out for itself in later years – could endure astonishing hardships. Even the Finns, a group of missionaries who had located their stations throughout the region, sometimes commented on the stoicism of the Ovambos. Those who had had dealings with them in the past recall an almost elephantine memory: an Ovambo would rarely forget a slight, was a comment made by one of these Holy Fathers. So it was that the Ovambo people built up a fearful hatred of those South African functionaries who had been posted to the northernmost reaches of the territory, ostensibly to "administer" to their needs.

I had a taste of this myself in the early days of *Uhuru*, a period in Africa associated with the symbolic casting-off of the British Colonial "yoke".

Having qualified as a Fellow of the Institute of Chartered Shipbrokers at the Baltic Exchange in London, I returned to South Africa. But I wasn't happy with a desk job and decided to head back to Europe. Several years before, I had gone overland through East Africa where, in 1960, I hitched a lift on a Norwegian steamer from Mombasa to Montreal. It was touch-and-go since even then not every ship's captain would take a total stranger on board: I suppose I was just young, innocent and lucky. The second time across Africa, I chose to go to Europe along the West Coast route.

That journey took me through Windhoek and on to Angola,

north to Congo-Brazzaville, Gabon and so on. Finally, having passed through the Ivory Coast, Liberia, Guinea, Sierra Leone and Gambia, I was able to cadge another maritime lift in Dakar from an oil supply barge that was heading for the Canary Islands.

It was the trip through Ovamboland that was the most instructive and, as I was to observe afterwards, indicative of more serious things to come.

In their wisdom, probably to impress their Portuguese allies, Pretoria had financed and built a fine new tarred road all the way from Windhoek, the South West African capital, to the Angolan border. Slightly elevated to avoid being swamped in the rainy season, this highway went straight through the Ovambo heartland, almost like a proverbial arrow. It ended rather abruptly in the village of Oshikango at an imaginary line in the sand which separated the Portuguese overseas colony from South West Africa. From there on, Lisbon took over.

Because I was hitchhiking, and there weren't too many vehicles about, I took advantage of what rides I could get after I'd left Grootfontein, about eight hours drive north of Windhoek. But there wasn't a single white man who gave me a second glance, although there were pitifully few of them about anyway.

Instead, it was the Ovambos in their beat-up old Ford and Chevvy pick-ups who, if they had the space, would haul this lonely white boy between their towns and villages, some of them so remote that to get about, the locals needed to create their own primitive paths by hauling a mopani stump behind a four-wheeled drive vehicle. Although clearly impoverished, not one of these generous souls ever stuck his hand out for payment when we got to wherever they were taking me.

So, what should have been a day trip, eventually took three or four times as long across some of the remotest meanderings in Africa. And for good reason. The Ovambos steadfastly refused to use that spanking new national highway provided by what they termed "the Boer oppressors". Dozens of times the drivers would cross and recross the main road and generally, with few exceptions, they would stick doggedly to their primitive bush tracks, never mind what these sandy, potholed excuses for gravel strips did to their engines and suspensions. Clearly, this was a nation that was damned if it was going to show those in authority that they'd been done any favours.

Interestingly, after I had again returned to South Africa and spent a while reporting on the South West African case before the International Court of Justice at The Hague with, among others, Pik

Chapter 12
SWAPO's first attacks in South West Africa

Botha (by then a senior civil servant), I cautioned him about taking too much for granted from the people who lived in this remote northern enclave. I knew immediately that it was a mistake: he had nothing but disdain for the Ovambos. But then that had happened during the lull before the real ground war started.

Pik and I had got to know each other quite well in Holland in 1969, where, as the case progressed, we stayed at the same hotel. Already a heavy drinker, he was not averse to careening down hotel corridors in his underpants in search of more duty-free grog that the SA Embassy supplied to its legal team. Being one of the hacks assigned to the case, I was both willing and able to share in this perk.

Once back in South Africa, Pik and I met socially a few times at his home in Cape Town's Acacia Park, where many government officials had the privilege of free housing. And there, one quiet Sunday afternoon, I did the unthinkable: I again broached one of the imponderables that surrounded the gathering Ovambo storm. Having previously mentioned my experiences while travelling overland through the region, I ventured that the ruling all-white National Party might be making a serious mistake by underestimating the measure of Ovambo resolve to be free of South African control. Of course, such reactionary sentiment was almost unheard of at the time.

To the surprise of everybody present, including Helena, his lovely wife, Pik Botha – the man who was supposed to be my friend – turned on me. His face, contorted into a ferocious scowl, spat out the words: "Venter, don't you talk shit to me ... you know nothing about the Ovambos. *Nothing*!"

He paused a moment to gather his breath, while the veins in his neck stood out like cords.

"Once we push our army into Ovambo, the war will be over in six months ... mark my words!" he bellowed, at which he turned away from me in disgust.

I got up and went home, never to speak to either of the Bothas again. Like so much else in the final years of the millennium, Pik Botha had already begun to believe his own propaganda, and while the incident is hardly likely to make the history books, we all know what happened over the next two decades of a full-blown, modern-day guerrilla war that sometimes went conventional ... tanks, jet fighters, the lot. Further, it is impossible to discount the lives of the tens of thousands lost on both sides of what was always a badly delineated frontier.

But then Botha's tirades were symptomatic of so many members of the National Party who, like today's Israelis, believed that they were inspired by some kind of God-given right to subjugate those less fortunate than themselves. To some of these perverse thugs, many of them erudite, some well educated and, granted, in their private lives probably kindly and genteel, apartheid was the talisman that would eventually allow the white man to stride tall across Africa for a thousand years. Ian Smith had said something similar in Rhodesia a short while before.

Still worse, I went on to write *Coloured: A Profile of Two Million South Africans*[2], one of the definitive books on the brutal iniquities of apartheid and my sentiments could hardly have rested easily among those who ruled. In one of the introductory chapters I highlighted something by Schopenhauer that, at the time, seemed to make a lot of sense. The quote stood on its own and just about says it all: "Suffering which falls to our lot in the course of nature, or by chance, or fate, does not seem so painful as suffering which is inflicted on us by the arbitrary will of another."

Such a work, coming from one of their own, was the ultimate outrage. Horror of horrors, moreover, it had emanated from somebody with an Afrikaans name (but who grew up English and was educated at Marist Brothers College), and at a time when it was not yet fashionable to criticise either *Afrikanerdom* or apartheid.

To many of these people I was regarded as the ultimate *verraaier* (traitor).

That these were difficult times for many African liberation movements is reflected in the scrabble games of acronyms that many of them adopted: SWAPO, MPLA, ANC, AFO, ZANU and dozens more up and down this vast continent.

Before SWAPO there had been several more from South West Africa, including SWANU (SWA National Union), SWA Student Body, the Ovambo People's Congress (OPC), SWA Progressive Association (SWAPA), CANU (Caprivi African National Union) and so on. Eventually, with the putative leader Sam Nujoma firmly ensconced in New York, SWAPO became the standard bearer in 1960.

By early 1962, some Ovambo dissidents had already been sent to Egypt for military training. A year later the organisation was given its own camp at Kongwa in Tanzania: others were sent to the Nanking Military Academy in China and still more to Libya and Ethiopia. Broadcasting from abroad, Nujoma used every opportunity to exhort his people to "overthrow the occupying Boers".

It was then, too, that "Namib" was accepted in Dar es Salaam as the future name of the country for which SWAPO cadres were fighting, based largely on the future potential of the diamond-rich coastal region. Only five years later did the name mutate into the Namibia that we use today.

By the time Ongulumbashe happened, the first confrontation between black political elements and the South African Police had already taken place a few years before. That was late 1959, when the residents of Windhoek's Katatura township were moved from their homes by force. Guns and dogs at the ready, a detachment of police moved into Katatura and ordered the community to pack its bags and get out. Incensed, the locals resorted to reacting with chunks of iron, slings, *knobkieries* and stones. In the clash that followed, ten rioters were shot dead.

The media, never shy to exploit something that was obviously newsworthy at a time when South Africa's racial policies were increasingly spotlighted abroad, the cameras were there as well. Overnight, the world was given some very graphic examples of Pretoria's brutal response towards a nation that it had been entrusted to protect by a mandate originally issued by the League of Nations.

The message was clear: this was an oppressed people "fighting for its rights". For the future SWAPO leader and the rest of his team, there was no looking back. Among those arrested at the old Katatura that day was Sam Nujoma himself, but he paid his fine in a Windhoek court and fled the country to take up the cudgels abroad and fight another day.

That was followed by an invitation to the SWAPO hierarchy from *Osajyefo* Kwame Nkrumah himself to attend what was termed a Freedom Fighters' Conference at Wineba, Ghana. Only months later, PLAN – the movement's military wing – was established. SWAPO had become a reality and its hopeful adherents basked under a new kind of nomenclature that included the term "freedom fighter".

Within about a year, almost 1,000 new recruits had left the country for training abroad. Many were students granted scholarships in just about every country in Europe, as well as quite a few behind the Iron Curtain. The largest group went to Moscow. Eastern Bloc nations provided the bulk of SWAPO's military training with intensive instruction in the sabotage of rail links and trains, the idea being to interdict troop and fuel trains. They were given the basics relating to mines and booby traps, many similar to those then being deployed against the Americans in Vietnam.

South African troopie early in the war on border duty. (Photo: Author's collection)

Concurrently, SWAPO's leadership was restructured along international lines with the appointment of foreign as well as domestic leadership elements. Offices were opened in the Tanzanian capital and in Egypt. While all this was taking place, more recruits were being processed for military training in Russia, Red China, Ghana, Algeria and North Korea and by 1965 almost 200 of these novice fighters had returned to Dar es Salaam for posting to camps adjacent to South West Africa, some in Angola and Zambia. Instructions were sent to recruit still more "volunteers" on home ground.

Sam Nujoma's original strategy was to have what was termed "a well-trained, fully fledged army" ready to take the military initiative within South West Africa's borders by the end of the summer rains in 1966. Initially the idea was to target tribal leaders, replacing, in the Marxist tradition, those who had been murdered, with party stalwarts before infiltrating southwards towards Grootfontein. About this time, the record shows, he envisaged several supply bases in Caprivi (which would also be used as both an infiltration and escape route to Zambia).

Documents that surfaced not long afterwards indicate that the rebels were confident that once the revolution got hold, the entire South West African nation would rise up in revolt. With a bit of prodding from Moscow, the leaders were confident that Pretoria would accede to SWAPO's demand of full independence and withdraw its troops to positions on the south bank of the Orange River. Nujoma was so convinced that this would happen that he even set a date: April 1966. On that day, he declared in a clandestine broadcast beamed into the territory, he and his governing entourage would arrive in Windhoek, by air no less.

However, long before that happened, many of the movement's international and internal leadership had been either betrayed or arrested. One immediate consequence was that four months before all this was supposed to have taken place, only 16 insurgents were picked to infiltrate south-westwards from Zambia. Another group of 20 fighters under Tobias Hainjeko – part of the original invasion group – were held up at their Zambian base because the money intended for them had disappeared into somebody's pocket somewhere along the way from Tanzania.

Significantly, Rhodesia's war had also tentatively taken off in April 1966, with the first spate of terror attacks in the Sinoia area.

It was about then that reports started to emerge from some of those arrested about the presence of a permanent base on South West African soil. The name Ongulumbashe also appeared on a few

SWAPO documents that reached Police Headquarters in Pretoria. (In the Othiherero language it was spelt Omugulu-gOmbashe, which means "leg of the giraffe").

Interestingly, in the years before the real war started, there was a lot of wild-life in Ovamboland. Police documents talk of herds of wildebeest meandering past their camps and, occasionally, elephants. There was enough antelope to keep a minor insurgent army supplied with red meat.

But in other respects, Ovamboland was among the most backward of any of the regions in which Pretoria had an interest.

At Ondangua – soon to become the busiest military airport on the African continent – the entire expatriate community comprised a police station with two married officers and about a dozen unmarried NCOs and other ranks. There was also what was termed at the time a Bantu Affairs Commissioner: a political appointee from Pretoria, together with his entourage as well as a handful of others.

All that the nearby village of Oshakati could boast about at the time was its state hospital with two white doctors, two nursing sisters and a handful of assistants, again all state-appointed. Their Ovambo staff was in the majority. Oshakati was also home to the Ovambo Commissioner General, a couple of technicians attached to Water Affairs and a white "postmaster", who, anywhere else, would have been regarded as little more than a glorified postman. If he handled a thousand letters a month, it was a lot.

Bush patrols following SWAPO's incursion into the northern reaches of South West Africa were the everyday norm for most of the troops. (Photo: Author)

Chapter 12
SWAPO's first attacks in South West Africa

The actual war in South West Africa began with an attack by six SWAPO terrorists who killed a Portuguese shop owner and four others (almost all of them bystanders) at the Ovambo village of Odimbo. It was a silly mistake because the village was actually in Angola.

The original idea had been to get funds for the movement and locals had put out the word that the store owner was "fabulously wealthy". That he worked from dawn to dusk and lived in a grimy shack in what were clearly grim circumstances, didn't register with this gang of criminals who, for good measure, murdered another shopkeeper as well. Worse, the second victim, an Ovambo, was one of their people. Also gunned down were three African bystanders. For all that bloodshed, the killers got the equivalent of about $200, which was all the money in the trader's strongbox.

Having accepted that both their geography and navigational skills were lacking, it wasn't long before the group had crossed into South West Africa near Rundu. There they were arrested, not by the authorities but by local tribesmen. Unceremoniously, the group was handed over to the police.

More isolated attacks in the region followed, including one on the tiny Oshikango border post in September and, two months later, attacks on two Ovambo tribal leaders. By December a small SWAPO strike force had ambushed a farm owner in the Grootfontein area. By then too, the first of many landmine incidents that were to follow were recorded, both in Ovamboland and in Caprivi, further towards the east.

By the end of that year, a total of eight SWAPO insurgents had been killed and 59 taken into custody. Though still at a low level of intensity, something resembling a war had started.

By now, South African security elements had recruited a few spies of their own, including Major Leonard Shuuya, alias "Castroli", an insurgent defector who had completed his training abroad and entered the country from Zambia. While Shuuya told his new bosses that he was extremely well connected within the SWAPO command, he wasn't too explicit about what he'd been doing until then, or even where he had been for the previous two or three years. What was clear was that he had been trained abroad and he gave as his reason for defecting that communism, per se, disillusioned him.

What should have rung a bell early on, but didn't, was the fact that Shuuya suddenly appeared out of nowhere and offered his services to the security police. He was able to prove fairly early on that he had solid links to people like Herman Ja-Toivo, one of the early revolutionary leaders and as a result somebody in Pretoria was impressed enough to get him taken on in the force.

Encouraged to maintain and further his ties, Shuuya was also tasked with finding the location of the permanent base that Pretoria was aware of having been established somewhere in Ovamboland. For several months he travelled extensively with elements of the SWAPO underground, at one stage even visiting Windhoek. He was authorised to handle money and issue instructions in the name of the SWAPO command, something he couldn't have done if he wasn't kosher. Indeed, it was he who instructed Comrade Nankudhu, the original commander, to dig defensive trenches all the way around the camp and to prepare the cave which was to be used to cache weapons. The idea of camouflaging it from outside was also his.

As a traitor, Shuuya didn't always make sense to his SAP handlers. At one stage he inexplicably disappeared into Zambia and for a couple of months wasn't able to account for all his movements. There is some evidence that he spent part of the time back in Dar es Salaam planning for the next phase of his role in the counter-revolutionary struggle. At very least, Shuuya's actions as a spy were erratic, and sometimes made little sense, because although it was only discovered later that he was a double agent (and had twice warned the insurgent commander at Ongulumbashe that they were about to be attacked) he quickly gained the trust of the South Africans by accurately pinpointing the camp's location. The area was subsequently discreetly overflown by a SAAF Cessna: it finally confirmed its position and took aerial photographs.

With that, Pretoria set in motion its own sequence of events. The first was to plan for the attack. Immediately afterwards a small force of security police was sent into the territory under a cover story of having to make preparations for the erection of a radio station. They put the word out that they were doing surveys necessary for erecting transmitting masts throughout the area and several times even approached local chiefs about hiring "strong young men" who would be able to help with construction. Interestingly, there were no takers.

The group moved about western Ovamboland for several weeks, very much aware that they were under surveillance. Several times their camps were visited by senior Ovambo headmen and they were questioned about their intentions. But the South Africans stuck to their story: most working days were intensively spent in their newfound roles.

At this stage, the group visited a local mission station run by Finnish nationals: there must have been a dozen such stations throughout the area. A subsidiary idea was to try to establish some kind of connection between the SWAPO leadership and the Finns, of which Pretoria was aware but never able to conclusively prove.

To the surprise of the South Africans, the mother superior greeted them in fluent Afrikaans. Clearly sceptical, she asked them what exactly they were doing in the area. Not satisfied with their answer, she started berating the South Africans for not granting the Ovambo people their independence. When the visitors requested water, she refused, saying that she and her charges had too little of their own. Things were getting tight. The unusual South African "radio mast" presence had generated a lot of suspicion, coupled to pretty obvious surveillance efforts on the part of the Ovambos.

With the position of the camp confirmed, Pretoria issued an order to prepare for the attack.

Meanwhile six SAAF Alouettes had already been made ready for action: on 22 August, all were partially dismantled and airlifted to Rooikop army base near Walvis Bay in SAAF C-130s. A couple of days later the entire force flew by a circuitous route to Ruacana, where they were joined by two more Alouettes, then operating out of Windhoek's Eros Airport.

On the ground, events started to gather a momentum of its own. Three more C-130s arrived at Ruacana with three 3-ton SADF Bedford trucks (painted to look like civilian vehicles) together with the weapons and ammunition needed for the operation as well as the rest of the strike force: their numbers included radio communication as well as medical elements. In overall charge of the attack was police Brigadier P.J. Dillon, with Air Force and Korean War veteran Colonel Jan Blaauw responsible for air operations. This was the same man who was awarded the American Silver Star, the highest US award to members of foreign armed services for bravery in rescuing one of his pilots who had been shot down behind enemy lines[3].

Also seconded to Brig Dillon's staff was Major W.H.J.F. Paetzold, GSO2 South West Africa Command.

Curiously, the SWAPO defector Shuuya had also been busy. On 24 August, immediately after returning from a night-time recce of the terrorist camp, he sent a letter to the Ongulumbashe camp commander not only telling him that his camp was about to be targeted, but he also gave him the exact timing. It was to take place at dawn two days later.

The reconnaissance of Ongulumbashe is notable for the fact that it was the first time that an insurgent camp was actually reconnoitred by whites. Two SAP officers, Major Theunis Swanepoel and Warrant Officer Piet Ferreira (who was promoted to Lieutenant soon afterwards), together with two Ovambos, Shuuya and a black SAP Sergeant, E.K. Johannes, left base at Ruacana early in the afternoon of the 22 August. They had to cover a distance of about 60 kilometres, two-thirds of it by truck, literally bundu-bashing through a thickly overgrown area to avoid Ovambo settlements in the area.

The final stage took place after dark, with everybody in old clothes and the whites disguised (with the help of shoe polish) as Ovambos. That lasted several hours, with the two black men keeping to footpaths and their officers walking parallel, but about 20 metres out into the bush on either side of the lead pair. Several times they encountered locals walking in the opposite direction and the policemen would melt further into the bush.

That first night was a disaster. Although they traced and retraced their steps, Shuuya was not able to get them to the camp. Early the following morning and for the rest of the day, the group laid up in thick bush. They finally got to Ongulumbashe about three hours after dark on the second night.

Armed with sub-machine guns which they secreted under their coats while on the march, the foursome immediately split up, with Major Swanepoel and Shuuya creeping forward on their hands and knees until they were about 20 metres from the perimeter. Immediately ahead of them they spotted their first sentry, armed with an AK. The guard moved around the camp in a circular pattern. Beyond him, they could hear voices: there were obviously a lot of people there.

About a half-an-hour later everything in the camp went quiet. Then somebody switched on a radio and they listened to a transmission from Radio Tanzania in English and for the duration, the major lay flat on his stomach. The broadcast over, he and Shuuya joined the others and they made their way back to base where they reported back to Colonel Dillon.

It was then that the overall commander had to make a decision. He had the option of attacking Ongulumbashe with the force being ferried in by vehicles from the tiny Ovambo settlement of Otshande (about 25 kilometres from the target) but the disadvantage there, was that there were many villages along the way that might sound the alarm. Or their dogs could give them away. Like most tribes, the Ovambos still used drums to send their messages and there would have been enough time for those in the camp, having been tipped off, to bombshell and head back across the border.

The colonel finally settled on using the helicopters, a logical alternative since just about everybody involved had been training with choppers for the past two days. And instead of rappelling out of the helicopters, as had originally been suggested, the troops would simply jump out in full gear from a meter or two above the ground. The order went out and the group prepared for action.

For some days already there had been intensive training under the command of a youthful Parachute Regiment officer Captain (later Colonel) Jan Breytenbach. He vigorously put the men through their paces with classes and practical demonstrations in the handling of the R1 rifle as well as hand-carbines, day and night route marches, navigation in the bush as well as the full gambit of counter-insurgent techniques, or as much of what was known about the subject at that early stage. This was a thorough and intensive phase. It might also have set the scene, inadvertently perhaps, for the subsequent establishment of South Africa's much-vaunted Reconnaissance Regiments.

Meanwhile, on 24 August, Comrade Johannes Otto Nankudhu got Shuuya's latest letter warning of the imminent attack. The commander immediately called for a war council with all foreign-trained SWAPO members in the base. The debate that followed – loud and vituperative on occasion as arguments were sometimes ridiculed and often shouted down – lasted most of the day.

Several members of the group were convinced that being in such an isolated area, the police would never find the camp. Other argued that even if the "Boers" arrived by truck, they would be able to put up a stiff resistance before disappearing into the bush. However, Nankudhu gave the order that if that were to happen, the men were to grab their things, and with that the insurgents got their possessions and weapons together, hid some of it in the bush and settled down to see what the morning would bring.

Preparations for the attack were finally completed on the evening of 25 August.

By then all eight helicopters had been serviced and, for a final check, test-flown. Also, to avoid any possible confusion that this might be a military operation, all eight Alouettes were given SAP call signs and the police crest prominently painted on their fuselages. In addition, SADF personnel involved wore police gear. The three "civilian" Bedfords were readied for action and the entire "small

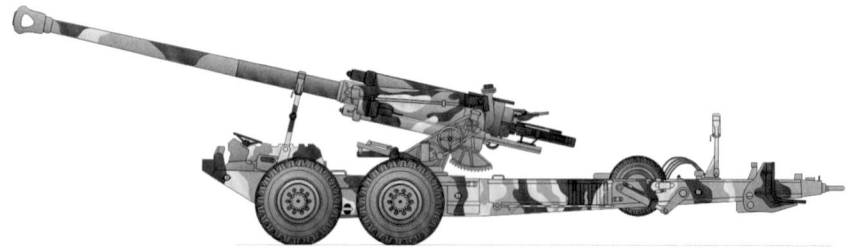

Within a comparatively short time following the first SWAPO incursions (which was followed by Operation Savannah), South African engineers started work on a range of new weapons that included what was soon accepted as one of the best artillery weapons in any man's army, the 155 mm G-5. That was followed by the G-6 motorised version. (Illustration & photo: Pierre Victor)

force" given its final briefing just before sunset.

As soon as it became dark, a dozen members of the police backup, together with the four members that made up the operator's radio and medical team, set out by road for Ongulumbashe. Their orders were to pull off the road 18 kilometres from the target and set up a temporary base in the bush until an hour or so before daybreak.

With the 29-man attack force the choppers – all with troops, except the command and control chopper – left Ruacana for Ongulumbashe just before seven in the morning. They moved in light formation along the border with Angola to the point where it dissected with the irrigation canal out of the Kunene. From there on in, it was south all the way. Perhaps ten minutes later they were directly above the terrorist base. Colonel Blaauw fired a signal flare that the attack should begin.

By now the Alouettes were already taking incoming fire, but having moved into set positions around the circumference of Ongulumbashe, they immediately put men on the ground. The first priority, apart from returning fire which was heavy to begin with, was the establishment of a blocking cordon that extended all the way round the base about 400 metres out. Each section had its own radio and was in contact with the others, as well as with top cover.

From the start it was clear that the Nankudhu group had been surprised. There had been no warning and no indication that anything untoward was happening until they heard rotors and the flare that followed moments later. What emerged afterwards in the debrief, was that in spite of Shuuya's warnings, some of the insurgents were still asleep when the Alouettes arrived overhead.

Comrade Nankudhu's first reaction was to order his troops to disperse into the bush, though this was already difficult because quite a few were hit in the first salvos fired by the attackers, including James Hamowayo, who took two shots in the chest from an FN rifle. He was eventually flown back to South Africa and hospitalised at Voortrekkerhoogte Military Hospital. Brought to trial later, he ended it all by hanging himself in his cell in Pretoria Central.

By now, something of a pattern had emerged among the attackers. The exchange of fire had become sporadic. There were also a number of insurgents wounded and those that could be patched up were walked or carried to a temporary casevac station established in the middle of the camp by Colonel Klomp, a doctor who went in with the first wave. Meanwhile, two choppers were ordered back to the trucks to fetch the rest of the medical and radio teams.

Other helicopters extended their search range beyond the *cordon sanitaire* and Captain Jan Breytenbach apprehended one of the insurgents who had fled north after cornering him in a thicket. Three more were spotted on the run and moving in the general direction of Angola. Although a strike team went after them, only one was killed while returning fire. The other two got away.

Firing stopped about 30 minutes later. The SWAPO group had one wounded and eight captured. For their part, the South Africans suffered no casualties.

Nobody is quite certain what eventually happened to the SWAPO double agent Shuuya. The fact that he had warned that an attack would take place, emerged in the cross-questioning of some of the prisoners. He was never arrested, but the man vanished again immediately after Operation Blouwildebees, probably back to Zambia. And although the police used him in an operation after he returned to South West Africa in 1970, he disappeared again, this time for good. Having been exposed as a spy, he was probably "taken out" by one of the SAP special squads like Koevoet. What you won't find today is anybody who might be prepared to comment on the matter.

Interestingly, the day on which that first attack took place, August 26, was declared a public holiday in Namibia shortly after independence.

1 Paul Els: *Ongulumbashe – Where the Bushwar Began*: 290 pages, order direct from the author at paul@who-els.co.za.
2 Al J. Venter: *Coloured: A Profile of Two Million South Africans*, Human & Rousseau, Cape Town, 1970.
3 SAAF pilot Jan Blaauw in the Korean War led a four-Mustang mission into an area north of Seoul, then heavily protected by communist forces. During the raid, his wing man Vernon Kruger was shot down. Blaauw stayed to provide top cover against encroaching enemy troops. Eventually, because he had run out of fuel, Blaauw crash-landed his plane alongside where his buddy had taken refuge. He dressed Kruger's burns, prepared a landing pad with stones and waited for a rescue helicopter to arrive, which came soon afterwards. The full story is contained in Dermot Moore and Peter Bagshawe's epic book *South Africa's Flying Cheetahs in Korea*, Ashanti Publishing, Johannesburg, 1991.
4 http://www.nshr.org.na/modules.php?op=modload&name=News&file=article&sid=128

CHAPTER THIRTEEN

WAITING IN THE GROUND IN KOSOVO FOR THE DEMINERS

> There's an aphorism about landmines in the Balkans. The Good Lord, say the Croats, created Hell. The Serbs reciprocated and devised the PROM-1, the worst in bounding, anti-personnel mines and not very much bigger than a beer can. A vicious weapon, its shrapnel can penetrate almost any body armour and cut through the average Kevlar helmet like cardboard, as it does often enough among those who try to clear these deadly little bombs. Until recently, Kosovo was full of them …
>
> Al J. Venter went into the Balkans twice during the war: once with the United States Air Force in a Joint-STARS operation (detailed in his book *Barrell of a Gun*) and, after hostilities ended, he visited some of the Serbian minefields where he was able to observe the landmine threat from up close.

There aren't many mine-clearing specialists working in the Balkans who don't have a favourite story about the PROM-1. By the time the Allies have cleared all those laid in Kosovo, there will be a stash more. But that will take a while.

The Yugoslav PROM-1 is a deadly and menacing all-purpose, anti-personnel mine, even if it is dislodged and ends up on its side. This mine has killed or injured more clearance personnel in the Balkans than all the other Yugoslav mines combined. The worst in bounding, anti-personnel bombs were laid in many parts of Bosnia and Croatia and elsewhere in the Balkans where war raged, though mine-clearing operations are finally having some affect.

When one of the teams working there is lucky enough to spot one before it "finds" them (and sometimes there are several, usually laid in clusters) the word is whispered down the line and most of those on the ground will wait to see what action is taken. Obviously, all mines must be cleared and that's official. How this is done tends to focus the mind, because the PROM-1 is among the most lethal.

After Dayton, there were a lot of casualties among those trying to clear PROM-1s. In the words of one American specialist, "They're a bitch to disarm. We just like to blow 'em where we find 'em." As he also said, PROM-1s are difficult to spot, especially when the ground is thick with grass and shrubs, as it is in the summer in Kosovo. The business part that protrudes above the ground can fit in the palm of your hand.

In recent years, during the course of a succession of Balkan wars, it quickly became apparent that most PROM-1s were so unstable that the only way to handle them was to destroy them on site. Anything else was invariably a disaster. You only need to brush against any one of its tiny prongs and it's over. When that happens, the bounding mine is hurled a couple of feet into the air and kills everything nearby.

According to Colonel Richard Todd, a 23-year American Special Forces veteran with experience in mines and ordnance dating back to Vietnam, you have about a 60 per cent chance of being killed if you are within 50 metres of the explosion. "It happens so fast," he explained, "most of those involved aren't even aware of what happened."

Todd worked with mines in the Balkans for several years and explained why the PROM-1 is so dangerous. "Unlike the 'popular' Yugoslav PMA-2 – the blast mine you find just about everywhere in Bosnia, Croatia and Kosovo – the PROM-1 is a group fragmentation mine, originally designed around the original German 'S' mine which caused terrible damage in World War II. The Allies notoriously dubbed it the 'Bouncing Betty', but that's the kind of language carried over from the Vietnam era and is in little use today among mine-clearing specialists," he declared.

"What makes the PROM-1 different from others is its devastating effect when it blows...it can possibly be likened to a proximity fuse on a mortar or artillery shell exploding a few feet above the ground," he stated. "And because it can be laid with multiple trip wires, it soon became the rather obvious weapon of choice among the Serbs...they like it because a single PROM-1 can take out a group of people, or disable a squad of soldiers on patrol," he said.

"Towards the end of the war, it was increasingly used in urban areas, and to pretty deadly effect … they were laying them in Kosovo as if they had a licence to do so," he said.

Small as it is, the PROM-1 – a bottle-shaped, olive green, cast-steel mine – is a complex device. Designated in the textbooks as a "buried, tripwire-activated, bounding anti-personnel fragmentation mine", the device weighs in at almost three kilos. Its half-kilo of embedded explosives is a combination of Trotyl and RDX in about equal proportions, while the fuse contains an integral percussion cap "which is what makes it so damned unstable," said one authority. Most of the people who have tried to disarm it have come short while fiddling with the business end.

There is also some controversy about its plastic-coated tripwire. Some say dogs can detect it and others reckon they can't. Usually the same colour as the terrain, tripwires are difficult to spot under the best conditions and the Kosovo Liberation Army had major problems because of the foliage. A large proportion of the casualties taken by that guerrilla group before the Allies went in, was from mines, some PMA-2s but also PROM-1s.

The problem is that, once tripped, it is impossible to differentiate between the small blast that lifts the bomb out of the ground and the full effect of the explosion, which is devastating. More uncommon versions of the same mine, such as the PROM-1P and PROM-2 tend to bound a little higher, but they kill just as efficiently.

"Some mean weapon, and not to be trifled with," Todd warned. He was head of the UN Mine Action Team in Zagreb at the time of our visit and had files full of PROM-1 incidents, a lot of which made for grim reading. Despite multiple warnings, he told us, casualties with PROM-1s continue to take place. A crack international mine-clearing team working under UN auspices in Croatia had one of its members killed shortly after we were there.

Operating with dogs in what was termed "an area reduction programme", the operator couldn't have spotted the one that either he or his sniffer dog tripped. Two shards of shrapnel penetrated his brain and he was killed instantly. Miraculously his dog, working only yards away, was unscathed.

Almost all the countries that once comprised the old Yugoslavia and that have seen military action in recent years have problems with landmines. In parts of Bosnia it is still dangerous to venture off the road. The same holds for Croatia. A succession of minefields, some Serbian, others laid by the Croat Army, stretch almost the entire length of the country in a half-moon pattern that extends over 800 kilometres. The minefields run from Vukovar in the north-east to the Montenegro border further south. Only the narrow coastal corridor between Sibenik and Sipa remains uncontaminated.

While there are minefields in dozens of other countries, those in the Balkans seem to have acquired a notoriety of their own. What the Serbs did with mines in Croatia and Bosnia, they repeated in Kosovo. It is also no secret that Croatian minefields became the subject of close study by a variety of NATO security and intelligence organisations, because all the major powers are aware that this sort of thing could happen again.

The reality of that lot is that the Serbs have been doing this kind of thing for decades, and their weapons, mines included, are good value to those who need these things. By the early 1990s, Yugoslavia was earning $2 billion a year from weapons sales, mostly from Third World buyers. Even today, it is easy to buy any number of Yugoslav mines in East European arms bazaars.

Like it or not, some mines, like the PROM-1 and the anti-tank TMRP-6 (and TMRP-7) as well as the full range of TMA mines, are as good as anything produced in the West. UN mine-clearing teams are encountering Yugoslav mines in just about every international trouble spot, and that includes places like Angola, Cambodia, Afghanistan, Ethiopia and Mozambique, often in very substantial quantities. In Kosovo, until fairly recently, landmines were arguably the single most serious obstacle to resettling the region. As someone suggested, "mines are cheap, need no food ... moreover they remain silent, inactive and potent for years. And landmines have the ability to do great damage."

Mine-clearing teams who worked under UN or World Bank auspices in Bosnia and Croatia made a number of observations about Balkan minefields. Clearing them often involved (and in some instances, still involves) complex and sometimes frightening problems. More to the point, some of those doing the work are getting hurt. There have been numerous fatalities. "There is simply no magic bullet for clearing landmines," Todd reckoned.

"In order to do the job effectively, you need to draw from a 'toolbox' of three fundamental disciplines. These are human and mechanical deminers, as well as dogs trained to find them. None of these assets on its own can do the job properly ... you need the one to check the efficiency of the other."

Nor are these disciplines either free or inexpensive. "It costs money to run and maintain a decent demining operation. The specialists doing the job come at a price and so does the insurance to cover them in case of an accident. Similarly, you constantly need to train more people to do the job ... that, too, costs money," he stated.

By the time that we got to the Balkans, there were then a number of countries clearing mines, all involved in seven-figure dollar contracts and usually linked to foreign aid. In Croatia, the Russians were followed by Italy, Germany, Israel, the Netherlands, the United States' RONCO (an American company involved in mine and UXO clearing) as well as Mechem of South Africa. In addition, there were at least a dozen Croatian firms, which included Mungos, said to be one of the largest companies in the world specialising in this sort of work.

Mechem, following contracts in Angola and Mozambique, operated with a project leader plus seven: that included two team leaders, a pair of dog handlers, a driver/mechanic and a couple of demolition specialists with Johan "Sakkie" van Zyl running the show. As he explained, all his men had good military experience and almost all had been trained in trauma medicine. "There have been times when these attributes have been handy," he explained.

The men worked seven days a week until the contract – in this case 60 days – was complete. To save money, they lived rough, usually starting their day at six and working through to seven or eight at night. They would eat something before they started work and the next meal was often only after they were done for the day. Time lost to rain was made up afterwards.

Operating under contract with this foreign mine-clearing team were 40 Croat deminers headed by four team leaders. Additional crews (according to Croatian law) included two each of doctors, medics, drivers, dog handlers and ambulances, plus an interpreter, all of whom had to be paid by the contract company, in this case Mechem. In Van Zyl's view, it was a massive waste of money because most of these people simply hung about and did absolutely nothing.

Other companies were similarly bound by red tape, which most foreign contractors believed was a legacy of the old Yugoslavia's socialist mindset. It didn't take any observer long to see that the majority of ancillary personnel were superfluous, but there was nothing they could do about it. Foreign mine-clearing specialists with whom I spoke, said that while the quality of Croatian mine-clearing was good, their rate of clearance was mediocre; again, reflecting residual communist ways.

Almost all expatriates who would talk about it ventured that if they had been able to bring their own people into the country to do the work, they would have been able to eliminate much of the crap. And the job would have been completed in half the time …

There were several categories of mine-clearing in the Balkans. The first was humanitarian. Consequently, most effort was invested into commercial projects, with economic goals such as the one around Gospic, about 180 kilometres south of Zagreb. This involved clearing anti-tank (AT) and anti-personnel (AP) mines around the only rail link running from the capital to the southern coastal cities of Split and Dubrovnik.

The problem here was that contractually, clearance only extended to 15 metres on either side of the line, which meant that minefields fringing the line – some of them extending many hectares – remained uncleared because there was simply no money. The World Bank gave Zagreb a $7 million loan for clearing the bombs and because the money eventually had to be repaid, the Croats weren't falling over themselves to get the job done.

While it was clear that the mine-clearing teams had a handle on the job, the civilians who lived and worked in these areas did not. After the first year of operations, their casualties hardly made the national news. A few days before I arrived in Gospic, a local was killed after tripping a PROM-1 within a hundred metres of the rail station while walking home from work. A huge hole gouged from the turf was still visible while mine-clearers worked around the spot. There wasn't a newspaper in Zagreb that carried the report.

While driving on some isolated country roads around that town, we were told that another problem facing mine-clearing teams was the lack of patience among local residents to finish the job. Pointing to fresh tractor tracks on both sides of the road, my guide explained that quite often the farmers did not even wait for them to complete the job. "They just drive around and occasionally they'll trip a TMRP-6, which can reduce a three-ton truck to scrap." Or their animals do it for them, he added: the Gospic countryside was littered with the bones of dead cattle and horses and apparently it was much the same in Kosovo where locals were anxious to get back into their old routines again.

One of the more difficult problems in the heart of the Balkan countryside was coping with natural growth of foliage and bush. After five years of waiting for the mines to be cleared, some parts of what had once been farmland had almost reverted to forest. Consequently, before any clearance could be done, small trees had to be removed to allow teams to haul in their equipment.

In some places the undergrowth was so thick, it had become impossible to work there. Also, it was dangerous. Everybody involved in this business was aware that mines laid a decade before did not, with time, become inactive. Van Zyl was considering hiring a Caterpillar tractor to help him clear the terrain, though he wasn't at all certain what the authorities would say or how the owners of the machine would react.

One of the observations during our visit was that because the region in which the Mechem team worked lay on a main road heading towards the Dalmatian Coast on the Adriatic, the town of Gospic was often crowded with German and Scandinavian cars heading south for summer. Very few of these people were aware that there were mines in the surrounding countryside, and the reason was simple: Zagreb did not allow the authorities to put out any warning signs, nor does it do so today.

Consequently, said a UN official, most people passing through the country and perhaps picnicking en route, have no idea that they might have stopped on the edge of a minefield. "Sometimes I see cars parked with children playing in the nearby fields. It's only a question of time before there is a disaster," he intimated.

Most of the minefields, both Serbian and Croatian, are mapped. Todd made the point that just about every day he received calls from former Yugoslav soldiers offering him information about old minefields. "There is a price, of course," he continued. "Some want cash, others try to use it as leverage to return to their old homes."

It was notable, travelling about Croatia, that every third or fourth house or farm that we passed had been broken down, burnt or trashed. All had formerly belonged to a very large Serbian community that lived there before the war and most of the families had been there for centuries. Like the Albanian Kosovars, almost all had become refugees.

Postscript: *Since visiting the Mechem operation around Gospic, the company finished its contract and in that two-month time frame, they were able to lift about 60 mines, of which about two-thirds were anti-personnel. There were no casualties in that period. The contract, though comparatively small by international mine-clearing standards, was worth $1,3 million and was also the largest single mine-clearing contract to be awarded in Croatia that year. Mechem subsequently tendered for two more mine-clearing projects, both successfully as it turned out. One was in the north-east of the country near the Hungarian border, which Van Zyl reckoned was "a bastard of a job because of all the booby traps". The other was close to the Dalmatian coast, to the immediate west of Gospic.*

1   Al J. Venter: *Barrel of a Gun*, Casemate Publishers, Philadelphia US and Newbury, UK, 2010, Chapter 26. pp 455 – 466.

CHAPTER FOURTEEN

GUNSHIP FOR HIRE: SIERRA LEONE (AUGUST 2000)

"If we ever catch you, we'll cut out your heart and eat it!": a very real threat made by people who are to be taken seriously – the rebels of Sierra Leone's Revolutionary United Front (RUF). The intended victim that time was Neall Ellis. To those involved in this secretive business, Ellis is a "private military contractor". To the rest of the world, he is a mercenary who pilots a helicopter gunship.

> Australian Broadcasting Corporation's Mark Corcoran reports from West Africa after flying with Neall Ellis in a helicopter gunship foray against the rebels in Sierra Leone.

Ellis had been living with this threat for five years by the time we met for the first time at Paddy's Bar in Freetown.

In Sierra Leone, Paddy's is the watering hole of choice for mercenaries, spooks, peacekeepers and aid workers, all the usual suspects who seemingly materialise at every Third World conflict, now spilling out of this noisy, sweaty, open-sided shed, perched above the appropriately named Pirate Bay on Freetown harbour.

It is a typical Paddy's night, reverberating to dance music, war stories and bar girls on the make. All the clichés of airport fiction, straight from the pages of the Frederick Forsyth's novel *The Dogs of War*. Except here it is all very real, and the patrons of Paddy's are doing their best to intoxicate themselves against the horrifying reality that lies outside.

This port city was founded in the 18th Century by freed slaves from America. The mood and look of the streets seems more Caribbean than African.

Nursing a large beer, Ellis explains that his opponents in this latest dirty war are best described as Africa's Khmer Rouge, without the ideology. The RUFs only clear objective seems to be controlling the country's fabulously rich diamond fields.

Even by the brutal standards of African civil wars, this conflict is terrifying. The RUFs trademark punishment is amputation or worse. Out in the darkness that night, just beyond the bright lights of Paddy's Bar, are the camps and slums, home to thousands of men, women and children who have had arms, legs and even lips hacked off by teenage rebels.

Ellis talks about it all in a dispassionate tone – much the same way he reflects on the country's unpredictable tropical weather – which can be just as deadly to a helicopter pilot.

This bespectacled, 50-something South African is totally unassuming. He displays none of the "hard-man" qualities that make him a legend in mercenary circles. Short and stocky, he has, like so many South African mercenaries, the air of a social rugby player on tour, perhaps a Johannesburg dentist, cutting loose for a couple of weeks away with the boys.

But his reality is quite different. Ellis is a former South African colonel. One of the world's most experienced combat helicopter pilots, he fought in apartheid South Africa's toughest and dirtiest battles, flying gunship missions in support of a variety of feared Special Forces units at the forefront of Pretoria's secret war against Black Africa's frontline states, which included 32 Battalion, Koevoet, the Parabats as well as South Africa's crack, long range-penetration Recce Commandos.

In Angola he was the only helicopter pilot to survive being targeted simultaneously by three surface-to-air missiles, fired by Cubans, who lived to fly another day. He also, single-handedly at the controls of the Mi-24 gunship, forced major rebel concentrations away from the gates of Freetown. Twice!

When apartheid ended, most of these military specialists quit the army, effectively privatising to form the nucleus of Executive Outcomes which quickly established a reputation as perhaps the most ruthlessly efficient private army in the world. Ellis also resigned, at first trying his hand at farming and commercial fishing, before being lured back to "the job", signing on as a soldier of fortune in Bosnia and the Congo.

He was then lured to Sierra Leone by an offer from Executive Outcomes and, afterwards, by the similarly minded British outfit Sandline – all big names in the mercenary world. These days they prefer to be called Private Military Companies, or, as operators sometimes prefer, Private Security Companies.

To paraphrase one mercenary executive, "The dogs of war now live in a corporate kennel." Ellis agrees: "The job, I think, is the same, but the image has changed. Now it's suits and briefcases. You are more professional. I think the days of the Congo and Angola, when you had the image of mercenaries as drunken guys going around shooting up the place and having a fine time has long gone. The people involved now, generally speaking, are well-trained professional soldiers, the majority with Special Forces experience."

Ellis is keen to display the "new professionalism" of his calling. A few days after our drink at Paddy's, we're on the helipad at Cockerill Barracks, the Freetown HQ of the Sierra Leone Army at Aberdeen, on the eastern fringe of the capital. Cameraman Geoff Lye and I have been invited on a combat mission.

In the course of a nine-year civil war the rebels have defeated the national army and confounded two peacekeeping forces. Now in mid-2000, the guerrillas fear only one thing: what Neall Ellis calls his office – a Russian-built Mi-24 Hind helicopter gunship which he flies under contract to the Sierra Leone Army. With flying helmet in one hand and assault rifle in the other, Ellis strides towards the Hind helicopter which squats on the tarmac, not dissimilar to a large menacing camouflaged bullfrog.

Ellis boasts: "The RUF call this aircraft *Wor-Wor* boy. It means 'ugly' in the local Mende language and we're not arguing. They fear it, they are frightened of this aircraft whenever we get overhead. They used to shoot at us quite a bit, mostly small-arms fire, but now they run and duck for cover all over the place."

His nine-member team was recruited from around the world – a veritable United Nations of mercenaries. The mechanics scrambling over the helicopter making last-minute checks are Ethiopian. Loading a machine gun is Fijian Fred Marafano, a grim hulk of a man in his late fifties who served in the British SAS and won an MBE in London's Iranian Embassy hostage drama of the 1970s. The other door-gunner stacking ammunition is Christophe, a short, wiry Frenchman who insists that he's holidaying in Sierra Leone. Everyone wears flying suits, except Christophe. Determined to maintain his vacationer alibi, he fights in jeans and a T-shirt.

They've run out of ammunition for the big nose-mounted cannon, so there's no need for a co-pilot gunner on this mission. Ellis gestures that this vacant front seat should be occupied by Geoff and his camera. I'm to ride in the back with the door-gunners. Fuelled, armed and strapped in, we lurch off the helipad for a heart-stopping 160-mile-an hour ride, just a few feet above the jungle canopy.

Chapter 14
Gunship for hire: Sierra Leone (August 2000)

The Sierra Leone jungle is unforgiving to those not accustomed to this tropical backwater. Movement can be extremely difficult because much of the country is swampland and, in places, almost Vietnam at its worse. (Photo: Author)

"It makes it harder for them to hit us with a missile or rocket," offers one of the crew as reassurance. The rebels have just overrun an army-held village. Ellis has been called in "to sort it out". Rice paddies and coconut trees flash by, so close that I flinch, to the amusement of the door-gunners. The margin for error is zero. Our lives are in the hands of pilot Ellis. If he flinches, it will be all over in an instant.

The back of the helicopter is stacked with rifles and grenades. If we are forced down in a rebel area, there will be no prisoners, the crew will fight their way out, or die. Ellis's view: "If you do this job and worry about dying, then you should stay at home and do an eight-to-five job back in the First World."

The RUF rebels, vow to cut out the hearts of captured mercenaries is no idle threat. In 1995 the rebels ambushed a mercenary force of ex-Ghurkas led by a former American Colonel Robert MacKenzie who was wounded in the subsequent battle. According to eyewitness reports, MacKenzie was dragged back to the rebel base, horribly tortured in the presence of seven Roman Catholic nuns being held hostage and his heart carved out and eaten by the men who killed him. In a sense, it was a mark of respect: his killers believed that by their actions they would absorb MacKenzie's power and bravery.

"Five minutes to target," warns Ellis on the intercom.

Time enough to briefly ponder the ethical issues. If I survive a crash landing, should I pick up a weapon in self-defence, sure in the knowledge that as a European, the rebels will assume me to be a mercenary? Or will I maintain my non-combatant status to the end, hoping that some drugged and dreadlocked teenage rebel, going by the name Commander Superhero, will make the distinction between media and mercenary? I need not have worried.

Later, Ellis reveals that if Geoff and I were to face imminent capture, he'd given orders for the crew to shoot us. He smiles when he says this though I'm still not sure whether he was joking or not.

Smoke from burning houses marks the target village. "Are you going to fire?" asks Fred on the intercom.

Ellis: "I see them. I'm not sure if they are civilians or not ... there are not supposed to be any civilians here ... it's all supposed to be a rebel area."

Seconds later he unleashes hell. A volley of 80 mm rockets shreds a row of houses. "These rockets were used very effectively in Chechnya," says Ellis. Now they very effectively shred a row of houses and anyone hiding inside. "You can tell the difference between a rebel and a civilian, you get the feeling, you can discern," Ellis insists. Arbitrary decisions of life and death at more than 150 miles an hour.

The door-gunners open up, picking their targets with slow deliberate aim, tracer rounds arching towards the ground like a

There were many freebooters who joined the Sierra Leone Air Wing in the hope of seeing action, including this white mercenary "Christian" who regularly flew with Ellis in the Hind as a side-gunner. (Photo: Author)

deadly garden hose. There's no Hollywood bravado, just a cold clinical efficiency to it all. This is the business of contract killing.

To many it is morally reprehensible. Human Rights Watch accuses the crew of indiscriminately killing civilians by targeting marketplaces. Ellis says the RUF use villagers as human shields. If he's fired at, he shoots back.

"Rebels are carrying guns. Civilians aren't carrying guns. If a civilian is carrying a gun he is a rebel, so he is a target."

But the rebels are also armed with shoulder-fired missiles. Ellis takes no chances, throwing the aircraft around the sky. The floor is awash with hundreds of expended machine-gun shells, a sea of brass, rolling from side to side as the gunship lurches at high speed.

The crew spots figures huddling under a river bridge. The cabin shudders as another deafening rocket salvo is fired, the barrage sending sheets of water high into the air. "The rebels are terrified of this aircraft – when they see it they just run," says Ellis. From my position in the back of the gunship, it's impossible to determine what they're shooting at. All I see is the occasional flash of movement through the tree canopy below.

Then it's all over, and we're tree-hopping back to base, over villages where the people don't run away. They recognise *Wor-Wor* Boy, everybody smiling, waving and cheering for the unlikely saviours of Sierra Leone.

Fijian Fred, hunched over a still-smoking machine gun, is transformed. Minutes ago he was wild-eyed with controlled aggression. Now, he's a laughing, grandfatherly figure waving to the kids below. The other door-gunner, Christophe, remains expressionless. He stares blankly at the passing scenery. I wonder what these men dream about at night.

In one sense this is a mission of redemption for men more accustomed to being vilified. In other parts of Africa mercenaries are, with considerable justification, accused of perpetuating rather than ending conflicts. But here in Sierra Leone, they are for many, heroes who stood and fought when everyone else had fled.

Ellis and his crew first arrived in Sierra Leone in 1995. Like so many other mercenaries, he came for the money. Hired by Executive Outcomes, his crew joined a force that in just a few weeks drove the RUF out of the diamond fields and to the brink of defeat.

Then the soldiers of fortune were forced out of the country after allegations that the mercenaries were receiving diamond-mining concessions, dubbed "blood diamonds" as payment. Ellis claims this wasn't true. They'd demanded and received cold hard cash for their efforts.

"It was pressure from the international community for using a private military organisation," Ellis says. "I think the World Bank had some input on that. Executive Outcomes had just about achieved their aim when they were forced to leave."

The South Africans departed, replaced by more chaos and bloodshed. Eighteen months later Ellis was back, this time flying for the UK-based mercenary outfit Sandline International and providing air support to a West African intervention force. That contract also crashed amid political uproar in Britain, when it was revealed that Whitehall had tacitly approved Sandline's involvement, while publicly supporting a UN arms embargo on Sierra Leone.

Yet, when the pay cheques stopped, Ellis and Fijian Fred kept flying and fighting. At one stage he and the rest of the crew were owed more than a million US dollars by the Freetown government. But that didn't stop them doing what they believed was right.

With the rebels in the suburbs of Freetown and the West African peacekeepers in disarray, it was Ellis, at the controls of a lone helicopter, who was widely credited with saving the capital, driving

A Sierra Leone ground-crew services the four-barrelled 12.7 mm Gatling in the nose of the Mi-24 gunship. The gun often jammed and it was Al J.Venter's job to fire the cartridge mechanism that unjammed it, not always successfully. (Photo: Author)

the rebel columns from the city – but not before thousands were slaughtered – with many of the survivors wishing they too were dead; bloodied and limbless after encountering their RUF "liberators".

After the smoke had cleared in Freetown, and rhetoric in Whitehall ebbed, Sandline quietly gave Ellis the helicopter, an aging Russian Mi-17 – the military aviation's equivalent of a flying dump-truck – as payment in lieu. Although long overdue for a new engine, Ellis and crew used the overworked Hip that had been dubbed "Bokkie" by its original EO crew to evacuate almost a thousand civilian refugees in the face of the advancing rebel army.

Then, when "Bokkie" could do no more, Ellis says he simply parked the disintegrating, battle-damaged chopper on the tarmac at Freetown's Lungi Airport and walked away.

In turn, the West African peacekeeping debacle was replaced by international concern. Something must be done, declared the United Nations, suddenly horrified by the bloodbath. First World nations provided the angst, while it was left to the developing world to send the peacekeepers, a poorly equipped, faction-ridden force with no clear mandate that quickly found itself in the middle of a civil war with no peace to keep.

It was early in the year 2000 that Sierra Leone's tragic cycle repeated itself. The rebels took 500 peacekeepers hostage, and with the UN mission in chaos, were once more at the gates of Freetown.

A United Nations convention bans the use of mercenaries, yet Ellis, at the controls of *Wor-Wor*, came to the rescue of embattled UN units on several occasions, buying valuable time until Britain could land paratroopers to defend the city.

As one of the new breed of "corporate soldier", Ellis insists he only works for legitimate governments. But down in the jungle below us are others who work for the highest bidder. The rebels control most of the diamond fields, smuggling out up to $100 million worth of stones a year, so there's plenty of money for hired help.

"An Israeli and a Russian were arrested for giving assistance to the RUF rebels," he admits. A couple of Ellis's old comrades from South Africa are training the rebels. If they get in his way during a day at the office, "it's just bad luck".

While the Sierra Leone government is willing to hire "private military contractors", God help any foreigners caught working for the other side.

A senior Sierra Leone police intelligence officer later tells me that during a rebel assault on Freetown in 1999, his men captured six Ukrainians, acting as combat advisers to the RUF.

The senior officer reveals that the Ukraine government was formally notified, but denied any responsibility for the men. The officer says there was no hearing, no trial. The six were simply taken outside and shot. Government troops brought their heads back to the city, ostensibly for identification. Being a mercenary pays well, but only if you are on the winning side.

I raise this story with Neall Ellis shortly after we've landed safely back at base, but it's not something on which he wants to dwell. "I don't know that it was six ... I don't think anyone was actually arrested ... I don't know anything about that ..." Ellis stumbles, his quiet, assertive manner momentarily fails him.

Uncomfortable with his local hero status, Ellis acknowledges the moral ambiguity of his calling. Working for Zaire's President Mobutu Sese Seko in 1997, Ellis found himself on the losing side, his employer overthrown, and the helicopters he was supposed to fly inoperable because of a lack of spares. He and two others spent a week fleeing through the jungles on foot, outwitting a posse of rebels in hot pursuit. They eventually escaped across the Congo River in a stolen pirogue, having been robbed of everything but their underpants.

This adventure, certainly worth a film treatment, reinforced his legendary status among mercenaries, but perhaps also explains why he is so reluctant now to accept the mantle of Freetown's local hero. Mobutu was a murderous despot and Ellis was being paid to keep him in power.

As he shuts down the aircraft, and the ground crew sweep out the bullet casings, another helicopter with civilian markings lands nearby.

Two European men dressed in polo shirts and chinos stride towards us, beckoning Ellis over for a chat. They exude the purpose and manner of the social rugby set. It finally dawns on me why a group of mercenaries who once attempted to launch a coup in the Indian Ocean state of Seychelles attempted to infiltrate the country by posing as a touring rugby team. But there's no sporting bonhomie today. For the first time since meeting, Ellis waves the camera away, warning us, for our own safety, not to film his mysterious visitors.

There's a brief discussion, they shake hands, and Ellis returns to tie down his helicopter. The pair are South Africans, recruiting for an upcoming "job" in a nearby African country. Ellis has declined the offer of work. From such casual meetings are born so many of Africa's coups and wars.

There's another revelation in store as we walk back into Ellis's operations room, wallpapered with maps, buzzing with radio chatter.

The Sierra Leone government regards this mercenary helicopter operation as the country's only effective defence against the RUF. So too apparently, does Whitehall.

Across the room, I spot a figure in a British camouflage uniform with the rank of Royal Air Force Squadron Leader issuing orders down the phone. We both do a double-take. My obvious surprise, only matched by his instant recognition of a journalist. At this point I'm about as welcome as an RUF guerrilla.

There's a flicker of dismay on the face of the British officer before he decides to ignore me. Perhaps he has a premonition of what will inevitably follow my reporting of his involvement here ... the heated questions in the British Parliament on yet another covert entanglement with mercenaries, and the London tabloid headlines screaming "Britain Backs Aerial Killers". Neall Ellis finds it all mildly amusing. "He is technically an adviser, but he's basically running the show," he laughs.

Apparently the British had tried to stop Ellis from taking us on the mission, an order he ignored. No one is going to argue with the man who saved Freetown.

Back at Paddy's Bar that evening, the crew, still in flying suits, are propping the bar, and ignoring the spectacular tropical sunset. Only Christophe, the self-proclaimed tourist, has changed into evening leisure wear. It's another *"Dogs of War"* moment.

Fijian Fred no longer glowers at us. He cracks a smile and backslaps. We now have the bond of shared adversity. I laugh out of relief that I'm still alive. But Fred seems to crave the adrenalin surge of combat to come to life. "I enjoy this job," proclaims Neall. Fred agrees.

Now, out in the darkened jungle there probably lies the mangled human wreckage of their "good day's work". There are no regrets. I'm told the RUF are vermin, can't be trusted and are treacherous in negotiations. What jars is that this view is privately shared by UN officers and foreign-aid workers who come over to pay their respects to the crew.

In Sierra Leone, compassion died a long time ago.

The mission had taken barely an hour. One crowded hour, as the saying goes. Tomorrow morning the crew of *Wor-Wor Boy* will be back at the office to do it all again. But for Neall Ellis, this is the last campaign, one that he hopes to transform into a lifestyle.

CHAPTER FIFTEEN

PORTUGAL'S WARS IN AFRICA

> If your intervention force is small, like Guevara's or the British in Sierra Leone, you are greatly at risk. So, inevitably, you have to bargain, seek allies, make deals. This means that you, too, have to work on the basis that you are an armed group with certain irreducible interests – that is, that you are just another piece in the factional jigsaw. The only way out of this is to dominate – if necessary, to suppress and destroy the factions.
>
> R.W. Johnson: "Playing with Fire in Africa", *The Daily Telegraph*, London, 29 August 2000.

Contemporary Africa has a predilection for violence not always evidenced elsewhere. Coups, insurrections and other forms of carnage are commonplace. People are killed, sometimes for the clothes on their backs, yet the international community tends to look the other way. Darfur, the Congo, Chad, the Ivory Coast, Zimbabwe and the rest make the news these days, but almost grudgingly.

The Middle East and Central Asia have a history of conflicts, but these are mostly brief, intense conflagrations like hostilities between India and Pakistan, or those short, sharp wars that involve Arab and Jew. We experienced ructions in Vietnam and the contemptibly destructive Pol Pot regime in Cambodia, but those countries are stable today, their troubles relegated to the history books. And things have been looking up in Sri Lanka for a while now. The same applies to regional wars in other corners of the globe such as in Central America and the Philippines, where low-level insurgencies continue but seem to be contained.

That has not always been the case in Africa. In Angola, after almost four decades of fighting, a peace of sorts has settled on the nation, but even there, another civil war is barely a whisper away, the brutally impoverished kept in check by the routine excesses of a police state that include a no-nonsense, black-clad paramilitary security group that everybody refers to as the "Ninjas"; truly a modern African version of the Nazi German *Shutzstaffel* or SS. Small wonder then that the life expectancy of the average Angolan these days is barely 40 years.

The same applies to the Congo, which has been ablaze for decades and where life expectancy is even less. Mayhem has become so much a part of everyday life in this vast Central African country that the majority of its citizens regard it as totally normal, a tragic condition that evolved almost within days of the Belgian Congo having been granted its independence in 1960 and some years before the tyrant Mobutu Sese Seko seized power. Unbridled and unmitigated by any kind of reason, carnage has continued ever since.

Even worse has been a series of military struggles that have blighted Khartoum since the 1950s. In reality, what is happening today in Darfur in the Sudan is an extension of a series of conflicts in the south of the country that have left more than a million people dead and who knows how many more millions homeless or displaced.

Then you have Nigeria, currently struggling with a low-level insurgency that has festered for years. Hostilities have blighted this oil-rich West African nation that supplies the United States with more than 20 per cent of its imported crude, and cut domestic oil production by about a third.

For the observer, the scenario for Africa is a sobering reality that appears only to get worse each time a new assessment is made. Despite hopeful projections (where, in any event, only the fat cats score) it will become even more so with a deteriorating international economic climate that will ultimately affect just about everybody on the planet, and Africa most of all.

Yet, much of the violence that has ravaged this volatile continent during the course of the past half-century had its roots in a series of liberation wars launched in the early 1960s in Angola, Mozambique and Portuguese Guinea. All three countries were part of Lisbon's overseas provinces in Africa, or more appropriately, what the Portuguese liked to call their *metrópole-províncias ultramarinas*. Britain had to cope with its Mau Mau insurrection in Kenya in the 1950s, but that was low key by comparison and the British Army was able to draw on extensive experience gained from the Malayan Emergency a short few years before.

The first of the anti-Portuguese rebellions was launched in 1961 in Angola, when groups of rebels invaded the country from an already-destabilised Congo Republic. More upheavals took root in Portuguese Guinea in 1962, followed by Mozambique the following year.

Unlike Kenya's rebellion, which was countered by stern measures implemented by Whitehall, all three Portuguese conflagrations gradually evolved into fully fledged military campaigns that involved hundreds of thousands of troops on both sides of a series of largely undefined "front lines". There were thousands of casualties during 13 years of guerrilla warfare and while agreements of sorts were eventually signed by the warring parties, the peace that followed was fragmentary.

What Lisbon's campaigns did do for Africa was to forever change the political face of this inordinately unstable continent. Effectively, Portugal's African conflicts were the beginning of the end of white rule on the continent.

One needs to carefully examine the nature and extent of Portugal's wars in Africa to properly appreciate the consequences of these struggles, although this can be difficult since so little has been recorded. In his dissertation on Portugal's African wars, William Minter stated: "Even in Portuguese, the written material for a more careful judgement is sketchy. The gaps in the history of the Angolan conflict are larger than the patches of reliable information or systematic analysis[1]. This is true both for the pre-1975 war against Portuguese colonialism and even more so for post-independence strife."

Look at the facts: Lisbon, a tiny nation of less than nine million people fought twice as long against its African foes as the United States did in Vietnam. Moreover, they did so in regions where populations aggregated roughly 12 million, spread over regions half the size of western Europe. Yet today, little more than a generation later, there might be one in a hundred Americans who are even remotely aware that Portugal not only once had colonies in Africa, but were actually involved in a spate of military upheavals on the continent. Moreover, this was guerrilla warfare on a massive scale.

Brigadier General Willem "Kaas" van der Waals, the last South African to serve as Vice Consul tasked with military liaison in Luanda prior to the Portuguese finally leaving Africa, encapsulates it neatly in the preface to his book on Portugal's wars[2]:

> ... from the 1960s, revolutionary warfare, insurgency, guerrilla war and national liberation movements were to

become the major form of strife on the southern African subcontinent. This type of conflict in the Third World, symptomatic of the international Cold War scene after World War II, erupted in Angola in 1961. It was soon to spread to Mozambique, Rhodesia (Zimbabwe), South West Africa (Namibia) and eventually to the Republic of South Africa.

While other colonial powers progressively retreated from Africa, Portugal weathered the storm for several years until its capitulation in 1974. This was followed by decolonisation at an unseemly and ill-prepared pace, the result of more than a decade of costly warfare in three of its African possessions, stretching its material, human and moral resources to the utmost and creating a climate of psycho-political collapse. While not defeated on the field of battle, Portugal ultimately had to give way."

The brigadier general goes on to say that the military coup in Portugal in 1974 and the withdrawal of its troops from Angola should have resulted in peace in that country. It did not. He declares that the ensuing chaos left a power vacuum and caused this area to become a physical and psychological battlefield involving international as well as regional forces and influences.

The original accord initiated by the Portuguese stipulated that there be a power-sharing agreement between the three ethnic-based liberation movements in Angola, pending a general election. But that was soon breached and fighting between the factions continued for another 30 years.

What happened after independence in Angola in the mid-1970s, he tells us, is that "with the United States paralysed after its mortifying Vietnam experience, the USSR moved quickly to capitalise from the situation in Angola, using its resources to install its own protégé, the Marxist-oriented MPLA, in power. The Portuguese buffer disappeared virtually overnight, and strategic Soviet bases were set up in Angola and later in Mozambique, from where the Soviets and their surrogates were to pursue an intensified revolutionary onslaught against the remaining white regimes in southern Africa."

This was all Cold War stuff and, sadly, much of it still has to be properly recorded.

For all its problems, Lisbon did have a considerable amount of material support from much of Europe, their NATO allies (including the United States, depending largely on who was in the White House

Guerrilla fighters attached to the PAIGC in Portuguese Guinea attend an order group deep in the jungles of this tiny West African enclave. Amilcar Cabral's rebels were by far the most effective rebel fighting force in any of the overseas territories. (Photo: Author's collection)

at the time). Much of it was discreet, but it arrived in solid amounts that enabled the Portuguese to counter the efforts of three large Soviet-backed insurgencies in the African provinces. There were also a variety of Western-oriented nations such as Morocco and one or two Middle East states – including anti-communist Saudi Arabia – that provided Lisbon with a measure of covert assistance.

Almost all weapons and aircraft deployed in the three overseas territories had North Atlantic Treaty Organisation hallmarks and while NATO was not an active participant in Portugal's colonial wars, it was no secret that there were many American and European specialists who were able to spend time in the various operational areas. Washington's attention tended to focus on the kind of weapons supplied by communist states, in particular, some of the hardware used against American Forces in Vietnam.

For their part, the rebels in three overseas provinces got their help from Russia, China, Cuba, Vietnam, Algeria and most Eastern European states, the majority channelling their wherewithal through Dar es Salaam in Tanzania and Sekou Toure's Guinea (from where rebels were able to hit at Lisbon's resources in the tiny enclave of Portuguese Guinea. As with Angola, Mozambique and Namibia's South West African People's Organisation (SWAPO), a good deal of assistance came from moderate liberal nations such as Sweden and Canada, as well as churches and philanthropic organisations throughout North America.

While hostilities in Africa continued, racial overtones remained a feature of the struggle, although it was never a convincing argument. At the beginning the conflict was propagated by the various liberation movements as a confrontation between black and white. And while this ploy had its adherents, it didn't work because the Portuguese had long ago reduced colour to economic, and to a lesser extent, social considerations.

What did emerge soon enough was that Lisbon was obligated to rely increasingly on black volunteers who, because there was little other employment, were never in short supply. In line with this approach, some of the best counter-insurgent units in the Portuguese overseas empire were created from the bootstraps up, the majority of them predominantly black. There were African Commandos (*Comandos Africanos*) and Special Force units composed entirely of black soldiers, including their officers, as well as *Fuzileiros Especiais Africanos*, a specialist marine unit composed mainly of black soldiers.

In contrast, the only white faces in the ranks of the guerrillas were their Cuban and Russian advisers and the very occasional Portuguese defector who had joined their ranks. There was also a bevy of British journalists who propagated the cause, including the British writer Basil Davidson, regarded by the majority of his peers as a socialist "fellow traveller", with strong links to the Kremlin. Occasionally a member of the French Left, customarily a follower of Regis Debray or some other revolutionary would appear among rebel forces.

In the eyes of rebel central committees, said one neutral observer at the time, a white Portuguese would always be exactly that: a white Portuguese, even though, over the years, there were quite a few Portuguese soldiers and airmen who deserted and went across to the enemy. Curiously, the desertion figures for the Portuguese army in Africa were modest; there were only 103 desertions throughout the 13-year period of the war in all three African territories.

While the intent of a fugitive from the Portuguese army might have been sincere, rebel leaders considered these defectors of more value outside the fighting zone, preferably behind the Iron Curtain or, in the case of the PAIGC – the Freedom Army in what was to become Guiné-Bissau under the control of the exiled, communist *Frente Patriotica de Libertacao National* (FPLN), with its headquarters in Algiers.

A constant preoccupation with enemy agents was a trait – not necessarily peculiar to the PAIGC High Command – that was almost certainly inherited from the Portuguese. In this regard, the movement's internal security could almost be equated to PIDE, the Portuguese secret police. Equally ruthless, an individual might easily be liquidated if even suspected of collusion with the other side.

Also damaging to Lisbon's cause was the number of its nationals who voted with their feet. Douglas Porch told us in *The Portuguese Armed Forces and the Revolution* that as the war crept on, more and more good officers began to slip away, usually into the metropolis. He maintained that while some were politically motivated, many more were spurred on by economic considerations. Then there were those officers that failed to return from holidays abroad …[3] That was followed by an incident involving 15 engineering cadets – all of them regarded by the establishment as the "cream of the Military Academy" – who, after completing their four-year course in 1973, one dark night walked across the frontier to Spain.

Economic factors were destined to play as significant a role as politics in the outcome of Lisbon's colonial conflicts.

For a start, these were exceedingly difficult times: after Albania, Portugal was the second poorest nation in Europe. Yet by 1971, it had committed nine-tenths of its military resources to its colonial wars.

The Cambridge History of Africa[4] is piquant when it declares that "together with the conscription of settler manpower in Angola and Mozambique and of African service units and local militias (including "commando" type units at special rates of pay), Lisbon then had in Africa a total force that was probably equivalent, by ratio of the Portuguese and American populations, to at least seven times the United States force in Vietnam." In the same year, 1971, it says "the Portuguese spent 40 per cent of its national budget on military purposes".

Captain John Cann, a former US Navy aviator who served in the Pentagon subsequently wrote *Counterinsurgency in Africa: The Portuguese Way of War 1961–1974*, one of the definitive books on Portugal's African campaigns. What he has to say is instructive[5].

For Portugal in 1961 "to have mobilised an army, transported it many thousands of kilometres to its African colonies, established large logistical bases at key locations there to support it, equipped it with special weapons and material, and trained it for a very specialised type of warfare, was a remarkable achievement.

"It is made even more noteworthy by the fact that these tasks were accomplished without any previous experience, doctrine, or demonstrated competence in the field of either power projection or counter-insurgency warfare, and therefore without the benefit of any instructors who were competent in these specialties. To put this last statement in perspective, other than periodic colonial pacification efforts, Portugal had not fired a shot in anger since World War I, when Germany invaded northern Mozambique and southern Angola."

Consider too that all three wars were great distances from the Metropolis. Portuguese Guinea – or as it is known today, Guiné-Bissau – is almost as far from Lisbon as Nairobi is from Johannesburg.

Luanda, Angola's largest city and the major resupply point for the war in the interior, lies more than 7,000 kilometres from Portugal, or roughly speaking, the distance between Washington and Berlin. Mozambique, twice the size of California, lies several thousand kilometres further east.

Of all the European countries that established Imperial dominions in Africa, Portugal's colonial traditions lasted the longest. Lisbon was the first of the seafaring nations to establish a foreign base in Africa when it captured Ceuta, a tiny enclave in the north-west corner of Africa in 1415. It was also the last to leave.

These weren't the first attempts to colonise Africa. The Arabs – both from Egypt and the Gulf – had made serious inroads from the north for millennia. In fact, much of East Africa was ruled by Omani Arabs by the time the British and Imperial Germans arrived in Kenya and Tanganyika towards the end of the 19th Century. From the Dark Ages the Chinese had been intermittent visitors in their periodic global voyages of exploration, but they didn't choose to stay. Consequently, when Prince Henry's navigators first arrived in Africa in the late 1400s, they discovered a continent that had already had some form of contact with what might have been termed the "developed world" of the day. Quite a few of their countrymen who followed in their wake were to put down roots in the new-found settlements.

Lisbon ended up ruling its African possessions for more than five centuries, eventually driven out by the combined forces of an impoverished economy, political impasse at home, coupled to the kind of domestic upheavals that had already characterised post-World War II developments in French Indochina, Indonesia (against the Dutch) Malaya and Algeria.

And when rebel groups in the *ultramar* took up the cudgels, they did so with a determination that was ferocious enough to take the world totally by surprise. For more than a decade it was these small bush wars that eventually bled Lisbon dry.

Portuguese colonial history, though tarnished by self-interest and, some might say, delusions of grandeur, was as illustrious a colonial chapter as anything launched over the centuries by Madrid in South and Central America and by Amsterdam, London or Paris on the great unexplored continent that lay south of Europe. It was a historic epoch that was to have far-reaching and historic effects on the globe. For a start, it opened up trade between an isolated Europe and the East and once initiated, there was no going back.

Until other European states arrived with their so-called "civilising missions", the Portuguese were active, even before Spain, Britain, the French, the Dutch or the Italians had established permanent outstations in their respective possessions, several motivated by a burgeoning trans-Atlantic slave trade. Lisbon went on to leave its identity – and its blood – in all its former possessions[6].

In one respect, this ethnic footprint is still there. Portuguese remains the language of choice in all three of its former African colonies. The same holds for Brazil, where there are as many Ferreiras, Delgados, Rodrigues, Alcadas in the telephone lists of Sao Paulo and Rio as in Lisbon or Oporto. So, too, with Portugal's other erstwhile colonies, like Sri Lanka and Goa in South Asia, Macao off the Chinese Mainland and Timor, within the ambit of present-day Indonesia, since renamed West Irian.

It was Africa's Liberation Wars – *Guerras de Libertação* in Angola, Portuguese Guinea and finally in Mozambique – that brought this remarkable epoch to an end. None too soon either.

France and the United Kingdom, Africa's two other major colonisers (if you don't count Italy and Spain) had already been made aware of the "Winds of Change" in the 1950s. Most of their African colonies were consequently quietly prepared for self-rule and in the majority of cases – there were dozens of countries involved – independence, or *uhuru* as it was phrased in East Africa, became a reality a little more than a decade later.

Effectively, the Gold Coast became Ghana, Tanganyika was renamed Tanzania (after thousands of Arab residents on Zanzibar had been slaughtered) while Basutoland and Bechuanaland became Lesotho and Botswana. Almost overnight, a host of brand-new Francophone states were created, among them Niger, Chad, Upper Volta, the Ivory Coast, Central African Republic, Gabon and others.

Lisbon, in contrast, resisted these changes and it did so with indignant fury. Power-sharing or even limited autonomy in the African colonies was never considered an option in a colonial policy that was strictly in line with the *Estado Novo*'s narrow vision of what some of its adherents believed was a divinely-inspired Imperial mission. This was one of the reasons why the bureaucrats along the western shores of the Iberian Peninsula would refer to their African struggles as Colonial Wars, or more colloquially *Guerras Colonial*. Overseas War or *Guerra do Ultramar* also became part of the Lusitanian lexicon.

While war raged in Angola, we'd hear the catch-phrase everywhere, on the radio, at public meetings, and more often than not on billboards posted on every vacant space in cities like Luanda, Silva Porto, Nova Lisboa, Sá da Bandeira and others: *Angola é Nossa!* – "Angola is Ours!" was the cry.

In truth, as the nation was so often reminded by the dictator Antonio de Oliveira Salazar, "the three African 'provinces' represent a powerful motive for national pride". Then the wily old fox would subtly add that Angola, Mozambique and Guinea not only sustained Portugal's economy, but for centuries had symbolised a heritage of a great and glorious past. He was only partly right because he ignored the reality of history: while cultures might remain mired in the past, ideologies and the people who shape them constantly change. More to the point for Salazar, who had an old-fashioned notion of what constituted the wealth of nations, he would tell his people that the overseas colonies were what made his nation great. Angola, Mozambique and, to a lesser extent Portuguese Guinea, all helped to provide captive markets for home-produced goods, ready sources of cheap raw materials and foodstuffs as well as an outlet for the homeland's surplus population.

Consequently, when Angola was finally invaded by a rag-tag rebel army that emerged out of the recently-independent Congo, Lisbon retaliated by sending to Africa an inexperienced conscript army and as many aviation and naval elements as it could afford. The same happened shortly afterwards in Mozambique and Portuguese Guinea, the conflicts escalated and were to evolve into a grim series of military campaigns that went on for half a generation.

Curiously, Lisbon's African travails received scant attention beyond its own frontiers, in part because Southeast Asia was hogging the headlines. Were that to happen today, these military struggles would almost certainly get the attention they deserved, but in the 1960s almost everything was focused on Vietnam and, to a lesser extent Algeria. Nor were matters eased by Lisbon's reluctance to provide journalists with the necessary facilities to report on them. More salient, it was also a time of dissension at home, with a growing body of radical, left-leaning military officers who believed that the military campaigns should be terminated and Africa left to its own devices.

With time and numerous assignments as a foreign correspondent, I got to know some of the members of the junta that eventually overthrew the Lisbon government quite well. It was interesting to glimpse the machinations of the revolt from the inside, especially since Captain Vitor Alves, with whom I spent time operationally in eastern Angola and Captain Otelo Saraiva de Carvalho, an aide to General Antonio de Spínola and my escort officer while I covered hostilities in Portuguese Guinea, were among them. While Captain Alves was relatively moderate as revolutionaries go (he was eventually to serve his country in the European Parliament), that did not apply to De Carvalho, who was both an insurrectionist and an anarchist. General De Spínola's aide was eventually jailed for sedition by the government he'd helped create.

There were many reasons why Lisbon eventually bowed out, with politics and economics featuring in roughly equal measure. The reality is that Lisbon's initial impetus disappeared in a quagmire of conflicting ideologies, in large part because the majority of the young conscripts called to spend three years in Africa, saw absolutely no sense in losing their lives in wars in which they had neither interest nor enthusiasm. The majority had never even seen Africa. Almost to a man, they couldn't wait for their military service to end. And to that mix, there were increasingly radical Moscow-fed influences that began to surface within the country's officer corps. By the time of the coup there were quite a few senior commanders who were members of the Portuguese Communist Party, the most prominent being Admiral António Alva Rosa Coutinho, who, after Angola's independence, became president of its Council of Governors. It was not by accident that the man who steered the MPLA to hijack the government of Angola (where it has been ensconced for almost 40 years) earned the nickname "the Red Admiral" (in Portuguese *o almirante vermelho*).

All these interacting factors, together, eventually caused Lisbon's colonial empire to disintegrate in 1974. Within a year, the Portuguese army, navy and air force had packed their bags and were headed home.

Portugal's guerrilla wars in Africa were fought under horrendous conditions. They were made worse by a continent that has never been kind to the interloper.

Interestingly, things weren't nearly as bad in Angola, where generations of young Portuguese had lived and worked in this remote and remarkably wealthy bush country. Primitive it might have been, but Angola's natural resources included diamonds, gold, oil, hardwoods and the kind of quality coffee and other produce that achieved top market prices abroad. The country offered undreamt-of rewards to those who persevered, and many did, for a dozen generations. More to the point, the always-hardy Portuguese appeared to adapt easily to adversity. Those who had been there long enough tended to understand conditions better than their black compadres, which was a reason why the war in Angola ultimately went a lot better than it did in Mozambique.

The majority of young conscripts taken off the streets and from homes in Oporto, Sintra, Coimbra, Figuera de Fos and elsewhere often faced a host of uncompromising options. Like many American GIs in Asia, the majority were still in their teens, thrust into a series of bitter conflicts that ultimately went on to claim more than 3,000 lives. There were 13, 000 more casualties – apart from those who were struck down in accidents or by disease. Stuck in the African bush, sometimes for years at a stretch, coupled to austere living conditions – as well as the prospect of contracting any one of dozens of tropical illnesses – their options were limited. Malaria, tick bite fever and other insect-borne diseases were always a factor and although Lisbon seemed to cope, a steady toll was extracted.

No wonder then that tens of thousands of young men of military age from the western fringe of the Iberian Peninsula refused to don uniforms. Most slipped quietly across the border into Spain and made their way to Germany, France, Scandinavia and elsewhere to find jobs for themselves and their families and sit out the war.

I spent a lot of time with Portuguese units in the field, first in Angola and later in Portuguese Guinea, where I was to write a report on the war for the Munger Africana Library of the California Institute of Technology[7]. On my first Angolan trip, I was accompanied by Cloete Breytenbach, one of South Africa's best-known lensmen (and brother to peripatetic Breyten, who vigorously opppposed the apartheid policies of the white South African regime). Cloete's third brother, Colonel Jan Breytenbach went on to become the founder-commander of South Africa's first Special Forces unit, the Reconnaissance Regiment, more popularly known as the Recces.

My time spent with Lisbon's military in Mozambique, in contrast, was fragmentary and usually centred around units based at Tete, in the Zambezi Valley or on the isolated road that linked Malawi with Beira. We called it "The Highway to Hell", and that it was. About the only thing that was certain about travelling between the Rhodesian border post at Nyamapanda and Mwanza – at the southern tip of Malawi – was that someone in your convoy was bound to be blown up by landmines.

Conditions everywhere were tough. In this regard, there is nobody better than Ron Reid-Daly to offer words about the kind of circumstances that might have been encountered, especially along the southern approaches to the Zambezi Valley[8]. I deal with his comments about the Portuguese fighting in Chapter 10.

The Tete Region of Mozambique – through which the great Zambezi flows out of Zambia to the sea – rapidly developed into one of the most disputed zones of the war. The most important role of Portuguese forces there was to guard the strategic Cahorra Bassa hydroelectric dam, then under construction.

Over several years, I went in, both by road and by small plane from Tete and as everybody knew, the defences – and the minefields – were extensive. I was to see the results of some of these encounters in the military hospital in Tete and it was a grim, sobering experience.

At the end of the war, early in 1974, after the ceasefire had been signed, I returned to the now abandoned air force base at Cahorra Bassa by car.

Still intact, the place was deserted. It was almost as if the local natives, fearful of intruding on something that had been forbidden for so long, were hesitant to disturb yesterday's ghosts. Hangars, mess halls, sleeping quarters and engineering shops were all intact, but there was garbage everywhere. The only call came from a go-away bird precariously perched on an abandoned radar antenna. Flies milled about as if there were no tomorrow. In a sense, it was like something in those early British films made after World War II, where the main character would go back to one of the airfields where he'd spent time and find only faded photos on the window sills, broken cups and doors, partially off their hinges banging in the breeze.

It was much the same on the long journey between the camp and Tete, a distance of a couple of hundred kilometres. Mine was the only car that I saw in a journey of several hours there and back, and because the road was tarred and I was struck by the insecurity of an isolated countryside, I travelled fast. I never encountered a single domestic animal along the way. At one stage I was stopped by a lone FRELIMO soldier who first apologised for halting me and then asked politely whether I would give him a lift to town. It wasn't the first time I'd given a revolutionary cadre a ride while travelling around Mozambique: I'd done so a few years before on the road between Tete and Rhodesia, only this one was a full-blown rebel commissar who waved me straight into his camp. For my efforts he offered me a cold beer from the comfort of his headquarters.

Some idea of the intensity of these African conflicts, particularly in Portuguese Guinea, might be gauged from what has been listed in the record books as "The Battle of Como Island". It was a series of grim battles that involved Portuguese land, sea and air forces and provides a valuable insight to rebel determination to win, at all costs if necessary.

By early 1964, the rebel movement *Partido Africano da Independência da Guiné e Cabo Verde* or, more commonly, the PAIGC, had captured parts of Como Island. A counter-attack by Portuguese forces was swiftly repulsed and even the deployment of F-86F Sabres by the *Forca Aerea Portuguesa* (FAC) from Bissau using heavy bombs and napalm were unable to change the outcome of the battle. On the contrary, it soon became almost impossible for the Portuguese troops to operate in relative safety anywhere in Guinea or at any distance from their well-fortified bases. For a while the anti-guerrilla campaign stuttered along. A few *colons* were moved to safety – usually under control of the regular army – but very little else happened that might disturb the connection between the local population and the insurgents. The war developed negatively for the Portuguese from the start.

As it became clear that a better-organised operation was needed to attempt the liberation of Como Island, military headquarters in Bissau prepared Operation *Tridente*, which was to involve army, naval and aviation elements. The battles that followed were fierce and progress was slow, with the Portuguese suffering heavy casualties in combat and still more from disease and malnutrition.

After 71 days of bitter fighting, the island was cleared of rebel forces – but at a terrible price.

During the course of Operation *Tridente* the Portuguese Air Force flew 851 combat sorties. These were detailed, with numbers of sorties flown, in a subsequent report:

F-86F Sabres:	73
T-6 Harvards:	141
Dornier Do-27:	180

Auster:	46
Alouette III Helicopters:	323
PV-2 Neptunes:	16
C-47/Douglas Dakotas:	2

Almost all this effort was in vain. Barely two months later the rebels recaptured some of their original positions on the island, in part because the Portuguese Army had to redeploy forces elsewhere. This time, there was no counter-attack: due largely to the PAIGC establishing new important positions in the south of the country, especially on the Cantanhez and Quitafine Peninsulas, where strong contingents of the Portuguese Army at Catió and Bedanda were encircled and put under a siege. As a consequence, Como lost much of its strategic importance.

Besides, in October 1964, the FAP was forced to repatriate all 16 of its F-86Fs based at Bissalanca because of pressure from the United States. By deploying these Sabre fighters to Africa for use in counter-insurgency operations against the rebels, Washington maintained that Lisbon was endangering NATO defences along Europe's Atlantic coast.

Peculiarly, the USA had nothing to say about the deployment of Portuguese Air Force F-84Gs Thunderjets to Angola further south, but then Angola had gold, diamonds and oil …

1 William Minter (Ed.): *Operation Timber: Pages from the Savimbi Dossier*, African World Press Inc., Trenton, New Jersey 1988, p. 2.
2 Brigadier General Willem S. van der Waals.
3 *The Portuguese Armed Forces and the Revolution*; Douglas Porch, Croom Helm, London, 1977.
4 *The Cambridge History of Africa (Volume 8 c.1940 – c.1995)* by J. Desmond Clark (Ed.), J.D. Fage (Ed.), Roland Oliver (Ed.), Richard Gray (Ed.), John Flint (Ed.) and G.N Sanderson (Ed.), Cambridge University Press, 1986.
5 *Counterinsurgency in Africa: The Portuguese Way of War 1961 – 1974*; John P. Cann, Hailer Publishing, USA, 2005.
6 Several factors motivated the early navigators to explore beyond Europe's real or imagined frontiers. The first was the knowledge that somewhere beyond the horizon, towards the east especially, there were other great civilisations and cultures that were not only immensely enticing, but had an awful lot to offer. Make contact and there are fortunes to be made, was the dictum. It was these early voyages of discovery that ultimately caused Lisbon to establish a series of "replenishing posts" along the African coastline that became the basis of Portugal's colonial empire. So came into being countries that we recognise today as Angola, Mozambique and Guinea-Bissau.
7 Al J. Venter: *Report on Portugal's War in Guiné-Bissau*, Munger Africana Library, California Institute of Technology, Pasadena; Also published in South Africa under the title: *Portugal's Guerrilla War*, Malherbe, Cape Town, both in 1973.
8 Introduction to *Staying Alive: A Southern African Survival Handbook*, by Ron Reid-Daly, Ashanti Publishing, Rivonia, 1990.

CHAPTER SIXTEEN

DEATH OF A GUERRILLA FIGHTER

> Guerrilla warfare has one major advantage in this nuclear age. If employed as an instrument of foreign aggression, it constitutes an "ambiguous threat" by confusing the legal, political and even military bases for an effective international response.
>
> Peter Paret and John W. Shy *Guerrillas in the 1960s*

Captain João Bacar of Bissau, Portuguese Guinea – a country listed on the map of Africa today as Guinea-Bissau – was an incredibly brave man. He died brutally one quiet Sunday morning in April 1971. Only a week before, I'd been with him in the jungles of this remote West African country that had been at war for eight years, a colonial struggle that pitted all the forces of a profoundly Western nation like Portugal against what was then termed in some quarters as Moscow's Evil Empire.

This war had been a long time coming, very much a part of the gathering anti-Imperial struggle that had almost totally enveloped the continent of Africa. From passive or disobedient phases in the tradition of Mahatma Gandhi, the struggle in Africa – with strong support from the Soviets and its allies – had regressed to a succession of conflicts that stretched from Algeria on the Mediterranean to Mozambique – another Portuguese colony thousands of kilometres away, to the south.

By then Kenya's Mau Mau insurrection was history and Rhodesia's war was just starting. Nkrumah's dream of independence for black people all over the globe – by violent means if necessary – had taken fire. Ultimately, the Ghanaian leader declared, it would encompass the entire continent, including white-ruled South Africa. So, in the end, it did, but none of it was of Nkrumah's making because he was overthrown by his own people shortly afterwards.

This all took place in the 1970s and Lisbon had suddenly become engaged in a succession of wars in all three of its mainland African possessions. An indication of the intensity weathered by Lisbon came from American academic Douglas Porch who wrote a dissertation on Portugal's military role in Africa for Stanford University Press. Titled *The Portuguese Armed Forces and the Revolution*[1], Porch told us that with over 150,000 men in Africa by 1970, "the Portuguese deployment represented a troop level in proportion to the Portuguese population [that was] five times greater than that of the United States in Vietnam in the same year."

Throughout, Lisbon's leaders – and many of their people too, fought a hopeless rearguard action. They had neither the hardware nor the numbers to counter groups of rebels supported and more than adequately armed by Moscow and the rest of her Warsaw Pact Allies. Among these were Czechoslovakia, Cuba, North Korea, Poland, Bulgaria, East Germany as well as several radical Arab and African states that included Egypt, Algeria, Libya and Ethiopia.

With her young men dying in numbers, the impetus that drove Lisbon to continue in Africa seemed to most of us who knew anything about these military struggles as futile. Some regarded these ongoing conflicts as akin to an improvised death wish, because by then, a lot else had been visited upon the Portuguese nation. My Lusitanian friends have a name for this special kind of madness and it is called *Loucura*: a fatalism or super-optimism that while it lasted, was also reflected in the manner in which this nation fought its African campaigns ...

João Bacar, a black man and a full captain in the Portuguese Army, was one of those who died in the war. A brilliant tactical fighter and counter-insurgency specialist, he had been immersed in this guerrilla struggle since the start. He had seen it destroy his tiny West African nation as no other upheaval had done since the great Malian General Mansa Musa swept westwards, past Timbuktu, to bring the writ of his vast African empire to the verge of the great Atlantic, six centuries before. Short, lean and as tough as Muslim Africa makes them, Captain Bacar was a distant descendent of this astonishingly wealthy and influential civilisation which left its mark on Africa to this day.

He relished and vouchsafed its traditions, handed down through 30 generations, but still intact. He rallied to what he termed was the defence of the principles which had been laid down by his illustrious forefathers and which, in the present era as far as he was concerned, were being threatened by an alien, atheist and ungodly force from

Chapter 16
Death of a guerrilla fighter

beyond. He told his men that the enemy was nurtured by powers which had only self-interest and quasi-Imperialist designs in mind and they took him at his word because in their eyes, this officer was a person of substance.

Not for a moment did this commando captain – one of whose few gestures to the western society in which he lived was the small moustache he assiduously cultivated, very much like most of his other fellow officers – ever consider that this same self-interest could have been applied to the flag under which he fought. Bacar was born under that splendid green and red banner and considered himself proudly Portuguese. Nothing else would do and he often said as much.

The Europeans from the Iberian headland, 3,500 km to the north, qualified that fealty by treating this black warrior as one of their sons. Their mutual empathy peaked shortly before Bacar was killed, when they rewarded him with the country's highest military honour, the Portuguese equivalent of Britain's Victoria Cross or America's Medal of Honour. A member of the Futa-Fula tribe, the captain had become one of the few.

But then, as we should all know, death holds no awe for military immortality. Early one Sunday morning that April, João Bacar made his final gesture to the society in which he so implicitly believed. A week after I'd left him at Tite, while on an extended patrol in the same dense jungle area in which we had trudged and spent two days scouring for the enemy, he was killed. He died in an early morning skirmish with the black guerrillas of the PAIGC, a West African guerrilla movement that called itself *Partido Africano de Independencia da Guinee e Cabo Verde*.

Caught in the cross-fire of a heavy enemy ambush along a stretch of jungle south of Bissau, the colonial capital, his unit took the brunt of a well-planned and executed rocket and mortar attack. Aware that they were up against the man himself, the PAIGC guerrillas took great care in laying their ambush. Three "ballerina" anti-personnel mines – the same type known to the Americans in Indo-China as "Bouncing Betty" – were placed in shallow ground across the path along which Bacar's patrol was expected. None of the men in the column noticed the nine prongs – three to each mine – that bulged slightly in the red dirt. The first soldier to trip the bomb was also the signal for attack.

Curiously, and in keeping with the quirks of war, five of Bacar's soldiers managed to cross the kill zone without triggering any of the prongs. The sixth followed confidently, probably satisfied that if there were mines in the path ahead, they'd have been spotted or tripped by the usually eager-eyed scouts who led the way. He had long ago stopped following in the footsteps of the man ahead of him, for the unit was on its second day of patrol.

Number six was wrong. At the touch of his soft-soled rubber jungle boot – standard issue in the Portuguese Army – the "ballerina", with a dull thud, leapt upwards out of the hollow in the earth where it had been placed the day before. It was still spinning when it hit its shoulder-high apex and exploded, killing number six and badly mauling the man behind.

Numbers eight and nine received superficial wounds in their legs and thighs and for some minutes remained too shocked by the blast to comprehend the battle which raged around them and barely conscious of further explosions along the line.

Perhaps this shocked sprawl saved their lives, because two or three more soldiers were cut down by rocket and rifle fire in the minute or two that followed, because by then the ambush was over and the first of the guerrillas had started to pull away. One man, João Bacar, was killed by a grenade – his own.

Bacar's reflexes were functioning almost before he heard the muffled explosion that triggered the mine into the air about 100 metres ahead of where he marched. He was firing moments after the mine went off within touching distance of number six. So were 20 more of his unit, by now crouched low in the long elephant grass on the verge of a stretch of ragged palm-speckled rainforest which gave the jungle around them a crazy trunkular effect.

Once the first ammunition clips had been exhausted, fire wavered momentarily on both sides. Bacar didn't have to order his men to reload and keep firing their G-3s. They were the best of Portugal's commando force in Guinea and the swarthy captain must have been satisfied with their split-second reaction. The survivors recalled later that he issued no orders throughout the action because there was no need to.

For the two or so minutes that the battle lasted, the black Portuguese troops in Bacar's unit knew the routine: they'd exhaust a clip and hurl a grenade to back up the three bazookas that were retaliating with them and then they would revert to their G-3s again. The men had done it many times before, first in training and afterwards, for real. Mortars were out of the question at such short range and in any event, much of the action was random.

The enemy attack had slackened briefly after about a minute and, some of the troops recalled later, there was uncertain movement in

Chapter 16
Death of a guerrilla fighter

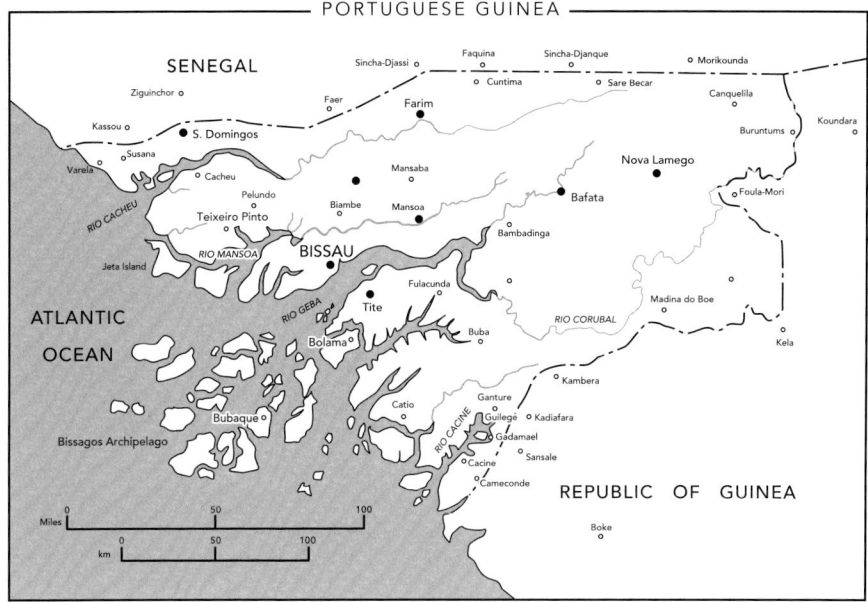

Portuguese Guinea, today Guinea-Bissau, where some of the worst fighting of the war took place.

the jungle ahead. One of them saw Bacar palm his second grenade and pull out the pin, after which he rose abruptly from his crouched position to hurl it. But then, it seemed, a silent, unexpected force knocked his legs out from under him: Bacar had apparently slipped on a patch of wet marsh clay, not unusual in a region that has more rain in a month than parts of Europe and Africa experience in a year. He hit the ground hard, the grenade still in his hand.

Now the normal firing time of a Portuguese hand grenade – a long tubular affair that looks more like a khaki can of shaving cream than a deadly instrument of war – is roughly four seconds once the pin is pulled. When Bacar momentarily came to his senses and found himself lying on his stomach with the grass above his head – the two men nearest him were only a metre away – he probably only had one of those seconds left. It must have been the longest moment of his life.

The way his superiors reconstructed the attack afterwards, he might theoretically have tried to disentangle himself and, who knows, possibly succeeded in getting rid of the grenade had he wished to do so. He must also have been aware that if he did that, there was a likelihood of others around him being killed in the blast. The decision he made could only have been immediate: with both hands clasping the grenade, Captain João Bacar pulled it close to his body and dedicated that last moment of his life to his beloved Prophet.

None of those around him at the time remember his last words, for they too, were frozen in terror. One of his men, a young corporal who had joined the unit from the north shortly before, recalls seeing Bacar's lips move and reckoned afterwards that it could only have been a final call to Allah. It was ironic too, that at that critical moment, Bacar was facing the rising sun, looking east, which was the direction of his much-revered Mecca. That was when the explosion flung his body into the air, smashing it as well as the firing mechanism of his carbine, its strap still slung around his shoulder.

Bacar had finally immersed himself physically, mentally and spiritually into what the Portuguese like to refer to as "This Christian War", even though his own divine beliefs differed radically from the deity of his Holy Roman Catholic patrons.

The news of Captain João Bacar's death swept through Portugal and her African Empire in a tide of shrouded sorrow and whispered dismay. João Bacar was dead, the people in Portuguese Guinea told one another in quiet tones, almost afraid the next man would hear, as if he had not already. By morning there wasn't a *tabanca* – a tribal village – in the country that hadn't heard the news. Drums echoed late into the night and sounded an eerie but pivotal role in passing the message along.

João Bacar's troops on patrol in the jungles of Portuguese Guinea. (Photo: Author)

Chapter 16
Death of a guerrilla fighter

Portuguese soldier in the jungle in Portuguese Guinea with one of the improvised rocket launchers that was developed to use a French air-to-ground missile. (Photo: Author)

Within the hour, the base camp at Tite from which Bacar and his men were operating – and where I spent a lot of my time while in this tiny country – had passed the word on to headquarters in Bissau. A few hours later they were setting the event in hot metal in newspapers in Lisbon, Luanda and Lourenço Marques, complete with comment and the eulogies of a dozen men who had lived and served with this remarkable Son of Africa.

The news was carried by the BBC shortly afterwards. Captain João Bacar, one of the most famous veterans of Portugal's war in Guinea-Bissau had been killed in action by a PAIGC guerrilla unit, the report read. Bacar had been a recent recipient of the coveted Gold Order of the Tower and the Sword, Portugal's highest military award. That he had been killed by his own grenade was inconsequential: the Futa-Fula officer was a victim of that war, as surely as if he had been killed by a guerrilla's bullet.

Many of his countrymen only believed the news when his shrapnel-torn body was flown back to the capital by helicopter the next day. He had often enough been reported dead before, usually by the enemy, who fanfared his death in Radio Conakry and the smaller guerrilla station just across the frontier, *Radio Libertacao*. But this time it was for real. In the eight years that he'd been fighting guerrillas in Portuguese Guinea, they had only succeeded in wounding him four times and he had reciprocated, always ruthlessly, by killing that many dozen of them.

It was a sombre 20-minute flight from Tite to Bissau, across swamp and river and probably a few enemy units huddled in the daytime-protection of some of the larger clusters of jungle. The helicopter swung low over the jungle to avoid taking enemy fire from the surrounding bush. Not for nothing had a few foreign correspondents recently in the country referred to this West African patchwork quilt of jungle and rice paddy as Africa's own Vietnam.

A deep sadness pervaded Bissau's Bissalanca Airport, with its rows of snub-nosed Fiat G-91 jet fighters and Harvard T-6's drawn up in echelon on the tarmac. Huge crowds of mourners were gathered in the road beyond the security fence. It seemed that the entire civilian and military population had turned out to greet the body of the hero as it was brought into town, his coffin draped ceremoniously with the flag of Portugal, a mantle so large it splayed out over the back of the truck. A train of military and private trucks and cars a kilometre long followed behind at walking pace. Two outriders led the way. There was no need to clear the route; the crowds stood grim, silent and respectful away from the road. With characteristic full-blooded Iberian emotion, men – black and white – cried like boys when he passed.

There are not many reports of what happened across the border in the Republic of Guinea when the news of the Portuguese captain's death came through that night. It was from this former French colony that the ambush unit had originally set out and it was in that direction that they returned after their mission had been accomplished. Some reports say that many of the younger guerrillas danced in the streets of Conakry as well as in Senegal's Dakar and Ziguinchor to the north when they heard the news. Bacar's name had become synonymous for all that Portugal's hated presence in Africa represented and now that that frightening symbol was gone, they rejoiced.

Yet, there was also some hushed talk and a certain undefined reverence for Bacar in a few corners, particularly among some of the older guerrilla veterans. They remembered him well, for they had crossed swords with this seasoned fighter often enough. They respected both his guile and his tenacity, even if they despised the

Chapter 16
Death of a guerrilla fighter

The army in Portuguese Guinea had a small unit of airborne-trained nurses on constant standby. Should conditions demand it, they could be dropped into the Sharp End after a battle. These brave women were constantly being flown out, usually by helicopter, to attend the wounded in outlying bases. (Photo: Author)

man for what he represented. At the same time, he was still one of them: in their native idiom, a man of the soil.

More important, his courage spoke the language often only understood by adversaries of long standing, especially in a war that had its own code of ethics and where the fighters were merely the pawns of other peoples' ideals.

There is a postscript to these events that is both contemporary and interesting. In 2007, more than three decades after Bacar was killed, I was sent a message by Manuel Ferreira, a former Special Forces operative and an old friend from several African conflicts. The attachment showed the headstone of João Bacar's grave in Bissau, still immaculate in spite of half a dozen post-independence revolutions that have rent this tiny country apart like few others on the African continent…

As Manuel commented, Portugal's colonial wars were long, but the conflict in some of the former possessions, Guiné-Bissau in particular, was longer: it still goes on, but in another guise …

A luta continua …

1   Douglas Porch: *The Portuguese Armed Forces and the Revolution*, Croom Helm, London and Stanford, USA, 1973.

CHAPTER SEVENTEEN

THE WAR IN PORTUGUESE GUINEA

> The future of Portugal depends on an adequate solution to the war in which we are involved ... it is not national unity that is at stake, but Imperial unity, and today's conscience does not accept empires.
>
> General Antonio de Spínola (from his book, *Portugal and the Future*)

Guerrilla conflict in and around the savage tropical swamplands of Portuguese Guinea was like none of the other colonial wars in Africa during the epoch that followed much of Africa achieving independence. It was the only military campaign in Africa in the modern period that was actually lost by a European colonial power.

Yet, through it all, not a single town in this tiny West African enclave was ever overrun by insurgents. Also, government casualties were manageable, the Portuguese Army never fled in disarray, nor were the few settlers that remained driven into the sea, though that was always the clear intent of the rebels. Considering the nature and extent of hostilities in Southeast Asia at the time, it is significant that the largely conscript army was never forced to abandon a single strategic position. Even though parts of Como Island were yielded to the enemy, it was never totally abandoned.

By the time the Portuguese Army mutiny had taken effect in Lisbon, hostilities in Africa were immediately halted. Almost as one, the troops called it a day and officers, NCOs and men grabbed their things and went home.

The truth is that things could have gone much worse had both sides not had a firm grip on their men. By the time young officers of the Portuguese Armed Forces Movement had seized power, many of those who had been active in Africa accepted that should the war

Chapter 17
The war in Portuguese Guinea

have gone on, conditions might easily have gone the other way. One young conscript was of the opinion that "defeat hung heavily in the air" in the streets of Bissau, Cacine and Bafata further into the interior.

Moreover, while the fighting cadres of the *Partido Africano de Independencia da Guiné e Cabo Verde* (PAIGC) knew they had the situation in hand, Luis Cabral, its leader (and brother of Amilcar, who had been assassinated in Conakry in 1973 by his own people) remained cautious. Having taken over the country as its first president after the Portuguese pulled out, he never allowed his triumph to give way to vengeance. Not yet, anyway. He told the nation in a broadcast that there were to be no scores settled, either with the vacating army or with indigenous members of the population who had sided with Lisbon. Instead, he allowed moderate minds to prevail and told them to wait for the handover of power, coupled to the formal international recognition that had been promised by those who had taken over in the Metropolis[1].

Notable about this conflict in West Africa was that it bore little similarity to other colonial struggles in Africa, or even the seven-year campaign that France fought against the FLN in Algeria. It also differed markedly from what had been going on in other Portuguese territories such as Angola and Mozambique and the struggles that had already emerged along the northern frontiers of Rhodesia and South Africa.

This war, in contrast, was a conflict that began almost overnight when small bands of well-armed and trained guerrillas crossed over from their exterior bases in Sekou Toure's Marxist Republic of Guinea in 1961. The insurgency gradually intensified until war was formally declared in January 1963 and it wasn't long before normally placid Senegal entered the fray. In effect, the guerrillas now had safe havens in both neighbouring states, to the north, south and the east: Portuguese Guinea was almost completely surrounded by hostile forces.

I recall travelling overland from South Africa to Dakar and getting to Conakry in January 1966, shortly before the death of former British Prime Minister Winston Churchill. I stayed with a group of American Peace Corps volunteers that I'd met along the way, including the scion of a very famous stateside family by the name of Vanderbilt. That was before I continued northwards towards the Senegalese frontier which I crossed near the small town of Koundara.

The three-day effort to cross into "friendly territory" was lurid. I was regarded as an object of some suspicion by a Guinean

General Antonio de Spínola was one of the most successful counter-insurgent specialists in Lisbon's wars. Towards the end of it, he wrote the book that resulted in the fall of Lisbon's civilian government and the Portuguese armed forces taking over. Their first job was to end all three conflicts, which paved the way for independence for Angola, Mozambique and Portuguese Guinea. (Photo: Author)

immigration official who made me return three times to Koundara because, he said, my exit permit wasn't in order. Each time, he would dismiss me by throwing my British passport onto the floor. There was no arguing either with the man or the soldiers who backed him, even though the town was 50 kilometres from the border post across some of the worst roads on the continent of Africa. It was clear that he didn't like white people.

On the positive side, I'd made contact with another Peace Corps couple who had been based in this unforgiving environment for more that a year. While their resources were sparse, they offered a roof over my head and a bed. Sadly, politics in Africa don't always make for convivial guests and I was pleased to finally say goodbye.

In a sense, the delay was fortuitous. Perhaps 100 metres down a rutted track from where these two volunteers stayed was a building that housed a sensitive electronic listening post manned by Soviet intelligence officials. Although my American friends weren't explicit, I soon gathered that all Portuguese Army radio broadcasts were being monitored from there. They also confided that there was regular movement in men and supplies between Koundara and Kantika to the immediate west, perhaps a couple of hours' march from Buruntuma, Lisbon's easternmost military outpost in the beleaguered enclave.

I ended up passing this information through the appropriate security channels and a commando raid was planned, something I dealt with in more detail in *Barrel of a Gun*, my last book on the subject[2].

Of all the states in West Africa during the 1960s and 1970s, the Republic of Guinea (Conakry) – formerly a French colony – might arguably have been the Soviet Union's strongest supporter. Ghana under President Nkrumah came a close second, but he overstepped the mark by fomenting revolution amongst his neighbours and he was soon overthrown by his own army.

For the Soviets, Conakry at that time might have been equated to the United States military base on the Indian Ocean island of Diego Garcia, for both had great strategic value. Conakry was not only a valuable monitoring station, it was also a refuelling stop for Soviet ships and aircraft that were keeping tabs both on Western shipping rounding Africa's bulge and American missile launches from Cape Canaveral on the opposite shores of the Atlantic.

In Portuguese Guinea – a tropical spit of land fringed by numerous islands – the PAIGC took the initiative from the start, leading to the partial occupation of Como Island which was the site of one of the first major battles with Portuguese forces. The guerrillas resisted a series of fierce counter-attacks, including air strikes by *Forca Aerea Portuguesa* F-86 Sabres.

Initially, the PAIGC was composed of a small group of disaffected African intellectuals, many of whom had been educated at Coimbra or Lisbon universities and then granted "most privileged" *assimilado* status prior to them returning home. It was these former students, later classified in the *ultramar* as dissidents, that as early as the late 1950s were already urging the Portuguese to leave Africa. A short time later these same nationalists, some of them having opted for self-imposed exile, started to issue decrees from Conakry. Portugal should vacate "our Guinea-Bissau" and hand over the government to the country's black population of about 600,000, they demanded.

Lisbon was unmoved, which was when PAIGC encouraged the enclave's black workers to embark on a programme of civil disobedience. The Portuguese reacted with force. Only after more than 50 dissident Africans had been shot by the Portuguese police during an ordered strike for higher wages at Pidjiguiti Docks in Bissau on 3 August 1959 – a date subsequently commemorated by the guerrillas – did the prospect of armed conflict become a reality. The country's Africans were obviously appalled by the killings and if many did not immediately become PAIGC members, the majority came to regard the movement as a hope for the future.

War broke out three years later and went on for more than a decade. The conflict eventually spawned other nationalist organisations, and, as with the PAIGC, almost all of this activity was underground. At the end of it, only two of these politico-military groups were to survive.

Amilcar Cabral's Conakry-based PAIGC headed the list and eventually achieved the distinction of being among the most successful black guerrilla organisations in Africa. While there were other rebel groups operating out of Senegal, Cabral's cadres were responsible for more than nine-tenths of all military activity in the country. The only other rebel movement of any consequence in the region was FLING *(Front de Lutte de l'Independence Nationale de Guiné)* then operating out of Dakar. This political and guerrilla force comprised at least four combined nationalist movements and was regarded by the Portuguese and the Americans as more moderate than the Marxist PAIGC.

Both groups nevertheless shared a determination that the Portuguese had to go, and by whatever means possible. Their leaders approved of the violence that broke out as a result of what they called Portuguese "brutality and intransigence". However, as with most revolutionary groups, disputes started to emerge on questions of policy, including leadership, the timing of the takeover and the nature of the government they proposed to establish once the colonials had been expelled: while the PAIGC wanted a communist state, FLING opted for ties with the West. It also indicated that it would not exclude the possibility of some kind of loose economic and cultural alliance with Portugal, similar to that between the Ivory Coast and France.

Chapter 17
The war in Portuguese Guinea

PAIGC had its own views and instead, embraced a strong Nyerere approach: Africa for the Africans. As the Cabral brothers and their lieutenants asserted, Africa was black and not part of Europe. Moreover, the PAIGC was resolved to put in place a radical government along Cuban or Algerian lines: all aspects of government, including politics, economics and military affairs would be answerable to the Party alone. Amilcar Cabral had always made it clear that he had learned much from Fidel Castro.

Despite their differences, the two organisations continued to cooperate while opposed to a common enemy. Apart from military actions, they launched a joint propaganda campaign that drew attention to the cartelistic nature of commerce, trade and industry headed by Portuguese commercial firms. Their principal targets were Portuguese cartels such as the *Banco Nacional Ultramarino* and Jorge de Mello's *Companhia Uniao Fabril* (CUF). Both enterprises had vast holdings in Metropolitan Portugal as well as in the overseas provinces and also had powerful sway on what was happening in Portuguese Africa, mainly through family connections at the highest level of government in Lisbon.

By the early 1960s, the CUF had accumulated a series of monopolies in Portuguese Africa that stretched all the way through to the Congo and the Rhodesias. A large proportion of trade and exports of Angola, Mozambique and Portuguese Guinea were channelled through company books and interests included diamonds, minerals and tropical hardwoods and were eventually extended to oil. Totally exclusionist, almost no foreign or domestic interests were tolerated, unless approved by the CUF. Percentage rake-offs – to government administrators, officials issuing permits and licences, and in some instances, even to military commanders in control of potentially lucrative areas to provide protection and convoys – were the norm.

Obviously, there were abuses; the majority targeted at those who could least afford them: impoverished African people.

From the start, conflict in Portuguese Guinea was bloody and uncompromising. Diminutive and with a forbidding tropical terrain – many low-lying coastal areas were impenetrable swamp or rainforest – an extremely difficult environment in which to fight a war. Conditions weren't helped by dismal communications. Also, experience from Angola, Malaya, Cuba, Algeria and Indo-China were put into effect by both opposing forces.

Further towards the east, on higher ground, things went a lot easier. In the interior, the country rose slowly to a small succession of savannah plains, which allowed for better roads and more regular army patrols.

One of the biggest problems facing Military Command in Bissau was getting the army to patrol the thousands of kilometres of waterways that spreadeagled out from the coast. Many small streams were entirely obscured from the air by the jungle; others became swamps at low tide and one needed to know your way about to avoid being stranded. Quicksand was commonplace. Here again the guerrillas had the advantage of local African help who had good experience in these backwaters. Tribal people had been through these waterways for generations and it did not take the PAIGC long to plot many of the more obscure trails in and out of the country.

The most notable difference of hostilities in Guinea when compared to Angola and Mozambique, was that there was little organised terror and mass slaughter. It stayed that way, but only until the colonial struggle had ended.

Throughout the war, conflict in Portuguese Guinea was characterised by both sides employing classical tactical actions in their efforts to make gains. On the one hand, it was a textbook guerrilla struggle in a pattern similar to what was taking place in Vietnam. On the other, it was a testing ground. Many insurgent tactics were later put to good effect in Rhodesia's war and in South West Africa. Widespread use of mines was both significant and often crippling, limiting transport options and lowering morale among the troops. Both anti-tank and anti-personnel mines featured prominently.

While the nature of this war was interesting, the fortunes of the two opposing factions were even more so.

Because of Lisbon's overwhelming preoccupation with security – and consequently adverse publicity – the struggle remained largely in the shadows for the duration of the war. Journalists were not encouraged to visit the place, and apart from a few Africanists who made it their business to keep themselves abreast of events, hostilities in Portuguese Guinea raged for years without attracting anything like the attention it deserved. Vietnam served to deflect much attention from what was going on in Africa at the time

Meantime, the war went on and until about the mid-1960s, things went dismally for Lisbon. While Salazar's often ill-conceived controls from abroad were at their harshest, Portuguese fortunes remained in flux. Only after he had been replaced by the more liberal Prime Minister Marcelo Caetano – a more progressive leader, still Right Wing, who promised a more relaxed and open regime – did

Chapter 17
The war in Portuguese Guinea

conditions improve. On the ground in the war, the ebb and flow was slight, but the advantage always seemed to be with the guerrillas.

Within a year of the first isolated FLING attacks on the two small towns of Susana and Verela on the north-western Senegalese border in late 1962, the Portuguese High Command was prepared to admit that the "terrorists" controlled about 15 per cent of the countryside, but not a single town. Yet, while hostilities in 1962 did herald an intensification of hostilities, attacks in the north were regarded as little more than "civilian disturbances".

And although war was never formally declared by Lisbon, a far more intense level of conflict was initiated with an attack by combined PAIGC forces on Tite, Buba and Fulacunda in January 1963, which was when Cabral made his commitment formal.

Tite – from where I was eventually to set out on patrol with Captain João Bacar – was occupied at the time by a battalion of two companies under the command of a major. Buba and Fulacunda were garrisoned by a company each. In a guerrilla attack that took place while I was there, only one Portuguese soldier was wounded at Tite, although rebel salvoes did manage to destroy the ammunition dump. Next day the guerrillas ambushed a car travelling between Tite and Fulacunda and killed all its occupants. At the same time they attacked a section of Portuguese soldiers on patrol near a village to the east of Tite. In this action two Portuguese soldiers were killed.

From then on conditions deteriorated further, both for Portugal and Cabral's band of insurgents. Two years later Cabral was asserting that the area under his control had risen to 50 per cent, when, in fact, it had diminished. By 1971 the PAIGC leadership liked to claim that all but the last 20 per cent of the country around the capital was theirs which was simply not true because I was able to travel freely throughout much of it, even if I had an escort as protection, which was always a formality with journalists.

That said, Cabral would make his declarations at public meetings and then challenge Lisbon to prove otherwise, which he knew they wouldn't do. He said as much when I met him at the meeting of the Organisation for African Unity in Addis Ababa in 1971. There he told me that he still only needed to take Bissau and "I will then have the entire country in my pocket."

The first time he made this statement was in 1965. He was still at it when he was murdered in Conakry two years later, in a PAIGC rebellion in which some of his most trusted lieutenants were involved.

The Portuguese in Guinea fought a different kind of war to what was going on in Angola at the same time. In all, there were about 4,000 black soldiers in the army, all volunteers. As one staff officer explained, this was very different from Angola where some indigenes were conscripted.

In addition to these African soldiers that had been effectively incorporated within the 30,000-man regular army, there were another 4,000 blacks in civilian militia groups defending villages and homes. These were not men on active service, he explained.

"Instead, they play a paramilitary role in their areas and like our troops, they have guns, mostly G-3 rifles and here and there automatic weapons, but only those who have requested them." Additionally, he explained, there were about 6,000 local men who had been given firearms for what he termed was "self-defence".

That the Portuguese Army preferred the safety of its camps and fortified *aldeamentos* villages after dark, there is no question. However, as I was able to observe during my own visit, there were large areas where movement at night was unrestricted and free from control.

To start with, the Portuguese had complete air supremacy and they used it to good advantage, sometimes even at night. This was to change when Russian SAM-7s drove the Portuguese Air Force out of the skies in Guinea and gave the insurgents an edge that was regarded at the time as "formidable". Soviet missiles first appeared in March 1973, with three PAF aircraft lost in two months. By September the PAIGC claimed to have downed 21 Portuguese aircraft, which was nonsense: there weren't even a dozen warplanes in the entire country at the time.

Foreign journalists who visited Portuguese Guinea included an American, Jim Hoagland, who eventually became the managing editor of the *Washington Post*, and the West German veterans Peter Hannes Lehmann and Gerd Heidemann of *Stern*, one, of whom was later prosecuted for trying to market bogus Hitler diaries. The consensus among us all was that there were few zones actually "held" by the black guerrillas.

Instead, guerrilla bands embraced one of Mao Tse-tung's more salient principles on unconventional warfare of always remaining on the move, making unexpected strikes and taking actual control of few areas. It was rare that they would hold an area in the face of counter-attacks. In 1971, when the rebels announced that their forces had entered the third or "mobile warfare" stage of this form of unconventional warfare – the equivalent of full confrontation – the

Brew-up time for the troops in the jungle in northern Angola. (Photo: Author)

statement was contradicted by the situation on the ground.

Basil Davidson's observations in 1967 concurred with those of the PAIGC, but then Davidson did not even concede that the Portuguese could fight.

The truth is that it matters little how well the Portuguese fought; they were at war in three separate and widely dispersed regions in Africa for 13 years and lost thousands of men on a defence budget in all three conflicts of less than $450 million a year. And while they fared badly in Guinea and Mozambique, the war in Angola was all but won when it finally ended.

By the time I arrived in Portuguese Guinea in 1971, things had changed much for the better from the heady days of 1967 when General Arnaldo Schulz held precarious command. It was then that a new man took command, General Antonio de Spínola.

Like his predecessor, he had originally distinguished himself in Angola and as with his Angolan successor, General Bethencourt Rodrigues in eastern Angola, De Spínola was remarkably adept at achieving results in this still undecided conflict, at least until the air force lost the initiative.

One of the conditions imposed by De Spínola on being offered the command in Guinea was that he should have total control of the country without direct supervision from Lisbon. He also insisted that he should be allowed to choose his own staff. Both demands were granted by the Ministry of War, which remains one of the main reasons why the war soon turned in favour of the Portuguese, be it only provisionally.

Among these men was a young captain, Otelo Saraiva de Carvalho, who was to be my escort or "minder" while I remained in Portuguese Guinea. A charming, effusive intellectual in uniform, Carvalho became prominent in Lisbon at the time of the putsch as one of the radical hardliners who demanded a full-blown communist government for the country.

After a series of bomb attacks in the early 1980s he was jailed for anarchy and little has been heard of him since, which was a pity since he was dedicated to change.

One of the first changes insisted on by General de Spínola showed his grasp of guerrilla warfare. Following the example of Sir Gerald Templer in Malaya in 1952, he assumed total responsibility for both civilian and military organisations. This proved valuable in his attempts to come to terms with the liberation forces. He also sliced through red tape and interdepartmental hostility which, until then, had become characteristic of the Portuguese war effort in Guinea, and to a lesser extent in Angola, largely because the latter was almost self-governing.

Schulz had been both civil and military governor of the region, but his hands were tied by Lisbon's bureaucrats. Many of the plans that he tried to put into operation were thwarted. In retrospect, since he was the boss, much of the blame for tolerating interference in a rapidly deteriorating military situation must be laid at his door.

Another result of De Spínola's rule was the execution of long-overdue political and economic reforms. The changes for the better came too late, but in the last analysis, De Spínola stole much of the rebels' thunder, for they too promised changes and were prevented by the war from carrying them out.

The PAIGC took their country into independence with an explicitly socialist programme. Since then, after several army mutinies and a civil war that lasted for years, the country lapsed into a sorry state. Bissau was a dismal backwater when I visited the place in 1971. It was also bankrupt.

So much then for the ideals of a forward-looking liberation army and an independent Republic of Guinea-Bissau.

The individual responsible for running the war during my visit was the ascetic and intellectual career officer General Antonio de Spínola, who was later to write the controversial book *Portugal and the Future* that was instrumental in ending it. His view that Lisbon could not afford to fight on indefinitely in Africa and that there could never be a military solution eventually altered the course of the political and military fortunes of the Portuguese, both in Europe and in Africa.

A taciturn conservative, General de Spínola was always seen in public with his monocle and, despite the enervating West African heat, his hallmark leather gloves. Certainly of the "old school" this senior officer was regarded unequivocally as a father figure by his men. Strong both on discipline and tradition, there were very few soldiers under his command who did not stand in awe of him. Yet, if it made sense, he wasn't averse to innovation, even within his own command, which was one of the reasons why he was so successful in the field.

He had other qualities at which he excelled. Few could match his ability as a thinker, tactician, historian and ultimately as a visionary. In this respect, he had a more enlightening effect on the future of Portugal than any other man in the previous century, including the dictator Salazar.

I met him several times, both formally in his office and in the

Discipline on the road while convoys were on the move was erratic. Known stopping points would sometimes be ambushed or there would be anti-personnel mines laid by the guerrillas. (Photo: Author)

more relaxed environment of the local festival. Each time I returned to Bissau, I'd be ushered through by Captain de Carvalho at Military Headquarters in Bissau.

We got on well, even if he refused to speak English which, I gathered, he understood quite well. We'd sit down in his office and he would offer me wine or coffee and ask about my trips through Africa and the various leaders I'd met. He was intrigued by people like Nkrumah, Kaunda and Nyerere as well as the Biafran leader Ojukwu and wondered how South Africa would eventually cope with its own disaffected black millions.

It was a constant theme: whether Africa would survive intact in the years ahead. While he was sceptical because of corruption and mismanagement, he had hopes for the continent on which he had spent a large part of his career. I thought him a delightful and enlightened individual. The last time we made contact was the day after I'd almost crashed into the Atlantic in a clapped-out old DC-6.

After a string of in-air emergencies, we eventually got back safely to Bissau but because it had taken us so long to get off the ground that morning, I asked Captain de Carvalho to put me on the next day's Boeing flight to Lisbon. I didn't want to wait for the old prop-job to be repaired and didn't have the funds to get to Europe. Since I had a meeting scheduled with the Ghanaian foreign minister in Accra in a few days, time was of critical concern. I hoped that by approaching the general direct, that the army would pay.

Only one man in the country could make that decision, so Captain de Carvalho and I went to see the General. I explained the situation and without blinking, he agreed. I was to be given a ticket on the next day's Boeing flight to Lisbon, he told the Captain.

1 Bitter fighting was to follow the formal handover of power to the PAIGC in 1974. Conflict engulfed the country, culminating in a series of battles that lasted more than a year. It ended with the defeat and death of almost all the black troops that had formerly served in Portuguese Army units. Still more revolution followed, well into the 21st Century and as we go to print, conditions remain unstable, almost 40 years after "independence".
2 Nothing came of the venture in the end. I was to have gone from London to Lisbon over a long weekend and joined a command group and gone in with them. But somebody in Lisbon got cold feet and the operation was canned.

Al Venter covered all three of Portugal's African campaigns over several years. He found conditions in Portuguese Guinea to be the most dangerous and rigorous and is seen here with a marine unit on a river patrol near the tiny harbour of Cacheu. (Photo: Author's collection)

CHAPTER EIGHTEEN

JUNGLE PATROL

> "... by 1966, Guinea already had 18 militia companies and the authorities were requesting funds to create more, although still acknowledging the risks involved in having to deal with a volume of people armed, equipped and trained ..."
>
> João Paulo Borges Coelho: *African Troops in the Portuguese Colonial Army, 1961–1974:* Angola, Guinea-Bissau and Mozambique; Eduardo Mondlane University, Maputo.

The patrol on which I was to go with Captain Bacar and his men would take me close to the proposed camp site at Bissassema (not to be confused with Bissau's Bissalanca Airport), which was actually an extension of the Tite operational area. We would circle the outer reaches of the zone and hope to achieve a "contact", which was basically what counter-insurgency was all about. Essentially, the idea was to find the enemy before they ambushed us.

Also, we'd been told in the briefing that ambushes would be set by our group when expedient. The captain would be guided by local trackers or scouts, experienced military personnel who accompanied every patrol, mostly Balanta natives from the area.

I was warned by Lieutenant Jimenez that we'd be out for several days; his men were fit and this was what they did and they'd consequently be moving fast. Earlier he'd quizzed me about my ability to keep up because the schedule he'd planned was unrelenting. He cautioned too, that this was a serious business: our adversaries were tough and fit, perhaps even more so because they didn't have the comfort of a local base to return to once they'd "walked their beat". We'd possibly rest every four hours he reckoned, but once on track, it was all systems go for as long as it took. Also, we'd sleep in the wild and haul our food with us.

"If things start to happen and it looks promising, we're going to go for it, even if it takes an extra day or two." He then posed the obvious: "You still want to go?"

Chapter 18
Jungle patrol

Civilians in Portuguese Guinea were a diverse, largely loyal community who had experienced five centuries of Lisbon's rule. The majority were Muslim. (Photo: Author)

I nodded, well aware that he didn't need a "passenger", which was when he said something about bringing in a chopper to haul me out of the bush if things got really bad or if I was hurt …

I told him not to worry. I was more than eager and had been doing 400 metres in the pool each day in recent months. Still, he was worried and as a concession, I'd be allowed two additional litre cans of water as opposed to the single water bottle issued to the rest of the squad and somebody else would carry them for me. They'd be refilled from streams along the way, which, for me, meant taking along a supply of water-purifying tablets. The rest of the group had been drinking unfiltered water all their lives and each time I filled my bottles and popped the pills, the procedure was viewed with quiet amusement by the rest of the team. Give them their dues, they never said a word.

It was clear that I faced a stiff challenge. Because of the heat, I was going through two pints of water before breakfast. It was worse in the jungle where conditions could be stifling. I'd sometimes find myself dehydrated after only an hour's march. More to the point, this operation would be more testing than anything I'd tackled so far – including a Kilimanjaro climb. Still, I was young and possibly a little overenthusiastic. And while everything pointed towards the impossible, I wasn't going to let up, especially since I might never get this opportunity again.

Much of the country we'd be passing through would be heavily overgrown terrain, some of it triple-canopied and interspersed by swampland or rice paddies. While there were paths galore, we'd avoid them if possible because of mines and since I'd managed under similar conditions in Biafra, Angola and Mozambique, I felt reasonably confident.

Each member of the 30-man patrol was handed his rations the evening before we left. This so-called rat-pack[1] consisted of a large box that weighed perhaps two kilos and contained a tin of sardines, two small cans of sausages, chocolate milk in a carton together with a number of tubes containing a fruit concentrate, marmalade and butter. Bread was issued separately, just before we pulled out in the morning, which was when each man was handed two loaves, according to our camp doctor, "more than enough for the time you'll be out".

The rations were expected to last a soldier two days. The package was standard issue and used throughout Portugal's African wars. More food would arrive by chopper.

Saturday morning – the day we were scheduled to depart – came and went without the unit pulling out. It was a bind, but we'd have to hold over for another 24 hours, the colonel explained. A patrol already out in the bush had made a tenuous contact with something and was working at an encircling move. Since there was the possibility of an ambush later, some of the squad were made ready for a heli-airlift: they'd be deployed in a stop-gap role.

Word came later that the unit already out there was having a particularly hard time. They'd been moving at double pace for several hours at a stretch and their food had run out, but the colonel said his men were accustomed to hardship. "This is how we normally operate, the good with the bad," were his words.

We left the camp in a long file before dawn on Sunday morning and grabbed our bread at the camp gate. Tite lay silent and unprovoked against a dark jungle screen that crept up on all sides. Occasionally a figure moved in the darkness as we passed and once or twice we could hear the guards as they shuffled at their posts. Nothing was clearly visible: the moon had long since faded.

Bacar took point from the start. He said little, except that I should stay near Lieutenant Jimenez who, for the first leg, would be my guide or, more appropriately, my mentor. In the end, young Jimenez

Chapter 18
Jungle patrol

was with me for the entire patrol and it was manifest that I was his responsibility.

The two of us pulled aside to let the column pass and took up our positions towards the rear. Tough, disciplined men shuffled past, their austere faces unsmiling, more because they were still heavy with sleep than because of what lay ahead. Only Tomaz, a young junior officer barely out of his teens, could manage any humour at this ungodly hour; the hulking youngster loped past as if he were off to Sunday school.

"Hi," he croaked cheerfully with a flash of white teeth. I don't know how he did it because he'd led the liquor stakes in the mess the night before. Tomaz patted his kit bag before hurrying forward with the rest:

"I'll have something for you here later," he grinned. "I've got a small carafe of wine … for our supper …"

The early morning was cool, but because of the humidity, it started to get uncomfortable within 10 or 15 minutes of leaving base.

The men in the patrol carried a strange assortment of weapons. Of the 30-odd black soldiers – I was the only white man among them – more than half were armed with a new weapon that I'd not previously seen in any of Portugal's wars in Africa. This was a rifle grenade about 25 centimetres long and which protruded from the tips of their rifle barrels. Its business end was oblong and distended around the middle, like a badly swollen finger that had been caught in a door.

It was deadly, I was assured by Jimenez. Known as the *Instalaza*, it was of Spanish design and manufacture and had an effective range of about 400 metres. The anti-tank version could knock out an APC or armoured car, but in Portuguese Guinea it was used mainly in an anti-personnel role. The colonel had explained earlier that the *Instalaza* was a relatively small weapon that gave the infantryman a bit of muscle. If the unit came under attack, a dozen men using this kind of retaliation would be enough "to send the enemy scurrying", he reckoned. They'd had remarkable success so far, he stated, but was not prepared to elaborate, except to say that it was not only handier than the bulkier Chinese-supplied RPG-2 rocket in everyday use by the insurgents, but was lighter and more portable.

Another piece of hardware in our ranks was a recoilless rifle adaptation which had been designed and built by Portuguese engineers around the 37 mm Matra aircraft rocket. Special firing tubes with dozens of ventilation holes had been built to make an improvised bazooka. Its firing pin was activated by a small portable battery fixed to the barrel, which made it look like an elongated kitchen utensil rather than a sophisticated device of war. The warhead was French and like the *Instalaza*, packed an even more destructive punch.

Each operator in the squad who carried the device had about a dozen rockets that he hauled about in special sleeves slung about his body. The two men on either side of him shared the load and carried more warheads. The downside was that if any of these projectiles took a hit, there would be quite a few more men hurt.

There were three mortars included in our patrol, one each fore and aft and another towards the middle of the column where I eventually marched. Again, the two soldiers on either side of the tube had more mortars strapped to their belts, which would sway to and fro. If not covered in swabs of sacking, the mortars would sometimes connect loudly with protruding bits of metal or their rifle butts and the captain and Jimenez had their hands full to start with getting it right.

Each member of the patrol was armed with two or three grenades, like GIs fighting elsewhere. These were customarily suspended from their uniform lapels or protruded from their top pockets. Grenade belts were provided, but the men preferred it this way: it made for easier access if things suddenly got hot, one of them told me.

It took about an hour for the mist to clear from some of the low areas we passed through. By then we were well away from the camp, moving west at a steady pace. We'd reach a position well to the south of Bissassema and then turn north, Bacar explained before we departed. After that, he'd told his troops in the pre-departure briefing, we'd double back on our tracks. "Hopefully somebody would be encountered on the run back," he stated and the interpreter translated.

Only when the first rays of the sun lifted over the horizon did the troops perk up a little: they had been silent until then. Light-hearted banter was tossed about in desultory Portuguese undertones and it didn't amuse their captain: the order had been strict silence all the way. They kept at it while still in open country, moving from one rice paddy to another, but went completely quiet as soon as the first stretch of jungle loomed up. This, Jimenez whispered, was PAIGC country: from here on in we were on our own.

Bacar worked to a plan based on previous experience. Whenever the patrol approached an area where an ambush might be expected, he would detach some of his men and send them forward independently

Chapter 18
Jungle patrol

One of the small air strips in the interior regularly used by Portuguese Air Force planes. (Photo: Author)

of the rest. Some of the heavier stuff would be brought forward to give fire support and others would go round the flanks.

Two or three times before, Bacar told me, he'd found that an enemy ambush group had withdrawn in the face of this kind of encircling action. In truth, the tactic was only possible in open country where easy movement was possible. In some parts it was impossible to leave the track on which we marched because there was heavy undergrowth on both sides, which sometimes tended to envelop the squad. At other times, the black commando officer would move his men carefully a kilometre or two down a jungle grove and then quickly double back. Once he deliberately flanked a huge patch of palms and bush, working his troops through an open paddy field, but out of any effective close-quarter contact range.

"We're waiting for them to present themselves," he told me later when we halted briefly for a break. "PAIGC uses the Maoist principle of tactical retreat. They strike only when they're certain of being able to knock us hard; then they pull back. This way we hope to draw them into a contact or perhaps making a mistake," he reckoned. He called the tactic "tantalising" the enemy. In doing this, his men took chances, but everything was pretty well calculated.

Part of the problem facing Bacar and other Portuguese officers in this war was that the enemy rarely stood and fought. They'd hit and run, strike at a camp and melt away into the jungle to avoid retaliation. It was a well-honed system, of course: feint, strike, retreat: or play possum in the tall grass or possibly come in again from behind.

"The guys are keen, you can see that, but we don't always get the chance to exchange blows, all good classical guerrilla stuff." Often they prefer to lay mines or booby traps; "then, having caused damage, they'll strike while we're waiting for an evacuation."

At base earlier, I'd been shown a set of PAIGC directives that had been captured the previous month. These warned that serious contact with government forces was to be avoided. As one of the Portuguese officers explained, Cabral and deputies had been trained in the Asian communist tradition of fighting a guerrilla war and it was all guile, stealth and the premise that it is better to live and fight another day.

We made our first long stop at noon for a meal and by then I needed it. Some of the men ate in small groups between the trees, while others stood guard out of sight in the jungle beyond. The next time the procedure was reversed. Smoking was prohibited for the duration of the patrol: according to Bacar, the guerrillas could detect tobacco whiff from kilometres away.

When everyone was done, we went on our way again, but I noticed immediately that our patrol had noticeably thinned. Following pre-arranged instructions, about a third of our group had disappeared into the jungle and set up an ambush position along the track by which we'd arrived.

"We're under no misconceptions that the enemy doesn't know we're here ... they've been conscious of that from the start ... their own intelligence system works well," was Bacar's laconic comment when I asked him. Though he spoke no English, his translator was an educated man and managed easily with the sometimes difficult diction.

Bacar explained that the idea was to move from one area to another, sometimes across open country and paddies. More often than not the guerrillas were able to observe the column as it moved. "Once we're actually spotted, they'll try to keep tabs on everything we do, day, night, every minute ... if they can manage that and, of course, if our movements allow it.

"When they are about, they're likely to do something. Then we act. That's why I have left some of the men behind. If they come in – wham! We'd have them, and of course we can follow up because we're in radio contact. Or we can call in air support, which they

Chapter 18
Jungle patrol

don't have. That's it, in theory, anyway," Jimenez elaborated.

We'd taken a short break about mid-morning and Bacar had sent off some of his men to check a booby-trap position. We'd been moving at a fast pace all the while and must have covered at least a dozen kilometres by then, some of it over difficult terrain that included paddies half-filled with water. There had been a few aircraft and choppers passing through our line of vision for some of the time, followed by concentrated strafing and rocketing towards the south-east. The targets, towards Buba and Fulacunda, were visual, Bacar reckoned ... another patrol must have had a contact. Or it had been ambushed.

Although our column must have been clearly visible by Portuguese Air Force pilots operating in the area, we were secure: our position was constantly being relayed to base and, in turn, passed along to Bissau. Prior to emerging from any area that was foliaged, he'd call in.

During several trips across the country while in Portuguese Guinea, I often spotted patrols out in the bush and at first it amazed me that the ops people could keep track of so many fragmentary groups in the field. But the tracking systems employed by headquarters were both old hat and efficient, even if the Portuguese Army and PAIGC guerrillas wore a similar kind of camouflage.

Still, accidents sometimes happened. More than once there had been men in the field who came under "friendly fire". Usually it was the air force responsible and then only because procedures weren't properly followed. But that too, is modern-day warfare.

In Bacar's words, the column's radio was the next best thing after his ration-pack. He made contact with Tite every hour, his radio operator always close on his heels. The man lugged a bulky American-built "Man-Pak" transmitter which, he said, could reach Bissau if necessary[2].

He also told me that there had rarely been a patrol where he hadn't called for air strikes in the past, especially if he saw a guerrilla group slipping away before his unit was able to close, but it required a reasonable amount of precision on the part of the aviators as his men were never far behind. The fact that a Bacar patrol had yet to be hit by "friendly fire" spoke volumes for this commando officer's direction, especially since there were times when his men were sometimes perhaps a hundred metres behind the guerrillas when on the chase.

Bacar also liked to keep in radio contact with the extremities of his patrol. This could be difficult because the column was sometimes spread out over more than a kilometre. The officers used handsets, something I hadn't seen Lisbon's fighters doing in Mozambique. "They're handy when the other people are about," Bacar said, stating the obvious.

Thanks to the sets, orders were given quietly and competently. Sound travels far in this humid climate and instructions were relayed by radio and then passed on down the line from man to man in whispers. There was rarely any need for more.

It was noon before we encountered the patrol that was waiting to be relieved. Almost gingerly, we met up with them as planned along an overgrown ridge of high ground that I'd observed from a distance earlier in the day. The feature was notable, because Portuguese Guinea must be the flattest country in Africa, without a single mountain, or anything resembling one. Bacar had deliberately avoided talking the shortest route on the off-chance that guerrillas lurking nearby might have been aware of the other group and possibly set an ambush.

The patrol which had preceded us into the jungle was led by two native Guineans, Lieutenant Alphonse and a young *Alfares*, like Tomaz, who called himself Manuel. Both men were dressed like us, with one curious difference: they wore gleaming black monkey-skins over their heads, like large shiny bouffants that gave them a distinct animal appearance when glimpsed from a distance.

The element of camouflage was obvious, but it must have been hell wearing those contraptions in that heat and they didn't smell too hot either. For these officers there was more to the skin headdresses. Monkey skins have significant tribal overtones in Africa, part of it sexual because simians are prolific breeders and therefore potent. After the lion and the leopard, the skins of certain anthropoids hold a distinct mystical charm for some of the coastal tribes in West Africa. There are those who believe they're the reincarnation of departed souls and are to be accorded reverence whenever encountered in the forest. In certain regions of the Niger Delta, Liberia and Congo, monkeys are only killed for food, or to provide the chief or an Oba with a badge of office. In Guinea the ritual has similar connotations.

The troops we encountered that day were bushed. They'd been out on their own for three days and were tired and hungry. On top of it, they'd not had a single contact, though it'd been close. Lieutenant Alphonse didn't elaborate. Because their stay had been longer than expected, Bacar had brought along a few supplies, handed over with little ceremony.

Chapter 18
Jungle patrol

Like our own unit there were no white faces among them and they were surprised to see mine. Words of parting were cursory: a raised hand, hardly a salute. Then they were gone, very much as we'd arrived, melting silently into the jungle. They were keen to get back to their families, Bacar said.

We passed several villages during the course of our trek. A few were abandoned, though there were those that thrived and were typical of *tabancas* throughout West Africa. The majority would comprise a medley of children, goats, chickens and a skeletal hound or three. Occasionally there would be a monkey or a parrot at the end of a rope.

There'd always be women pounding corn or millet somewhere near the verge of the settlement, usually within sight of the roadway or track. If there was trouble, they'd be the first to sound a warning. The villages were domestic and fairly secure, reflecting a deceptive laid-back approach which had settled on this land wracked by almost a decade of war.

Jimenez and Tomaz took few chances in some of the remoter areas where loyalties followed the traditional jungle law of not having to take a chance if you don't have to. Whenever we approached a *tabanca* that might not be familiar to the men, they'd go ahead after leaving a detachment on the fringe for cover. It was the same pattern as before, since nobody was fooled that there hadn't been PAIGC reception committees in the past.

Only after friendly contact had been made did we pass through. It was no secret that the enemy covered this ground as often as the Portuguese did – sometimes many times more – because their secure bases lay across the border. The civilians that we encountered had long ago accepted the philosophy of extending a hand of friendship to all newcomers, which was fundamental if you were going to survive in a region where political differences could be terminal.

Once we stopped at a *tabanca* fairly close to Bissassema. It was late afternoon and we would rest and eat there before going on for the night. The village was evidently visited by both enemy and government forces as they welcomed us with a courtesy that was friendly but guarded. Bacar accepted the gesture in good faith. It was an uneasy symbiosis but a pragmatic one in the fluctuating fortunes of war. These people, Bacar felt, would eventually choose for themselves on which side their allegiance lay and if things continued as they were, he said, it wouldn't be with the PAIGC.

The patrol mixed easily with the local tribesmen and their families.

They were accepted with amity; some even shared their food as they probably would with the next PAIGC patrol that might arrive out of the dark. Our intrusion lasted barely an hour. Bacar handed over some money for the effort and we went on our way.

Apart from trying to improve relations between the government in Bissau and the ordinary folk "out there", Bacar insisted that his men always be cordial with the peasants. Any kind of intimidation or heavy-handedness was unacceptable. So was fraternising with the women, which he always held, might be somebody else's wife. Now and again some intimacy would take place, as it always does in Africa, although in this regard Bacar, faithful to the Qu'ran to the end, followed stringent personal dictates.

On how the enemy operated, the black commando officer was specific. The PAIGC, he said, followed General Giap's theory on how relations with the civilians were conducted. A rebel directorate had declared early in the war that PAIGC forces were to be concerned with establishing and maintaining good relations with all country people, whatever their political affiliations. PAIGC policy was based solely upon the identity of their aims, or so it was declared. He would then quote Amilcar Cabral, who echoed Mao's words about "the people being to the army what water is to fish". He'd included this maxim in the PAIGC code of honour, which, like the Viet Cong, took the form of an oath.

It declared that "in contact with the people, each comrade would follow three recommendations: to help the people, to respect the people and to defend the people."

Bacar: "You see, we have to fight fire with fire and the terrorist is pretty subtle at times," the black Portuguese officer remarked as we marched away through a large grove a short distance from the last *tabanca* we'd visited.

The village stop was the first time I'd been able to refill my water bottles that day and locals, astonished at the presence of a European among all these black troops, provided fresh water from a pump set in the ground; as much as I liked, they said. The troops could drink it as it came. I filtered mine, an agonizing 30-minute wait since I'd finished my original set of cans some time before.

We set our ambush for the night shortly after leaving the *tabanca*. Bacar marched us due south in the bush alongside a well-used track for about an hour. He then abruptly left the route and doubled back towards the village we'd just vacated, keeping to cover all the way.

Chapter 18
Jungle patrol

If the enemy was to follow us to the settlement that night, we'd have them, was the idea.

We could hear village activity in the distance as we approached again on our turnabout. They too were preparing to settle in for the night. There was music, laughter, conversation. Someone banged a gong in the distance, another called on a bugle-like instrument that I had spotted earlier and which was fashioned from the horn of an antelope; a single discordant note that carried deep into the night. I was to hear it afterwards in Bissau, a call that couldn't be mistaken for anything else once you'd heard it the first time.

There were more noises somewhere to the left of us. In the far distance the women of another *tabanca* were singing. This was Africa talking – melodious and harmonious in some regards, guttural and bizarre in others, but generally not unpleasing. These were simple, human sounds signifying age-old settlement in the bush. It was the same primitive discordant symphony one sometimes hears in Kenya, or Zululand, or Togo or even the Congo in places. They speak different languages, all these people, but on hearing sounds dissipated by distance and the irregular countryside, we could have been in any one of them.

Bacar carefully spread his men out a short distance off the track. We were about a kilometre from the village, with the troops on a small rise and the men on the ground roughly equidistant from each other. Riflemen were spaced between some of the others handling heavier weapons. Behind them were the rocket carriers and bazookas. At both extremities were positioned the light machine-gunners, their muzzles trained in a wide arc that, in theory anyway, could cover almost every point of the compass.

Behind were his mortars and these were positioned in a clearing just beyond some low trees over which they would fire. The men worked out direction and elevation while Bacar directed elsewhere. They also needed to have their backs covered and several pairs of soldiers were detached from the main group for that purpose.

It was an ideal site for an ambush. To cover any eventuality, the Futa-Fula officer sent two more men into the jungle behind us to cover the distant rear. They disappeared into the bush where they would lie up secreted for the rest of the night with only a small hand-held radio to make contact if things should happen.

Bacar didn't again have to explain the need for silence. It was to be absolute, he'd told me earlier and applied as much to me as to them.

No talking! No smoking either ...

The men settled down silently in groups, first the one lot, then another, leaving about a third of the patrol awake at any one time while some of the officers moved silently between their charges. Only Allah could help the man who snored, never mind anybody caught sleeping on his watch. Bacar had his own brand of punishment for this offence and it was ruthless.

It was a long wait till dawn. Ants and mosquitoes, some as big as houseflies together with other jungle insects were resolute, with the crawlies particularly fierce, especially since we lay on bare ground with no netting. There was no question of using any kind of lotion or cream: the enemy would smell it before the mosquitoes did.

Nobody thought of spiders or snakes, or even scorpions – of which I'd been told there were a lot – or if they did, they kept it to themselves. They were there, to be sure, but it's different when you're with a large group of men; it's usually the other man who will get bitten …

Earlier in the evening, before everybody had properly settled in, Tomaz had approached and produced his elixir and it was like magic. We each drank a little wine that night and had a couple more sips after it got light in the morning. I'd never handled wine for breakfast before and it made a change, especially since I'd hardly slept. It was a good substitute for coffee under the circumstances but I'd have preferred water. Again, mine was long gone.

The night was uneventful and I found it difficult to stay alert, even though we had the moon for company for more than half the time. Occasionally there'd be a rustle in the night to our left or to the right and one of the men would start. There were few other distractions and the men who needed to piss did so where they lay.

All weapons were already cocked; any metallic click can be heard over hundreds of metres by a trained ear and it was an effective measure. Bacar had imparted his basics well.

Shortly before midnight we heard a muffled explosion somewhere to the south. It came as a dull thump in the dark and Jimenez who was dozing alongside me looked up but said nothing. I knew what was going through his mind. Someone had probably put his foot on a mine …

One of ours? Or theirs?

Capitao Bacar's circuitous jungle safari followed a set pattern. The entire route had been detailed between him and the colonel before we left camp and they'd taken a while to settle the route, Bacar's boss wanting the men to go in one direction and Bacar in another.

Chapter 18
Jungle patrol

The black officer must have made good tactical sense, because he ended up winning the day.

The route had to be established for two reasons. The first was to advise air force command at Bissalanca, so the men wouldn't be rocketed while out patrolling. Second came mines – Portuguese landmines this time that had been set along some of the routes we would traverse. Quite a few tracks had already been booby-trapped by government forces.

But then we all knew that two could play at that game, Bacar reasoned when he explained. To avoid injury to the civilian population, tribal leaders were ordered to keep their people within the bounds of the territory they normally frequented. They knew the paths that led to the watering points or to the next village and so did his people. Beyond those limits, he would warn, their safety could not be guaranteed.

Obviously, the Portuguese Army also had to observe these strictures. Shortly before I arrived at Tite, a soldier had his leg blown off trying to return to camp along a route which had been mined by Colonel Lopes's men: he had been screwing somebody else's wife and it was rough justice. It was also a vicious cycle.

We left our positions in the jungle at the first hint of a false dawn. Like an effulgent curtain, a quiet glow crept slowly over our position, diffused and evocatively beautiful. One moment Africa is jet black and then, within minutes, trees suddenly appear 100 metres away, as if through a London smog. The men were up and on the move even before many of the birds had stirred. Like phantoms we slipped silently onto the track and were on our way again.

It came as a surprise to us all to learn a little later that morning that a PAIGC unit had set up an ambush only a short march from us and on the very same track. But Bacar said nothing to me, nor did Jimenez. Not then, anyway. Apparently, shortly after we'd left our ambush site, our trackers discovered the evidence.

The unit had been large – two bi-groups – about 60 men in all, the scouts had estimated. Had contact been made it would have been vicious. Like Bacar they'd used an L-shaped position from which to prepare their ambush and it might only have been the luck of the draw that we stopped where we did for the night. Or perhaps it was the PAIGC on whom the lady smiled, for this was the same bunch of guerrillas that ambushed Bacar seven days later.

I was to return to this country quite a few times in the decades that followed. Twice I went in to make television documentaries of the country whose representatives now sit at the United Nations with the name tag Guinea-Bissau on their desks before them. It's turned out to be an extremely difficult transition because the country teetered from one violent insurrection to another with tens of thousands of people killed. It continues intermittently to do so.

The lovely old town of Bissau is a macabre shadow of what it was when Lisbon was still around, its buildings battered or imploded as factions battled in the downtown areas for control. Many of the old historical structures have been purposefully defaced, some of them five centuries old.

I wandered about the interior with my film crew for weeks, though not to Tite. That, some of the locals told me, had become one of the biggest "killing fields" in Africa, with the rebels initially ranged against the same black troops who had once fought for the Portuguese until they were all wiped out. One source said that in the end, anybody even vaguely linked to *Comandos Africanos* had been slaughtered. So were their families. There was no word of young officers like Tomaz or Jimenez or even the monkey-skin-clad Lieutenant Alphonse or the rest. Memories die hard in Africa.

I also went north to Bigene, where the early Portuguese navigators landed on this stretch of coast six centuries before. The old fort still stands, today a repository of some of the old colonial relics that couldn't find a home elsewhere. Many of the bronze statues were

After Lisbon had vacated its African possessions, the communists were waiting in the wings to take over: a local newspaper follows the party line

lodged there, behind two-metre-thick granite walls, including one of Vasco da Gama, the first man to round the Cape on the sea route to India. By now, with metal prices hitting the rafters, they've probably been melted down and sold as scrap.

Half a kilometre away, along the narrow estuary that leads into the sparse interior, there was one of the original Alvor Class gunboats used by the Portuguese Navy in the closing stages of this colonial war. Lying high and dry on the beach, the craft had been stripped, its aluminium plates long ago oxidised all the way through in places.

These were proud little fighting craft in their day and had been handed over intact to the new regime. Within a year, they'd been beached and left to rot, their engines sold to a passing Chinese fishing boat.

1 Ration pack.
2 Not to be confused with Manpad – shoulder-fired anti-aircraft missiles like the SAM-7 or Stinger.

CHAPTER NINETEEN

IN THE HEART OF AN AFRICAN MILITARY STRUGGLE

> "However long [these African guerrilla struggles] take, they will sooner or later involve everyone in Africa, south of the equator. Already some have died for a cause that is barely understood by the mass of the people ... at the same time it is only the beginning of the story."
>
> From Al Venter's prologue to *The Terror Fighters*, one of the first reports to appear on Lisbon's wars in Africa when it was published in 1969.

The sound came as a heavy coughing grunt from somewhere in the tropical darkness outside, followed by another, then another. Moments later, a high inrushing noise like a sheet being ripped culminated in an explosion nearby. A powerful blast swept through the officers' mess where we were sitting at dinner and shattered windows on all sides.

More shells started falling around the camp, followed by the irregular dull plops from remote mortar positions beyond our barbed-wire defences. These only helped to accentuate the pattern of heavy artillery directed our way; we were under attack.

It is strange, but whatever the origin of a mortar — British, American, Iranian, Russian or Chinese — they all have that same hollow "plop" when fired, probably because the mortar is such a simple weapon, a tube with a firing pin fixed to its base. These bombs, I knew, were Chinese. I'd gathered that much from one of the officers who'd rushed out into the night as soon as the first blast sounded.

"Chinese," the man screamed above orders being hastily issued by the camp commandant. Moments before, he'd been sitting at the head of our table and we'd actually been enjoying both the meal and the *vinho tinto*, backed by plaintive strains out back of the winsome

Chapter 19
In the heart of an African military struggle

Portuguese marines on river patrol in Portuguese Guinea. (Photo: Author)

voice of Amália Rodrigues singing fado. By his almost casual reaction, there was no mistaking that the major had experienced this kind of onslaught before.

"Get under the table and stay there until it's over," another of the officers screamed. Yeh! like I want to miss the action ...

Shortly afterwards our camp batteries opened up from several points along the perimeter.

Bacar, meantime, had also rushed out into the night. It'd be over in minutes, he shouted over his shoulder as he scuttled for the door. I learnt later that it was his job to assess the direction and distance from which the attack was made. The idea was possibly to send out a patrol if he thought contact could be made and this time, apparently, it couldn't. I gathered afterwards that the attackers were more than an hour's hard march away and there was swamp country in-between. It would have been impossible in the dark: the enemy had chosen their positions with discretion.

I'd been left alone in the mess as everyone rushed out to cope with the emergency. Out of curiosity perhaps, or maybe fearful that the Tite officers' mess would take a hit from one of the shells, I followed the men outside, crouched in the shadow of a huge baobab and watched as a 105 mm howitzer crew loaded, fired their gun, reloaded and fired again. They let loose 15 or 20 rounds at potential enemy positions that had been pre-plotted to hit likely strike points in the bush. Degrees and elevation were called out by the officer in charge as he called out compass readings and elevation from a board in his hand that was lit by the pencil beam of his pocket flashlight. His specifications were repeated in a gruff, bucolic voice by the gun aimer who hardly seemed to appreciate the urgency of the occasion for his gestures were slow and deliberate. Cool, some would say; the man was in no particular hurry.

Three shells were fired at one position, three at another, then back to the original target again; all barrels were aimed south, the direction from which the attack had come.

Much effort was put into teaching the locals to defend their homes against guerrilla attacks. Willing volunteers were given weapons and instruction to achieve this objective. (Photo: Author)

The men worked to precision. The only sounds above the roar of the big guns and exploding shells were readings given by the officers and answered by the men, navy fashion. They knew exactly what they were doing because they'd started firing before the fifth or sixth enemy shell hit the base.

In three or four minutes it was over. A cloud of white and orange smoke hung in the air and the acridity of cordite burnt our nostrils. Although the camp was blacked out, the scene was lit by a diffused light from an almost full moon which had started moving towards its apogee late in the afternoon. Only much later would an inky blackness descend, but by then the moon would have disappeared over the horizon.

A short while later the officers ambled back to the mess in small groups, about 20 of them in all, their conversation animated. Others were elated because there hadn't been a casualty.

"Terrorists," João Bacar laughed as he walked in again. The tension had emboldened his usually passive character. His black face glistened in the light of an oil lamp a steward had placed near the bar: it was too soon to start the generators again, one of the other officers commented.

"There might be another attack later," was his comment. There usually was. The captain's beret was perched at a cocky angle on the side of his head. "The bastards said they'd hit us and they did ... we'd had a tip-off," he told me through the interpreter. "Perhaps someone informed them that we have a foreign journalist staying with us ... and they want to give you something to write home about," he chuckled.

He turned to talk to his commanding officer in Portuguese. "The hour of seven had arrived when those shells started falling," said another officer to my right. Many Portuguese soldiers say you can almost set your watch by it; roughly an hour after sunset was when most of these attacks took place.

"The big guns that hit us were Russian," the commandant told me later after he'd assessed the damage. Then the mood dampened after word came from the gate that two civilians in a nearby *tabanca* alongside the camp had been killed; their home had taken an oblique hit and there were seven wounded, including a woman who'd lost a leg.

More serious, he commented, was that the guns were 122 mm Russian artillery, long-range stuff and it was the first time they'd struck so deep into the enclave, although Lisbon's intelligence services had been aware that they'd been around for a while. They'd originally been landed in Conakry, the strategic Guinean port city further to the south that was being used by the Soviet Navy. But that was not the end of the story. The following morning two Soviet-supplied MiG-17 fighters flew low over Tite on their way to Bissau. The jets circled once, their pilots probably intent on seeing the extent of damage inflicted the evening before. The airmen, it was ascertained later, were Nigerian, although the planes were sometimes flown by Algerians, all of them operating out of Sekou Toure's Guinea.

PAIGC guerrillas didn't hit Tite again while I was there. Also, the onslaught had borne indifferent results. Altogether 24 shells were fired and almost all landed beyond the defence perimeter.

The garrison at Tite, I was told by the commanding officer, Lieutenant Colonel Baptista Lopes — another Mozambique veteran — worked to a routine that was invariably predetermined whenever an attack was launched, on average once a month.

"The first shells we fire from each of the large guns are geared to go when the gunner is given the signal by his officer. They're already in the breach and aimed at a predetermined target; we just have to pull the trigger. When we've fired our first three shots, we realign the sights and fire three more at a new target, and so on. We go on until we think we've covered the full gambit ... it's all quite simple."

There were not many places in the surrounding jungle from which the insurgents might have been able to launch their shells, the colonel affirmed. Each of the sites needed to be close to an access route so that the weapons could be manhandled into position. These locations had been carefully surveyed and pinpointed and designated responding targets.

"They always seem to go back to the same positions. Tomorrow we'll go and have a look."

How effective were his howitzers? I queried. Under the circumstances, Colonel Lopes reckoned, he couldn't think of anything better for countering this kind of irregular warfare; neither too large nor too small. In any event, the insurgents rarely attacked up close: they'd usually stalk up to within a few kilometres and use their guns and for this reason his retaliation had proved adequate. Problem was, they still had to make their escape and the guns were bulky, so nothing was easy, he added.

One of the conclusions reached later was that the long-range artillery presented a new kind of problem because the PAIGC was now able to attack from further away. "That's sometimes beyond the range of our weapons, but of course, greater margins would proportionately lower their accuracy," was the off-the-cuff comment from another Portuguese officer.

The heavy artillery was all part of Portugal's multinational armoury, the colonel told me the following day. The guns were originally German, and actually dated from the pre-World War II period. "But we've replaced their original barrels with American ones and the ammunition we manufacture ourselves, in Portugal."

Seated around the mess table at lunch the following day, the colonel

Chapter 19
In the heart of an African military struggle

A protected village in the African war zone, or what Lisbon referred to as an *Aldeamentos*. While similar to what the British instituted with its Protected Villages Programme in Malaya, this African version produced few dividends, largely because of inadequate security. (Photo: Author's collection)

spoke about Bacar's role in the war.

Captain João Bacar, he declared, indicating with a nod towards the Futa-Fula officer across the table that was almost respectful "is part of what I like to call my First Team". He explained that the captain, at that moment, was outlining a plan of counter-attack to another officer and was almost oblivious that he was the subject of discussion.

This African officer, said Colonel Lopes, headed a recently established fighting unit known as the *Comandos Africanos*, an elite group of hand-picked black soldiers who, in the short time they'd operated together, had distinguished themselves as an aggressive bunch of front-line fighters. Their ability in the field and tactical prowess was almost as renowned throughout the colony as it was in the Guinea Republic and Senegal, he reckoned, adding that they enjoyed an élan of their own, not matched by any of the white or mixed-race metropolitan units then active in the region.

"And let's face it, that says a lot," declared the colonel, who spoke excellent English because he'd been to school at Marist Brothers College in Johannesburg in South Africa.

Five other black commando officers were attached to the same mess. One of them, Lieutenant Jimenez who was to accompany me on patrol, was a Futa-Fula like Bacar and sat opposite me. He didn't have much to say, but was friendly, smiling and nodded each time our eyes met.

"A good fighter, that Jimenez," one of the other officers acknowledged quietly when he heard I was to go out with him on patrol in the morning.

"He's as unconventional in his tactics as he is in his dress...prefers a woollen astrakhan to a cap and you'll never see him without his AK. That gun is his Excalibur; he took it from a man in the jungle after he had killed him with his knife."

The other black officer present in the group was a friendly hulk of a man, *Alfares* Tomaz who, although only commissioned shortly before, had come through a number of scrapes. Tomaz had been recommended for a decoration after a particularly weird attack in which one of his men was wounded and dazed by an enemy RPG-2 rocket. Instead of lying low and waiting for a medic or for the enemy to withdraw, the injured soldier staggered, shell-shocked and aimless through the trees with bullets popping all around him. Unbidden, Tomaz left the safety of his own position, sprinted through the jungle towards the man, picked him up like a bag of string beans and returned with him to his own lines.

Tomaz was of Sierra Leonean stock. Of that much the youthful officer was aware, but he confided, had no idea how his parents had come to Portuguese Guinea or why they'd done so. "It certainly wasn't for money," was his comment.

Tomaz spoke good English and knew some Freetown Creole which his father had taught him. At the same time, this hulking black officer was proudly Portuguese, and like Bacar, willing to fight to uphold that identity which he considered sacrosanct for reasons of his own. It was an unrealistic and, some would say, unwise dedication which few Europeans or independent Africans understood, but, as I was to discover, it was possibly linked to that same irrefutable quality that caused so many black men to fight valiantly for the British in Malaya, with French troops in French Indo-China and, more recently, with white South Africans in their own border wars. Also notable was the fact that here were many more black soldiers in the uniforms of Rhodesian security forces than whites, all of them actively combating African ZAPU-ZANU insurgents in the Zambezi Valley.

In sheer size and physical strength, young Tomaz was probably bigger than Jimenez and Bacar together. He had the power, they'd joke, to lift them both – and perhaps another like them – and carry

Chapter 19
In the heart of an African military struggle

all three to the edge of the base. They hadn't tried it yet, Jimenez quipped, because he reckoned it would have been too darned uncomfortable.

Tomaz was known among his friends as the "gentle giant", although he was considered "frivolous" by some of the senior men in the mess.

"It's his youth ... he does crazy things at times," said the colonel. Tomaz was only 21 and, as young as he was, he was regarded by his colleagues as a master of the art of practical jokes. He'd once offered his commanding officer an exploding cigar and got a week in the cooler for that stunt and also had some of his pay docked, but it didn't affect his rank. The man was too valuable a combatant, somebody at headquarters had argued.

Although a Muslim ("but not a good son of the Prophet", he'd confide), he didn't hide the fact that he enjoyed his liquor. In contrast to Bacar and Jimenez, both of whom abstained, *Alfares* Tomaz drank just about anything handed to him, and in the words of some of the men who shared the mess, Tomaz was "quite a guy".

Those who served under him, even some troops who were considerably older, held him in deep respect, for in the short time he'd been commissioned, he'd proved himself a leader of men.

I'd arrived at Tite in the long-disputed Quinara region after returning to Bissau with an officer who'd introduced himself as Captain Alcada. I was offered another aide, but refused his services, at least for the time being. I thought I had an adequate grip on the war, I told Lieutenant Colonel Lemos Pires, my liaison officer in Bissau. If he had no objections, I'd prefer to make my own way about the country.

All I asked for was transport and, surprisingly, he agreed, although obviously I'd be passed from one military unit to another and radio messages would take care of the details. The units I'd be visiting obviously needed to know about this hack by the time I arrived.

In part, my gesture was self-serving. With another man as part of my retinue, I couldn't cadge lifts on the occasional chopper as easily as if I were alone. The same with small fixed-winged planes like the Dorniers. I had to be constantly on the move and one interloper instead of two was the obvious way of doing it. There would always be somebody waiting for me at whatever destination I chose and clearly, I'd have to tell headquarters where I was heading each time.

Captain Bacar was waiting for me at Bissalanca Airport the morning I was lifted into Tite by helicopter. The captain had come across the river to greet me because I'd specifically asked to meet the man who was already more than a legend in his own lifetime.

This Futa-Fula officer didn't have much to say on the way over, but he kept his eyes on the jungle below as we sped south. This is "my area" he explained through his interpreter and at one point he thought he'd spotted movement in a thick clump of palms about 15 kilometres from our destination and ordered the pilot to turn around and make a closer inspection at tree-top level. Bacar was right.

Tiny figures scattered in all directions as we shot past, barely a metre above a ragged row of tall palms which surrounded a nearby paddy. We circled a few more times while the pilot gave directions on the radio. Bacar identified the clump on a large-scale map which the pilot handed to him and passed on a row of digits to base. The first T-6s could be seen approaching the site before we moved on.

At Tite, the regional headquarters – and eventually, following this colonial war, the scene of huge battles between competing liberation groups that left thousands dead – it was business from the start. Two Daimler armoured cars greeted us at the helipad and our little party was taken past some pretty formidable defences to the mess.

Colonel Lopes had about 500 men under his command, of whom about 200 might be in the camp at any one time: it was indeed very different from Mozambique, where most of the Portuguese Army was base-bound. His was an important zone in the middle of Balanta

Portuguese Navy patrol craft on one of the rivers in Portuguese Guinea. The author visited the country decades afterwards to find these boats lying broken and abandoned on the shore. (Photo: Author)

country and his men were often in contact with "hostile forces". The Balantas, he explained – there were about 20,000 of them — were a cautious lot because they were neither for the enemy nor against.

The position was best summed up by the officer who spoke to Jim Hoagland of the *Washington Post* who covered the war shortly before I did; he was speaking about Balanta country: "There are villages where we go in the day and receive a very good welcome. At night, the terrorists receive a very good welcome, too."

According to the Portuguese, the men of the Balanta tribe were a gregarious, generous lot. They were good workers, good drinkers and good fighters with whichever side they chose to embrace. It was not surprising therefore that many PAIGC members were from this tribe, which was also scattered north of the Geba River. There were also a good many Balantas in the Portuguese army, so you sometimes had brother fighting brother, or a father ranged against a son. As a people they enjoyed life and they showed it. When they threw a party it went on thumping hard, drums and all, sometimes for more than a day.

The Balantas had some peculiar customs. Every man, woman and child in the community were animists. They worshiped Ira, their god of fate.

Essentially, the nucleus of their belief was that worn old maxim: what will be, will be; it was Ira that decided which way the cookie crumbled. It was up to the individual to appease his god in his own way in his or her day-to-day considerations and this was done by making regular offerings of rice or palm wine at a succession of tiny shrines in every Balanta *tabanca*.

It was interesting to observe that the authorities – the majority of them staunchly Roman Catholic — rarely attempted to tamper with these tenets. Since most indigenous rituals fringed on voodoo or black magic – called *ju ju* throughout much of West Africa, with rites conducted by the local Balanta witchdoctor who charges a small fee for his services — it had long been evident that there were Balantas among the slaves who were shipped westwards from Africa two or three centuries ago. It is to be expected therefore that some of the customs observed in Haiti, Jamaica, New York, Savannah and elsewhere in the US, Caribbean and Brazil suggested Balanta overtones, even today.

Full-scale Balanta ceremonies are held at all stages: from birth, early childhood up to puberty and the circumcision stage. Boys as well as girls were circumcised at a certain age, usually about seven or eight and the tradition continues.

The operation on young boys is simple enough and is usually performed by the resident medicine man with the help of a piece of broken glass, a razor blade or a jagged jam tin lid. It becomes a lot more complicated with the girls.

The procedure – today the subject of a United Nations campaign to eradicate practices that are universally regarded as inhuman (except in much of primitive Africa) – is to "surgically" remove the clitoris, almost always without an anaesthetic. In later life, this is supposed to preclude coitus during intercourse which, Balanta men believe, results in their women remaining more faithful to them than would otherwise be the case.

It's all nonsense, of course. It was curious that the Portuguese in their part of Guinea were divided as to its purpose. There had been debates about the debilitating effects such abuse would have in later life, for the long-term effects as we now know, are serious. In Nigeria's Calabar area, the suicide rate among those who have had a clitoridectomy have been the highest in the nation for a while now.

For the rest of it, the Balanta community appeared to live and work willingly enough under government control. At Tite they were administered by a rather obese, self-important district commissioner who ran local affairs from his office in the base. He struck me as distinctly pachydermic, in both senses. He, in turn, was aided by tribal leaders, most of whom were based on the nearby *aldeamentos* or *tabancas*, the former being what was termed "the bringing together of rural communities under one command". The idea was to avoid the guerrillas enjoying the support of unprotected communities in the bush.

Tite had formerly been a regional capital and was still an important agricultural area with rice paddies stretching away in all directions. Coming in from Bissau by air, we spotted them just about everywhere and I couldn't help comparing the scenario to what I'd experienced in Southeast Asia.

I should have arrived the week before, I was told. The previous weekend had been the annual crop festival known locally as the *Quesunde*, the most important of all Balanta feasts. Because of the war, there had been no *Quesunde* for seven years and the colonel was proud that he'd been able to bring back something that the locals hadn't enjoyed for a long time.

But it hadn't been all one-sided. PAIGC command in the area had served notice on tribal elders that they would sanction no festivities while the Portuguese ruled. Countering, General de Spínola took the initiative and ordered Tite and other encampments to go ahead

Chapter 19
In the heart of an African military struggle

The author changing film while moving through the jungle with an armoured column.
(Photo: Cloete Breytenbach)

anyway. Consequently, the first *Quesunde* festival for a while went off like a charm.

A lot of it had to do with the annual crop that had been the best for some years, and also that things seemed to be improving all round, even the outcome of the war. Consequently, the message came through that there was no time like the present for a little frivolity. The guerrillas retaliated by warning that anyone taking part in the festival would be killed. The feast went ahead and something like 15,000 Balanta men and women kicked up their heels for three days and nights and significantly, the colonel said, there were no insurgent antics.

Immediately afterwards, during my visit to the camp, they hit Tite. That was the attack I'd experienced.

The onslaught graphically illustrated a remark made by one of the officers at Tite, Major Art Valente. He spoke excellent English and served on and off as an interpreter for much of my stay in a region that stretched from the Atlantic to Fulacunda and Buba further towards the east.

For every action made by the Portuguese, he said, the enemy would react, even if it took a bit of time to do so. If General de Spínola endorsed a fiesta, the PAIGC would demonstrate its disapproval by hurling shells at the camp. And if he happened to visit a region outside the capital, the guerrillas would retaliate, if only to make it known that they disapproved of his presence and were still active militarily.

De Spínola did, in fact, visit Tite while I was in the country. It was the last event I covered before returning to Lisbon and it took place in the presence of thousands of local tribesmen, with the general handing out certificates and medals to local civic dignitaries who had stood fast with Portugal during difficult times. The guerrilla ambush in which Bacar was killed, followed shortly afterwards.

"It's really a point of honour as far as those bastards are concerned; they counter our every move," Major Valente explained. "And if they haven't the manpower available just then, they'll send for reinforcements and do it later."

PAIGC attempts to stymie events at Tite reflected only one aspect of the kind of clandestine operations conducted by insurgent forces in this Portuguese colony. At the same time, it barely concealed more noteworthy characteristics of guerrilla strategy: that apart from the military effort, there were also economic and political considerations

The aftermath of the mutiny by the Portuguese Army in 1974: there were riots in all the major centres in Angola, Mozambique and Portuguese Guinea. This scene of destruction was in Lourenço Marques, Maputo today. (Photo: Author's collection)

that involved a huge measure of intimidation of the locals. If someone was believed to be colluding with the government, at whatever level – attending a government clinic, visiting a relative in a military camp or perhaps paying a government tax — a brief Comintern-type "show trial" would be held in the village and that person would be executed. Kafka wouldn't have been pleased to recognise the pattern had he been able to visit the place.

Unarmed civilians had long been a focus of PAIGC attrition. So had public services, lines of communication, transport, commerce, industry and agriculture — the warp and woof of everyday life in Portuguese Guinea and, to a lesser extent, in Angola and Mozambique.

Such operations as the rebels conducted against the hated colonials were directed — it was repeatedly claimed in their communiqués — to attain greater freedom of action with regard to the real objective: the destruction of the fabric of the nation. By then these same arguments were being bandied about in other guerrilla struggles in Southeast Asia, Indonesia, Tanzania, and later in southern Africa, almost as if they had emanated from a single source, which they probably had, although clearly, Beijing by then had almost as much influence in some of these Third World conflicts as Moscow.

The guerrilla strategy in Portuguese Guinea was neither offensive nor defensive: principally, it was evasive. For example, in areas where government control was relatively weak, the insurgents would go onto the offensive. But that rarely happened. It was more a case of seeking out your adversary's soft underbelly, which wasn't difficult in a country so grossly undeveloped.

Elsewhere, evasion remained the keynote of PAIGC strategy.

CHAPTER TWENTY

SIX SOVIET CHOPPERS AMBUSHED IN ANGOLA

During the final stages of South Africa's cross-border operations in Angola, the Angolan Air Force, supported by the Soviets and its allies – and in particular, the Cubans – became increasingly active in the south. Backed by advanced MiG-23 jet fighters as well as a range of Sukhois, the South African Air Force had lost air superiority over Angola. Simply put, the SAAF was outmatched. Then somebody got the idea to ambush a bunch of enemy choppers. In the skirmishes that followed, four Soviet-built Mi-25 Hind helicopter gunships and two Mi-17 Hips were knocked out in two five-minute sorties.

Wars have spawned anecdotes since the beginning of time. So, too, did hostilities in Angola while the South Africans were fighting there.

One of the most notable events of the conflict – the shooting down of six Soviet helicopters – took place in October 1985. A SAAF fighter squadron equipped with Impala Mk-2 strike aircraft destroyed six Angolan Air Force (FAPA) helicopters while they were operating routine sorties near the South West African frontier, effectively bringing to an end the Moscow-backed and supplied Operation Second Congress. Composed of a series of armoured strikes, the ground effort had initially been launched to cripple Dr Jonas Savimbi's UNITA guerrilla movement.

For several years, UNITA rebels had been making gains from their bush headquarters at Jamba in the extreme south-east corner of this vast country almost twice the size of Texas. A remote and isolated region of Angola, it had been known since Portuguese colonial times as *Terras do Fim do Mundo* (Land at the End of the Earth). Operation Second Congress, conceived and put into effect in Luanda, took the form of a two-pronged armoured strike, designed primarily to regain control of the Cuzombo Panhandle and recapture Mavinga. It was intended, as one Luanda newspaper phrased it, to "impale Savimbi on his own defences".

The combined Angolan Army, known as FAPLA, would launch a final assault on Jamba, the idea being to destroy its main base of operations. That was the intent, but this being Africa, there were problems.

In all of south-east Angola there were only two airfields which could be effectively used by the Angolan Air Force in most weather conditions. The biggest was Menongue (called Serpa Pinto during colonial times). The other was at Cuito Cuanavale, which lay further towards the east in the direction of the Zambian border. Cuito was demarcated specifically for helicopter operations during the course of the operation, while jet fighters would be based at the "more secure" Menongue.

Throughout, Angolan choppers would move between both airfields in communications, support and re-supply roles. For all that, Luanda tended to keep its air assets well away from the frontline and there were only four Mi-25 Hinds, a pair of Mi-8s as well as four Mi-17s routinely based at Cuito.

Anyone who has seen the Angolan hinterland is aware that this is an extremely difficult country in which to wage a war. Roads, even today, are sparse and hardly maintained. Apart from some large rivers, the terrain is almost featureless, with no tropical jungles like those found further north towards the Congo. Instead, the region is characterised by huge expanses of sparse mopani forest that can sometimes reach upwards to about 20 metres and much of the rest is savannah. The topography of pancake-flat eastern Angola barely varies by more than 30 metres for as much as five or six hundred kilometres north of the South African Air Force base at Rundu in the Caprivi Strip. Originally listed on the charts as the *Zipvel* – which was what Imperial Germany called this narrow sliver of land – it snakes eastwards all the way to the great Zambezi River where the frontiers of three nations – Namibia, Zambia and Zimbabwe – conjoin at Kazungula[1].

Hence, the Angolans and their allies could take little comfort from the fact that overland travel and navigation in eastern Angola has always been an appalling experience, and it goes back centuries. There are no outstanding geographical features, no escarpments nor any major settlements of consequence. As the South African pilots would say, the safest navigation method was always to stick to the

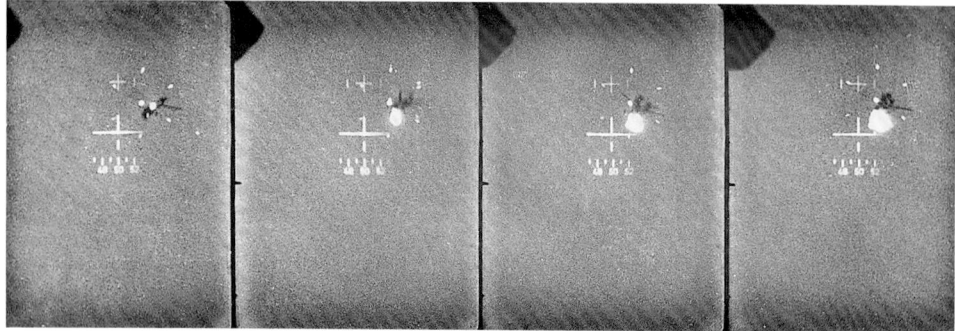

Gun-camera sequence of photos which show the destruction of a Soviet-built Mi-17 (Hip) helicopter after it took 20 mm cannon hits from SAAF Impala fighter/trainers in South Africa. (Photo: SAAF Archives)

river lines, or possibly follow the few "roads" that criss-crossed the region like spider tracks.

In the Angolan context even today, the word "road" is loosely used. Most are sandy tracks, and if the ruts become too worn or too deep, it's easier to bundu-bash a new one alongside the old ones. Because bedrock, as in any semi-desert region, lies 60 metres below the surface, more often than not you are likely to spot a dozen different sets of tracks in the sand, all lying parallel to one another and all leading in the same direction. And while Angolan military vehicles were used for ferrying in most of the heavier supplies needed by outlying military camps and moved in heavily protected convoys, regional logistics was largely dependent on what the rotor-wings and the occasional Antonov transport plane could haul in by air.

The South Africans had their problems as well. As the war progressed, Caprivi – with its army and air force base straddling the single strategic east-west road across the north of the country – became increasingly critical to the military effort in Ovamboland, where most of the fighting was taking place. For much of the conflict *Oom Willie se Pad* (Uncle Willy's road) remained unsurfaced, which meant that it was regularly mined. Also, Zambia lay just across the broad Kavango River that separated the two countries and Rundu was only minutes' flying time from Robert Mugabe's Zimbabwe. To the south lay Botswana, then also hostile towards a South African military presence, but never a real participant in the military struggle. In short, none of these countries were in any way well-disposed towards the South African apartheid regime.

One of the more prominent features of eastern Angola, even today, are the vast open grasslands that often stretch for hundreds of kilometres and which are referred to as Chanas by the Angolan Ovimbundu tribal people. Even then, there was an argument that ran along the line of isolating an army – or perhaps a squadron of tanks or infantry fighting vehicles in these open areas that offer very little cover – and using a handful of helicopter gunships to cause an awful amount of damage.

The South Africans had long been aware that in Angola's Cuito Cuanavale area – to the immediate north of Caprivi – hostilities had always dictated a vital need for helicopters to resupply Angolan garrisons in the region. They were aware too, that the situation was fraught and it didn't always work. A chopper would be lost to ground fire or one or more would be grounded because of lack of spares. Consequently, there were times when some FAPLA brigades were desperately short of essentials, especially since Savimbi's tenacious policy of ambushing road convoys was not only effective but commonplace. He chose the time and the place and hardly any of those road convoys got through intact. While Luanda controlled the towns and had air dominance, UNITA guerrilla units governed the countryside and the rebels had long ago mastered the art of shock and surprise.

Nonetheless, Angolan Air Force assignments in the area were a daily affair. They provided such necessities as fuel, vehicle spares and medical supplies. Weapons and ammunition, in contrast, were too heavy to be ferried in by air in any quantity, except in emergencies.

Medical evacuation or "Medevac Missions", as they were called, would also be launched when necessary, but to spend time and fuel on bringing out somebody wounded or ill by helicopter meant that that individual had either to be a political VIP or a high-ranking army or air force officer. It was not surprising that all Soviet political and military personnel fitted into this category. Troops on the ground were regarded as expendable and nobody wasted any fuel on them.

Aware that the South African Air Force operated in this southern region with a measure of impunity, it was left to Angolan Air Force Hinds to provide cover for the lumbering rotor-wing Hip transporters, as well as giving close-air support for ground forces. These gunships would sometimes offer "flushing fire" onto remote landing zones during troop deployments and on these missions 57 mm rockets would be used in shallow dive attack profiles and, on rare occasions, cannon fire.

Chopper formations would transit at between 3,000 and 6,000 feet above ground level (AGL) with escort helicopters following a minute or two later. The formation would fly in line astern for the transport helicopters, with the Mi-24s customarily maintaining a loose echelon pattern with roughly 1,500 feet separation.

Depending on the threat, helicopter formations would often be escorted by MiG-23s flying at about 15,000 feet and customarily orbiting towards the rear. Yet, for all that sophistication, Soviet advisers were also sometimes heard to mutter that the threat of RPG-7 rockets was a bigger problem than Moscow was prepared to accept, which was surprising because in Afghanistan it had long been the Mujahadeen infantryman's weapon of choice.

South African intelligence learned early on that the pilots at the controls of Angolan helicopters feared UNITA ground fire a good deal more than any real or perceived threat from a fixed-wing formation, in large part because of the Stinger anti-aircraft missiles that Washington had delivered to Savimbi's forces a short while before. This was then also taking place in Afghanistan and there was no question that these deadly little SAMs (or in the lingo, Manpads) did a lot of damage. It didn't take long for the Angolans to revise their operational tactics, which necessitated their helicopters flying at high altitudes.

Going by reports since made public, the Stingers originally arrived at Jamba in US military aircraft, together with American instructors who were responsible for training UNITA missile crews. Those of us who were able to visit Savimbi's home base knew that they were around somewhere in that southern bush area, but we were never able to set eyes on them.

There were other problems, including some serious ones with the Angolans themselves. It soon became evident – even to the Russians and their Cuban and East German allies – that accepted standards of flying competence within the Angolan Air Force was dismal. Navigation among these aviators was so bad that their foreign advisers prevailed on them to use physical features such as river lines, bush tracks and "roads" to reach their destinations.

South African intelligence briefings would often mention the fact that the Angolans would very rarely fly on a direct route to any point. Also, it was clear fairly early on that the basic lack of navigational competence was another reason for flying at height. Even then, pilots often failed to find their LZs and more significantly, following the Soviet pattern of going strictly by the book, missions tended to be planned for the same time of day.

Radio procedures and discipline within Angolan Air Force ranks was poor. However, this improved as losses increased or when Russian pilots flew as formation leaders. It is interesting that only

Chapter 20
Six Soviet choppers ambushed in Angola

The photo above shows an Mi-24 (Hind) helicopter gunship about to land. The second helicopter (below) is an Angolan Air Force Mi-17, but this one was flown by pilots attached to the South African mercenary group Executive Outcomes. (Photos: Author)

two radio frequencies were used by operational aircraft; one for fighter and helicopter operations and another for transport aircraft ops. Night flights were unheard of: all rotor craft had orders to return to base before last light.

By October 1985, South African forces were heavily involved in supporting Savimbi's guerrilla units in a bid to stem the flow of FAPLA forces heading southwards towards Jamba. At about this stage Pretoria decided that it was essential to deploy a squadron of their Impala (Macchi 326K) ground strike aircraft to Air Force Base Rundu, in Caprivi, largely to give own forces close-air support when requested to do so. It was a calculated move, since South African Army elements engaged against FAPLA brigades were only a fraction of the number of the enemy; the ratio being something like one-to-twelve in favour of the Angolans. By the last week of October 1985, it also became clear that the Angolan ground offensive had fallen behind schedule, badly so.

Intelligence sources indicated that FAPLA had decided to change its basic plan and launch a significantly bolstered strike, backed by armour, to capture Mavinga to the north of Cuito. Jamba, the intercept indicated, would come afterwards. Clearly, it was a softening-up process, but these sources did mention that Angolan helicopters were flying daily to resupply their ground forces.

With these facts in mind, Dr Savimbi, in a surprise move, approached his South African counterparts with a proposal: Why not shoot down the helicopters being deployed against him in south Angola using the Impala jets based at Rundu? Clearly, the idea had merit.

Word has it that the first reaction from Pretoria was one of stunned silence. Then someone said something about such a move possibly escalating the war and bringing MiG-23s over South African air space. Someone else talked about that not being necessarily so, especially if the Angolans were not made aware of the fact that it was jets that had been used to down their choppers. UNITA could claim to have shot them down with their Stingers …

And so the discussion went on until everyone sitting around the table on that momentous day agreed that perhaps this was an idea that might work. The proposal was referred back to headquarters and a signal was sent out 24 hours later with the authority to proceed.

Pretoria made a single stipulation: UNITA was not to be involved in the strikes. In fact, Defence Headquarters was adamant that Savimbi was not even to know that the go-ahead had been given. There was good reason, including the fact that nobody was certain to what extent UNITA's command structure had been infiltrated by MPLA intelligence agents. In any event, the South Africans always tended to play their cards close to their chest, so the prerequisite was nothing unusual. What it came down to was that Pretoria did not intend to tell its principal Angolan ally that it intended to shoot down what amounted to almost a squadron of Angolan helicopters and so, perhaps, alert the Angolans to the coming strike. Should Luanda have word of it, they would obviously take appropriate counter-measures.

Military headquarters in Pretoria immediately instituted intensive flight evaluations to determine the most efficient method to use jet fighters to destroy helicopters in the air. It was accepted that they would do this without giving the Hind pilots an opportunity to fire back; or to establish exactly what it was that had destroyed them. To determine the profile to be used for this action, SAAF Puma helicopters were drafted in to simulate enemy chopper flying techniques and formations used.

The first problem encountered by the Impala crews was that while in Angolan air space, they would be forced to ingress at extremely low levels (50 feet AGL) in a bid to avoid enemy radar coverage. That would be the *sine qua non* of the entire operation, first to maintain surprise and second, to prevent MiG-23 escort fighters from taking any kind of retaliatory action during the approach and return legs.

The most suitable profile determined was to attack from either the flank or from behind, and perhaps slightly above the target helicopters.

The altitude that Angolan choppers maintained in their daily operations presented the South Africans with several problems for

Chapter 20
Six Soviet choppers ambushed in Angola

the hoped-for standard-quarter attack. If this was attempted with an Impala jet with full underwing stores, the speed at the top of the pitch tended to be a bit low and should the helicopters be alerted, they might accelerate away from the attacking aircraft. Naturally this involved a potential tracking solution.

A decision was finally reached to reduce the rate of pitch once the attack had been initiated and to flatten out at its peak so as to maintain speed. The aircraft were to fly in pairs and, when going in, a type of "scissor" pattern would be maintained with the lead aircraft knocking out the rearmost helicopter first, and the wingman moving into the kill on the next chopper in line. This pattern would be repeated, depending on the number of helicopters in formation.

For the South African fighters there was no problem with the route likely to be flown by the Angolan Air Force helicopters; they knew about their pilots' preference for visible features.

Once most of the preliminary planning had been settled, the Impalas were split into four sets of pairs, three for reconnaissance and attack and the last as backup and, should it come to that, to be used for "search and rescue". Additionally, a couple of Puma helicopters were tasked to be airborne during the mission for similar reasons.

Timing would be vital throughout and was calculated in seconds. The combat zone was 35 minutes' Impala jet flying time from Rundu, while the "time gate" (when enemy choppers would be in the most remote area between Cuito Cuanavale and the combat zone) was equally critical. Pairs of Impalas were to take off at four-minute intervals: they would fly more or less the same route to the anticipated contact area and back.

Six headings were calculated to give most area coverage without placing crews' lives or aircraft safety in jeopardy. Pilots were instructed to make one pass over the route and not to loiter if enemy aircraft had not arrived when expected. Most importantly, radio silence would be maintained throughout. Pretoria had long been aware that Luanda had deployed the most sophisticated Soviet monitoring equipment and that they were able to pin-point a position with direction-finding (DF) equipment from a single radio emission.

To inform the South African pilots of the status of enemy choppers and their fighter escorts, a fixed-wing single-engine aircraft was positioned nearby the area to pass on codewords; a not-unusual precaution as these aircraft were always in the air, day and night. With that, Impala crews were placed on standby at Rundu; they would be scrambled as soon as word was received of any enemy helicopter movement.

At approximately 16h00 hours Bravo on the afternoon of 27 September, a brief radio message, in code, was received at the SAAF ops rooms, Rundu. Two enemy Mi-24 attack helicopters were airborne. They were moving from Cuito Cuanavale in the direction of the war zone. The Impalas were scrambled and headed north towards the previously designated area of operation.

It seemed as if only minutes had passed before the wingman of the second pair of Impalas made visual contact with the helicopter formation directly ahead and above him. The Hinds were flying at approximately 2,000 feet AGL.

Since he was in the most favourable position, the wingman initiated his onslaught by pitching up towards the rearmost aircraft. He came in from behind and above the target helicopter and his initial burst of fire was observed by the lead aircraft to strike towards the rear of the chopper's fuselage. Moments later, the Mi-25 started to burn and its pilot initiated an emergency controlled descent. The helicopter then started to burn furiously and the pilot fired off a clutch of FFAR rockets normally fitted to the underwing pods before jettisoning all his underwing stores and continuing with the descent.

The leader of the Impala formation then saw the first helicopter initiate a steep descent towards the ground. He immediately began his quarter attack and approached the descending helicopter from below and to the side. By then, the helicopter had turned a full half-

Four South African Impala jets flying in formation during training. It was these aircraft that shot down the Angolan Air Force helicopters flown by Soviet pilots. (Photo: Author).

Chapter 20
Six Soviet choppers ambushed in Angola

circle through 180 degrees and was still in a steep, nose-down diving attitude.

Using rotor diameter, and not the size of the sight reticule relative to the helicopter to estimate his range, the jet leader pegged the firing distance on the sight at 500 metres. His aim point was at a spot just below the main rotor gearbox. Fixing his gunsight in air-to-air mode, he only fired when the diameter of the diamond on the sight was less than the rotor diameter and the pipper on the exhaust port. Although he wasn't counting, it was established afterwards that 19 rounds were fired, and as he confirmed, he could clearly follow the strikes on the starboard fuselage of the target, exactly where the pipper had initially indicated. The attack was carried out at approximately four-to-five Gs.

Recounting the event afterwards, the Impala pilots got the impression that suddenly everything had gone into slow motion; they could observe every detail, including the detachment of a side panel of the helicopter, at which point the machine immediately adopted a nose-high position and the rotor blades separated. The chopper went into a tail slide, hit the ground and exploded, sending a tall plume of smoke and flames into the air.

By this stage the wingman had repositioned his aircraft for a second pass on the leading Mi-25 and shot it down. With the second strike, its rotor blades also separated. The Russian-built helicopter crashed into the ground nose high and exploded. Both SAAF pilots descended to a low level to evade any potential MiG-23 threat and returned to base at Rundu.

A report went out, again in code: "Mission successful."

Two days passed before another strike was possible. At approximately 09h00 hours Bravo on 29 September, word was passed to the operations room at Rundu that a formation of helicopters was airborne out of Cuito Cuanavale: all were headed for the war zone and consisted of two Mi-8/17s and a couple of Hind gunships. The Impalas were scrambled and the same procedures used before were observed. This was almost a carbon copy of the first attack, only it took place in the full glare of the morning sun.

It was not long before the crews spotted their objectives; all four helicopters were flying along the Lomba River at approximately 3,000 ft AGL.

Drawing closer, the Impala pilots saw that the two Mi-17s were flying in a line-astern formation, roughly 1,000 metres apart. The Hinds, about a kilometre behind them, were in an echelon formation and separation was approximately 500 metres. Then everything happened quickly.

The wingman of the formation was in the best position to attack and immediately initiated a quarter strike on the rear chopper. Pitching upwards to a position approximately 1,000 feet above the Angolan chopper, he waited until he was within range and fired a long burst of cannon into its fuselage. The helicopter immediately caught fire, but instead of losing altitude, it continued straight on course.

The long burst of fire coupled to the extremely low airspeed following the pitch, suddenly caused the engine of the attacking Impala to flame out. The South Africans suddenly had a serious problem of their own, compounded by the need to maintain radio silence.

By now the Impala formation leader had also come into position and set himself up for his attack on the second-last helicopter, another Mi-25 gunship. During that run-in, he crossed ahead of the burning rearmost helicopter and, for a second or two thought that the Angolan pilot might try to squeeze off a burst. Nothing happened.

Approximately 500 metres from his target, the leader fired and he could see that his rounds struck the helicopter's tail boom and rotor. Moments later the helicopter's entire after-section separated and the Hind spiralled into the ground without catching alight. It exploded on impact.

There were still two helicopters ahead; the two Hip transporters. By now they were well aware of what was taking place, having almost certainly been warned by the first Hind: there was furious radio chatter among the Angolan pilots, all of which was probably being picked up by the Soviet monitoring bases in the north.

Having meantime re-lit his engine, the Impala wingman attacked the rear Mi-17. As he did so, the chopper pilot carried out what could best be described as a full rudder turn in a desperate effort to get a proper view of his attacker and possibly be in a position to retaliate. It was futile: the Impala opened fire and the helicopter flipped onto its back, falling towards the ground upside down and exploding on impact.

Only one of the original four helicopters remained airborne; the last Mi-17. Having observed what the Impalas had done to his comrades, he immediately lost altitude and went down almost flush with the ground at tree-top level, an exercise he completed just as the lead Impala came in. But the Hip was too low for the leader to track properly and the jet's rounds exploded harmlessly into the

Chapter 20
Six Soviet choppers ambushed in Angola

Much evidence of Angola's war with South Africa was left littering Angolan airports airport long after the hostilities had ended. This is one of the sophisticated air-to-air supersonic missiles which would have been fired by MiG-23s. (Photo: Author)

ground behind the target. That was when the two South African pilots determined that the single survivor could not be allowed to escape.

Breaking radio silence, the leader called to the other formations flying nearby, but by now he had lost visual contact with the Mi-17. It had effectively disappeared into the tree-line in a desperate bid to elude its pursuers.

In the debrief that followed later, it was noted that the Hip pilot had turned towards the attacking Impala, forcing him to overshoot. The South Africans were convinced that since FAPA pilots had received no aerial combat training, it could be assumed that that chopper was being flown by a Russian. His escape tactics suggested a good understanding of anti-fighter evasive training.

It was minutes before the next pair of Impalas arrived on the scene. By now the Mi-17 pilot — believing that the jets had withdrawn — decided to take his chances and managed to regain some altitude. It was clear to the South Africans that he had a course for his home base, a bad mistake. The Hip was immediately spotted by the leader of the newly arrived pair of jets who prepared to go in on the attack.

By now, also aware of the threat because he had been flying a zig-zag pattern, the Mi-17 pilot spotted the predator on his tail and abruptly put his nose down. In a desperate bid to escape, the helicopter hit the ground hard in an open space between the trees in what he had obviously hoped would be a controlled crash. Instead, his main rotors separated from the fuselage before the hulk finally came to a halt and the helicopter toppled over onto its side.

The third pair of Impalas arrived moments afterwards, but they decided that it was perhaps time to move out; there were just too many aircraft over the target area.

The South Africans had barely started to egress for home when the leaders spotted two MiG-23s flying over the burning wreckage at about 200 feet AGL. The Soviet jets did not orbit, but carried out a single pass over the wreckage, probably in a bid to ascertain whether anybody had survived. Surprisingly, this was a new tactic; SAAF pilots were aware that Angolan fighter aircraft had never previously been observed at heights lower than 15,000 feet, probably because of the threat of Stingers which, by then, was a constant.

Having passed once over clumps of burning wreckage that lay scattered about the bush, the MiG-23s lit their afterburners, folded their wings and shot up to an altitude that was less intimidating.

There were two consequences as a result of the loss of the six helicopters. The Angolans immediately stopped deploying rotor-craft during Operation Second Congress. They did send in their French-built Alouette helicopter gunships to pull their Russian advisers out of the front-line when the South Africans threatened to overrun their positions, but there was no other helicopter activity.

Second, it was acknowledged that this was the first time in history that an Impala jet fighter, originally built by the Italians – and ostensibly a trainer – had managed to destroy enemy aircraft in aerial combat. Although jet fighters ranged against helicopters hardly rates comparison, it nonetheless happened and the event is listed in the record books.

It also remained one of the contradictions of a war that had been on the go since 1961 – first against the Portuguese colonials who had ruled their three African fiefs for five centuries – and later, through a succession of civil wars between the various political factions. Effectively, it was an unbroken 40-year period of hostilities, one of the longest in modern times.

1 Germany originally colonised South West Africa (Namibia) until it was overrun by the South African Army in World War I. The territory was then handed to Pretoria as part of a League of Nations trust mandate (in the same way that Tanganyika, also formerly German, was administered by Britain until independence in the 1960s, ultimately to become Tanzania). The South African government refused to relinquish that responsibility after World War II, and it formed the basis of the bush war that followed.

CHAPTER TWENTY ONE

WILLEM STEENKAMP – REPORTING ON SOUTH AFRICA'S BORDER WARS

It was Holger Jensen, the much-wounded Associated Press staffer in Vietnam and *Newsweek* correspondent who made the rather innocuous comment while reporting from South Africa that "you really do not get a good press by lying to it ..."

It appears that most of today's younger media practitioners have a rather distorted idea of what their predecessors had to contend with, or got up to, during the "apartheid era". This is hardly surprising.

First, because that same "apartheid era" ended when the main run of them were still at school; second, because almost every day brings more outpourings from self-seeking politicians and people who did very well in the "apartheid era" and are now busy with a frenzied self-exculpation process; and last, because, in retrospect, the South Africa of 1965–1990 was a strangely schizophrenic state with racial priorities, hidden political agendas and an ingrained *baasskap* mentality which intruded into the very being of the country's psyche. Indeed, it is difficult to compare the South Africa that we knew then with any other community I know of.

Therefore, under the circumstances, it is hardly to be wondered at that South Africa – and South Africans – tended to baffle first-time visitors of all shades of opinion unless they arrived with their minds already made up. It could probably be said that the South Africa of the 1965–1990 epoch quite often baffled South Africans as well, and continues to baffle the journalistic generation that grew up after it began its slow march into history.

The nature and manifestations of South Africa's schizophrenia were both various and complex. That was perhaps to be expected in a country which was not so much a nation as a crazy agglomeration of peoples and territories, converted into uneasy bedfellows as a by-product of the age of imperialism and then hurried into statehood.

With hindsight, its internal contradictions are possibly easier to discern. And to understand how us scribes who covered military affairs operated between 1965 and 1990 – and how it felt to be doing so – it is necessary to know something about those contradictions.

- The political system was both democratic and undemocratic. There was a functioning parliamentary system, with reasonably free, fair and transparent general elections based on what the politicians of the day liked to refer to as universal franchise. At the same time, it had several major shortcomings: the universal franchise was only for whites (plus, latterly, coloured and Asian-origin voters, by way of separate chambers) but excluded what might be termed "pure" blacks. In typical British style, Parliament and not the constitution was the supreme authority on all matters. Also, it should be remembered that certain political groups like the South African Communist Party were excluded, regardless of ethnographic composition.
- There was a genuinely independent judiciary, whose verdicts, interdicts and judgments were (unlike those in modern Zimbabwe) scrupulously abided by. However, at the same time, the judiciary's hands were partly tied because there was no supreme constitution, and therefore no body of written precedents to consult or from which to seek guidance. Judges and magistrates were sometimes obliged to try people for contravening laws that were blatantly undemocratic in spirit or intent or both, or undermined long-accepted but uncodified precedents.
- There was a strong and very vociferous trade union movement whose existence was enshrined in legislation. At the same time, many unions made no bones about supporting the banned African National Congress, to the extent where it was the basis of the ANC's internal operation. This was an unanticipated result of the government's banning of the ANC and other organisations, together with its legalisation of black union membership. Deprived of other forms of political

expression, the organisations turned a large sector of the trade union movement into their chosen vehicle and rode it with grim determination, using every legal loophole and platform in spite of detentions, bannings and worse.

- There was genuine freedom of religious practice, although the National Party government made no secret about its Christian nature. In addition, while many churches and preachers were deeply involved in political activities, the various widespread monotheistic fundamentalist movements of today did not exist as such, and no-one (a few maniacs aside) had any inclination to foment a classic religious war (as we've seen in Iraq). Possibly this was also due to the fact that, with so much else to be divided about, nobody really noticed that the fundamental religious strife angle was going to waste.
- There was a large and obedient defence force that, by the late 1980s, had long since ceased to be all-white as a result of an on-going integration process that had kicked off in the mid-1970s. By the final stages, the Permanent Force of the South African Defence Force (or regular component) contained a substantial number of members who were other than white, some of them holding fairly senior commissioned and non-commissioned ranks in both combat and combat-support arms. It was still white-dominated, especially in the top echelons, and although the army was based largely on racially segregated units, the country's Special Forces were increasingly multiracial, as were ships' companies in the South African Navy. One of the part-time components, the Citizen Force, was still mainly white, while the other, the Commando Force, had a strong representation of non-white members.
- There was a large national police force which was in an even more advanced state of integrationist evolution, especially at the coal-face, although also still dominated by whites at senior and top levels. What few people noticed was that the police, heavily overstressed by unrest and subversion — not to mention tasks for which they were not geared — were not only beginning to lose the war on non-political crime but had acquired some very dubious fringe structures.

- The government's security services were in plain sight: the Security Branch of the police and the National Intelligence Service (NIS), the latter established as the Bureau for Security Services in the early 1970s (to the frustration of its founder, Lieutenant General Hendrik van den Bergh, the media promptly nicknamed it "BOSS"). At the same time there arose over the years, a variety of highly clandestine bodies of one kind or another that were completely invisible to members of the public and all but a very few members of the security services. Eventually these included the NS's StratKom section for special operations, including covert political action and psychological actions; the Directorate of Military Intelligence's Civil Cooperation Bureau, the Directorate for Covert Collection, the Directorate for Special Tasks and 7 Medical Battalion Group. The Security Branch — in addition to its long-standing intelligence and counter-intelligence sections — also maintained a Technical Section which, in turn, formed part of its Special Task Force. Quite possibly others existed that remain top secret to this day. There were some that carried out fairly straightforward intelligence collection and related tasks, while others, like clandestine bodies all over the world, went rotten. At least one became a scam operation into which tens of millions of rands vanished without trace, while in other cases actions ranging from farcical to atrocious were committed. The Truth and Reconciliation Commission exposed many of these crimes.
- Classic apartheid caught a cold in the late 1960s. By the late 1980s it was dying by inches. Formally introduced as a concept after the National Party's narrow 1948 election victory (the NP actually lost the election to General Jan Smuts's United Party, but gained a slight parliamentary majority by making a deal with a splinter third party). Contrary to what many people now seem to believe, it was not a changeless monolith but a mutable entity, and within a few years entered a long period of evolution that resulted from a variety of internal and external onslaughts. The onslaughts were changing social mores, national and international agitation and sanctions, the demands of the Cold War and inexorable marketplace

pressures together with an array of nonsensical policy measures that either could not have worked properly even under ideal circumstances, or had effects unforeseen by their initiators.

For example, Prime Minister Hendrik Verwoerd's mad-scientist scheme of creating notionally independent black "homelands" were not only economically handicapped by his disapproval of "white" investment but also firmly established the universal-franchise principle.

Eventually apartheid was more of a mess than a policy or even a philosophy. A glut of apartheid laws coexisted in the statute book with a large body of exceptions to those laws, always the sign of bad legislation. Scores of other measures were struck down, some very significant, like the abolition of influx control aimed at keeping down black emigration to urban centres. There were others of much less moment. While it is now forgotten, these latter-day abolitions actually helped to prepare the way for President F.W. de Klerk's

Helicopters were always an important part of reporting the Border War, but while the SADF would fly correspondents to the areas where military activity was taking place, getting photos on operations involving helicopters was a rare event. Because of possible negative reaction from France, Pretoria never allowed the media to show their Alouettes with weapons mounted, as seen here on ops in Ovamboland. At the same time, they couldn't stop us from taking our cameras along.
(Photo: Author)

turnaround of February 1990. The cold reality of it all was that simple segregation itself was on a heart-lung machine.

By the late 1980s grand apartheid had become an embarrassment. It was a burden to those who had inherited it from the 1948 generation, but no one in government knew what to do about replacing it, or what to replace it with, other than the ANC's option, which was simple black majority rule. Sadly, few observers accurately gauged apartheid's advanced degree of debility; we were all too busy with other things of immediate importance. Yet the signposts were there.

Watching over and commenting on all this was an active and long-established independent press, both the mainstream component and a fringe element, which reflected many shades of opinion.

However, at the same time, its elbow-room was restricted in some areas, particularly those relating to security (although not much in others), and when it overstepped the mark it suffered the legal consequences. But it never ceased pushing the envelope, its practitioners adroitly ducking and diving their way through a minefield of security legislation, outbursts of urban unrest and, not least, the normal laws of libel to which all journalists are subject.

The bottom line was that South Africa, for all its problems, boasted the most liberated press in Africa, although this is not saying much, since for most of the period in question virtually the entire continent was firmly in the grip of an assortment of autocrats of one shade or another. While these dictators differed with regards to aims, ideologies, methods and agendas, they were unanimous in their convictions about the undesirability of free media.

The antics of African leaders such as Idi Amin, *Osajyefo* Kwame Nkrumah of Ghana, the Central African Republic's "Emperor" Bokassa, Mobutu Sese Seko *et al* completely overshadowed the achievements of enlightened rulers like President Sir Seretse Khama of Botswana and his successors. There is a line of thought about these matters that some of these demagogues and tyrants actually prolonged the existence of apartheid. So did the perception that the ANC was a communist organisation.

Subsequent events have of course proved that this was not so; but that was the impression created, inadvertently or not, by the ANC's propagandists, who never made any serious attempt to woo white South Africans. This is not to say that the then National Party government's spin-doctoring contraption was exactly subtle; one would not be far wrong in comparing it to a sledge hammer.

Take one example, when two African National Congress operatives accidentally blew themselves up during a bombing attack. That it was an "own goal", and an embarrassing one at that, was transparently clear from the stumbling statement issued by a spokesman in Dar es Salaam.

A reporter I knew called the minister in question, Louis le Grange, to ask for permission to quote the statement. No, said Le Grange, the most intransigent man in the Cabinet. The reporter pointed out that the ANC would be deeply embarrassed to see the statement in print but Le Grange was not interested. The ANC was the ANC, he declared, and it was not going to get a word in edgeways.

No doubt one could say that people should have looked below the surface and accepted inter alia that the ANC had to talk the talk because it received most of its help from the Soviet Union. But as any competent journalist will tell you, most people are prone to base their perceptions on what they personally see or hear, whether that is superficial or not.

An additional aggravating factor was the Cold War, in which the sense of a titanic struggle between the world's communist and non-communist nations permeated just about everything.

South Africa was obviously a significant strategic prize, not only because of its minerals but also because it lay halfway across the only sea route between West and East that was open all year round. This was why the Soviets supported the ANC while top Western nations cultivated extensive links, mainly clandestine, with Pretoria. Ideologues and opinion-formers on both sides frequently misinterpreted the motivation for this support, whether deliberately or through sheer ignorance.

These issues aside, there were few signal victories in this protracted press struggle, although the media did manage to hound a couple of cabinet ministers and other pooh-bahs out of office. This small band of scribblers also managed to exhume some major dead rats from their carefully concealed coffins, such as what was termed at the time the "Information Scandal" of the late 1970s when the then Minister of Information, Dr Eschel Rhoodie, was revealed as the author of a vast, very clandestine and very free-spending propaganda machine.

In-between such much-savoured coups, the press also managed to keep the public informed about the vigorous debates and scandals within and outside Parliament, not to mention an excess of other things that, strictly speaking, were prohibited by existing security legislation.

Pre-1990 South Africa was a hectic and sometimes perilous place for the media practitioner – reporter, commentator, stills photographer

Going on actual operations with military units took time and patience to organise. The author was eventually accepted by the officers and he often went on patrol with units, such as this day/night operation that involved an ambush with SWA *Spes Magte* (Special Forces) – an elite South West African unit composed of black and white troops. (Photo: Author)

or television cameraman. It might sound callous, but the country provided the average journalist with an array of subject matter, professional challenges and outright problems that today's young journalists – operating in a country which is at peace and regulated by a comprehensive supreme constitution – would find difficult to imagine.

Remember, there was an external, albeit undeclared, war (in the territory variously called South West Africa, South West Africa/Namibia and just plain Namibia). There was also an increasingly intensive internal insurrection led by the ANC, coupled to the pressures of the Cold War mentioned above, wholesale collapse and chaos outside South Africa's borders (including fighting in Rhodesia and Mozambique) as well as the bogey of international sanctions. And heading it all was a government, which, like all governments, was exceedingly reluctant to have its internal scandals hit the headlines.

This is not to mention several fiercely contested general elections and the usual share of scandals coupled to natural and human-made disasters that are the journeyman reporter's normal fare. Small wonder then that the South African media in the 1965–1990 era was a happy hunting-ground for adrenalin junkies and assorted

Captain João Bacar of the Portuguese Army was one of the most celebrated – and highly decorated – military men in Lisbon's military forces. Among a slew of decorations, he was a recipient of the coveted Gold Order of the Tower and the Sword, Portugal's highest military award and roughly equivalent to Britain's Victoria Cross. A brilliant tactician, he led his commandos on dozens of raids against PAIGC guerrillas and was killed in a contact a week after the author had been on patrol with his group of fighters in the jungles of Portuguese Guinea. (Photo: Author)

CLOCKWISE, FROM TOP LEFT: Captain João Bacar's patrol moves through fairly open terrain an hour or two after leaving the military base at Tite. • Ambush positions were taken up at dusk and we didn't move till daybreak. • Journalists who covered the war in Portuguese Guinea often equated its low-lying mangrove swampland with Vietnam: the terrain was ideal for the kind of insurgency employed by Amilcar Cabral's PAIGC rebels. • Monument to early maritime explorer Bartolemeu Diaz was removed from its prominent position in the centre of Bissau after independence. • Bacar's men on the alert after someone had radioed in an enemy sighting.
(Photos: Author)

CLOCKWISE FROM TOP LEFT: Portuguese marines on board a rubber duck retaliate at a sniper with a bazooka: hits were rare on both sides in these fleeting contacts. • Portuguese troops guard the waterfront near Bissau from their antiquated armoured car. • The ancient fort overlooking Luanda harbour, with its original iron guns still in place. • General Antonio de Spinola addresses a community meeting of loyalists in the interior. (Photos: Author)

CLOCKWISE FROM TOP LEFT: Unsurfaced roads through the interior of Portuguese Guinea were always problematical – you invariably had the twin option of an ambush triggered by a landmine, usually a Soviet TM-46 anti-tank. • Portuguese garrison commander sits atop his stock of newly delivered ammunition at a base near the border with Senegal. • One of the airborne-trained nurses based at Bissau and on regular call-out after contacts or ambushes. • A Portuguese Army truck reduced to scrap by a mine. • Frontier post with Senegal in the north of this tiny country. (Photos: Author)

Portuguese Guinea was the only one of Lisbon's three African possessions where heavy artillery was in regular u— against PAIGC guerrillas. Salvos were most often directed at predetermined positions, usually following enem— Katyusha rocket or BM-21 attacks. Almost all the aircraft deployed in these anti-colonial struggles – as with thes— guns – were NATO supplied, much of it American. (Photo: Author)

Hairbreadth Harries. Nobody seemed immune to the rush.

Obviously, this kind of confusion sometimes led to brash decision making. Take one of my more liberal-minded colleagues, who in the early 1980s got so fed up that he sold everything and emigrated with his family to Britain to work on one of the larger provincial newspapers. Six months later I ran into him in Cape Town. I discovered that he was back for good, at great financial cost and, naturally, I asked why.

"Because," he said, "it's so damned dull over there. All the newspapers get worked up about are things like the bad state of the sewage system." This, mind you, from a person who was not particularly adventurous by nature; which proves my point about the degeneration of adrenalin-immune systems in the old South Africa.

By and large, journalists covering pre-1990 South Africa could be placed in three broad categories.

First of all there were the pseudo-journalists. These were the agents-in-place for a variety of organisations, ranging from the government security agencies and foreign bodies like the Central Intelligence Agency and Britain's Secret Intelligence Service (MI6) to the African National Congress and related groups. I call them "pseudo-journalists" because although some were trained media

The media never did get to see the destruction of Angolan jets or helicopters. Apart from six choppers brought down by SAAF Impalas, most were destroyed by American Stinger missiles: American instructors were actually resident at Jamba, the UNITA headquarters in the extreme south-eastern corner of Angola. (Photo: Author's collection)

practitioners, objective reporting and analysis of the news was not their primary objective except when it suited their cover. Some of these were speedily unearthed by the Security Branch; others had a long run for their money.

My colleague Tony Holliday spent years at the *Cape Times* as a senior editorial staffer, producing excellent and very balanced work. Then he was arrested and exposed as a long-time ANC operative. He went to prison, emerged some time later and settled down to become an incisive and fearlessly non-partisan commentator on current affairs.

Then there was the community of foreign correspondents. Many were not living in South Africa, but descended en masse whenever it looked like the manure would hit the air-conditioning, which it did with great frequency. Some were great and good journalists that I was proud to know and work with. These were people like Australian-born John Monks, the son of Fleet Street's celebrated Noel Monks (who lost his wife to the unfettered charms of Ernest Hemingway), Fred Bridgland, René McColl and *Time* magazine's Peter Hawthorne. Several, like the *Telegraph's* Chris Munnion, Peter Younghusband of *Newsweek* and the London *Daily Mail* and Hawthorne, who, though British-born, ended up living permanently in this country.

To others South Africa was just an evergreen target of opportunity, ideal for a cheap shot at reputation-building because almost anything they cabled back would not only be used but believed.

One such gentleman arrived in Johannesburg with the openly stated aim of launching his career by winning a Pulitzer Prize, come what may. He succeeded, got his Pulitzer and went on to become a great man at, I believe, the *New York Times*. Another time a friend of mine saw a Swedish television crew callously pay a group of black urchins to scratch, allegedly for food, in the rubbish bins behind one of Cape Town's better hotels. I am sure it went down a treat in Stockholm.

The third group was made up of resident journalists like myself, Don Marshall, Bob Hitchcock, Henrie Geyser, Mervyn Rees, Helmoed-Romer Heitman and a host of others, some of whom worked for local newspapers and broadcast services or were resident correspondents for foreign news services or newspapers.

These were the journeymen of the free press in South Africa, covering events large and small continuously in spite of difficulties, obstacles and dangers, not to mention the liability of being called up for compulsory military service. The majority were all-rounders, while others had specific beats (for example, Venter and I specialised largely in issues related to defence).

These were interesting times and there was plenty of action to be had in almost every field. There was also a downside, because sometimes one got more of it than one bargained for – particularly in areas such as riots and unrest, and, to a lesser extent, defence. The likelihood and implications of being detained under some or other multifarious series of security laws were inevitably much greater for us locals than in the case of, say, a visiting staffer of the *International Herald Tribune* doing a quick in-and-out.

It could also be dangerous. Several old Africa hands died simply by being in the right place at the wrong time. Among them was television cameraman George d'Eath who had already survived numerous wars including a stint with Venter making documentary films in wartime Beirut. Not very long afterwards he was mutilated by a panga-wielding mob in Cape Town while filming. There was also the inimitable Ken Oosterbroek, one of the most enterprising photographers of this age. Ken was killed in security force cross-fire on the Reef. There were several others who died on the domestic front, although not one in the Border War. However, Venter was blown up twice while accompanying military units in cross-border operations and, as a result, he is all but deaf.

What comes across somewhat forcible is that spending one's time on the news-gathering beat often required a good bit of old-fashioned guts. Journalists could be, and indeed were, arrested or detained for a variety of reasons, and were not infrequently beaten up for one reason or another. It was a given that they would sooner go to jail than reveal a source, whether the story concerned was political or not, and occasionally they did.

The so-called "cut-line", a very clear demarcation of the border between South West Africa and Angola. (Photo: Author)

For many of the journalists who visited the Sharp End, the war along the Angolan border was a bit of a jolly. It wasn't all work, as can be seen here along the Kavango River. Al Venter (centre) with his hand on the shoulder of Bob Poos, one of America's most famous Vietnam correspondents who had come to South Africa to cover hostilities for *Soldier of Fortune* magazine. (Photo: Author's collection)

My editor at the *Cape Times*, Tony Heard, once ran a lengthy interview with ANC leader Oliver Tambo, not because it had any spectacular intrinsic news value but because he had decided it was time to take a stand against the blanket ban on such news items, which was not only a bad law but very badly applied as well. The result was a good deal of consternation and, so it seemed at first, the normal route of trial and prison was on the cards. Saner counsels prevailed however, and the powers-that-were let it go. The point was that whenever Heard took a stand, nobody really knew how it was going to end.

I might add that although I covered a number of riots and near-riots I was never touched by the police; I suspect this might have been because, being large, short-haired and invariably dressed in jacket and tie, uniformed cops tended to think I was either working undercover or a plainclothes-man. In fact, on one occasion a very new-looking constable came up to me and panted: "I'm looking for Warrant-Officer So-And-So!" To which I said, giving him a why-aren't-you-saluting-me look: "Not me, son. But carry on," and he rushed away, babbling: "Oh, thank you, sir!"

News coverage problems were also affected by the primitive state of the media technology of the era, descriptions of which tend to send today's young journalists into fits of apoplectic laughter. And remember, this was not all that long ago either …

- There were no cellphones, so half the task was to get the story and the other half was to get it out, which often meant having to find a public telephone, or persuading a private owner to let you use his, which was not always easy, particularly if you reeked of tear gas or showed signs of a close encounter.
- There was no Internet. Communications from, say, Johannesburg to London came down to one of two things: using a teleprinter or dictating your story over the telephone, in either of which cases it usually took about an hour to get through. Things started to change when the first faxes surfaced in the mid-1980s, although the first models were large, unprepossessing cabinets that ground out reams of slimy paper on which the copy was often partly illegible. Also, we used an esoteric journalese called cablese, with one word truncated into another to cut telegraph costs. This was essential with longer messages where newspapers were charged by the word.
- Black-and-white photographs could be land-lined between Johannesburg and Cape Town, but not colour, and in the early days it was common practice to buttonhole airline passengers and persuade them to carry packets of film to wherever they were going, to be picked up there on their arrival. Imagine trying, in this post-9/11 world, to find an air passenger at the Johannesburg end that would actually be willing to carry a bulky sealed envelope to Cape Town on the mere say-so of a stranger claiming to represent a newspaper. But those were more innocent times, and this gimcrack courier system worked quite well. While working in Lagos, Nigeria in the 1960s, Al Venter would regularly approach passengers about to leave for Johannesburg on the weekly Pan Am flight out of New York (it refuelled in Lagos) and ask them to take with them his copy and a couple of film spools. At the same time he would give them Wilf Nussey's telephone number at the Argus Africa News Service, adding that the goods would be fetched from their hotel. Not one of his dispatches ever went awry.
- Desktop computers started surfacing from 1978 onwards — the *Cape Times* was one of the first South

African newspapers to computerise — but laptops were still a long way into the future. So were satellite communications, which are today part and parcel of the baggage of any responsible foreign correspondent.

- Videocams had yet to replace the big, suitcase-like TV cameras of the day, which used so much power that a cameraman — especially when operating far from his base — would sling bandoliers of extra batteries over his shoulders like some old-time Boer rifleman. Even that didn't always work: I have a vivid recollection of one cameraman, standing bolt upright in the middle of a lethal skirmish in the bush, profanely begging the 16 mm Arriflex SR camera on his shoulder to find just 30 seconds' worth of life in its batteries. Alas, the Arri was *kaput* and so, very nearly, was the cameraman, since exposing yourself during a free-for-all fire-fight could sometime be life-threatening.
- Digital cameras did not exist either, and from early on in every assignment one's photographer would start whining about getting back to the darkroom to develop his negatives and print pictures. If he was shooting colour instead of monochrome, the whining would start even earlier.

All this backwardness could be exciting in a negative sort of way, in the same way that an old-time duel might somehow seem more romantic than a modern shootout.

Take the assassination of Prime Minister Hendrik Verwoerd in 1966. It was a drowsy day in the United Press International offices in Troye Street, Johannesburg, and my colleague Erik van Ees and I were engaged in desultory conversation when, far away in Cape Town, a parliamentary messenger named Dimitri Tsafendas blew his addled top and handed Verwoerd not a glass of water or a note from the Speaker but several blows with a large hunting knife.

We had two moles (neither of whom knew about the other) on the newsdesk of the SABC building, which was just across the street. Simultaneously they telephoned us while Tsafendas was still being wrestled out of the National Assembly. Erik and I each answered a telephone, barked "fuck me!", bellowed "Verwoerd's been murdered!" at one another and burst into hysterical laughter. Then our professional instincts clicked in and we rushed to book a teleprinter call to our immediate head office in London. By a never-to-be-repeated miracle we were connected within five minutes, and scooped everybody in the world.

Having got off the first urgent bulletins, we kept the line open for the next couple of hours, periodically punching in new flashes, or sometimes just a lot of gibberish to make sure we weren't cut off. This cost UPI five pounds a minute, which amounted to a very considerable sum of money in those days, when there were only two rands in the pound (my monthly salary, as I recall, was equivalent to about $200). London never minded splashing out on big stories, although it would fight for months about a taxi fare.

I left UPI after three years, during which time it had done such a thorough job of snatching away my journalistic maidenhead that no crisis I encountered in the rest of my professional career ever phased me. The problem was that I had become an adrenaline junkie. I spent a couple of years in a pleasant nine-to-five job at a magazine, got tired of the leisurely pace and in 1973 snatched at an offer from my old colleague Tony Heard, who had meantime become Editor of the *Cape Times*, to come back as his defence correspondent.

Tony had read the entrails, divined the general shape of things to come and wanted to be ready for whatever the future might bring. And he was right. The war business, as they say, was about to boom. In early 1974, the SADF took over border-control duties from the miniscule South West African Police and a year later, found itself in the middle of a genuine shootout in neighboring Angola.

Once on Angolan soil, things often got serious: an Angolan Army APC that had taken a direct hit from South African artillery; in this case a 155 mm shell. (Photo: Author's collection)

One of my first tasks was to thoroughly acquaint myself with the Defence Act (No. 44 of 1957, as amended several times).

The Act was by no means the only law that was directly applicable to the press, and more kept coming as the years passed. By the mid-1980s, for example, the average defence correspondent had to wend his way through a minefield which hid at least a dozen major security laws and all sorts of lesser nastiness. These included the Official Secrets Act, the General Law Amendment Act, the Terrorism Act, the Criminal Law Amendment Act, the Unlawful Organisations Act, the Affected Organisations Act, the National Supplies Procurement Act, the Armaments Development and Production Act, the Riotous Assemblies Act, the Gatherings and Demonstrations Act and the National Key Points Act. And not to mention the Atomic Energy Act and a couple of others.

However, the Big Daddy remained the Defence Act, whose stringent provisions and prohibitions overrode a plethora of existing laws or regulations governing defence-related matters or postal, telephone, telegraph or broadcasting services. All this thunder and lightning made defence reporting a daunting but certainly not impossible task, provided one was always prepared to take a gap.

For example, free debate took place in Parliament, and the rule was that anything said in Parliament could be reported; so on occasion we would ask a friendly opposition MP to raise a certain matter we had been restricted from publishing. Once this was done, it was no longer sacrosanct and could be reported and commented on. Then again, an authoritatively sourced report from overseas about South Africa's nuclear energy programme could usually be published ... though the same story might well be suppressed if of local origin. Crazy, but that was how it was in the great State of Schizophrenia, aka South Africa.

Reporting on defence matters tended to be a fairly relaxed affair for my first couple of years on the beat, with the Defence Force's public-relations mechanism consisting mainly of the energetic and generally helpful Brigadier Cyrus Smith and a couple of assistants.

The first sign of things to come was in April 1974, when the SADF flew a bunch of us to remote Katima Mulilo in the Caprivi Strip, one of many odd places I was to visit in the next few years. Among other things on the fringes of what was then still Black Africa, they would send out an armoured car on Saturday afternoons to chase elephants off the soccer field. It was also the sort of place where one bored old timer had installed a flush toilet in the trunk of a huge baobab so that he could tell visitors it was a "lavatree".

Most of the work on patrol was routine. A contact or fire-fight with SWAPO was a rarity: here troops check a village in Ovamboland. (Photo: Author)

The purpose of that visit was specifically to announce to the world that the SADF had taken over the main responsibility of patrolling the borders of South West Africa (the use of the word "Namibia" then still very much *verboten* in official circles).

But it was not all work, since there was a rip-roaring party that evening at which one of my colleagues, sloshed to the gills, tried to take a fishing boat over the adjacent Zambezi River to "find some stories" on the Zambian side. Because he was more likely to find a fusillade of bullets from the Zambian garrison, we alerted the orderly officer, who turned out the guard and dragged him away as he was fumbling at the mooring rope of a rickety boat.

A little over a year later, all this was changed by a watershed event: Operation Savannah, the first major South African incursion into Angola that took place between September 1975 and March 1976.

Against his better judgment, Prime Minister John Vorster allowed himself to be sucked into the Angolan civil war late in 1975, following urgent pleas from a number of other African states and various inducements and/or pressures (the nature of which we can only guess at) from none other than the American Secretary of State Henry Kissinger. As a result the SADF spent the next seven months

– successfully for the most part – in a small but wide-ranging semi-conventional bush war against a Cuban expeditionary force which had been summoned by the Marxist member of the three parties in the dispute, the Popular Movement for the Liberation of Angola, or MPLA.

My personal recollections of Operation Savannah are of a military escapade that had two distinct components.

From September to December 1975 I covered it as best I could, more than somewhat handicapped by the almost total news blackout imposed in terms of the Defence Act. Tony and I had a pretty good idea of what was going on, and after some hedging, the editors were finally given an off-the-record briefing by the government. That done, we couldn't publish much because our hands were still tied by the Act. Then, just before Christmas 1975, I was called up by the army and spent the next three months swanning around Angola as an infantry lieutenant (the same thing happened to various other reporters, then and later).

This was to be the first of a series of mobilisations over the next dozen years or so. The army made strenuous attempts to persuade me that my best place would be in the Troop Information Unit,

Camp life could be pretty basic. Visiting journalists would be shown most routines, including mortar positions in the camps they visited. (Photo: Author's collection)

Chapter 21
Willem Steenkamp – Reporting on South Africa's border wars

Colonel Robert K. Brown, the owner/publisher of *Soldier of Fortune* magazine (centre) was a regular visitor to these shores. He is seen here, shortly after crossing into Rhodesia at Beit Bridge with John Donovan (right) the magazine's "Demotion/Explosives editor" and "Fat" Ralph Edens. The Americans would arrive in southern Africa with an array of firearms and carry them everywhere.
(Photo: Author)

a satellite, as it were, of the Directorate of Public Relations. But I rejected that overture because such a transfer would obviously have constituted an impossible conflict of interest. So the army washed its hands of me and I saw out my time as a flat-foot infantryman.

Meanwhile, I was enjoying the dubious pleasures of Defence Minister P.W. Botha's magical mystery tour to places I had never heard of. For his part, the ever-helpful Brigadier Cyrus Smith and his small staff worked like stakhanovites at Defence Headquarters to handle endless enquiries that flowed in from all over. Eventually, even they were overwhelmed by the sheer volume of interest in what was going on "along the border", to the detriment of both the SADF and the government.

In March 1976, South Africa withdrew its forces from Angola and Washington dropped any support – clandestine or otherwise – for Pretoria when it became clear that the astute Dr Kissinger had failed to achieve his objective in this handy little surrogate war. Always the survivor, the Secretary of State had cut his losses well before the upcoming presidential election and as soon as large amounts of domestic dust raised by Operation Savannah had started to settle, the government took stock.

The bottom line, I imagine, was fundamental. The government's small expeditionary force had won almost every important combat encounter in Angola, but at a price: South Africa had lost the media war. Its ham-fisted attempt to keep a lid on Operation Savannah by invoking the full powers of the Defence Act resulted in a victory that was both partial and pyrrhic.

What had not been taken into account was that throughout, South African media continued to enjoy free access to news from overseas, even though most of it was unpublishable in the local press. There was no stopping South Africans enjoying unrestricted access to the BBC and other foreign radio news services, so that those who wanted to know what was going on in the world outside could easily remain in touch with events that weren't reported in their own country. The immediate result of government interference and the resultant news brown-out was a backlash of fairly serious proportions.

In the absence of any kind of help from Pretoria, even the most lurid and improbable overseas report tended to be widely believed. Incredible scare rumours flashed around the country and quickly became fact, for no better reason than that scare stories usually do.

There were lighter moments along the border as well: Al Venter spent a week with an army mounted unit on patrol in South Angola. Here he is "examined" by the unit mascot, a frivolous young baboon. This could also be dangerous work: shortly after he left the unit, one of these horses triggered a Soviet TM-57 anti-tank mine and the mounted soldier was killed. (Photo: Author's collection)

This was something the Americans discovered to their cost during the Vietnam War and, more recently, in Afghanistan. Equally worrying was the fact that a significant number of people – among them some usually fervent government supporters – were expressing strong doubts about the whole affair. There was consequently a demonstrable drop in the credibility value of official SADF statements.

At the end of it, though, we muddled through. We had no option but to continue doing so, even though some members of the media were harassed at home, while others working in Africa north of the border sometimes had to contend with even more draconian restrictive measures.

CHAPTER TWENTY TWO

"THE INCREDIBLES": RHODESIAN LIGHT INFANTRY

> To paraphrase the old aphorism, Rhodesia in its glorious, impetuous heyday, as old timers like to recollect, was the best of times, the worst of times. Hannes Wessels, himself "one of the few", looks back on some of his experiences with the RLI.

He recalls:

My time with the Rhodesian Light Infantry, or more familiarly the RLI, began in January 1974 when we arrived at Heaney Junction, just outside Bulawayo. Rain poured down and one got the impression that Llewellyn Barracks was one gigantic bog.

We were apparently the largest intake yet and there was a lot of improvisation, what with the weather and a lot of young men who had been called up and were waiting for their first set of orders. Tents had been erected to supplement barrack accommodation, but most of these were flooded. I stood for a long time in the rain thinking that by going into the army, I might have made a mistake. Perhaps I should have gone to university after all ...

To ensure that our spirits remained low, we were eventually dressed in oversize combat-jackets which hung to our knees. These were accentuated by baggy shorts that hung even lower, as well as black athletic trainers, or "tekkies" in the lingo, that were distinctive because the guys would wear them on ops in the bush without socks.

So too with headgear, which was disparagingly referred to as "cunt caps", in symmetry with the people they adorned. Studying myself in the mirror – and bearing in mind that I went into this business in the admirable quest for glory – I felt like a rat that been

Chapter 22
"The Incredibles": The Rhodesian Light Infantry

dragged through a sewer. There were moments that I could quite easily have had a quiet weep.

Three days into this miserable gloom and it was announced that a few of us were to be given the chance to get into either the RLI or the SAS, the country's ultra-elite Special Air Service. The process would involve a series of interviews, followed by a selection course for one or the other. Volunteers were called for and I all but tripped over my laces to get out front. It was a regular rigmarole and for me, ultimately, it turned out that 2 Commando of the Rhodesian Light Infantry was to be my "home".

1st Battalion of the Rhodesian Light Infantry was nicknamed alternatively the "Saints", or with time – as they gained a reputation for defying remarkable odds – "The Incredibles". The unit was a regular airborne commando regiment in the Rhodesian army that had become a parachute battalion in 1977. Regarded in its day as one of the world's foremost proponents of counter-insurgency warfare, its regular duties included both internal operations and external preemptive strikes against guerrilla units based in the neighbouring territories of Mozambique and Zambia. The format was always the same: if the gooks were within striking distance, the RLI would be called upon to deal with them.

Organised into four company-sized sub-units called commandos, their average fighting strength was about 70 men, with their characteristic deployment being the Fire Force, a reaction operation called out by radio whenever enemy units were spotted, more often

RLI Fire Force deployment. (Photo courtesy of the Hannes Wessels Collection)

than not in remote and most-times isolated locations in the bush.

RLI "troopies" soon became the country's most effective rapid-deployment helicopter strike unit, a versatile and effective shock force. Small combat elements would consist of four men in what became known as a "stick". Basic weapons were the 7.62 mm FN rifle, as well as a single belt-fed MAG machine gun – both of which were Pretoria-supplied – and which became the hallmark of military ground operations throughout southern Africa for the next quarter-century.

It didn't take the RLI long to become remarkably adept at this type of warfare. The men were trained to shoot by double-tap on semi-automatic and the idea was to follow up without giving the enemy a chance to react. Fully automatic fire, in contrast, was almost unheard of.

For his part, the MAG gunner worked short bursts from the hip and, correctly handled, he had more stopping power than the rest of the stick together, especially at short range. It was a good combination because in the environment in which these troops operated, the system was both simple and effective. Most times squads were dropped from two or more Alouettes, while another chopper – designated the G-Car (Gun-Car) – would hover over the scene of the action and with its twin 7.62 mm machine guns (or later in the war, 20 mm cannon) provide top cover.

Alternatively, if the occasion warranted it, a larger force would be dropped by parachute from an antiquated DC-3 "Gooney Bird", that almost half a century after they were first taken into service, always provided us with excellent backup. The problem for the boys was that they would often be dropped into the lap of the gods from heights of about 160 metres (500 feet), sometimes less, which meant there was simply no margin for error.

Chris Cocks's book *Fireforce* deals with his wartime experiences while serving with the RLI, and to my mind it is still the best work to emerge from that conflict. He makes the case for the Rhodesian Army having been second only to the French Foreign Legion in assimilating into active combat units large numbers of foreigners. As he recounts, the RLI had a bigger proportion of expatriates than any other military force in modern times. I quote:

"There was a wide diversity of characters in 2 Commando. By tradition, most foreign volunteers served in the ranks and at one stage I was the only born Rhodesian in 11 Troop.

"There were Americans, almost all of them Vietnam veterans,

Chapter 22
"The Incredibles": The Rhodesian Light Infantry

RLI on parade, inspected by Ian Smith with General Peter Walls behind. (Photo courtesy of the Hannes Wessels Collection)

resplendent with their impressive arrays of medals. But we were not overly impressed by such dazzling displays and told them they looked like Christmas trees. Understandably, they ignored our taunts and wore their decorations with pride.

"There were Canadians and Australians and New Zealanders, some of whom had also fought in Vietnam. And we had Frenchmen, Belgians and Germans too, many of them ex-Legionnaires. Earlier there had been a lot of South Africans, but their numbers began to dwindle as their own bush war in South West Africa and Angola started to intensify.

"The majority of overseas recruits came from Great Britain and Ireland, drawn from a variety of units like the Parachute Regiment, the Royal Marines, Special Air Service and the Brigade of Guards. The British adapted well to Rhodesian conditions and many served with distinction and were decorated for valour.

"All foreign volunteers, in the main, were professional soldiers. It is true that a few liked to think of themselves as mercenaries (or mercs) but they weren't really … if they had been, they would have been soldiers 'without fortune' if only because they got the same pay and served under the same conditions of service as Rhodesian-born regular soldiers. Like everyone else, they paid income tax to the Rhodesian Exchequer. Added to that, they were allowed to remit only a small percentage of their salaries to their own countries.

"The volunteers came for many and varied reasons. For some it was for the action and adventure. For others it was glory. Many came in the belief that they were fighting to stop the spread of international communism. And there were a few who were there just for the love of killing …"

One of the illustrious figures to don a uniform in the Rhodesian Army was British national André Dennison who, before arriving in Rhodesia, had served with distinction with 22 Special Air Service Regiment in Borneo. His exploits while penetrating dense jungle on patrol in South Asia with the legendary Sergeant Eddie Lillico earned him high praise from General Walter Walker. He was then detached as part of a contingent of 80 British officers and senior NCOs seconded to the 3rd Battalion of the Malaysian Rangers. After that, there were stints in Europe, Cyprus, the Malawi Rifles, Northern Ireland and elsewhere.

Major Dennison joined 2nd Battalion Rhodesian African Rifles in October 1975 and commanded A Company, until he was killed in action almost four years later.

An interesting aside here is that while serving in Rhodesia, Dennison met the illustrious American war photographer Sarah Barrell, who had spent a lot of time in Vietnam. As one wag wrote, "her obituary described her as a beautiful blonde … who collected wars and war heroes". John le Carré is believed to have cast her as the American photo-journalist Lizzie Worthington in *The Honourable Schoolboy*.

Having arrived in southern Africa after seeing a lot of action in Cambodia and Lebanon, Barrell moved onto Rhodesia, met Dennison and fell deeply in love with him. Her friends believed that he had given some meaning to her life at last. Then Dennison was KIA, an incident compounded by the fact that he was accidentally shot by one of his own men during a contact. Two days after his funeral, Sarah Barrell returned to her apartment in Salisbury and shot herself with the same .38 that her lover had given her for protection. She was 33 years old.

Richard Wood documents all this in another fine book to emerge from that period titled *The War Diaries of André Dennison*[1].

The man from whom I took my orders while I served in the RLI was an illustrious character by the name of Sergeant Fouché. A formidable non-commissioned officer, this sergeant was always immaculately turned out and quintessentially, the kind of military man that us youngsters looked up to. He was precise on parade, his orders were crisp and clear and he wielded his weapon as if it were an extension of one of his limbs. That said, his marksmanship under all conditions was, as one of our officers phrased it, "phenomenal".

Add to those combinations some of best tracking and bushcraft skills in the business, combined with several years of combat experience and you had what any officer commanding would regard as a valuable attribute to the unit. He was regarded by his peers as among the best instructors in the army.

Sergeant Fouché in those early days had a profound impact on me and it stayed that way when I arrived at Mt Darwin to join 2 Commando at the Fire Force Base that had been established on the edge of that ragtag little town in the middle of nowhere. Even getting there had its moments: one of the vehicles in our convoy detonated a landmine along a lonely stretch of road, but nobody was hurt.

I think my youth – I was barely 17 years old – and obvious lack of operational experience might have caused the older soldiers a little concern. After waiting in the canteen a while, I was brought before Lieutenant Nigel Theron. He told me that I would be in his troop and answerable to Corporal Jan de Beer, who was in charge of the tracking stick. I was then directed towards a shell-scrape, given a small canvas shelter to erect and told to go and make myself comfortable.

Just before dark a helicopter landed and De Beer disembarked with his team. Short, stocky and with sharp blue eyes and close-cropped blonde hair – and like Fouché, professional to his fingertips – I immediately liked the man. He flashed me a big smile and told me to fetch some beer. I was introduced to the rest of his team, of whom two were foreigners: "Frenchy" had originally served in the Foreign Legion and had seen action in Chad and elsewhere, while the other man was an American by the name of John Coey, a soft-spoken former US Marine just out of Vietnam.

Over a few ales Jan told me we would be reacting to callouts by helicopter. When the alarm sounded, he expected his men to come running, "no matter what they are doing just then". He explained that our job was to track down terrorists "wherever and whenever they're encountered".

Over the next week or two, a spate of landmine incidents blighted our days and nights, and though we were called out, the culprits usually walked straight out of the bush and into populated areas. There they would change their footwear and effectively disappear into the crowd. It was the same old story on half a dozen continents all over again: as Mao would say of his own forces, being like the fishes in the sea ...

It was obviously frustrating. During the course of my first deployment of over a month, I did little more than trudge around a section of north-eastern Rhodesia that fringes on Mozambique achieving almost nothing. It was as if we were trying to pursue a phantom enemy, all the while running from elephants on the rampage because we'd accidentally intruded on their feeding grounds. Or swatting tsetse flies and occasionally coming down with malaria. We'd eventually return to base more fearful of buffalo beans than the enemy.

Then a report came in of an incident near a mission involving some native villagers. There was nothing explicit, except that there had been some trouble, we were briefly told prior to lift-off. The helicopter dropped us nearby and, weapons ready, we headed towards a hut complex not at all sure what to expect. On the face of it, everything looked normal: there were a few locals around and there was smoke from a simmering fire, but then an unusual smell wafted over the area.

I spotted a woman sitting uncomfortably on her haunches. Her head hung low over her chest and she was clearly in distress. While the rest of my group split into flanks to encircle the huts, I walked towards her, curious to see what her problem was. I greeted her, as I customarily did in her own Shona language and noticed that the eyes of the other villagers were on the pair of us. But nobody moved.

When I called to her again, she lifted her head slowly and I was overwhelmed. She presented a terrible image, her lips having been savagely cut away with a knife or a blade to reveal a mouth full of teeth that flashed white in the sun. To the uninitiated, she might have been displaying a grotesque smile, but it was obvious that she'd been horribly tortured: slicing off facial parts was something that the terrorists did with a peculiar relish.

Only when I stopped and bent down beside her did I smell burnt flesh. I suddenly realised that whoever had subjected her to this lunacy, had also viscously abused her private parts. The top of her thighs were savagely burnt. I called forward an old man who explained that the terrorists had hacked off the woman's lips with wire-cutters, which are part of the bayonet of an AK-47. They'd then forced her to eat her own flesh before they shoved a chunk of flaming wood into her vagina. The poor soul had been accused of sleeping with a policeman.

Others had been similarly tortured, and some of the guys found a hut on fire nearby that, once the door had been forced, revealed a pile of dead bodies. A family had been locked inside and burned to death. We did our best to follow available tracks, prying some information out of the locals as we went, but to no avail. The terrorists had made their point and the survivors were terrified.

We were airlifted back to base by chopper that evening and for the first time in that war, things had become personal. I was now ready to react and if it meant killing some of these bastards along the way, then so be it: *bellum se impsum alet*[2].

My chance came pretty soon, following a sighting of a terrorist camp in the Kandeya Tribal Trust Land.

The siren sounded and Sergeant Fouché was given the task of attacking the temporary base. For the first time, I was included in the assault group. There were 16 of us that ran towards the helicopters and within minutes we were airborne. The pilot took us in low, doors off and rotors slashing through the warm, bushveld air.

As the machine gunner, I sat at the door facing the "chopper-tech" who was hunched over his twin-Brownings while calmly scanning the countryside. I would surreptitiously watch the others, absolutely amazed at their nonchalance. They had done it all before and it showed. I turned frequently towards Corporal De Beer in search of a reassuring glance, but his bright blue eyes were set outwards, steeled in resolve. I drew on his demeanour and reminded myself that I was where I'd wanted to be; in the company of a few hard men. Moreover, we were going to do battle with the people I'd learned earlier that day to despise.

Suddenly the Alouette banked sharply, its blades clattering as they often do when the pilot abruptly turns the nose of his machine around. I looked askance at him but he was cool, talking into his "mike" and his right hand, as they say "gentle on the stick".

Then, to my astonishment the Perspex immediately in front of me was punctured by a bullet. You couldn't miss the crisp crack of rifle fire below, or our "tech" retaliating with bursts from his own twin barrels. Meanwhile, between shouting into his mouthpiece and gesticulating furiously downwards, Jan de Beer was urging the pilot to put us down. His message was clear: the guys had work to do on the ground. To my dismay, I saw two of the other choppers in our group soar away to a higher altitude, clearly avoiding the ground fire that had suddenly become quite intense. We just continued lower, descending off the cusp of a *koppie* where the gook camp, discovered earlier by a Selous Scouts quartet, came into view.

Waving an orange "Day-Glo" patch on a stick, I spotted a burly black soldier pumping the air with his fist, a huge grin on his face. He was actually cheering us on.

My emotions surged, but this was momentary because the pilot had all but levelled off with the ground. I looked towards the corporal who was shouting at us to jump, even though we were still hovering several metres high. I hesitated, looked at the "tech" waving me on and leaped out anyway. I hit the ground hard, where I crumpled, winded, into the dirt.

The chopper's downdraft kicked up billows of red dust and for a little while I was blinded. Unsighted I waited, and then, becoming aware of where I was, I turned and fired into some nearby trees. In the meantime, having deposited its load, the chopper soared away, its guns chattering.

Moments later everything went quiet and in the kind of unfamiliar panic that overtakes those who are plunged headlong into something totally unfamiliar, I realised that I was on my own. The rest of the squad had already moved on.

Jan de Beer's feet must have barely touched ground before he led a charge into what we recognised afterwards must have been some pretty awesome enemy fire. Moments later, I saw Sergeant Fouché's slim, sinewy figure among some heavy overgrowth ahead, which was when I gathered my weapon and the rest of my gear and hurtled through the bush after him. This was one time I had no intention of becoming a straggler.

Finding it difficult to make up the distance, I cursed my tardiness. But suddenly, dropping down to one knee, the sergeant targeted a bevy of shadowy shapes moving at speed through the bush ahead. The enemy was on the run and I joined in by emptying a belt into the brush.

By now Fouché was well forward and moving ahead into the tree-line. Between running towards the enemy and firing hard, he stopped several times to change mags. For the rest, he allowed nothing to break his momentum, confident that the rest of us were providing support. Moments later the insurgents broke ranks and bombshelled in multiple directions, only for the majority to be cut down by our guys who, going by past experience, had been waiting for this to happen.

It was obviously all new to me and I admitted afterwards that I was amazed at what was clearly an astonishing display of firepower. At one stage I saw Fouché swing his rifle around and fire two quick shots through the branches of a nearby tree: the rebel that spilled out was dead before he hit the ground.

Ordered by Corporal De Beer to clear a nearby ravine that lay across our path, I covered the distance in several strides and fired volleys into several likely positions that might have provided the enemy with cover. Still more fled straight into Fouché's line of fire as a helicopter roared low over our heads and sent me sprawling as its Brownings rattled. That was when I spotted the body of another gook that had tried to dodge the sweep line and was being shredded.

Perhaps a minute later the shooting stopped and I was able to take stock. Unbridled aggression combined with fine musketry resulted in our tiny squad of eight to annihilate a group more than twice its size and it had all happened within minutes. The battle was over and the only underperformer, I realised, was me. I was mortified, but not for long.

My spirits soared as Sergeant Fouché approached, his purple birthmark glistening with sweat and his face one big happy smile. He slapped me on the back and his only words of encouragement were that I should run faster next time. I promised never to take cover again.

That was my first experience with this unusual body of men and I remember it like it was yesterday. Any baptism of fire, like our first tentative moves at sexual dominance, tends to stay with you, but it does little justice to what the RLI were actually capable of.

There were "troopies" from all four RLI Commandos that stormed into action every single day in that war, sometimes two or three times in succession, and on a few notable occasions, even more. In the tradition of this kind of "shock troop" retaliation – that sometimes employed reckless aggression combined with excellent combat drills – such actions would almost always deliver the goods. Of course there were casualties, as well as the occasional setback when things went seriously wrong, but the idea throughout was to unnerve and intimidate the enemy – to force them into a flurry of disordered panic and invariably, defeat. In that, "The Incredibles" almost always excelled.

My first contact that bright August winter's day might have encapsulated the classic RLI role in this extensive bush war. But the battalion's finest hour came on the edge of a large town in central Mozambique on 23 November 1977. That was at Chimoio: during Portuguese colonial times it was listed on the map as Vila de Manica.

The target was colloquially referred to as "New Farm" and early intelligence reports indicated that it was able to muster an estimated 10,000 enemy troops. A secondary objective was Tembue, home to about half that number of rebels.

For the planners of the operation back in Salisbury (Harare today) the odds were absurd. If they were to conform to the conventional military logic of a three-to-one ratio for the kind of attack that was envisaged, roughly 30,000 Rhodesian troops would be needed. That was about 29,815 short of what was available. All we could bring to the fray was a paltry 185 men, split almost equally between the RLI and the Rhodesian SAS. Yet, the ground assault went ahead anyway and an event without precedent in military history went into the record books. With the Rhodesian Air Force providing back up, about 3,000 insurgents were to become casualties at Chimoio, and that for the loss of only two Rhodesians: one a soldier, the other a pilot.

"The briefing officer advised all stick commanders that we would be working with our own sticks," remembers Corporal Jimmy Swan of 2 Commando, "… but the bad news was that we would be woefully thin on the ground and when he presented his details, the immediate reaction was a stunned silence, followed by a low rumble which grew into a roar. Everybody in the room was incredulous."

There was more bad news. In addition to the defenders at Chimoio — mainly expatriate Rhodesian ZANLA forces — the Rhodesians had to be prepared to deal with a FRELIMO support group armed with mortars and anti-aircraft weapons. In addition, there was a company of Tanzanian troops and over a hundred Soviet advisers, all of them backed by a squadron or two of T-54 tanks, BTR-152 armoured personnel carriers as well as SAM-7 batteries. The odds against us were enormous.

"The obvious plan would have called for a simultaneous hit on both targets," recalled Ground Commander SAS Major Brian Robinson. "However, we hardly had sufficient resources to hit one objective, never mind both."

Robinson explained that at the initial planning stage, headquarters worked on a 48-hour-turnaround from Chimoio, with the possibility of then going on to Tembue. Every aircraft in the Rhodesian Air Force was to become operational, without a single reserve. "That effectively meant that the rest of the country would be severely exposed."

The operation, he said, was called "Dingo" and it was accepted that on its outcome rested the immediate future of the beleaguered country. The basic idea was to give the enemy the kind of defeat that would both upset their plans and undermine their resources for at least a year, possibly two.

The target area had been abandoned by a fleeing Portuguese farmer several years before and spanned approximately five square kilometres. There were a number of buildings that consisted of the old homestead, some offices and sheds as well as tobacco barns, all of which had been converted into military facilities. There were rooms and offices for the guerrilla leader Robert Mugabe, as well as some of his top commanders, including Josiah Tongogara, Rex Nhongo and the rest of the guerrilla top echelon. Since the camp was the administrative centre for ZANLA in the region, which gave it a high priority rating, the Rhodesians hoped to collar them all, as somebody phrased it, "in situ".

Aerial photographs of the Chimoio base showed a labyrinth of trenches, revetments and defensive lines. These were backed by a variety of guns, including multi-barrelled 14.5 mm and 23 mm AAA, as well other heavy weapons. Everything was pretty well dug in, and from long-range observations made by Ron Reid-Daly's Selous Scouts, an efficient early warning system of sentries in towers with whistles was in place.

The gooks had another early warning system that proved remarkably effective. They would tether baboons at strategic points around the base and the animals would react the moment they detected the sound of approaching aircraft. It was a passive alarm system, but with time, it proved extremely effective. Salisbury was horribly aware from the start that without the element of surprise, the attack could develop into a fiasco: the moment the insurgents heard aircraft coming in, they would quickly go to ground in their warrens of bunkers and tunnels that straddled the area.

The man tasked to deal with the critical problem was Jack Malloch, a World War II fighter pilot who had flown on the wing of Ian Smith's Spitfire during the course of the Italian campaign. No longer a youngster, Malloch devised a cunning strategy to use his noisy DC-8 former passenger jet that he had been using to trade with the rest of Africa as a decoy over the camp immediately before we went in. As he explained, he would arrive over the site a minute or two before the choppers and the Dakotas ferrying the bulk of the raiding force were due to show up.

The veteran pilot accepted that his was both a shrewd and a risky ploy. The gooks could easily turn their guns on the jet, but, he told Ian Smith, it was a chance they would have to take.

What was finally agreed was that he would over-fly Chimoio at exactly 07h41, at which time the insurgents — as was their routine — were expected to be on parade. They would hear the sound of jet engines and scramble for their trenches, only to discover it was a commercial aircraft. Hopefully they would relax and return to their previous positions. Moments later Rhodesian Air Force warplanes would be onto them.

Hawker Hunters of No. 1 Squadron would initiate the attack with bombs, rockets and cannon, followed immediately by the Vampires and finally a bunch of ageing Canberra bombers. The intent was for the squadrons to keep enemy heads down so as to cover paratroop deployment. Immediately after the Canberra strike, all airborne troops would be dropped, while 40 more RLI commandos would be deployed by the helicopters as "stopper-groups" on the periphery of the base.

Once all the escape routes had been "sealed", more assault-troops would advance to flush out the trenches and gun-pits.

Those who chose to flee rather than fight would head straight into our RLI stopper groups. Machine gunners would be loaded with all the belts they could carry. They were briefed beforehand that because there was no chance of resupply, they would have to replenish with looted ammunition, which didn't exactly help us because almost all our weapons were South African-supplied R1s that used 7.62 mm NATO ammunition.

John Ngwenya, one of the defenders who survived the onslaught, recalls the period immediately before the attack.

"I had just arrived from Nachingwea in Tanzania and was awaiting my first mission that would take me into Zimbabwe. Our commanders told us the Rhodesians were not to be feared. Despite this I did hear some talk: some of my comrades had been involved in actions against Rhodesian soldiers and it had been tough. As a result I was apprehensive, but at Chimoio there were many of us and we were well armed, so we were mostly of the opinion that they would not attack us there.

"As a result, I think we were not as well prepared for them when they did come because most of us just believed it would not happen. Comrade Mugabe visited us once while I was there and he was very aggressive. He told us the Rhodesians were tiring and we would be victorious because our cause was just."

While the enemy slumbered, 40 helicopter-borne troops of 2 Commando assembled along the shores of Lake Alexander on the eastern border of Rhodesia before dawn on 23 November 1977. They were destined for a ridge on the northern side of the camp where they would be positioned into "stop-lines" to gun down those fleeing the 145 attacking paratroopers made up of 97 SAS troops and 48 men from Major Jeremy Strong's 3 Commando.

The paratroopers had already gathered at New Sarum air-base in Salisbury a day earlier and the primary order to the troops was unambiguous: to kill and capture the maximum amount of terrorists.

Andrew Standish White remembers the prelude at New Sarum: "The hum of voices, the snapping of clips being tested and fitted, that funny sweet smell of the parachutes, the nausea of one too many the night before. There was no missing the morning chill that caused the shivers that were so desperately suppressed lest anyone watching thought it was from nerves," he recalls.

It was the same each time, he said. "You quite often needed a bloody pee after being fitted and checked, and what a pain it was to get to the necessary 'apparatus'! Everyone was thinking about dying but trying not to let on.

"Some fiddled with their weapon — was the gun tight enough behind the shoulder? Was the pistol well secured but still easily accessible? Should you stow the metal feeder strip of the RPD belts in the webbing pouch or have them protruding for instant access? The smokers all had to bugger off outside once fitted — NO SMOKING in the hangar – heaps of them stood outside puffing hard."

Brian Robinson had his own views on preliminaries. "It was an emotional time," he recalls today. "We estimated 30 per cent casualties and expected worse. The odds were frightening."

Across the country at Thornhill Air Base, outside the central midlands town of Gwelo, the pilots of No. 1 Hunter Squadron who would initiate the attack went over details of what was termed their AIRTASK. Led by Squadron Leader Richard Brand, these were all experienced combat aviators, but they were aware too that first light would arrive with the most challenging target of all. They accepted too, that ground fire was one of several problems and that they would have to be mindful of possibly being intercepted by Mozambique Air Force MiG-21 fighters.

At New Sarum the pilots of the Vampires and Canberras went through a similar process. There were six of the old wooden Vampires left, but only two had ejector seats.

At 03h00 Robinson and Air Commander, Group Captain Norman Walsh stirred, dressed and joined their officers in the hangars as they prepared for battle under overcast skies. Bad weather

RLI Fire Force deployment. (Photo courtesy of the Hannes Wessels Collection)

notwithstanding, the order had come through: they were going to go for it and the survival of the country — as they knew it — lay in their hands.

The helicopters went airborne first, flying almost due east in waves of five for security reasons. Bush telegraph amongst the locals – always by word of mouth – was legend for the speed it travelled and sight of an aerial armada would trigger a quick response that might be communicated to the enemy in time to warn them.

The Dakotas followed, heavy with fuel and troops and their pilots used the full length of runway to get aloft. Soon they were all airborne, following carefully selected flight-paths to avoid being observed from the ground.

Charlie Warren, a 3 Commando NCO, remembers it well: "The atmosphere in our 'Dak' was one of nervousness, a bit of light-hearted humour and I suppose, of concern ... this was a big camp and we were headed a long way into Mozambique. So if you got a 'third eye' or were wounded, we'd ask ourselves whether they'd be able to get us out ... to hospital ... or retrieve our bodies for burial inside Rhodesia."

Jimmy Swan recalls flying out from Lake Alexander at first light. "We did our final checks in the choppers, gave the thumbs up and eased forward. We were headed for the border and then onto our target."

Squadron Leader Harold Griffiths was at the head of a formation of 30 helicopters, all of them flying line astern from Salisbury. He map-read his way through a succession of valleys that led towards the target. In a remarkable feat of airmanship he managed to negotiate a route through some pretty poor visibility while reading the 1:50 000 map on his lap, and he did so in an open cockpit.

Behind him came the command chopper flown by Norman Walsh, with Brian Robinson alongside him.

"There was light on the horizon," recalls Swan, "but as we got up over the tree-line, it was a proud moment. We were part of the most extensive raid made in Africa since World War II and all around us were lines of aircraft silhouetted against the horizon.

"It was all tree-top stuff … and the roar of so many choppers must have been frightening for anyone below. We flew over the lake off the Rio Pungue, with some of the guys leaning half out the doorways of the choppers craning their necks to get a glimpse of what lay ahead."

Arriving over the target at the predetermined time in the commercial jet, Jack Malloch opened his throttles for maximum power and lowered the flaps to increase noise. The ruse worked. Unseen by him and blinded by cloud, an army of terrorists on the ground below were on morning parade and the sound of the aircraft triggered an air-raid warning that sent the entire camp scurrying for refuge. Moments later, as the four-engine jet came into view, those on the ground accepted that it was a false alarm. Their officers ordered them back to their stations.

Through a break in the clouds Richard Brand's "Red One" Hawker Hunter got a clear view of the barracks at the western most side of the camp. He immediately called "target visual" over the radio, put his nose down and screamed in out of the sun with his four 30 mm cannons blazing. That was followed by two 50-gallon napalm canisters which exploded in a huge sheet of fire over the complex. Behind him the second Hunter deposited two half-ton "Golf-Bombs" onto the headquarters and a third jet bombed Chitepo College where 250 ZANLA students and staff huddled, as was disclosed later. They were there to be lectured on why Marxism would dominate the world, but few would survive that initial attack.

At H-Hour, and still a short distance behind, Norman Walsh looked nervously at his watch. Unable to bear the tension but desperate to know if the Hunters had found their targets, he broke radio silence.

"Red One … are you on target?" he asked. He waited nervously and then smiled when he got a reply. "What a question," said Brand laconically as he pulled up steeply and prepared to run-in again.

Following Brand onto the target, the Canberra pilots were pleased when they emerged through cloud cover to find a thousand faces looking up at them from the ground. Thousands of kilos of high-explosive, home-made Alpha Bouncing-Bombs thundered down.

"We felt the 'Dak' alter its route," remembers Charlie Warren, "and were told to get ready to jump. While we were still tightening our helmet-straps and checking equipment, 'Action Stations' order was given and before we knew it we were out the door and on our way down.

"I followed Major Strong with my machine gunner behind me. Once I'd checked that my canopy had deployed, I looked at the camp below and saw palls of black smoke where the bombs had been dropped. The place was huge and I could see the enemy running in all directions. They looked like ants at first, but as I descended their size grew."

"The sight that greeted us was awesome," wrote Jimmy Swan afterwards. "Just streaks and hisses from the ghosts of the sky, and then flashes on the ground. We knew the jets had started the assault ... then came the thumbs-up from the cockpit and we prepared to jump. In the gloom at the back of the 'Dak', I could see only the gleam of white teeth and the eyes of our guys who were covered in camo-cream. We sat on the edge of our seats, adrenaline rushing, a cocktail of fear and excitement that early in the day. The truth was, we were ready for them. ...

"As we came over the last rise we pulled up off the trees ... at approximately 1,000 feet ... it was Armageddon ... flashes, smoke and people running ... the stench of napalm was incredible.

"We now had all the light we needed and it was a perfect day to kill. We jumped ... dashed into cover ... and the heat and humidity, even that early in the day, was unreal. We kneeled at the ready ... the paras dropped from the 'Daks' effectively completing the 'box-cordon'. These were moments when we felt that we really were untouchable."

For Charlie Warren the descent was difficult. "There were cracking sounds around our heads going into the parachutes. I looked down and saw a group of about a dozen 'terrs' legging it towards where Keith and I were going to land, firing at us as they ran. Before I knew it, I was coming in fast and hadn't yet prepared for the ground rush ... I was too busy concentrating on where this 'welcoming party' was going and if they were to come back, whether I'd have to deal with them.

"I landed hard and winded myself. I looked around for Major

Chapter 22
"The Incredibles": The Rhodesian Light Infantry

Strong and we linked up with the OC. There were contacts all around us."

Despite having no overall control on what was going on around him, RLI Battalion Commander Colonel Peter Rich went in shortly after his son Michael, a 2 Commando troop commander parachuted in, though the senior officer was dropped onto the ground by one of the Alouettes. Shadowing him as he fought his way through a series of fire-fights, he would later express disappointment when he noticed that his son "tended to snatch the trigger".

Airborne in his antiquated Vampire jet fighter, Steve Kesby's weather worries dissipated as he closed in on the camp. As he recalls, "we left our IP on time and on pull-up, I searched frantically for my target. Once I'd spotted it, I experienced a sense of relief at finding it exactly as it had appeared in the aerial photos. On turning into the attack, I saw numbers of 'swastikas' (insurgents on the move) bomb-shelling in all directions. That was when I called my number two and told him to concentrate on the parade square. We'd been briefed to re-attack from several different positions in order to confuse the anti-aircraft gunners.

"As soon as I'd fired my rockets and positioned for a re-attack with the front gun, I heard Phil Haigh call in that his aircraft had been hit. I formatted on him climbing through the cloud, which was

Dead ZANLA insurgents. (Photo courtesy of the Hannes Wessels Collection)

when he came through again and said he had a very high jet-pipe temperature, which was when I did a close formation evaluation of his aircraft but couldn't see anything untoward. Undeterred, we headed back to Salisbury.

"I crossed the border back into Rhodesia and informed them we were 'feet dry' but Phil never did check in". Kesby immediately went down to search and found a pall of smoke where his wingman, trapped in his cockpit, had gone down. The Englishman had left the relative safety of his homeland to fight in an unpopular war for Rhodesia and he had flown his last mission.

For those Chimoio defenders who had survived the initial attack, there was more pandemonium to follow as bombs continued to thunder down and the ground-assault gradually unfolded. There was little cohesion among the insurgents: one trooper barely touched ground when he was bowled over on landing by a panicked gook that ran headlong into him. Momentarily flattened, he looked up helplessly. Then one of his oppos who had landed nearby, killed the man in a burst of fire.

Tony Coom of 3 Commando, clearly recalls that moments after landing, his team formed up in a sweep line that was commanded by Lieutenant Mark Adams. "We started moving up and there were bullets cracking all around us. Adams shouted the order to advance and fight our way through, which we did, killing those ahead: then we reformed again and advanced once more to a new position. We managed to shoot our way through whatever and whoever was in our path and ended up clearing what appeared to be our temporary objective."

"They (the enemy) just ran about like headless chickens, all of them in disarray," recalled one RLI officer, adding that his men could hardly change magazines fast enough to cope with the numbers coming at them. "God knows what had become of their command and control, but they were a shambles. With thousands of them and less than two hundred of us, all they had to do was take up a decent defensive position and fight. Had they done that we would have been in serious trouble."

The officer explained that his assault group included a single machine-gunner for every two rifles, "so our fire power was hugely enhanced … and obviously, our fire control was outstanding".

Within five minutes of battle being joined, there wasn't an aircraft that hadn't been holed by ground-fire. The command chopper flown by Norman Walsh and carrying Brian Robinson was almost shot down when its main rotor took a hit from a 14.5 mm DshKa, but

Chapter 22
"The Incredibles": The Rhodesian Light Infantry

nevertheless had to make a precautionary landing. Walsh nursed the stricken craft skilfully to the ground and no one was hurt, but for a short time the battle seemed to lose direction while he and Robinson were out of the command loop.

Jimmy Swan, a member of the RLI stopper group that had been deployed around the periphery of Chimoio recalls going to ground as they had been instructed to do and in absolute silence, watching the panoply erupting around them.

"Then, as predicted, it happened. The bush in front of us just opened up and we had hundreds of the enemy running towards us in the crouch. All hell was let loose as we fired into them from 30 or 50 metres away and within moments they were forced to reel back, shouting and screaming in a confusion of shock and panic. Some of them fired at us, but without effect ... we took them out with volleys of fire from the gunners and riflemen on all sides of where we were positioned.

"None of us fired on full auto, as I might have expected some might. The guys resorted to the good old tried and trusted 'double-tap' which is marvellously accurate and always results in a kill. We had them dropping all around us and for a long time the bush was alive with movement and screams. Then some of the enemy tried to get back to their original positions, but they were being annihilated. We'd stop briefly and hurl HE (high explosive) and white phosphorous grenades and it became a massacre.

"That done, we ran through their positions and then went to ground awaiting the next wave. Other gooks hearing their comrades making contact, headed off in different directions and ran straight into a bunch of 2 Commando sticks on the left flank. It was a full-on killing ground, from start to end."

In desperation some of the enemy shed their ZANLA uniforms and fled stark naked into the bush. It was pointless: the initial order had been concise: all adult males were to be dispatched no matter how they presented themselves.

The wife of Rex Nhongo, one of the most senior ZANLA commanders, jumped into a latrine and submerged herself in human faeces. Quite correctly, Mrs Teuri (Spillblood) Nhongo believed it was the one place in the camp that the soldiers would not want to investigate too closely. She survived.

Initial radio intercepts indicated that following the onslaught, 3,500 men had been killed and approximately the same number wounded. The Rhodesians lost two and for the soldiers of the Rhodesian Light Infantry, it was their finest hour. When news of the defeat reached Mugabe it was said that he was close to despair. Commiserating with his close confidante Edgar Tekere, as it emerged years later, he confessed that he was "...beginning to wonder if this armed struggle is worth pursuing".

Looking today at the unmitigated human and economic disaster that has been allowed to follow the transition from Rhodesia to present-day Zimbabwe, Rhodesia's conflict should never have ended the way it did.

1   Richard Wood: *The War Diaries of André Dennison*, Ashanti Publishing, Johannesburg, 1989.
2   As the Romans would say, "War will feed on itself."

CHAPTER TWENTY THREE

SURVIVING AFRICA

> "Your visa is not in order," the immigration officer told me when I passed through Conakry on my way to join gunship pilot Neall Ellis in Sierra Leone. I replied that it was. It had been issued at the Guinea Embassy in London the day before, I told him. "You are wrong," was his curt reply. I asked him why and he snorted: "Because I say so!" A 20-dollar bill changed hands before I was allowed to make my way through the airport terminal.

An American journalist on the *San Franscisco Chronicle* once asked me whether I'd had any close shaves while working all those years in Africa. "I've had a few," I replied. He eventually got me to open up a little and I ended up putting pen to paper. The events that follow describe some of them.

One of the most telling events took place while I was covering the war in Angola with South African forces during Operation Daisy, a long-ranged armoured strike deep into the Angola's interior that lasted a week. As attacks went, it was a catastrophe: somebody had tipped off both SWAPO and the Angolans that we were coming. By the time we reached the target, just about everybody had fled. The South African Air Force bombed and strafed the base and a few people were killed, but very few of the enemy became casualties. Instead, a lot of landmines were left behind and they ended up causing damage galore.

I was standing on top of a Ratel command car that had been put at the disposal of our television crew and we hit a mine. It was still early in the morning and as some of the vehicles in our column started moving off, five were destroyed by anti-tank mines in about as many minutes. It was a sobering experience and not a little unnerving, even if there were no fatalities.

Then came our turn to thread our way through what was clearly a pretty extensive minefield and moments later our front wheel detonated a Soviet TM-57. I'd been standing immediately behind the driver and must have travelled horizontally through the air for four or five metres; when I got up off the ground I found that my arm was broken. I didn't complain because it could have been worse.

During the course of covering numerous wars in southern Africa and the Middle East, I've had more than my share of brushes with mines, four or five of them altogether, some of which involved fatalities. In this regard, I consider myself fortunate.

Twice while on operations in the southern African bush I was woken in the night to massive explosions nearby. The first time it was near Chiredzi in Rhodesia and a few years later outside a remote camp in the northern reaches of South West Africa. When we investigated at first light, both blasts suggested that somebody had been trying to lay mines on the tracks we might have used the morning after. Those responsible had probably seen us mooching about with our cameras and hoped to make an impression. That they certainly achieved.

The perpetrators in both incidents were killed outright. In fact, at Chiredzi it was the first time I'd seen a man's intestines spread all the way across a thorn tree. I was actually astonished to see how extensive a human's entrails actually are. As for those responsible, not much else of either was recognisable as human, apart from their legs, of course.

Operation Protea followed, and having reached the target area, it was curiosity that took me down some primitive steps that had been dug into one of the underground bunkers in the SWAPO camp we captured: one of many. I crouched low, went in, looked about for a minute or two and then headed out into the sunlight again. It was as simple as that and nothing happened. But the young troopie that followed after I'd exited the bunker tripped an anti-personnel mine. Obviously he couldn't have been following exactly in my footsteps and he ended up taking the full blast in his face.

By then I'd moved away a short distance and there was no mistaking the muffled thump of an explosion, after which everybody came running. The youngster was killed by what was later identified as a pressure-activated PMA-3. For me, it came as a shock and I recollect thinking afterwards that it was astonishing what damage a miserable 35 grams of Tetryl explosives could do.

More recently, in Croatia with Richard Davis, the man who invented

Chapter 23
Surviving Africa

the same concealable body armour that is worn by just about every law enforcer in the United States, we once found ourselves in the middle of a minefield.

Now Richard had been involved in a few scrapes himself in a fairly adventurous career, including being shot twice by gangsters in Detroit, but not before he gunned down two of his attackers. That alone might have suggested that the man is pretty laid-back when it comes to such things, but, as he admitted later, landmines were altogether something else. I deal with his Michigan gunfight in some detail in my book *Cops: Cheating Death*, in part because his invention followed that incident and concealable body armour – discreetly worn under the shirt or vest – has so far saved the lives of about 3,500 law enforcers in North America[1].

We'd been spending time with a group of South African mine-clearing engineers from Mechem and they were showing us around. Not unexpectedly, Richard was researching the use of the same Kevlar that he customarily incorporates in his vests to devise some kind of anti-blast system that might prevent mine-clearers taking the full impact of a mine explosion in the face.

There was nothing particularly threatening about the stretch of uncleared land in which we found ourselves on our last evening with the mine-clearers. It lay adjacent to the main railway line leading south towards the coast out of Zagreb, but had long been inoperable because of the mine threat. Still, we both had to gingerly "feel" our way out of the area because there were anti-tank mines peppered with anti-personnel (AP) mines all over the place.

Perhaps my nearest brush with the inevitable was when I was with a bunch of Charlie Company's Parabats that had been tasked to attack an Angolan strongpoint through three lines of trenches outside the hamlet of Cuamato in southern Angola.

The attack itself (detailed in Chapter 1) was pretty straightforward. We were led by Peter McAleese, a British mercenary who had served with the SAS and who wrote about his own adventures in his book *No Mean Soldier*, published in London by Orion some years ago.

As we'd already discovered – several of the attacking group had become casualties, with two of our men killed – the enemy base was pretty well defended. Consequently, though not strictly in accordance with the Geneva Convention, I carried an AK: you never knew who was going to rush out of the bush at you.

Anyway, we moved in line-ahead and when the mortars started coming in, I found myself in a trench which, to my mind, the enemy seemed to have taken a particular liking to because there were mortars popping off all around us. Without much ado, I jumped out of the trench and moved forward, hoping that by doing so, such action would take me out of the line of fire. But just then one of the bombs landed behind me and I was hurled forward onto my gun which went off in my face. The bullet missed my head and the alternative option is hardly worth contemplating, but the incident did leave me permanently deaf in my left ear.

The second most exhilarating – and dangerous – experience was flying combat with South African mercenary pilot Neall Ellis in the Sierra Leone conflict in 2000. For our efforts, we used an ageing Russian Mi-24 helicopter gunship that leaked when it rained.

Although the chopper took a lot of incoming fire and because I was in its nose (under what is termed "the front bubble") I could hardly miss what was happening all around us. Green tracers are the hallmark of the AK and there were a lot of them: also quite a few 12.7s and now and again a 14.5. But at the end of it, I – like the others – emerged intact, although I'd put it down to luck.

On reflection, the closest I possibly came to being killed must have been in Nigeria shortly after the Christian-led army mutiny that was about as brutal as these things go.

That series of events ended up with the deaths of some of the

Movement about the continent involves using local transport – so-called "mammy wagons" in Nigeria (trucks with seats at the back), "bush" taxis and even scooters to gad about in towns, as seen here in Djibouti, on the Red Sea. (Photo: Author)

Chapter 23
Surviving Africa

country's most prominent leaders, including Alhaji Sir Aboubakar Tafewa Balewa, Knight of the British Empire and the only prime minister of an independent Nigeria (the leaders that came afterwards were presidents, more-often-than-not self-declared). And, as we are all aware, people of Islamic persuasion have inordinate long memories and all those bloodlettings eventually led to the Biafran Civil War.

My office in Lagos at the time was at Ikeja Airport, on the outskirts of this populous Nigerian city and since that was where the army mutiny started, I was right in the middle of it from Day One. A series of attacks were launched by mainly Muslim Nigerian Army troops at dawn, with the objective of killing every single Christian soldier that came their way.

Twice on that historic first day of violence – which involved a spate of attacks and counter-attacks, I was a whisker from getting shot. The first time, not aware of the fighting ahead, I'd turned my car off Lagos's Ikorodu Road in order to get to my office at the airport, thinking that once there, I'd be safe. My reasoning was based on the fact that Ikeja was the biggest international airport in West Africa and usually a very busy place: Pan American and British Airways, among others, were using it as a hub at the time.

Too late did I realise that a very large battle had just taken place along the same road along which I was then driving. In fact, I'd landed in a clear line of sight of an attacking force that was perhaps 500 metres away.

There was evidence of heavy clashes everywhere, with trucks and bodies strewn all over the place. Overturned armoured cars and burning half-tracks littered both sides of the road as well as the verge: it didn't seem likely that anybody could have survived such carnage. Here and there flames and smoke curled intermittently from some of the vehicles that had taken hits and there was no missing the cries of the wounded.

At that moment, I couldn't help thinking that I was in serious trouble. I must have been the first non-combatant to arrive on the scene, and while the thought crossed my mind, I knew that I could hardly stop the car and get out. Had I not kept moving forward, it might have looked suspicious. I knew too, that had I stopped or tried to turn around, the soldiers at the far end that had caused all this mayhem might have reacted: in fact, any unexpected gesture on my part could have resulted in some trigger-happy Nigerian soldier opening fire.

But, I reasoned, it was a clear day, the shooting had stopped and probably because I had no real option, I knew I had to keep on driving straight ahead. Whoever was waiting for me at the other end of that long, lonely straight stretch of road could see that I was unarmed. More to the point, I was neither black nor was I in uniform. Just then, seated in a blue civilian sedan, I was probably very pale indeed. As gingerly as possible, I put my foot down on the pedal and continued slowly ahead.

When I came to the final turn in the road that led to the airport (and safety, I hoped), I could see a bunch of heavy machine guns lined up under the trees alongside the road, muzzles outward and ammunition belts glistening. The troops manning these weapons were watching me, as were their officers. It was obvious that they were puzzled by the actions of this lunatic white man who'd suddenly arrived from nowhere.

Though it was still early in the day, it was already hot: the kind of torpid West African heat that makes life unbearable in what the expatriate community in Lagos liked to refer to as the Armpit of Africa. Consequently, in the days before automotive air-conditioning, the windows of my car were down and my radio was blaring *Hi-Life*.

As I pulled abreast of the emplacements, I did the only thing left. With one arm hanging casually out of the window, I waved at the gathering of soldiers as I passed. Smiling broadly I offered them all a cheerful "Good morning, gentlemen".

With that, I went on my merry way.

I was to spend a month at Ikeja after that historic battle which changed the face of Nigeria forever. It was also at the airport that I started writing seriously: I was the only person who was doing any reporting because journalists were prevented by the military junta from entering the country, not that I made too big a thing of it because I would have been deported or worse if they discovered the source of some of the stories then appearing in newspapers abroad.

There was no shortage of newsworthy events, as well as quite a few unexpected "scoops". Also, getting my missives and photos out of the country was not a problem, bearing in mind, as Willem Steenkamp earlier reminded us, these were times when fax machines hadn't yet been invented, never mind cellphones.

Each time I had something ready for one of my editors, I'd sidle up to a departing Pan Am passenger waiting to check in his or her baggage. Totally incognito, I'd ask them to take my little package out of the country: it would usually contain a roll or two of film and, of course, my story. But they didn't know that and nobody ever

Chapter 23
Surviving Africa

The African traveller constantly comes into contact with scenes that might be a century old: an old hunter in the Kenyan outback. (Photo: Camerapix, Nairobi, compliments of the late Mohamed Amin)

refused. It says a lot that not one of my reports went missing. Try that at any international airport today ...

Those were exceedingly interesting times. I cut my teeth as a journalist on reports that went to Wilf Nussey of the Argus Africa News Service in Johannesburg and worked for Otto Krause's *News Check* as well as *Huisgenoot*, while my old friend Klaas Steytler – the husband of author Elsa Joubert – was still editor of the biggest Afrikaans magazine in the country. United Press International came into the picture soon enough, and being the only person with any kind of access to what was going on at the time in that West African state, I not only made a packet but learnt bucketsful about the news-gathering game.

Then, a day after those momentous events at the Ikeja Airport in Lagos, I was again almost shot, this time at a Nigerian Navy installation at Apapa where I was living at the time. But that's a story for another day.

A couple of years later, after the civil war between Eastern Nigeria's Biafra and the rest of the country had become a reality, I had another narrow miss. By now, a fully fledged reporter, I'd been reporting on hostilities from the embattled enclave, already completely surrounded by the Nigerian Army. One of my colleagues was a youthful British scribe by the name of Frederick Forsyth, who went on to write his bestseller *The Dogs of War* three or four months later. Also in the mix was Italian photographer Romano Cagnoni who helped make world headlines of Biafra's starving millions, not that it made any difference in the end because a million innocents – more than half of them children – ended up dying in that dreadful internecine conflict, most of them starved to death.

My closest brush at the time took place one fine morning in that same Biafra. Having had my breakfast of sawdust cakes and what passed for a jungle tea (the country really was ravenous, and it affected us all) I cadged a lift in a civilian car to get to the next town. We were halfway there when we were strafed by a Russian-built MiG jet fighter and everybody in the vehicle had to decamp at very short notice, head first, straight into the jungle. Fortunately, the pilot missed, narrowly as it turned out, but being Africa, we all thought it worth a chuckle afterwards.

Later I was to meet Ares Klootwyk, the pilot who'd done the dirty deed. He was a South African mercenary employed by government forces and we had a few ales on the event. It was actually the first time that any Western pilot had been able to fly a Soviet MiG-17 jet fighter which, until Ares got into the cockpit, had been totally under wraps. Small wonder that Nigeria was crawling with spooks.

Talking about espionage, an equally frightening event happened when I was arrested and jailed for "spying" in the Congo. A French journalist with *Le Monde* and I had been trying to get into Angola but had been stopped. So we headed north, through Zambia and then into Mobutu's war-wracked Congo Republic. A bunch of government functionaries thought we were up to no good and they led us to the local secret police headquarters, the *Centre Nationale de Documentation* (CND) in Lubumbashi to be interrogated, after which we were jailed.

What made the experience unnerving was that anyone committed to a CND establishment in those days very rarely came out alive. Once inside, we could hear the screams of other unfortunates being tortured, but thankfully, they spared us the pain and the indignity, although we did take some thumps.

To cut a long story short, my colleague and I managed to smuggle a message out of our holding cell to the Belgian manager of the local Katangese copper mine; it was written in French and English on two sheets of toilet paper. Eventually the word got out and a second or third secretary from the British Embassy in Kinshasa flew down from Kinshasa to check us out … or at the very least, alive.

Chapter 23
Surviving Africa

I've since heard that it was the French Premier Francois Mitterrand who, on very good terms with President Mobutu Sese Seko, used his considerable influence to get us released.

In terms of escapes, narrow or otherwise, I'm not sure where I'd place an event that led to us being ambushed by rebels in northern Uganda. I was with a crew from French television and we were all heading back to Kampala when a rebel group then operating in northern Uganda opened fire. These were the forerunners of the notorious Lords Resistance Army.

I'd hired a South African film crew and the little shits told me they were too terrified to leave Kampala. Too late to make alternative arrangements, I managed a discreet deal with the French producer: he'd shoot footage for me each time he'd completed a sequence of his own and I'd pay him by the 400-foot reel of 16 mm film (we hadn't yet graduated to digital cameras). In the end the documentary was flighted on SABC and quite unexpectedly, came out much better than expected. There was nothing about the ambush though: brave souls that we were, we were all cowering on the floors at the rear of our getaway cars.

Having left Gulu in great haste in a two-vehicle convoy after the Ugandan Army had tried to arrest us all for disobeying orders not to film in the town, we headed into the countryside on the only road leading south, the French crew way out in front. So I missed some of it, except that we were a couple of kilometres out of Gulu when the first shots rang out and my new-found French pals wasted no time in picking up speed and disappearing over the next hill.

With that, my extremely nervous driver did the only thing possible: he, too, put his foot down!

We must have travelled on our own for about five minutes before we got to the next settlement, which lay on a low hill. The French crew had arrived intact and the entire populace had gathered on the edge of town to greet them: they'd watched it all go down from a distance and offered us some pretty lusty cheers.

Parts of that event were also used in one of my productions screened nationwide in the United States by Public Broadcasting Service. The documentary was called *Africa's Killing Fields* and according to the PBS website, there are still copies of the programme for sale[3].

Apart from that, I've had three pretty serious run-ins with sharks, twice with great whites, and once chased out of the water by a pack of Zambezi (Bull) sharks while diving along Protea Banks with

So-called "child soldiers" might not be an everyday event in Africa, but the youth – and sometimes very young children with guns – are still to be seen in some of the ongoing wars, like the Congo or Ivory Coast. (Photo: Author's collection)

Graham Powell of Aliwal Shoal fame. The problem there was that I'd just survived a serious dose of food poisoning and, as we all know, predators – both on land and in the sea – have a highly developed sense of who or what is old, or sick or ailing. That meant that this pack of about six or eight "Zambies" came right at me and I had to scarper back into the boat in a hurry. I found myself on deck without even having removed my dive gear …

Frankly, that little run-in with sharks was much scarier than any military adventure. I've had more than a dozen of my diving pals attacked by sharks, the majority of them while spearfishing; there have also been three people that I knew killed by them, one while diving in Mombasa. He and Conway Plough were working in shallow waters alongside the local yacht club and both divers were savaged. Conway had a large section of his calf removed by what was later determined to be a Bull shark (Zambezi) and the other diver was killed.

Chapter 23
Surviving Africa

With all this in mind, I am only too conscious of what can happen, usually unexpectedly, with these critters. But then you are bound to bump into sharks if you've dived off the southern tip of Africa for almost half a century and end up writing six or eight books on the subject.

In a more serious vein, there have been a number of other incidents, like being sniped at by anti-government rebels in El Salvador and a few experiences in Beirut and elsewhere in the Middle East that could curl hair. In retrospect, I suppose I've been extraordinarily lucky.

Moving about in today's Africa can be tough. It is often dangerous. There are a thousand reasons why, although very few African safaris in this age of global travel and instantaneous communications end badly.

In the 1960s and 1970s – and even more recently – I could move around without fear in both East and West Africa. I hiked to London through Angola, the Congo, Gabon, the Cameroons, Nigeria, Ghana and all the way on to Senegal. In Gabon I was to meet *le grand docteur* Dr Albert Schweitzer before he died; that was shortly after his 90th birthday. In Liberia I travelled a week totally on my own in the jungle as I slowly worked my way towards the capital, and I came out unscathed from there as well. But those days are long gone. Now, in order to achieve any kind of progress in modern-day Africa, you need to grease palms. Lots of palms and excessive amounts of silver-coloured grease!

Case in point was when Abidjan airport was closed and I was obliged to go overland between Ghana and the Ivory Coast. For no apparent reason, my wife Madelon and I were held up at the border. After a five-hour delay, I asked to speak to the senior man. It wasn't a clever move, since nobody likes to be upstaged.

Once in the colonel's office, I explained that I had urgent business on the other side of the frontier. I desperately needed to get through, I said, clearly exasperated. With that, I opened my briefcase to show him details of a meeting we had planned with four others, two of whom had flown in from Europe. Like a banner, a copy of *Penthouse* loomed prominently on top of my pile of papers and I could immediately see that it had the same effect as a strobe beam in a midwinter Arctic blizzard. To the exclusion of all else, the magazine with its scantily clad bimbo on the cover became the single focus of attention of this head honcho's mind. All conversation had stopped and the man's breathing became laboured. He was clearly transfixed

Violence in Sierra Leone was fanned by civil war for many years, but these days its capital, Freetown – seen here – is a quiet but noisy backwater in West Africa. You need dollars to get around, but rarely travellers cheques. (Photo: Author)

by this relatively innocuous skin magazine that wouldn't have turned an eye anywhere else.

Hello, I thought, here's trouble! After an interminable silence that was punctuated only by a wheezing electric fan that ruffled papers each time it swept over us, the colonel got up from his chair. He loomed ominously over me and pointed.

"You give me *that*. You go!" he declared forcefully and it was the first time he even deigned to speak English. Then he smiled, almost like a schoolboy embarrassed to be caught with his hand in the cookie jar. Ten minutes later Madelon and I were on our way. Because things sometimes work that way, it is one of the reasons why I rarely go into Africa these days without the requisite dollop of smut.

I long ago concluded that Africa is the continent of contradictions. Tom Staley spent a while in a succession of strange wars on the West Coast and he tells of a flight crew on a relief mission in Liberia a few years ago. They were in an antiquated Russian Mi-8 that had probably seen service in Afghanistan.

The three men took their chopper into a remote corner in the interior near the Nimba Mountains in the north, unloaded their cargo and prepared to head back to Monrovia. While all this was going on, the proceedings were watched by a group of soldiers who were supposed to be government and probably weren't. One of the crew recalled afterwards that they'd obviously been smoking something devious, or worse. Which was when they started waving their Kalashnikovs about like people possessed. "We were pretty damn glad to be getting out of there," recalled Tom when he told me about his little adventure.

All three aviators were already strapped into their seats in the Hip's cockpit when the leader of this ragged band — gimlet-eyed and brutish — stepped forward and used his weapon to indicate that their helicopter wasn't going anywhere. The crew got away eventually, but not before they were stripped. They had to fly naked all the way back to Monrovia.

The deployment of UN troops to Sierra Leone — many of them British and quite a few from Europe, Asia, the Middle East as well as some Canadians — resulted in a rash of questions about those intending to visit West Africa. Because of ongoing violence and a level of volatility that is totally unpredictable, there is barely a Western government that actually encourages its nationals to travel to many parts of the region. Gambia, Senegal, the Cameroons and Gabon might be all-right, but perhaps not Nigeria, Mali, Guinea, Sierra Leone, Liberia, Chad, the Ivory Coast, Upper Volta, Niger, Mauretania ... the list goes on.

For all this, Africa remains a draw card. You can fly to both Kenya and southern Africa for about as much as it will cost you to get to Hong Kong, but much of it boils down to personal security. Things have deteriorated so much in recent years that in some African states, muggings, robberies, hijackings and even senseless murders most of the time don't even make the news.

Take the most recent example. Almost nobody outside South Africa was aware of one of the biggest jewellery heists ever that took place in broad daylight at a shopping mall near Johannesburg. About 20 robbers — some of them armed with AK-47s, others with automatic pistols and revolvers — stormed a complex of about 200 stores and held more than a thousand shoppers at bay. The majority were ordered to lie face down on the ground. That done, the gang ransacked three shops and at gunpoint stripped them of all their precious wares.

Why didn't anybody call the police? Good question. Or rather, as someone caught up in the drama said afterwards, "What police?".

A couple of police cars showed up after a while, but by then the

And then the headlines – a gory photo from yesterday's Liberia when mayhem ruled! (Photo: Craige Grice)

gang had fled. The first arrest in the case still has to be made and this, irrespective of the fact that Johannesburg has one of the highest per capita cellphone rates in the southern hemisphere. It's infra dig *not* to have one! That kind of incident scares a lot of people, some of them into leaving South Africa permanently. It also highlights selective reporting by the media.

Now, had it been a gang of white thugs ...

While that sort of thing is happening in "sunny South Africa" it's a lot different in parts of West and Central Africa that have become increasingly mired in revolutionary conflict.

In much of West Africa, and to some extent in the central and eastern regions of the continent as well, there have been conflicts that the international media remained tentative about while it lasted. Sierra Leone and Liberia received a lot of publicity as their wars dragged on, while others, like the guerrilla struggle in Senegal's southern Casamance Province, hardly rated coverage, though there were people there being killed. Still, the violence hasn't stopped Europeans and Americans visiting many of these places.

For all this, most former British and French colonial possessions in West Africa retain a certain ineluctable Third World charm. Graham Greene, for instance, loved Sierra Leone and apparently did some of his best writing there. The same with Senegal and the Ivory Coast.

Chapter 23
Surviving Africa

In the old days, I would never give Dakar and Abidjan a miss: both were islands of *francophonie* far from home. But more recently, things haven't gone all that well.

Also, when it comes to money, observe the basics. For a start, keep something in your back pocket to appease the knife-wielding thug: just enough to keep him happy. Secrete the rest in your underpants or in a sock: everybody else does!

Also, avoid using credit cards north of the Zambezi. During my stay in Sierra Leone not so long ago, I met a Scandinavian officer attached to a UN contingent who, on his previous deployment to this posting, had used his American Express card at a Freetown travel agent before going home. The first thing his wife did when he stepped in the door was to berate him for buying a new car in Sierra Leone. The details were clearly reflected on his latest bank statement, she told him.

Of course he protested, but it was all there, signatures, the lot. Obviously the man got his money back in the end, but it took months and the hassles that ensued were endless. Meantime, his credit rating was downgraded. Also, it's not wise to change money with the first man who accosts you in the street in Nairobi, Ouagadougou or Luanda. Most countries have exchange control laws in place and it could be a sting that might land you in jail. And having spent

Roadblocks manned by soldiers are still part of the everyday mix in many parts of the continent. Approach with polite confidence and never argue with these troops: it is their country and they like you to know it! (Photo: Author)

Megalomaniacs like Zimbabwe's Robert Mugabe do not like visitors coming to Zimbabwe and even innocent visitors are sometimes subjected to scrutiny. You need to tread lightly in some of these countries. (Photo: Author's collection)

much longer than I would have liked in a Congolese prison, I am able to testify first-hand that they're nothing like the penitentiaries we are likely to see on the BBC or any other European or American network. African prisons can be like taking six steps backwards in time, with dungeons, violence and unsanitary conditions that defy description. The food's not all that good either.

There are other pitfalls. While West African ladies are lovely to look at, touching them with anything other than your hand can present problems, especially in some of the countries where you can have three whores hanging onto each elbow as long as you're buying. Truth is, Africa has some remarkably exotic sexually transmitted diseases, one or two which could prove fatal if not promptly treated and I'm not talking about Aids. It gets worse in places like Freetown where encephalitis and Hepatitis B are both endemic and can be transmitted by a kiss.

In Nigeria these ladies are euphemistically termed "Night Fighters" and they're a resilient, persistent bunch who will come knocking at your hotel door four or five times before dawn if you appear in any way "approachable". The fact is, almost every one of these hookers is selling the only commodity they own and they regard white transients – who they refer to disparagingly as "White Monkeys", "Weebos", "Do-Ums" and the rest – as easy meat, if you'll excuse the pun.

One way of avoiding them is to tell them you are gay, but that doesn't always hold water either, because there is usually somebody in the gang who is willing to prove that she has the charms to "convert" you. The trouble is they go at it with an almost Baptist commitment rarely found outside the Midwest Bible Belt and given half the chance, they'll spend hours telling you that you don't know what you're missing. You can even have it for free the first time round, is the usual ploy.

Also do not underestimate Aids. The disease is rampant throughout sub-Saharan Africa and one example will suffice. Three years ago, six Danish businessmen visited Zambia to explore business interests at Kitwe, a moderate-sized mining town near the Congolese border. They got home a few weeks later to discover that five had Aids and sadly, that only came to light a month later. But not a word about how their wives fared.

Strange things can happen when societies go berserk, so expect the worst in any country that might be facing insurrection.

During one of several bouts of fighting in Sierra Leone, in late 1998 – it followed another change of government — Henry Kenealy held the lofty title of communications officer at the US Embassy in Freetown. As he recalls, things very quickly started to go sour.

"With our telephone and satellite links down, I managed to get onto the 40-metre amateur band using the embassy's old off-site Transworld (TWC) 500W high frequency station," he told me. "I called 'CQ emergency/mayday … any US station, this is 377 US Embassy, Freetown, Sierra Leone requesting phone patch assistance."

Kenealy was finally answered by one of the amateur radio stations in America. The operator – by then, joined by one or two others – asked whether he perhaps had a local amateur call sign that he could use. He did and it was 9L1HK. For the next 12 hours, while stray rounds smashed into the embassy and the diplomatic compound was looted, two-short-wave enthusiasts across the Atlantic relayed phone messages between Kenealy and the Pentagon as well as the State Department in Washington.

"Three days later, through the same channel, we received orders to evacuate the mission. We were told to execute emergency destruction procedures. Unfortunately, in the process, my station log was destroyed and I lost the call sign of the operator who assisted me," Kenealy recounts.

Networking internationally as radio amateurs do, the two Samaritans were eventually traced and commended by State.

Food can be a problem in most African states where hygiene might be suspect. If in doubt, try to frequent local markets and wherever possible, observe the maxim: "If you can't peel it, don't eat it!" This market is on the Red Sea. (Photo: Author)

Chapter 23
Surviving Africa

The name of the game in Africa, essentially — as Ron Reid-Daly titled one of his books – is staying alive.

For instance, there are basics that need to be observed, if only because things can get nasty if you don't react properly. Experience has proved often enough that it can get worse if you actually display fear. So, you need to smile, no matter what. Be friendly and make conversation, even if circumstances are inane. More than one life has been saved on the "Dark Continent" by acting friendly and respectful towards crazies with guns. Remember too, that there are enough loose cannons with weapons in their belts in the streets of Freetown, Lagos, Johannesburg, Nairobi, Luanda, Abidjan, Kinshasa and a lot of other places to arm a succession of minor battle groups.

For all this, Africa can be an enjoyable experience. It is also reasonably safe if you observe a few fundamental ground rules, each one predicated by common sense:

- Anybody contemplating visiting tropical Africa needs to start an anti-malaria regimen several weeks before setting out. Remember that there are more pet theories about what to take for malaria than there are listed tropical diseases. Check out the latest in Artemisinin anti-malarial herbal treatments – they really do work and are now manufactured in the European Union – and instead of being incapacitated for three weeks, you are back on your feet in days. The last time I contracted malaria in Zambia, I was incapacitated for only 48 hours ...
- Don't wander about any African city alone after dark. The chances of a woman being raped in West Africa (as opposed to South Africa) varies somewhere between zero and nil. But if you're carrying a bag and strolling about the back streets of some of Africa's bigger cities, it'll almost certainly be snatched. Don't fight it because having something minor taken from you under duress is better than getting an eight-inch cut stitched up at arguably the most unhygienic clinic south of Suez. Also it can be prohibitively expensive.
- Never take wads of cash with you: traveller's cheques are safer because they're guaranteed. Also, once off the beaten tourist track, there are many African states that won't accept credit cards. Check all valuables into the hotel safe, though even that isn't foolproof. I lost more than $5,000 while filming in Abidjan: the money was

stolen from my safe deposit box to which, I was assured, *only I had the key*! Try getting the local police to accept that for a line!

- And if you're thinking of slumming it, don't! African countries are not the same as Europe or America. As a tourist, you're not in the same bracket as the average American Peace Corps or British VSO volunteer, most of whom don't have a bunch of beans between them and are invariably embraced by the communities in which they work because they are helping local people. In this regard Nigeria must be the worst and the sanest advice here is not to go anywhere near Lagos – it has been the world's largest suppurating slum for more than half a century where raw sewage is still pumped into the lagoon between Apapa and Victoria Island. Both Britain's Foreign Office and the US State Department will tell you as much in almost as many words. Also, though things have improved, it is still easier to be robbed on the way into town from the Murtala Muhammed International Airport in Lagos than it is to hail a cab at JFK.
- If you can't afford the kind of amenities offered by the average Western hotel, you shouldn't be contemplating the trip. Just getting back to the quasi-antiseptic environment of a clean, air-conditioned room after a day in the average African city is an essential break from a ruthlessly demanding unhealthy and unsanitary environment. You only need to get the whiff of a public toilet in any one of these places to get the message.
- Watch what you eat. Once you emerge into the street from your hotel, observe the fundamental principle that once on the road, don't eat it if you can't peel it. There are no health controls like we know them back home. Also, in most African cities north of the Limpopo, meat is slaughtered on the hoof. And it hardly takes a quantum physicist to discover that refrigeration is a luxury that the masses simply cannot afford. Anyway, who really knows what other contagion was washed in that basin out back from which your glass has just emerged.
- Everybody needs water, but spend the extra and buy it bottled. Also, establish beforehand that what you pay for isn't recycled. First law is to ensure that each bottle, can, jug or container that is handed to you is factory-sealed.

If the bottle arrives with its screw cap or cork unsealed, reject it. At bars or restaurants, drink your beer from the bottle. Forget about ice: what does it help if you observe the rules and use ice to cool your drink that came from the local tap water?
- Take with you at least three types of medicine for stomach bugs: anything mild for the "runs" as well as a powerful antibiotic for a serious amoebic infection and finally, a binder like Lomisol for afterwards.

These are only *some* of the basics. Observe them and you will survive, hopefully in relative peace. Ignore some of these elementary warnings – about malaria or drinking untreated water – and you might be dead in a week. It happens far too often …

1 Al J. Venter: *Cops: Cheating Death*, Lyons Press, New Haven, 2007.
2 Duncan Rykaardt has since been killed: he died tragically in 2009 after the Russian plane in which he was travelling to Mogadishu, Somalia crashed into Lake Victoria immediately after take-off from Entebbe International Airport in Uganda.
3 The US Public Broadcasting System network can be accessed on the Web at www.pbs.org and the one-hour television documentary titled "Africa's Killing Fields" can be historically traced on "Search".

CHAPTER TWENTY FOUR

AN AMERICAN HOSTAGE OF HIZBOLLAH

Colonel William R. Higgins of the United States Marine Corps was 43 years old when he was murdered by Hizbollah zealots. At the time he was the commander of Observer Group Lebanon, or as we would call it, OGL. Still operational in areas adjacent to the northern frontier of the Holy Land, it is a United Nations body responsible for "supervising the truce" between Israel and Lebanon.

The word "truce" in the context of this United Nations body is anomalous. In typical Middle East gobbledygook there might have been something written on paper at some stage or another, but as experience has proved in the past, it is as worthless as the peace it was supposed to have guaranteed.

I met Colonel Higgins only once at a function at Naqoura that I attended while at the South Lebanese UN base. He was then just another faceless functionary and only after he'd been abducted and I spotted his picture in the papers – a strong round face, with bald forehead and the stock grey Marine Corps moustache – did I realise who he was.

To the Arabs holding him hostage, Bill Higgins was not only a prize, but a senior American military officer and hence of inestimable political or blackmail value. To Hizbollah, the Party of God, he was a spy. It was as simple as that, they said. They reckoned that within the vagaries of Middle East politics, it made him "fair game".

As they still describe the incident at OGL headquarters at Nahariya, on the Israeli side of the border, Colonel Higgins set out to meet some unknown individuals on a blustery morning in February 1988. He'd mentioned that there was a meeting planned with Arab leaders about a problem, though he wasn't specific. Overnight, an icy

Chapter 24
An American hostage of Hizbollah

Almost all of South Lebanon at the time of the abduction of Colonel Higgins was under the control of the Iranian-backed Pasdaran, forerunner of today's Hizbollah. Huge billboards of the Ayatollah Khomeini were erected all over the countryside.
(Photo: Author)

wind had swept in from the Syrian highlands and by all accounts, it was cold, so the American wore his standard UN blues together with a heavy winter greatcoat.

There is no question that he intended to raise the issue of the eight Americans being held hostage by fundamentalist Muslim groups, the most prominent only much later identified as Hizbollah. The Party of God was not yet the most important player in this filthy Middle Eastern game, but with solid Iranian help, its predecessor – Pasdaran, which is Iranian nomenclature for a specific security body – was inordinately active and increasing its sway in the region at a pace. Also, Pasdaran making a name for itself. Clearly, Colonel Higgins had a role in those aspirations because he was to become its Hostage Number Nine.

Once in custody, the American was held in isolation for two-and-a-half years. They killed him early on the morning of 6 July 1990. In this time, in my own meanderings about the region, I was made aware afterwards that once or twice I must have been only yards from his improvised prison. Had I only known ...

Subsequent interrogations of Hizbollah prisoners by the Israelis have revealed that the captivity of the Colonel was both brutal and indeterminate. It was often cruel, often mindlessly so and, reports have it, he was regularly beaten and starved. Throughout his ordeal, he was bound, gagged, most-times blindfolded and kept in solitary confinement. In short, the man who had served with distinction in several military campaigns during the course of an illustrious career, suffered the most horrible privations.

It is also worth mentioning that the Israelis made it known afterwards that his tormentors never ever managed to break him. He was finally murdered in Tyre with a *Nackschuss* – a single bullet in the back of the head or neck – curiously only a short distance from where the original meeting was scheduled to have taken place. A spokesman for Hizbollah later tried to dismiss this horrific chapter by declaring that Colonel Bill Higgins was an agent of the CIA and as such, it was deduced that he was "an enemy of Islamic people everywhere".

An immediate consequence of Colonel Higgins's death was that from that time on, no member of Observer Group Lebanon ever again travelled solo in Lebanon. These days, meetings are held in the presence of at least two members of the team, routinely backed by a radio check to base every 30 minutes or so. The same procedures are followed when OGL staff travel on the roads in that country, though not when on business in Israel.

Even my own movements with members of OGL in August 1996 were invariably in the company of two of their officers, and sometimes with a member of the UN spokesperson's staff. The last time I was there, a couple of years later, two New Zealand Army officers escorted me.

We'd drive throughout the region, from Naqoura eastwards towards Shihin where Team Zulu had its observation post and our route would take us past Bint Jubayl, where we were regarded with great suspicion.

From there we'd wend our way on lonely roads to the position of Team Victor, another concrete bunker fitted with a powerful pair of binoculars on a metal stand. Then we'd turn north-east, where Team X-ray had a base that overlooked the heartland of Upper Galilee. This was on the fringes of ground that had come under heavy Israeli gunfire during Operation Grapes of Wrath some years before.

The largest United Nations military base in the world is at Naqoura, on the narrow coastline in South Lebanon. It was from here that Colonel Higgins went out to meet with a group of unknown individuals. (Author's photo)

Chapter 24
An American hostage of Hizbollah

Although we travelled through terrain dominated by Hizbollah, we passed unhindered, even though those members of the Party of God who we met along the way knew exactly who I was and why I was being escorted by members of the Observer Group. They'd been formally told so by Naqoura, as is the custom with the UN, and while we were never really challenged, we remained cautious.

Along the way we passed several South Lebanese Army (SLA) mine-clearing squads and each time we'd stop until we were waved on. One of the Australian officers had unexpectedly become a target of one of their soldiers after suddenly coming over a rise. Although his vehicle was white and he was in his customary blue uniform, he was shot at despite his conspicuous UN identity. The man wasn't seriously hurt, though the car was hit a number of times: one lucky Australian!

The most active of United Nations Truce Supervision Organisation (UNTSO) observation posts was Op Mar, manned by Team X-ray which comprised two more New Zealanders with an officer each from France, Canada, Belgium and Finland. The OC was another Australian, Major Frank Kalloway RAAC, from Tasmania. Arriving there after advising beforehand by radio that we were on our way, I was immediately struck by the fortifications around this tiny base – essentially a cluster of concrete blockhouses, some of them underground; all were surrounded by staggered layers of razor wire.

Op Mar had come under fire many times in the past few years, usually from Israeli Defence Force (IDF) artillery units and Jerusalem would afterwards declare that it was either accidental or inadvertent fire. During the Grapes of Wrath Israeli invasion, Op Mar was hit – purposely, the UN charged – by two IDF airbursts at very close range.

This kind of incident happens all too often and is customarily dismissed as irrelevant by the authorities in the Jewish State, which

is unfortunate. But then the Israelis invariably take a cavalier approach to the problems of others and obviously, United Nations soldiers, or any other soldiers "across the line" are not among their most favoured people.

One consequence is a groundswell of deep resentment towards the Israeli people that has taken root among many of the UN troops stationed in the Middle East and it persists to this day. The base commander submitted at the time of the attack that if the observers at Op Mar had been in their usual monitoring positions on the morning the shells were fired – they were in their bunks, down below – they might have all been killed. Damage had been severe, Major Kalloway confirmed.

"What really pissed us off about those bastards," said Captain John Doran, a New Zealand reserve officer from Otago, "was that they didn't even ask whether any of us were hurt. Then, not long afterwards, it happened again, and once more the issue was broached with Jerusalem."

Doran, like many other UN troops who were fired on by Israeli artillery, believed that none of this was accidental. Certainly, he felt, the hit on Op Mar was intentional. "They're one of the most advanced military nations in the world ... that's simply not the kind of error they would make ... remember, their own people are around here too, and you very rarely hear of friendly fire losses among IDF units."

I afterwards asked several Israeli officers about the incident. Either they didn't know anything or they weren't telling. The complaints were dismissed with a shrug and a wave. These gestures of contempt remain one of the reasons why United Nations-Israeli relations are as bad as they are.

At the same time, give the IDF its due. Israeli Captain Shimon who accompanied me into one of the border camps had his own views when I broached the subject:

"We must have fired at least 10,000 rounds of artillery during Grapes of Wrath. So a couple of rounds fell short. What can we do? This is war. What do these people expect?"

Captain Shimon was less forthcoming about the half-dozen or so shells that landed in the Fiji Battalion camp (FijiBatt) at Qana, east of Tyre. Historically, the Bible tells us, this is where Jesus transformed water into wine.

More than 100 Lebanese men, women and children were killed in the attack that must be chalked up as one of the most serious peacetime military blunders committed by the IDF. Apart from the loss of life, it cost the Jewish nation an inordinate amount of goodwill among many of the countries that might have tolerated the occasional excess in the past. But certainly not on this scale.

As was to have been expected, CNN made a meal of the slaughter among viewers in more than 100 countries in broadcasts that went all over the globe.

Situated on the Israeli border about five kilometres east of Qiryat Shmona and with the Lebanese hinterland stretching behind, Op Mar had been the focus of much attention by Hizbollah in the period leading up to Operation Grapes of Wrath. All the towns in the region, the majority Islamic and pro-Shi'ite, had been targeted by ambushes, mines and roadside bombs or what is more commonly referred to these days further to the east as IEDs. These included Bani Hayyan (from where a group of Palestinians had tried to launch a microlight, immediately shot down by the IDF with a six-barrelled Gatling); Markabe (where a car bomb was detonated) and Houele, the source of at least two Hizbollah suicide bombers and other acts that caused the death of children a few months before I arrived.

The region is characterised by a series of wadis or river valleys running from east to west, almost none offering natural cover of the kind needed for guerrilla operations. These natural defiles are nonetheless used to penetrate as close to the Israeli border as possible and the deepest of all, officially listed on the charts as Wadi Salaq, is referred to by both the UN and the Israelis as "Hizbollah Highway".

It says a lot that the IEDs currently causing casualties among Coalition Forces in Iraq and Afghanistan were initially field-tested against Israeli Forces in these same areas by Hizbollah's forerunners a quarter-century ago.

Many of the United Nations officers whom I met during my trip with Observer Group Lebanon maintained that Hizbollah was making serious inroads wherever it had influence; including its social, political and military domains. They noted too that suicide bombings had become the norm.

One example displayed remarkable guile. In its bid to foil Israeli remote-piloted vehicles (RPVs) – which use infrared instruments positioned at 18,000 feet in its bid to seek out hostile intruders making their way across country – Hizbollah commanders had acquired neoprene wetsuits for their men. Not only did the suits reduce heat emissions at night (when most of these raids took place) but they also kept their people warm, especially in winter. A

Norwegian intelligence officer suggested that when the IDF was still deployed in South Lebanon, a Hizbollah ambush group might lie in one position for three or four days without supplies waiting for an Israeli or SLA patrol to pass.

"They are totally focused in their determination to get at what they naturally regard as a 'blood enemy'," he declared

Since then, that kind of activity has stopped. Islamic attrition had increased to the point where the Israeli government finally decided that it would be in the country's best interests to withdraw its military forces back to positions behind its own borders. The gesture was immediately trumpeted across the Islamic World as a major Hizbollah victory, which, when you look at what has subsequently taken place, it was and has had a powerfully negative effect for the Israelis. Moreover, Hizbollah rocket attacks continue, somewhat more sporadically than before, only these days the bombs land on Israeli soil.

While the IDF was still stationed in South Lebanon – and during my own visits to the region – Hizbollah tactics evolved in several other directions. Besides taking along their own camera crews to record attacks at the "Sharp End", they would invite Lebanese television personalities from Beirut to position themselves at specific spots at designated times.

One such incident involved Israeli troops returning back to their base near the Metullah border-crossing. The Arab cameraman filmed sensational footage later acquired by CNN and again, beamed all over the world. Pictures of dead and dying Israeli soldiers, some still writhing on the ground, had a profound effect on Jewish sensibilities and there were many who expressed horror and despair at what was termed "these depravities". Predictably, air attacks on Hizbollah training camps in the Beka'a Valley intensified.

The cameraman involved was arrested by the Lebanese authorities immediately afterwards, but not before – as might have been expected – he was able to spirit away his tape. Naturally, after he was handed over to the Israelis by their South Lebanese allies, he denied any prior knowledge of the ambush, which was interesting: it had taken place near a busy road in an area where there was strict policy in force that mandated absolutely no casual movement of civilians on this or any other border road. In effect, the Arab cameraman was very much out of bounds.

He later added his own two bits worth, proclaiming loud resentment at the presence of Jews on Lebanese soil. On this issue, there were even some Israelis who had to acknowledge that it was his

Chapter 24
An American hostage of Hizbollah

The Israelis did what they could to try to track the last movements of the American colonel, who, Hizbollah later claimed, worked for the CIA. An Israeli helicopter returns to its northern headquarters having found no trace of the man. (Photo: Beata Hamizrachi).

right to say what he wished. The man was held for several weeks by the Israeli General Security Service (GSS) and then released, but not before strong protests were lodged by the Egyptian and Jordanian governments.

Such were the political machinations in South Lebanon while Israel still maintained a military presence there. The IDF went back in the summer of 2006 and, for the first time in the brief history of the Jewish State, its soldiers took such a pounding from Hizbollah irregulars that Jerusalem had to pull its troops back in disgrace.

The nearest Israeli fortified post to Op Mar towards the end of the "occupation period" is listed as Four One Alpha on operational maps of this corner of South Lebanon. At the time it was manned by about 20 IDF conscripts and supported by a single heavy tank that displayed an array of electronic equipment on its turret. There were also a couple of armoured personnel carriers.

At the time of my visit in the late 1990s, Four One Alpha was used for launching nightly Special Force patrols against Hizbollah, usually on foot. According to Major Kalloway, the heavily camouflaged squads would leave base at about eight in the evening and return before dawn. More often than not, they would have been extracted by helicopter. They often had mine-clearing equipment with them, he reckoned, "and you couldn't miss the occasional night-vision goggles about their necks".

He disclosed that it was Hizbollah's purpose to lay mines and booby traps in their efforts to hamper these patrols in and around

Houele. They also targeted them with their Iranian-supplied Sagger missiles.

In total, said the Australian officer, the Israelis maintained about a dozen camps (which he referred to as Permanent Violations, or PVs) in his area, which was a lot compared with a few years before when most of the work was left to the South Lebanese Army. He disclosed that Hizbollah became most active whenever Israeli forces were preparing to resupply their men.

"They don't always do damage, but the fact that they are able to attack, almost at will and quite often effectively, is a powerful boost to morale; it shows the locals that they can act in the area, if not with impunity, then with less risk than before. That, in itself, is a victory for the guerrillas," he stressed. Major Kalloway also made the point that some guerrilla strikes were causing the kind of problems that the Israelis needed to solve to avoid losing still more lives. And as we now know, they never did, having preferred instead to remove their army from Lebanon.

I was shown some of the positions where Hizbollah had laid their IEDs, including two along roads in the vicinity of Houele.

According to an OGL report published afterwards, the first bomb exploded in what was identified as "Echo Road". Its target was Captain Ali Abass, deputy commander of the SLA 70th Battalion.

The South Lebanese Army also entered the fray with little luck: two Lebanese SLA soldiers on board a Sherman tank that had originally belonged to the Egyptians at Outpost 301, Marj'Auoun. (Photo: Dave McGrady, formerly a mercenary with the SLA)

Chapter 24
An American hostage of Hizbollah

The first explosion had no effect, which immediately gave rise to a suspicion that it had been intentionally detonated to oblige SLA officers to use another route where a second IED had been laid. What happened next was not entirely clear, but to quote from the report, four children, three of them girls, apparently chased a snake into a hole in the wall about 100 metres from where it joined Echo Road. This wasn't all that unusual because there are plenty of snakes in the Levant and not all are poisonous.

They poked about for a minute or so with a stick when suddenly there was a powerful explosion: three of the children were killed outright. All that was left of Muhammed Talar Juwad, the only boy in the group, aged 12, were his shoes. These were still on the ground where he'd been standing. The remains of two of the girls were never found. The third girl, the 14-year-old sister of one of the dead, was unharmed but in shock and couldn't speak for days.

About 20 minutes after the explosion, Al Manaar, Hizbollah's radio station in Beirut announced that four "collaborators" [sic] had been killed by a roadside bomb laid by their guerrillas. When the extent of the mishap became apparent, the story abruptly changed: that evening the childrens' deaths were blamed on the Israelis.

What had actually happened, we ascertained much later, was that a Hizbollah group of three men had set up an OP on a hill with a clear view of a position in Shaqraq, the next village to the east. They'd set off their bomb in the belief that it had been found by security personnel who were dismantling it. In truth, they were too far away to see that the "intruders" were children.

It is one of the tragic quirks of this vicious struggle that the family of 11-year-old Hamama Ashad Hussein, one of the children who had died, had already lost three boys in the war. SLA engineers later produced fragments of remote-control equipment taken from the site of the explosion and a UN source confirmed later that it had all the hallmarks of bombs previously laid by Hizbollah.

Observer Group Lebanon teams with whom I worked were very much aware that roadside bombs were a danger to their safety. According to another New Zealander, Captain Charles Smith, also from Otago, bombs were seldom laid singly. There was usually a second charge, often detonated while the other was being investigated. And since it has always been the principal task of the OGL to look into such matters, you could easily become a casualty "by accident", he explained.

"The first is usually set off by a trip wire; the second is almost invariably command-detonated by radio from a mile or more away. At that distance all men in uniform look the same," was his comment.

I was to experience this for myself one morning when we set out from Naqoura for Majdal Zun. Word had arrived over the radio that a bomb had gone off in the next village to the east. Smith asked headquarters for permission to investigate; it was refused. Other bombs might have been laid, said his superiors. Let the SLA handle the matter first, was the order. As it transpired, the premise was correct. It was a Sunday and nobody went near the place until the following morning. When UN sappers did start scratching around, it wasn't long before a second charge was uncovered. It had apparently not been detonated because SLA units had fanned out into the surrounding hills and they'd probably disturbed those manning the OP who had been tasked to watch the place.

It was also confirmed before I left the area that a possible "armed element" observation post had been found in the hills nearby.

Many prisoners were captured while the Israelis remained on the wrong side of their frontier and there were a lot of questions raised as to who exactly could be construed the enemy since Hizbollah was operating on their own soil. To the Israelis the conflict was an "insurrection". To the Arabs it was a full-blown war, presaged by an illegal occupation. Which was why the question constantly arose: when was a man a prisoner of war or simply a plain prisoner? The issue gave rise to acrimony on both sides, as it still does today when the IDF crosses illegally into Lebanon.

During the earlier "occupation" period, suspects were customarily taken to the main South Lebanese Army prison at El Khiam, to the immediate south-east of Marj'Ayoun. It was a grim incarceration for those who experienced it and regarded as a hellhole by both local inhabitants and the UN. Also, not everybody who went in there came out alive and it was an open secret that El Khiam had been the subject of numerous human rights investigations and that it was the Israelis – and not the SLA – that actually ran the show.

The difference between prisoners taken by the SLA or the Israelis – and those grabbed by Hizbollah – was that there was an odds-on chance of being charged or released if the former got you. With the Jihadis it was enough to be *suspected* of treason (or of being fingered as a "collaborator") to die. Life, throughout the area was indeed precarious.

One of the most interesting towns in the region was Bint Jubayl, which was almost laid to waste during Israel's 2006 invasion of the region. Quite big by South Lebanese standards in the old days, I visited the place with the two New Zealand captains. It lay on a series of hills at the southern edge of the part where the Irish Battalion was then positioned. Although predominantly Muslim, there were some Christians, though I've been told that most have now fled.

Observer Group Lebanon logbooks, I found, contained dozens of entries that indicated Bint Jubayl as being linked to car bombings, roadside bombs or IEDs, unauthorised arrests of suspects, arms caches, as well as attacks on SLA or Israeli positions or patrols. One read that a car bomber had been intercepted outside the main SLA military base in the town shortly before I got there. Countering this activity, there were Israeli attacks on Hizbollah infiltrators in nocturnal ambushes on approach roads. Some left blood spoors that were followed up the next day and indicated that many of these tracks led to Bint Jubayl.

The history of Observer Group Lebanon is interesting. It dates back to 1948, when the Israeli state was founded.

As the convoluted politics of the Middle East evolved, so did the principal United Nations monitoring body which we all referred to as UNTSO. In the interim, hostilities went on almost daily, and lives were being lost.

Besides Colonel Higgins, dozens more officers with the force died on active service, the last time in the mid-1990s. Only six were OGL, including an Australian, Captain Peter McCarthy, killed on the last day of his tour of duty. He'd apparently sauntered up the hill overlooking Naqoura for a farewell look at the area and tripped an anti-personnel mine. To his colleagues, it was a sad goodbye.

The OGL came into its own in 1972, when the government in Beirut demanded that the UN should strengthen its presence along the southern border with Israel or get out. The first three international units were stationed at Naqoura (a nondescript place alongside the Shi'ite town of Marun ar Ras) and Khiam (where the prison is situated).

Three more posts were added later, although the Israelis never agreed to the presence of the OGL, which is why its activities have always remained restricted to Lebanon, even though most of its personnel spend their off-duty hours in Israel or actually live there. There were 36 observers until the spring of 1980, when increasing hostilities caused the unit's strength to be doubled.

After the abduction of Colonel Higgins, the OGL base north of the Litani River (in so-called "Free Lebanon") was closed because it was considered too dangerous to maintain effectively. More such kidnappings were feared. Its numbers were further reduced in

Arab terror groups based in Lebanon continued to try to effect a breakthrough in bids to drop their agents on the Israeli coast or possibly explode their boats in the approaches to Haifa or Eilat harbours. This boat was captured while tasked with a terror raid out of Lebanon. (Photo: Israeli Army)

1989 and although the OGL maintains a headquarters presence in Naqoura, it is rarely manned by more than an officer or two. Most of its duties appear to be carried out across the border in Israel, in a pleasant villa near the beach in Nahariya where it has a bar, entertainment areas and rooms for off-duty OGL members. Its radio room is manned round-the-clock.

The future of Observer Group Lebanon or even UNTSO, for that matter, is problematical. The UN constantly warns that it is running out of cash. Somehow, its tenuous life is extended year-by-year, vote-by-vote at UN Headquarters at Turtle Bay in New York.

OGL has also had its share of problems. There was one development that its officers were taking seriously when I joined two of its New Zealand officers for a swan around South Lebanon. Whenever we left our vehicles unattended, Captain Smith would clamp a metal locking device to the steering wheel.

"Orders," he explained. He disclosed that both the UN and the Israelis believed that the next attack would be a suicide bomber and could happen in one of the big SLA or IDF bases or in the border post at Rosh Haniqra. The only difference between those vehicles or buses that had been exploded in the past and the next one, he explained, was that this one would be white, with UN markings and a man in a United Nations uniform at the wheel.

Chapter 24
An American hostage of Hizbollah

"We know that they already have some of our uniforms in their possession. We're aware too that they have a collection of our types of vehicles, all painted and fitted with UN markings. What we don't want is for them to also steal one of our rigs and turn it into a suicide bomb," he added.

The Israelis, too, were conscious of the threat. Every vehicle that went through border control at Rosh Haniqra was searched, inside and out, all of it done some distance from the main control point. I spent an afternoon there once watching the process: some vehicles were driven onto a ramp where a soldier with a mirror at the end of a pole checked the chassis for explosives. Nobody was taking chances after a spate of Tel Aviv and Jerusalem bus bombings which have since been limited by the huge concrete wall that has been built between Israeli and Arab settlements.

For all that, there were many questions being asked about UNIFIL, not only in Israel but in some of the countries who share in "peacekeeping" operations. Most nations, Holland, Fiji, Norway, Ireland and others, ended up withdrawing their troops. Others accused UNIFIL of bias in favour of the Arab cause. There are some who still do.

Over the years I spent time in South Lebanon with many of these units. I even made a television documentary on the UNIFIL role in the mid-1980s, and while some national units performed admirably, others lacked fundamental military ability or even basic initiative. Some of the troops with whom I spoke made no secret of being terrified of even being in Lebanon, positioned as they were between two belligerent entities that regarded a day without some kind of military action as time wasted.

As I was to see often enough, some of these soldiers would look the other way whenever Hizbollah was around. The Ghanaians, for example, were constantly being accused of incompetence for letting "Armed Elements" through their lines. It happened so often that nobody took any notice of such charges anymore and anyway, as one IDF spokesman was heard to comment, "they shouldn't have been deployed in the Middle East in the first place..."

The Irish and the Finns were a little better, though there were competent, professional soldiers among them. More than once the Irish took me to task for highlighting their inadequacies, which, as the maxim goes, sometimes included their men looking a little too deep into the bottle.

An American observer made the point that while troops from those countries might perform competently in other conflicts, they were a waste of time and valuable assets in Lebanon. The majority were simply not interested in what was going on, he declared. Moreover, they reflected "neither the will nor the stomach for the job", was his view dispassionate but incontrovertible.

There were some nationals, the Fijians in particular, who were respected and trusted by all. Moreover, the Fijians were resolute and most times gave better than they got. It was a sad day when these island contingents were withdrawn from South Lebanon. Tough, aggressive and intolerant of any kind of obstruction in the performance of their duties, this was, and still is, a national army that has been blooded in numerous conflicts during the 20th Century.

As might have been expected, Fiji paid a price. There were more Fijian soldiers attached to United Nations units killed in action in Lebanon than any other country deployed there. What they did leave behind was a proud legacy of their activities in one of the most troubled regions of the globe.

Stories about FijiBatt are legion. At the height of Operation Grapes of Wrath, one of the Islamic groups set up a Katyusha rocket launcher in front of a control post on the main road south of Tyre. A Fijian soldier didn't like it. He first asked and then ordered the Hizbollah soldiers to move. Anywhere else in Lebanon, he told their senior man, they could do as they liked, but while he was on duty, it was his job to prevent that sort of thing happening. They simply couldn't shoot at Israel within sight of his post, was the thrust of it. The Arabs said nothing. Instead, they just carried on.

The man from Fiji tackled them again. One of the insurgents drew a pistol and shot the Fijian soldier in the chest. A shootout followed in which quite a few more Fijians were killed or wounded, but it tells you something that most of that Hizbollah squad was annihilated.

The Israelis likewise, have been guilty of infractions. In December 1995 an IDF artillery battery fired several 155 mm shells at four Norwegian soldiers on patrol along the east bank of the Litani River. This kind of monitoring activity was routine at the time and took place twice a day, once during daylight hours and again at night. Not everybody did it, though.

Of the half-dozen or so nations stationed in Lebanon at the time, only the Fijians and the Norwegians patrolled at night. The Irish, the Finns, the Ghanaians and the Nepalese didn't consider it necessary or, as one Israeli officer succinctly phrased it: "They'd shit themselves if they ever had to leave their camps at night-time."

All visits to UN contingents in Lebanon start and end at Naqoura, a couple of kilometres north of the Israeli border post at Rosh Haniqra.

Chapter 24
An American hostage of Hizbollah

On one of my many visits, I'd come straight in from Israel, through the "closed" border at Rosh Haniqra and Timur Goksell. The Turk responsible for media relations didn't like it.

He'd always suggest that it would suit him better if I came into the country through Beirut. But for me at the time, that would have meant an additional risk. Hizbollah knew very well who I was and what I was doing there: they had read my reports in several Jane's publications over the years. I was also aware of a UNIFIL communications infrastructure that had long ago been compromised. Some of Timur Goskell's messages were seen by Israeli intelligence officers before he'd even read them. I surmised, correctly as it later turned out, that Hizbollah was kept similarly primed of just about anything that the UN did.

Naqoura UN Headquarters is one of the largest United Nations establishments in the world. At best, it has almost 15,000 personnel, military and civilian, on its books. The base squats rather than sits alongside the Mediterranean, with the result that it has something of a holiday air about it. From the air, but for the armoured vehicles, it might be mistaken for a resort on the Côte d'Azur. Arab Naqoura, in contrast, the original old town, stands isolated on a hill that overlooks the base, the same hill on which the Australian Captain Peter McCarthy was killed.

In that little town, dozens of small stores line the road and you can buy most of what you need at a fraction of the price that it'd cost you in the Holy Land. Although things have changed, you can still get a suit made in a couple of days at Naqoura, or buy a complete range of the most up-to-date electronic goods and cameras, all duty free.

In spite of its role in a region that has been marked by hostilities for the past half-century, Naqoura strikes the visitor as being more of a civilian town than a military base in a war zone. It has more pubs than anywhere else in Lebanon outside Beirut. At the bar in the Irish Compound you sometimes buy several beers at a time to avoid standing in line. Irish officers drink in the appropriately named Irish House, a delightful little hideaway a little higher up, towards the main road. Next door the Fijian officers have their own boozer.

There is much movement between these national clubs and bars. In contrast, Italian aviators at the helicopter base tended to keep to themselves, though they were most hospitable to me, probably because I flew with them. Their evening meal was communal, invariably presided over by their commander, at the time, the genial,

An Israeli helicopter over South Lebanon. (Photo: Beata Hamizrachi)

soft-spoken Lieutenant Colonel Guaccio Aldo, a classical authority of note. When not flying helicopters in Lebanon, he liked to visit historic sites in Britain with his wife. It was he who first showed me the small Crusader fort that stands in the base grounds, close to the water and overlooked by the office of the local UN commander.

Having something pre-prandial in the Italian mess was almost like being in one of those upper-class places in Italy where form is dictated by unspoken ceremony.

In the broader context, life at Naqoura in those days was fairly easygoing. It probably still is. It was also unhurried. I, and other guests were billeted in fairly comfortable single quarters that will probably be turned into a Club Med clone after the fighting is over, if that ever happens.

Since most supplies for camps lying in the "interior" (the most distant was perhaps only 10-minutes flying time by chopper) were controlled from Naqoura, the base has always been little more than a transit camp. In a sense, it's a clearing-house for troops moving in and out. You headed for Naqoura if you had toothache, or you went on furlough, or had your weekly session with the unit shrink. It was significant that no senior UN commanders or civilian staff lived there.

Whether for convenience (which is improbable because of the hassle of crossing the heavily defended frontier twice a day) or doubts about the ability of UN soldiers to defend them, all senior UN officers based at Naqoura had set up homes for themselves and their families in Israel. The majority stayed in Nahariya, the northernmost town along the coast. The commander of UNIFIL on my last visit, Major General Stanislav Wozniak, a Pole, had a home there, as did those senior officers who came before and after him.

None of these officials sent their children to Israeli schools because, as one Italian officer suggested, such action might be interpreted as partisan by the Arabs in the region. Timur Goksell, the UN spokesman at the base, sent his two children to an International School in Tel Aviv every day and that was more than two hours by bus *each way*. To do so, Timur confided, the family had to get up at four in the morning.

Every UN battalion in South Lebanon had its own regulations about length of service, local leave, fraternisation with the inhabitants – which, as far as the Fijians were concerned, simply wasn't allowed to happen. Most of these tough, disciplined troops worked off excess steam in their unit's gym and their physiques were commensurately impressive. But then the Fijians have always been a remarkably physical nation and we've all seen what they can accomplish on the rugby field.

The Norwegians were quite different. They liked to mix with the local people. Some of their troops married Arab women.

On my first day at NorBatt we had lunch at a modest house outside Clea'a, a mainly Christian village. Outside there was nothing to show that the place was a restaurant. Inside, the lady of the house, a Maronite Christian, lit a paraffin stove. It was icy cold outside and it still took us about 20 minutes to feel its warmth, even at midday.

Our hostess was swarthy, friendly and enchanting. According to my escort, a reserve captain in the Norwegian Army, she was soon to marry one of his colleagues. At that stage already, something like 20 Norwegians had paired off with local women, some of them widows who seemed to be happy to move to the totally alien domesticity and climate of Scandinavia.

The restaurant in an Arab village that day was a charm. In a country where health-inspectors and veterinary controls barely exist, I was wary of the steak roll placed before me, until the officer with me assured me that the unit had its own vet. This was a revelation because almost throughout Lebanon in wartime there were no health controls with slaughtered animals. People often became ill because they'd eaten contaminated meat, or the animals had been diseased. Health checks consequently made a huge difference as to what we did or did not eat. While covering the civil war in the earlier period, I purposely avoided eating meat while working in the Levant.

Interestingly, that village also had the only working post office in the area and though it was Lebanese, United Nations post was dispatched as if it were in Norway, with Norwegian stamps and postmarks. Local townspeople took advantage of the service: there was no other means of getting letters out unless they went into Metullah across the border, and that was a schlep because of frontier controls that sometimes involved hour-long vehicle and body searches.

The job entrusted to the United Nations in the Levant is regarded by most of the officers involved as one of the international body's most challenging. In the decades that this multinational force has been active, it has lost about 300 of its men, plus a sprinkling of civilian aid personnel as well as locals in its pay.

There are few observers who have spent any time in South Lebanon who do not concede that any UN role in the Middle East is problematical. The Lebanese maintain that UN soldiers are biased against Arabs. Others accuse them of being partial towards the Jews.

Israeli sentiments are pretty well summed up by an Israeli officer who had close dealings with several UN units: "Ineffectual, apathetic and often in fear of getting themselves hurt," were his words. I'd heard the same kind of comment made about other UN "peacekeeping" troops in Angola where the soldiers, also Scandinavian, spent more time humping local ladies than on patrol.

UNIFIL soldiers, almost to a man, had a good deal to say about the almost total lack of civic probity among the majority of the Israelis they encountered in their routine dealings with the Jewish State. In the early days, United Nations troops on leave in Israeli cities left their uniforms back at base: stories about their troops being beaten up were regular. It still goes on, I'm told, but to a lesser degree.

What is manifest is that there are very few Israelis who respect what the United Nations is trying to achieve along its borders, whether it be in Lebanon or in Sinai. UN personnel, by and large, have even less time for the average Israeli.

To some of these United Nations soldiers, a Lebanese posting was – and still is – simply a meal ticket. Among most countries involved, it comes tax-free. In Norway, there was such a demand for six-month Middle East postings that for a long time the system was run on a quota basis. It probably still is … Yet, were the United Nations to pull out of South Lebanon tomorrow, the present low-level insurrection would probably result in a full-scale war.

As one British wag succinctly phrased it, UN troops might not be God's gift to maintaining equilibrium in one of the most volatile corners of the globe, but at least they're there …

CHAPTER TWENTY FIVE

GREG LOVETT: AN AMERICAN SOLDIER OF FORTUNE IN IRAQ

In former Police Officer Lovett, I discovered a man whose mind could best be described as a series of locked cupboards guarded by the cherubs of self-discipline. Someone in Arkansas had suggested that he was the original no-nonsense cop, in part because he'd worked undercover in the drug world for most of his life and then became a mercenary. Before Baghdad he had been in Kosovo, operating with 150 others out of Ferzi, a small town just beyond Pristina.

> At the time of writing, Gregory Lovett was in Iraq, having been there off and on since December 2003.

This American military freebooter and former undercover cop started working for a large United States conglomerate that had a multibillion-dollar security contract with bomb dogs searching for explosive devices. From there he was delegated to what the brass like to term Executive Protection. "I protected civilian contractors and now and again some foreign diplomats," he explained.

One of his everyday jobs involved taking people along Baghdad's notorious Route Irish, the road out of town, from the Green or International Zone to the international airport. It was a trip that had its moments because people died doing it.

"Most of us were ex-cops or former United States Marines. And who better to protect you running up and down the road at 100 miles-an-hour then a bunch of law enforcers?" The people he worked with knew what to look for on the roads and how to react when others drove menacingly.

"Also, we're pretty good at getting out of traffic jams: more importantly, we're taught how to make decisions on our own. The marines are a lot like cops: they're also an independent bunch and aren't afraid to make decisions when they have to. Not at all like some

Chapter 25
Greg Lovett – an American soldier of fortune in Iraq

military personnel who won't go to the bathroom without asking their officers for permission. Since there are almost no security companies who do not hire former Special Forces soldiers, they have their place in Iraq and Afghanistan, he reckons. But for the most part these otherwise crack fighters are clueless when it comes to running the roads in a wartime condition. As police, that's what we did for a living: we were trained in driving tactics and in the use of small arms.

"Most Special Forces guys, but obviously not all, have only been involved in training, some for almost their entire careers in the military. Until the Gulf War – and the conflict in 'Stan, there was little for them to do. Of them all, only an exclusive little clique had actually been onto enemy soil, or even got themselves shot at. Most had never exchanged fire with somebody who actually fired back." Those were Lovett's thoughts on the issue.

While in Special Forces units Stateside, many of the operators stayed only long enough to get the "badge", he reckoned. Then they left to do something else. "But if you ask them ... they'll tell you they're all Special Forces." Some, as a matter of course, are excellent soldiers ... they make for outstanding combat groups, for good security teams. But as with cops, there are some that really shouldn't be there. So it goes both ways and both groups usually bring an interesting mix to the table.

As for close calls while working in Iraq, reckons Lovett, there have been quite a few. He'd been in the country barely a week or so – early January 2004 – and was standing in line to make a call home.

"There were about 30 of us waiting outside the Bob Hope chow hall and that was when the bad guys started dropping mortars on us. The first bomb landed in a very large pile of dirt just across the way from where we were. Had it landed three metres in any other direction, it would almost certainly have hit the asphalt parking lot and our casualty rate wouldn't have been worth thinking about ... but it didn't. All we had to do was shake the dirt out of our hair and survive for a day or two with some ringing in our ears.

"Then, last summer, on a beautiful day in May, we were running Route Irish into the Baghdad International Airport Area – or more commonly among those who work the area, the BIAP when, about a mile ahead of us and going the same direction, was a group of guys from BlackWater, the security firm that has been much in the news, and they got themselves ambushed ... all four men on board their rig was killed. It resulted in a massive traffic jam, as it was obviously intended to do, with a lot of very well armed, very aggressive bad guys on both side of the highway. That meant we had to fight our way out of the mess, but the fact is, had we arrived a minute or so earlier, it could just as easily have been us.

"A month earlier, on April 9 – the anniversary of the fall of Baghdad in 2003 – we were in the Green Zone, again heading for the airport. We'd intended leaving from Check Point 12, but that gate was closed because the EOD guys [explosive ordnance disposal] were checking a suspicious car. So we waited, and we waited some more and finally decided to cancel the mission and return up north to Taji. When we got back to our camp we were told that there had been several convoys ambushed and hostages taken. Had we rolled out to BIAP as originally intended, we'd have been smack-bang in the middle of it."

Lovett's views about the vehicles they used in Iraq are interesting. As he says, most security companies prefer the Suburban or the Tahoe, which are six or eight-seaters, depending largely on configuration; all are quite spacious inside.

"We regularly used the Tahoe Z-71 because it got to be the toughest four-wheeler ever made for this kind of work. The way we ran the road was usually in three-vehicle convoys, where each had a driver and a first officer, together with one or two shooters in the middle seat and a tail gunner in the back. The principles – the people we were protecting – were usually in the middle vehicle and it's actually quite a sight when you run up behind one of these convoys on the highway."

Bandit Island 2004 K-9 mission. (Photo: Greg Lovett)

Chapter 25
Greg Lovett – an American soldier of fortune in Iraq

The main weapon of choice in Iraq for private military contractors has always been the AK-47, he maintains. It is both dependable and easy to acquire in-country, he stated.

"Our tail gunners, in contrast, preferred one of the belt-fed weapons, like the PKM or the RPK (which uses the same round as the AK). But we did have a lonely .30 cal Browning, which made some very reassuring noises ... kinda like the sound of freedom ..."

It is Lovett's view that what is going on today in Iraq, and to a lesser extent, in Afghanistan and other Third World deployments is of immediate consequence to the majority of private military companies and contractors, whether they be American, British or South African. Sources in Baghdad at one stage talked about something like 50,000 of these people active throughout the country, but, he reckoned, a more realistic estimate might be around 30,000, which was still a remarkable number of security personnel, all of them working for private companies, he conceded.

"Every one of these individuals costs money, some of them a lot, and the United States taxpayer is footing the bill for much of it," were his words.

I first made contact with Greg Lovett when he'd returned from Baghdad in the summer of 2004 and we've kept in touch. At that stage, with my son Luke in tow in the Hurricane luxury RV motor home which I'd used to traipse around North America for two years, we'd gone looking for him in a small town in north-west Arkansas. We soon discovered that while he was in the vicinity, he wouldn't bite.

There was apparently good reason for this. Greg Lovett had worked undercover for so long that he was as wary of strangers then as he is today, because, as he will tell you, strangers like to ask questions. Eventually I got to speak to him on the phone and we agreed to meet in New Orleans a week later. Because of that contact, Lovett features prominently in *Cops: Cheating Death*, a book I was working on at the time and which deals with men and women in law enforcement or in corrections who had been shot and survived[1].

He'd been doing school patrol work at the time and ended up intercepting a 12-year-old who was of the mind to kill his teacher. Instead the kid opened up on Lovett who took five hits from a 20-gauge shotgun. As this former cop admits, it shouldn't have happened, but, as with most shootings, it just did. The youngster had hunted a lot with his dad, so he could handle the weapon pretty well, he explained.

Lovett's views about hostilities in the Arab World are introspective, in part because his experience with the police allows him to see things more or less the way they are and not as somebody who *thinks* they might be. In a sense, he is the ultimate pragmatist. Moreover, he likes the job and, as the saying goes, he has no axe to grind. But he tends to be frank about the industry's shortcomings and I quote:

"Overall, private security companies seem to fall into two categories now that things are starting to get 'civilised' here in Iraq. We have certain rules that we're obliged to follow and our activities are carefully monitored by a myriad of organisations, quite a few of them eager to bring us freelancers into disrepute. As a result, our hardest task masters are our own bosses. Step out of line and you're on the first plane home.

"In both Iraq and Afghanistan you have your 'high-speed' companies such as Triple Canopy, MPRI, Armor Holdings and the rest. They are all reputable groupings or most of them, anyway. They do everything from executive protection to guarding ambassadors. Quite a few have their own dog units, which are called K-9 units. Others handle static guard duties at embassies and palaces. It can obviously be expensive, but these people are good at what they do because they've been trained for it.

"The companies involved in security work are usually hired by what is termed 'other government agencies', as well as larger entities that are not necessarily hampered by budget restraints, like the American State Department, or the Department of Defense, where they might do more 'unsavoury' jobs like supply runs, protect building site or handle civilian escort duties. Obviously, quite a few have the political pull to get the big-money contracts that matter, firms like Halliburton, and, in the past, BlackWater, now called something else. They're all here for the long haul and in this kind of unstable political and military environment; you kind of get what you pay for."

As Lovett explains, the vast majority of companies in Iraq are connected in some way or another with an American-backed programme termed "Reconstruction of Iraq". They provide protection for construction personnel: they guard their engineers or might handle road convoys that get these folk to work and back again, as well as a variety of ancillary activities.

For instance, construction companies with contracts to rebuild or refurbish facilities or installations have to provide protection for their workers. One example of money spent, as elucidated by Gregg Nivala, a spokesperson working out of the American Embassy in

Baghdad, was that $2 million of a $9 million dollar contract budgeted to exhume mass graves in the southern Muthanna Province of Iraq was paid to a security firm to guard the diggers who were pulling the bodies out of the ground. That, it was explained, was almost a quarter of the total amount. Without protection, he suggested, it could never have happened.

But, as Lovett points out, as with all private companies, the bottom line is profit and that, in turn, leads to something else in the jargon of multi-faceted security work called "acceptable losses". This refers specifically to equipment and personnel which can be written off, all of which needs to be factored in against what a company can make out of the deal.

On the negative side, he points to some construction and security companies that are of the "fly-by-night" variety.

As he explains, some of these organisations come into Iraq and get a contract with the Department of Defense. Or perhaps they'll acquire a security job with the State Department and to get this right, they need to underbid just about everyone, often by millions of dollars. Meantime, they know very well that they will only operate in the country for a year, or possibly two, at most. Then they'll take the money and run, especially since in this business, companies get a large proportion of the contract cash up-front. Also, they're usually allowed a generous period of grace to get things moving. In the real world, some of these groups never even get off the ground, while there are others that eventually get going – after a fashion – but are unable to provide the services for which they were contracted. It is these entities, he says, that end up giving those who are actually doing the work a bad name.

"What I have personally observed, is that these flighty companies will hire as the front man a security manager, usually a solid and experienced individual with good Special Forces credentials, coupled to a string of military qualifications. He is not aware at first that he is being manipulated, but his bosses end up relying on him not only to hire security officers but also to train them. This can be difficult when you're dealing with individuals who have little or no prior military experience, and more often than not come from Third World countries.

"And when you accept that the going rate for a 'qualified shooter' is earning anything from $500 to a $1,000 American dollars a day – which is average – you're talking about some pretty big money. But then I am also aware of companies that hire what is known as 'Third Country Nationals' – or TCNs – as shooters for as little as $50 a day: they pay even less for static guard work at checkpoints. Then they wonder why the so-called 'bad guys' – the al-Qaeda or Sunni insurrectionists are able to get into usually well-secured areas and create havoc. When they achieve that much, they end up taking lives in the process."

According to Lovett, the majority of TCNs are from India, the Philippines, Nepal and elsewhere, though there are increasing numbers of potential recruits from South and Central America and also some from Africa north of the Limpopo. Most of these people, he conceded, were hard-working people. They were doing a job to provide for their families. But at the end of it, the majority shouldn't have been at the business end of an automatic weapon because they had almost no combat experience and quite often wouldn't have recognised an ambush if they landed in the middle of one.

Brad Monore Taji Iraq 2004: Typical American PMC. (Photo: Greg Lovett)

Lovett: "As with one of the K-9 companies I was familiar with, they were charging their clients $2,000 a day *per dog*. Multiply that by 30 dogs and it comes to something like $60 000 a month, per animal. And since they paid their handlers a paltry $5,000 a month and provided only the most basic facilities and equipment, the profit margin was immense. That particular company had anything between 30 and 40 dog handlers on their books and was making a killing." Again, he stressed, it was all being done quite openly and once more, with American taxpayers' money.

What was happening, remonstrated Lovett, was that many of the qualified and reputable security companies that arrived at the beginning of the Iraqi debacle, established for themselves some very good and reliable bases of operations. These were the ones that were instrumental in getting construction and trucking companies up and running and, in turn, got the funding for these projects.

"But as everybody knows, in most cases, government contracts last perhaps a year, and as with every business involved in this scenario, they have to resubmit their bids annually. So now that these security companies are on relatively firm ground and operating smoothly, so it is perhaps only natural that they should look at ways of expanding their profits … it is all part of the Western economic system.

"At the same time, these firms have been good at what they do. Some were outstanding. With time, everybody makes a mistake or two, but generally things went pretty well. Moreover, it was axiomatic that since qualified security companies provided good protection, hostile actions and losses were kept at a minimum and it wasn't long – in spite of a lot of things that went wrong on the periphery of the civil war – that things appeared to be reasonably secure."

Indirectly, he added, you now had clients beginning to think they no longer needed the same level of protection as before. So they would toy with the idea of saving money by cutting back on operational or protection costs, which, of course, was absurd. It was kind of like cancelling your car insurance because you hadn't had an accident. Then things begin to snowball, he said.

Enter into the equation a host of security companies that start by underbidding their competitors, the very same security companies that originally paved the way under the most dangerous conditions. The newcomers are security firms that pay their shooters and static guards $50 dollars a day (and sometimes less) coupled to what can generously be termed "less than stellar" living quarters. It doesn't need a rocket scientist to see where all this is headed.

It is Lovett's view that concurrently, with most people in the United States wanting to pull their boys out and questioning the billions of dollars spent on these ancillary but vital security services, Washington simply has to find a way to cut down on spending and lower troop numbers. One of the immediate consequences is that bids don't go to the most qualified companies or individuals, but rather, to the cheapest, or what the politicians like to call most "cost efficient", which is ridiculous.

Greg Lovett's observations, made in an e-mail from Baghdad before his return to the United States, were instructive. The bottom line, he told me, was that the overall security situation was far worse than when he got there in 2003. "And it's not going to get any better soon," he reckoned.

He went on: "We have to face the fact that for a long time the civil war dominated just about everything and let's not kid ourselves, *it was a civil war*, not an insurgency. It is just that nobody wants to put that kind of spin on it with the media grabbing at anything that can make America look bad. Not yet, anyway.

"I used to drive from here at the airport area in Baghdad to the Green Zone on Route Irish by myself. I did so many times in the past. Naturally, it was risky, but that was the job … it came with the package. It wasn't long before that very same Route Irish was proclaimed the most dangerous stretch of road in the world.

"Curiously, we had a bit of the old déjà vu here: the same kind of problem that our people experienced in Vietnam. The enemy was extremely active. It changed its methodology and it's tactics, as well as its deployments almost daily. Being fanatical, it had a regular supply of human resources from which to draw, which was why we had so many suicide bombings. Those people take enormous risks and they are able to cause huge damage.

"On our side, some very experienced, extremely well-qualified people were brought in to cope with these troubles. They were the ones who were expected to turn things around. Then you heard them whisper about not being allowed to do their job. Others complained about the inability to complete their missions. But they weren't too vocal about it, because such things simply aren't good either for business or for career advancement.

"There are others, I fear, who would rather *look* good, which they feel is an alternative to *being* good. And heaven knows 'we' don't want to offend anyone while the nation is fighting a war. At that stage I was involved with the mail convoy security … although I had been moved up the 'food chain' and had been riding a deck for some time. I still managed to sneak outside the wire from time to time for some fresh air.

"In the past seven or eight years our operation lost nine personnel, all of them killed in enemy action. And that doesn't include the wounded."

Going back a bit, Gregory Lovett was in Kosovo for almost five months, from August to December 2003. Opportunities opened up to transfer to Iraq late in 2003 and though he took a few breaks home, he stayed there until April 2007, which was when he returned semi-permanently to the United States and went back to his old police unit.

"At first I wasn't really sure how I went from the north-western part of Arkansas to beautiful downtown Baghdad. Looking back, I'm also not sure that I had any choice in the matter. If the gods of war decide that you're going to be there, I doubt that you can change that.

"While in Kosovo I was assigned to base security at Camp

Bondsteele. It was all a bit of an eye-opener: a taste of what lay ahead. In Kosovo there were two types of people assigned to security, largely restricted to former military personnel and people who had worked in law enforcement. As soon as we hit the ground, we were given our uniforms, a room and a bunk assignment as well as a bunch of training schedules. I ended up going through two weeks of training before doing any proper duty like standing guard. However, for me, it almost ended before I started. On the second day we were being trained on base security rules and regulations when the instructor gave us a break. I walked outside with the rest of the class and was standing there talking to some of the other guys. The next thing I know one of the instructors or 'Black Hats' – a man called Ishun Richards – took up a position right in my face: his nose couldn't have been more than an inch from mine. Ishun was a former Marine DI or drill instructor and as they say 'Once a Marine, always a Marine'.

"Ishun demanded to know, but not in the nicest possible way, where my cover was? It's what they call body armour in this industry. Without thinking I replied 'It's inside'. You'd have thought I'd just insulted his wife.

"Long story made short, I never again went outside without my cover. On the flip side, Ishun and I went on to become good pals and when I moved onto Iraq, I was able to get him hooked up in the security business and we were soon working together again."

Lovett never regarded the security situation in Kosovo as too taxing. But it didn't take him long to appreciate that the Balkans wasn't exactly what he was searching for. The crunch came after a couple of months.

"Security is security, or so I thought. Our project manager was a former Delta Operator (or that was what he liked to put out). And though security affecting all those coming into the base was excellent and the only people who didn't get searched were the commanding general and his staff, everybody else was stopped at the gate.

"Now, like I said, being a cop and having dealt with criminals for years, you soon enough learn the way they do things, how they operate and their manner of thinking. All the civilian workers on the site were either Albanian or Serb and their vehicles were searched on arrival. The same with those arriving on foot: all were patted down on the way in. Notice that I said… *on the way in*.

"At the time I was working at the Base Defence Operations Centre, or as we called it, BDOC. One time, talking with the project manager, I asked him why nothing going out of the base was checked. That was when a look came over his face, like he had just been asked something incredibly stupid. "Now why would we want to do that? It would be a total waste of resources and man power," was his retort. My reaction almost got me sent home again and going by past experience, I suppose I should have learned by then to keep my head down and my mouth shut.

"Anyway, I explained to the man that the Kosovo Police as well as the UNMIK Police (US police assigned to train the Kosovo Police) had been doing raids and, in the process, had recovered significant amounts of American military-issued clothing and equipment, together with an assortment of other items which were government-issue. I explained there were only two US bases in Kosovo and it had to come either from us or the other one. Next thing I'm in his office and being told that everything I'd said was classified. He then asked me where the hell I'd heard all this 'rubbish'.

"It was common knowledge among the police, I replied. In fact, I went on, it had even become a topic of conversation in the chow hall. The man was adamant: he said I had to keep my mouth shut, not spread 'rumours' and get back to work. It was about then that I decided that the project manager was an idiot who would rather that we *looked* good than *be* good. So I started to search for other options

"Soon afterwards I was able to get hired by a K-9 company looking for dog handlers for explosive detection and it sounded like fun. So I asked to be signed up. I was sent a first-class ticket to fly from Kosovo to Amman, the Jordanian capital city and my instructions were clear: get yourself there by air, take a cab from the airport to a motel and check in. It all seemed pretty straightforward. I should have asked how I was going to get from Jordan to Baghdad and I'm glad I didn't: the answer would have scared the shit out of me.

"Everything went smoothly until my plane tried to land in Jordan. Heavy fog had closed the airport, so we were diverted to another airport where some heavily armed troops were waiting for us on the ground. I must have had this worried look on my face because the Arab sitting next to me spoke good English and gave me a two-minute crash course on Middle Eastern culture and customs. He told me to put my money in one of my shoes and leave about $50 in my wallet. This was for what he termed 'customs tax', which those functionaries on the ground waiting for us would demand once we got inside the terminal building. Of course, there was no argument about the money having to be paid, if only to get my passport stamped. Welcome to the Middle East!

"I then asked him to direct me to where I was supposed to be staying. He told me he'd get me a taxi and pointed the driver in the right direction, which was how I eventually arrived at my hotel several hours later. I left the driver arguing with hotel staff about who was going to pay for the ride, which the security company was supposed to cover.

"After checking in, I was told to eat, sleep and be ready to roll the following night. They'd be leaving the city sometime around two in the morning, the idea being to reach the Iraqi border at dawn. No problem, I thought: we were going to drive from Amman to the border with the military, or so I assumed.

"At the time set the following night, I walked out with my bags and saw three Jordanian taxis waiting, with spare tyres strapped onto their roofs along with six or eight fuel cans. That alone should have sounded an alarm, but the next thing I was in the back seat with two other Americans and this little convoy of cars was headed out into the desert for Iraq. Hopefully, I thought, we would meet up with the military at the frontier post and get escorted the rest of the way. The three taxis arrived at the border just as it was getting light and on walking into the checkpoint, all of us Americans were told to grab our weapons and all the ammo we could haul or drag. We were about to experience what one of them described the 'Desert Dash'."

As Lovett recalled, the vehicles involved drove as fast as possible and stopped for nothing and, in a sense it really was a miniature "Hell Run". What he didn't yet know was that ambushes were commonplace.

Bill Bell, another American contractor in Iraq on K-9 mission. (Photo: Greg Lovett)

"It was about then that I seriously started missing my old DI pal Ishun yelling at me and my warm bunk bed back in Kosovo. As it happened, our drive to Baghdad was without incident and we soon arrived at our new home."

For the most part, as he tells it, the K-9 operation involved some solid work, but it was also fun. His assignment was to monitor the Baghdad Airport and adjacent checkpoints. "But we were also assigned to military units running missions outside the wire, as well as to other bases. More often than not, we did patrols with them, which was actually beyond the scope of the original agreement."

Bill Bell, a former Vietnam veteran was another of the colleagues with whom he worked while on the K-9 dog handling unit and as he remembers, he was about as crusty and knowledgeable as they come.

"Bill was my mentor and he taught me some valuable lessons about how to survive. He also showed me a few tricks, like gathering the weapons we'd seized on our raids.

"The military at Baghdad Airport would confiscate firearms hand-over-fist, and for the most part, nobody wanted to mess with them. So Bill and I soon used our own connections with the 'system' and we soon had a nice stash of automatic weapons which we cleaned and resold to other American contractors. It was a good bit of extra cash and served a purpose as well: nothing like having shooters out there who have access to all the good stuff they need when they hit a problem.

"But then that private military company also started with its bullshit. Each month their directors would consider ways to 'deduct' more money from our pay. So once I began to have financial issues with them, I starting looking elsewhere for PMC work. During one of my missions up north to the city of Taji, I had dealings with a security company that had a good reputation for handling executive protection. They were looking for additional shooters and drivers to protect civilian contractors, as well as some foreign diplomats. This was a motley crew, but at a glance you could tell these guys were tight and knew their business. I was more worried about being able to keep up with their really professional operators.

"So I moved across to Taji and it was great. Our project manager who answered only to the name of 'Pat' greeted me when I got there, handed me four crisp $100 bills as a cash advance on my next pay and told me to get some chow and clean my weapon. Our little group was divided into four teams: Alpha, Beta, Charlie and Delta. The Delta team was regarded as the elite, and I was assigned to Charlie as a shooter and a driver and our team leader was a former marine by the name of Heath. Once again the majority of the guys were either cops or marines.

"One afternoon we were doing a run to Baghdad Airport and I was driving the lead vehicle. We were going merrily along when Heath suddenly turned to me and said 'Lovett, look around you'.

"As the driver, I replied firmly, you don't look round. Instead, I told him, I liked to focus my attention on the road and added: 'Your shooters do the looking and the guy behind the wheel keeps his eyes firmly on the road ahead. Period!'

"Still, it was odd for Heath to make that comment and I told him that I didn't see anything, which was when he said out loud: 'That's what I mean! There is absolutely nobody around … the streets are deserted.'

"And so they were, I suddenly realised. There wasn't a single vehicle on the road, nor were there any civilians within our view. And for those who have been there, done that, you simply have to accept that when civilians are smart enough to duck out of the way, it almost always meant that some big shit was about to happen. In the end, nothing happened and soon the traffic started to reappear and things went back to normal … makes a person wonder about what the other side was planning and why they didn't put it into effect: we could have been hit big time.

"As members of executive protection teams we often sent out our 'scouts' ahead to check sites on which the engineers would be working. We had several local vehicles that we used so that we could blend in with the domestic scene in the city and even had a small pickup with a stock rack on the back for sheep or goats. We'd joke about getting ourselves a goat or two to ride around Baghdad for recon.

"Then, one afternoon, with Billy, Chuck and David on a reconnaissance mission, I was driving one of our 'Hoop Dees' as we called it and which looked like a local vehicle. We'd all be dressed like Arabs, but only from the waist up, and obviously, we'd have a bunch of firearms on the seats alongside us. Anybody who has been to Baghdad knows that its traffic can be deceptive: in places it's a bit like downtown Dallas during rush hour, but with no traffic signals or any kind of control. That day though, while driving along, we noticed a car alongside us with two of the locals inside. There was nothing suspicious, until we looked at the load they had on their roof: strapped innocuously to the top, with rope, were several mortar tubes.

"Somewhere in the conversation that followed, my pals and I decided these were the same people that had been using mortars to blow up power stations: those power stations that our engineers had been working on and that we had been been protecting.

"What to do? We couldn't just shoot them ... that would attract too much attention. Which was when Billy suggested they toss a grenade in the car; when it exploded it would look like a car bomb. Great idea! So we tried to parallel the vehicle in heavy traffic, not an easy job even in good conditions."

Lovett: "We had just made a turn when we suddenly became gridlocked in traffic with nowhere to go but forward. At the next intersection ahead there were two more of the "bad guys", also armed to the teeth and going through the motions of checking cars. As with every good civil war, you can never really tell the goodies from the baddies and obviously we were in a fix: the roadblock could just as easily have been manned by Iraqi Police with no uniforms, or they might actually have been terrorists. But we'd already decided between us that we weren't going to give them the opportunity to explain. As we inched forward we made a plan, quite a simple one actually: it is known in the terminology as 'pray and spray'.

"We were aware too that if we couldn't get our vehicle out of the traffic, we could 'borrow' one from the locals. We were still about three or four cars from the checkpoint when an Iraqi Police vehicle pulled up and two more of their people got out. Suddenly we had four armed men with whom to deal, but it seems the gods were with us again: a brief conversation followed, after which they all loaded up in their cars, opened the intersection, the traffic moved freely and we were able to return to camp.

"It was a good story until Harris asked a simple question. 'What would have happened if that car had been actually loaded with mortars and rockets and the rest and you guys didn't put enough distance between them and you before it all went off?'"

In the end, all good times come to an end. A few months later Greg and his colleagues were told that the security company for which they were working wouldn't be renewing their contract with the State Department and once again he was looking for work. That was when he hooked up with Halliburton, the largest security company in Iraq and, he reckons today, it remained a learning experience.

"On arriving back at Camp Victory I was met by some former co-workers. Picked up at the airport by two associates, Ken and Robin, and taken to the camp, I was brought before Ray, the site manager, another Special Forces major in his day. His boss, in turn, was Dan, a one-time Navy SEAL. It took a bit of time for all of us to adjust to one another – them being military and me being a former cop – but once we got going and we learnt to accept our individual strengths, coupled to the basic resources available, it soon turned into an extremely effective operation. Issues and personality conflicts aside, the new posting became the best of both worlds."

Greg Lovett soon found himself assigned to mail convoy security, which coincided with other operations that included dedicated military escorts, most of which were US Army National Guard or reserve units. Until then, he had had almost no dealings with either and his overview of the average 'weekend warrior' had became badly flawed with time, even though these people were serving on active duty in Iraq. Like the rest, they, like us, were also taking the occasional casualty.

"I actually could not have been more wrong about them. One of the escort units had a female officer in charge, or as Lieutenant Fowler preferred to call it: OIC. Unusually attractive and under normal circumstances, amenable to deal with, she would smoke your ass in a heartbeat if she thought you might be hurting one of her guys, or even *wanting* to bother them.

"It took a while, but eventually I was to discover that guard and reserve units with whom I came into contact were some of the finest troops around. They handled themselves well whenever push became shove, and throughout, were never afraid to mix it. In short, these were enthusiastic troops and pretty well trained as well: I take pride in having known and worked with them. During the time I was with the mail operations we lost nine personnel altogether, some military and some civilian drivers. Not long afterwards, Ken, Ray and Robin were all transferred to other camps. That was when I met my next boss who was Mike, a former Special Forces medic."

At first he wasn't sure how to take the man since his handle was supposed to be medical. But as Lovett admits, first impressions are often deceptive.

"Mike pretty well knew the rules and expected everyone to follow them, but he had never spent much time around us law enforcement guys, so he wasn't sure how to take me either. After some give and take, Mike and I ended up great friends and we quickly learnt to trust each other. From him I learned more about the inner-workings of corporate security and its role with the military than from all the other operators together." As Greg Lovett commented in one of his many e-mails, "war sometimes makes for strange bedfellows."

He went on: "One night Mike and I were at the OSI camp for a cookout and there were all sorts of brass and others there, everybody dressed as civilians. We were talking to one of the translators, an Arab by the name of 'Tony' when I noticed three guys, also Arabic and standing over by the grill. They looked normal, but I could tell they were not from the camp. Also, they weren't mingling with the others. I asked Tony who they were. He looked furtively around, put a finger to his lips and whispered: 'Shhhh ... those guys are three of the best Iranian cooks in Baghdad.'

Lovett didn't enquire further as to what they were supposed to have "cooked".

After his three-years-plus of fun in the sun, this Arkansas native decided that perhaps the time had come to head home, although he wasn't sure for how long. He was aware he would have a hard time adjusting to civilian life, and as he commented at the time, "now that I am familiar with the process, I can only imagine what regular combat troops go through when they return from Iraq or Afghanistan.

"But I can confirm one important aspect. I'd always heard from the guys in combat that we were not fighting for our country, nor for any kind of cause. Instead, those people that find themselves in combat situations in strange corners of the globe today are fighting for the person right alongside them ... it's actually as simple as that ... "

1 Al J. Venter: *Cops: Cheating Death*, Lyons Press, New Haven Conn, 2007.

CHAPTER TWENTY SIX

FREETOWN: DIAMONDS, A CIVIL WAR AND AMPUTEES

> Sierra Leone's cornucopia of horrors, like most recent developments in Africa, has a track record that goes way back. It dates from long before its present travails. One needs to remember that, until fairly recently, this was still a rather primitive land.

Move about the streets of Freetown, the capital of Sierra Leone these days, and there is a constant array of images that are likely to assault your sensibilities. It has as much to do with the demands of daily living as the unbounded misery that smacks you in the face wherever you turn. The very existence of the majority of the sad souls who live there has long been pared to the bone.

Shortly after I arrived on a visit during the civil war, I was taken to see a little girl. She was tiny, nestling in the arms of her sister. Though clearly out of harms way, it was obvious that all was not well. Not yet a year old when she was brought out to meet me, this soon became a very unhappy child. I was a stranger, I was white and in her mind – right or wrong – these two issues promised the unexpected. The last time something like that had happened, she could not have been remotely conscious of any threat; she was two months old when the rebels chopped off her arm above the elbow.

Her sister explained: "We were in the town and this group of rebels came along, some of them barely ten or twelve years old. There were about a dozen of them, all doped on something, either gin or *ganga* (a potent local marijuana popular in Amsterdam coffee shops), or possibly both. We had heard about this sort of thing before, but I couldn't believe it was to be us this time," she said.

Working to a single-minded purpose, one of the youngsters shot

South African mercenaries played a very active anti-piracy and anti-fish poaching role after Executive Outcomes had pulled out. More than once they used machine guns mounted on the prow of their semi-rigid hulled rubber ducks to stop Chinese trawlers trying to make a run for it. (Photo: Author)

dead an old man. They then separated males from females and earmarked those they would take with them. Finally, they chose a few more victims. One of them lost a leg, another both his nose and an ear. They got to the infant last and did their worst. Before pulling out, their pubescent leader told the villagers that they were to tell others what they'd done. A lot of such acts perpetrated by the Revolutionary United Front defied any kind of rationality. Few of the photos taken by people who chanced upon this savagery can be displayed because they're just too grotesque.

While some of the barbarism dispensed by these rampaging "children" – in theory, according to some Western analysts, still not fully in control of their senses – might possibly be found in primitive or backward societies, the slicing off of children's hands and feet with machetes is certainly not. Yet, it is peculiar that many of those who were originally responsible and subsequently "came in from the cold" have not been able to answer for their actions.

Some said they were forced into these acts. Others claimed that they were under the influence of drugs, or possibly "controlled by the devil". Certainly ju ju or voodoo had something to do with it. So, too, did cocaine, though people, no matter what their age, will look at any excuse to avoid taking responsibility. This is a trend we increasingly observe elsewhere. That said, the plight of some of the pathetic little souls they left behind, some with injuries that simply defy description, will tear out your heart.

Chapter 26
Freetown: Diamonds, a civil war and amputees

The sick, the maimed, the halt and the war-wounded are today as much a part of everyday life on Freetown's streets as its legions of beggars. Each one of these individuals is a desperate soul. Many were abandoned and few have families of their own. Consequently, you cannot stop a car in the streets of Freetown without a dozen wheelchairs zooming in on you.

If their occupants believe there's a chance of you sticking your hand into your pocket – and they quickly discover who's good for a touch and who is not – they'll even lie down in front of your car until either you fork up or the police arrive. The first option is usually the easiest, though most would accost you for money in your bed in the middle of the night were they able to do so.

While many local or transient residents give something, there are others in this community that simply don't have enough for their own needs. Also, it's impossible to keep pace with demand. Quite a few of these people regard it as their inalienable right to be helped. After all, they like to say, *you* are not helpless. "*So give!*"

The first time the rebels were driven out of Freetown, everybody thought the war was over and that ordinary folk would be able to get on with their lives. It was not to be.

Knowing the country and its people since the old days, I never believed it could devolve into the kind of semi-organised chaos the way it did, and on such a horrific scale.

The New York Times at one stage labelled the Sierra Leone capital "The Most Dangerous Place on Earth". The outcome, paradoxically, was that after hostilities ended, there were many people in Sierra Leone who were quite outspoken about preferring British-style colonial order and tradition to the kind of mayhem that had overtaken them all.

Nostalgic links to the "old country" were everywhere in a country where traditions had not changed much since Queen Victoria buried her beloved Prince Albert. Royal Navy warships centuries ago landed freed slaves taken off the high seas in Freetown, as the French did in Libreville and the Americans in Liberia, a country whose name is evocative of loftier aspirations. Freetown reciprocated by giving its suburbs appellations associated with the old country: Waterloo, Wilberforce, Hastings, Kent, Regent, Wellington, Cape Shilling, Gloucester and others.

Augustine, my host's driver, told me on the day of my arrival that he would be happy to see the British return to rule in Sierra Leone tomorrow and he was dead serious. "At least it would bring an end to all this corruption," he ventured. Then, after a moment's prevarication he added gravely, "and, of course, we'd also be rid of all those corrupt politicians."

Yet, with it all, Freetown offers some curious anomalies. One is that, on my last visit, I started drinking water from the tap. Neall Ellis told me that it was just fine, and that he had been using nothing else for years. What he didn't disclose was that he was on a bi-monthly deworming regimen. I followed suit and, in retrospect, it was a bad mistake: I needed a month of clinical tests in London on my return.

Another is that there is still a surprising lot of life in the old girl. There were a lot of British servicemen who were able to testify to that after they arrived. Even with a war on the go in the back and beyond, Freetown still boasts some of the best watering holes on Africa's West Coast.

Chris's Bar on Aberdeen's Man of War Bay offered seafood dishes that would easily have rated a handful of stars in some of the better – known gourmet guides in New York. Paddy's, down the road – hardly as Irish as Paddy's Pig because the place has no walls and is open to the elements – swings every night: its fast and not-so-fast tarts are legion up and down the coast, and if that's your proclivity, you can have three whores hanging from each elbow every time you show your face at the bar. It's probably the only city in the world where, as long as you're buying, you can entice half-a-dozen women into bed with you – simultaneously – for less than $100, and as one of my colleagues commented, not altogether tongue-in-cheek; that's especially true if you're a hack and your newspaper is picking up the tab.

The downside is that Freetown has a few exotic attributes of its own, including being labelled the sexually transmitted disease capital of West Africa.

In Freetown it is invariably the ladies who make things tick. The friendliest greeting you're likely to get from the women is usually *"Awe di bohdi?"* (How's the body?)

I asked that of one of them and she replied *"di bohdi small-small"*, because, as she explained later, she thought that she might be coming down with malaria. I'd have preferred to hear *"di bohdi fine"*.

Pidgin (or Krio as it's called in these parts) can be expressive. *Piskoh* sounds obscene, but it is – or rather was – the local version of the American Peace Corps. And since "chop" is food in Krio, a chop shop is a restaurant, as it was in 19th Century London.

So it went, and an evening at Paddy's could pass quickly. Then,

Chapter 26
Freetown: Diamonds, a civil war and amputees

American freelance heavies were also active during the Sierra Leone civil war. An Oregon company ICI deployed Russian Mi-17s (with the stars and stripes distinctively featured on the fuselage) to ferry men and equipment in and out of Freetown. (Photo: Author)

just before curfew (while hostilities went on in the interior), both places fizzled an hour short of midnight. You rarely underestimated the consequences if you overstayed your welcome, if only because you did not want to argue with a Ghurkha patrol in the middle of the night. And if you got cocky with Nigerian soldiers manning a checkpoint, you were likely to get a rifle butt in your face.

"Stay low key," warned Ellis. "Say nothing and do little to attract attention … just try to became part of it all and we'll survive." Point taken.

With the war on, someone described Freetown as a city of soldiers, military checkpoints and a place where you were nothing if you weren't carrying a mobile radio. In contrast – possibly because of that same military presence – the place was a lot safer than Dakar or Abidjan, at least during daylight hours. It bore no comparison to what was then going on in Johannesburg and Durban, though nights were another matter. At the same time, any form of civilised life in Freetown hung by a thread, with intermittent power cuts around the clock. Last heard, the city had four generators, of which only one worked. The word was out that it was 1,000 or more hours overdue for a service.

For the duration of the war, Freetown was an unusually dangerous place and generally, the city wore its despair like a mask. You saw it splashed across the faces of the folks along Kissy Street, or those walking past Foulah Town. Or among the touts trying their luck with diamonds by the old pepper tree in the centre of town. The gemstones were there, all right. They're still there, all over the place, but only a fool would be tempted.

You've got to understand the business to even begin to make money and it doesn't rest solely on the four principles of colour, shape, purity and size. Instead, what most often passes for precious stones on Freetown's streets is ground glass, with perhaps a few carats of flawed specimens thrown in for effect. Fact is, just about everybody is selling something: often enough, their bodies and for those interested, they come in both sexes.

But even the bad stuff sometimes finds a taker. A case came to trial in the Freetown courts recently where a Saudi Arabian national, Mr Gazi ben Taleb, was gullible enough to return to Sierra Leone after being bilked of $1,5 million for a parcel of precious stones that contained mainly glass. Since it was classed as an illegal transaction, he was arrested after he'd gone to police headquarters to complain. They caught the rogues in the end, but of the money, nothing. Since the cons weren't throwing cash about, they obviously didn't have it either. That's about the way things happen along this coast.

Considering that until fairly recently, the city was caught in a vortex of conflict, the crowds are always awesome.

It's rare that any sort of stillness looms in Freetown's morning air. From first light, everything emits a hand-to-mouth squalor that

One of the rebel villages targeted by Neall Ellis's Mi-24 helicopter gunship in the interior. The author sat under the front "bubble" of the Hind to get his photos. (Photo: Author)

makes it such a desperate place. If you are to survive, there is simply no respite and it was much worse with the war: resources were few, which made Sierra Leone one of the most impoverished places anywhere.

Then and now, drive from Aberdeen towards Hastings during the day, and the masses on both sides of the road are sometimes five or six deep. There are groups of children heading home from school at all hours, underscoring a pathetically inadequate educational system where classes are staggered to cope with the flow. It's commendable that the authorities are able to keep the school doors open.

Some classes start early, others begin after lunch and it's that much more astonishing that the majority of kids are neatly turned out in their often-colourful school uniforms. Considering that there are many parents that can barely feed themselves, the lengths to which some of them go to conform to custom is salutary. There must be many instances where dress has become a priority ahead of food, but then keeping up with the Krio family next door was always a staple of the city's social scene.

While there are schools aplenty and some old establishments like the Annie Walsh Girls School muddle on, the majority are tumble-down, overcrowded affairs where the students lack such basics as desks and pencils, never mind textbooks. All are in desperate need. Several country schools have themselves taken refuge in Freetown. The Harford School for Girls was a graceful old institution in rural Moyamba, at least until the rebels overran it in 1995. After it relocated to the capital, it called itself the Nucleus Harford School, at least until everybody could return to the original campus, but then again, nobody is certain if that will ever happen.

Even the old Fourah Bay College, one of the most famous tertiary institutions in West Africa, is a shadow of its old self. In its day it was a place where candidates for the ministry would learn Latin, Greek, Hebrew and even Arabic. A degree from Fourah meant status and recognition, even abroad.

The country's early history reflects a lot on what is going on in Freetown today. The city is the site of some of the first efforts by the West to redeem 300 years of plunder, slavery and piracy. As always, the intent was honourable, but then we all know about the Road to Hell.

Many of the actions that followed abolition quickly became mendacious. What's more, it was something that took place on both sides of the Atlantic.

Take one example: The first strip of real estate used to set down slaves freed at sea was granted to the British Government by King Tombo, the Temne chief of the Sierra Leone mountain peninsula. He gave the British an excellent site in exchange for a load of trumpery that included some rum, muskets and an embroidered waistcoat. If it sounds like it has happened before, you've got it!

And so it went, with everybody making money except those to whom the country belonged. Nor was West Africa alone in this duplicity.

The city spread during the course of the next two centuries. From the first concessions to mainly European newcomers, it grew up and over the hills overlooking the giant harbour and around the bays where the pirates used to bring their boats ashore for water. When I spent time there in the 1980s, there were still no-go areas around Cline Town that were regarded as off-limits to the police. By then small-boat piracy along this stretch of coast had become a problem, though these days the army shoots such transgressors, and truth be told, they don't ask permission to do so either.

A lot of the country's history can be found by just wandering about some of the colonial graveyards, though one has to be careful of snakes: they are everywhere, especially on the edge of town.

In one of the old burial plots adjacent to Tower Hill, I found the grave of a woman, Elizabeth Murial Duncan, a mother from a small town in Essex who, at the age of 22, was "taken" unexpectedly. The 1822 inscription on her grave noted that she had become ill in the

"Bokkie", the ageing Soviet-built Mi-17 that Neall Ellis and his mercenary pals used to pull Lebanese refugees out of the path of advancing RUF rebels. Here the helicopter is refuelled at Lungi Internationl Airport on the far side of the bay from Freetown. (Photo: Author)

morning "and died of high fever" before the sun went down.

It must have been serious because Sierra Leone soon acquired a sinister reputation. In his book *Sierra Leone* published in 1954, Roy Lewis – then on the staff of Britain's *Economist* – said that the colony exacted a dreadful toll. He wrote that between 1814 and 1885, "five governors and seven acting governors died at their posts or on the ship home."

Harrison Rankin, in the appropriately titled *White Man's Grave*, which he published in 1847, records a discussion that went something like this: "One kind friend, more facetious than the rest, observed that, inasmuch as I was bound for such a deadly place, it would be judicious to include a coffin in my equipment, since it might come in handy at an early date."

Another visitor said at the time, that in the first years after its settlement, "it was quite customary of a morning to ask: 'How many died last night?'"

Health problems persist. Only a few years ago there was an outbreak of mosquito-borne encephalitis. At one stage, it was endemic enough to kill the popular resident commander of the Nigerian armed forces in the country, Major General Maxwell Khobe (although the grapevine has it that he was poisoned for being too politically outspoken). Shortly afterwards, British forces under the then Brigadier David Richards had barely arrived before an expatriate in the interior died of Lassa fever. We didn't hear the end of that one, except that it wasn't the only instance of a disease that has some of the symptoms of Ebola.

Lassa fever, endemic to many parts of West Africa, is a highly infectious rodent-borne disease. The Kenema Centre was treating 50 cases a month at one stage and infections were accentuated by overcrowded accumulations of displaced people due to the after-effects of the war. Obviously, the wraps went up immediately. Both the World Health Organisation (WHO) and Atlanta's Centers for Disease Control were involved in the monitoring process.

In theory, Sierra Leone should have been one of the success stories of Africa. With independence in 1961, London handed the fledgling government sets of books that balanced, a working economy, a relatively efficient civil service and even a thriving little three-foot, six-inch narrow-gauge railway line that stretched from Freetown to Bo, about 250 kilometres into the east. The rail service didn't make all that much money, but as one letter writer is quoted in a Freetown paper of the time, "it kept the nation's portals into the interior ajar".

There was even a branch line to Makeni, quite a big town that at one stage became the rebel headquarters during the civil war.

For reasons that remain obscure – because none of it makes any sense – the young parliament, having been made an offer by a Japanese conglomerate for the steel, voted to rip up all the rails and sell the lot. Almost overnight, some very rich politicians emerged.

Then they couldn't make up their minds what kind of bribe money had to be paid for use of the Pepel iron ore-loading facility, a major foreign exchange earner. So the German company responsible for originally building it at a cost of millions of dollars, packed its bags and went home. Obviously there were some easy backhanders involved and from then on, the country went the way of all of sub-Saharan Africa.

Tariq Ali, who appears to have assumed Basil Davidson's mantle as the guru of Africa, offered us his two bits worth on some of the continent's problems. These were packaged in a review of several books in *The Times*, London.

"Corruption", he suggested, "is both uncontrolled and on open view. The cancer has moved from the top down ... judges, generals, politicians of all stripes and senior civil servants are for sale in the market place." He was writing about Nigeria, of course, but what he utters also holds fast for Sierra Leone. In such situations, he reckons, there is nobody left to organise the mega-dosage of political chemotherapy required to stage a partial recovery and stave off death. Naturally, the war didn't help either.

"In Islam," says Ali optimistically – for once, raising his flag – "there is some hope in ending this never-ending cycle of political corruption, military coups d'etat, violence and separatism." He points out that religious fundamentalism caters to a desire for purity and the sweeping aside of all evils, if necessary by washing them in blood.

Like some of the panaceas that deal with the continent's many problems, he forgot to factor in survival. When people can't put bread on the table for their children, they do what they have to simply to get along.

Yet, it shouldn't have been so. Sierra Leone's economic potential – with some of the richest kimberlite pipes producing precious stones – is part of today's West Coast legend. There is also the gold, enough to have made the country self-supportive, had there been no diamonds at all. Add to all that huge deposits of bauxite, titanium, iron ore and much else. The problem, as always, is nepotism and corruption and the present situation might have been reversed had

A small group of mercs attached to Executive Outcomes in Sierra Leone enjoy an early morning cuppa in the mist above the Kono diamond fields. (Photo: Author)

these industries been properly controlled; although it would have taken a strong and honest hand to do so.

Instead, those who mine gemstones in Sierra Leone in the 21st Century invariably smuggle everything out of the country.

Historically, the most damning consequence of this activity is that the Freetown government has seen precious little of what should have been its rightful share of the bounty. This illicit trade has been going on for so long, that there have been times when there wasn't enough money in state coffers to maintain roads, hospitals, schools and other public services. At one stage the country couldn't even pay for its fuel imports. Lines at petrol pumps were sometimes a kilometre long.

Even today, getting the Sierra Leone Army paid is an effort, but at least that was rectified for a time because there was a British national in the seat of the country's accountant general. There was also Keith Biddle, formerly of London's Metropolitan force, who headed the country's police. That followed a BBC report about teachers in Sierra Leone going on strike because they hadn't been paid for months. How sad.

Perhaps the columnist R.W. Johnson was right when he wrote in *The Daily Telegraph* that "Africa requires a second 'soft' colonisation – a lengthy and UN-mandated affair. But do the old colonial powers

have the willpower to do that?" he asked.

"It is a matter of double or quits," he ventured.

Getting large parcels of diamonds out of the country, until fairly recently, was as easy as pie.

One of the dealers who stayed on in Freetown during the troubles, explained his modus operandi. When the time came to leave the country (with perhaps eight or ten kilos of uncut diamonds) he would discreetly negotiate his passage beforehand by going directly to the head of the country's security services. He wouldn't even bother with any minister: that was the other man's business in case something went wrong. Anyway, the fee was hefty enough to cope with such contingencies.

Having settled on a sum, the man would push through the usual pre-flight routines on the day of departure. This could include a physical search for diamonds by a special police agency either at Lungi or Hastings airports. Customs and passport control would follow. Once those preliminaries were complete and his flight was called, he would board with the rest of the passengers. Then, just before take-off, a uniformed officer would board the plane and hand over a package with goods that might be worth millions of dollars.

As he described it, "it was usually given to me with a smile and generous thanks." Just like that …

Chapter 26
Freetown: Diamonds, a civil war and amputees

The resources that left Sierra Leone illegally over 30 or 40 years were staggering. Some of it built a succession of fortunes throughout the Levant and in parts of southern Europe. There were few Lebanese involved in diamonds that did not have fine homes in Freetown and back home along the Mediterranean, some of them baroque mansions with the decadent style of the Bosphorus. Quite a few of them had villas on the Côte d' Azur, as well as apartments in London or New York or both.

While covering the civil war in Lebanon and the Israeli invasion that followed in the 1980s, I was to see a lot of these glass and marble palaces built on the proceeds of Africa's wealth. Many were destroyed in the fighting that followed, but then a vicious reverse of fortunes has invariably been irony's child.

Quite a number of Freetown's more impressive homes still stand, others rubbished by conflict. Proud, dilapidated and uninhabited, they perch proudly on the slopes of Freetown's Mount Aureol and other high points around the city, almost all looted. Others haven't been painted in years. In that climate, if you don't use it, you lose it: the majority are coated in a dark, tropical fungus that is symptomatic of most structures in that part of the world.

Early maps of the west coast of Africa, even as recently as a century ago, showed little detail of the interior of the vast continent. It was only the first major war with Germany that forced the pace of progress, both for Britain and France and, to a lesser degree, Belgium, Spain, Italy and Portugal.

British historian Roy Lewis takes issue with the colonial government in his book for so effectively "shielding the tribes from hasty interference in their settled customs". It was not until 1927, he said, that the world discovered that London "still firmly upheld the principle of domestic slavery" in the hinterland. As recently as the mid-1950s, the folk around Kailahun in the east of Sierra Leone (and for a long while a rebel stronghold during the recent civil war period) were still using the famous Kissi penny as currency. These were iron bars about 50 centimetres long and used for trade.

In this regard, several generations of Lebanese traders knowingly contributed towards the systematic deprivation of this tiny West African state. Discreetly at first, then quite blatantly, they seized Sierra Leone's resources, offering little in return and there was nothing the government could do about it. As it was, this kind of skulduggery had been going on too long for anybody to remedy. Still worse, the proceeds were in terms of billions of dollars over the past

Executive Outcomes had a preponderance of black soldiers in its ranks, both in Angola and Sierra Leone. A bunch of these mercenary troops guard the airfield at Angola's diamond-rich town of Saurimo. (Photo: Author)

five decades. Some critics roundly criticised actions referred to by the local media as "the ultimate rape of the continent". Obviously, local African communities suffered the most.

Using the Arab guile for which Lebanon has always been known, these Levantines would gradually ingratiate themselves into a society where they eventually controlled just about everything, politicians included. Their approach, as one commentator put it, "was many-layered and subtle". Then they started looking about at other options, including the country's leadership. Disarmingly persuasive, these same Lebanese eventually corrupted the political system as well: they had Momeh in their pockets from the first day of his presidency.

For their part, Sierra Leone's leaders – long accustomed to Whitehall's way of doing things – were far too trusting and naïve to comprehend the shrewd manipulations of these Middle Eastern interlopers. Checks and balances that should have been in place, simply weren't. Of course it was the bribes that did it, and in this regard it's a problem that is hardly restricted to Africa.

The truth is that the average politician in Sierra Leone grew up in a society where people always nurse what little cash they had. Bundles of American dollars, sometimes six or eight inches thick, would be bandied about by these Lebanese businessmen, an enormous temptation. Further, it was immediately negotiable and, as we have seen elsewhere, that sort of thing tends to turn heads. Still, considering the chronic shortcomings of Sierra Leone, this was economic perversion of the most damnable and with the benefit of hindsight, Whitehall should have done something about it. But then Britain wasn't even able to counter the excesses of people like Idi Amin and Zimbabwe's Mugabe, to whom human rights were never an issue.

Since the political ranks of Sierra Leone – then and now – were filled with ordinary folk, the majority of whom had grown up poor, one can perhaps understand the problem. It was just about impossible to refuse a favour of a man who arrives at your door with a large amount of money.

Within a few years of independence in April 1961, dozens of Lebanese diamond consortiums began to wield a burgeoning power base in bids to persuade Freetown's leaders to abrogate ongoing contracts in the country's diamond industry, especially the hold that Britain's Consolidated African Selection Trust – part of the De Beers

Two members of Neall Ellis's helicopter gunship crew in Sierra Leone, with Fijian and former SAS operator Fred Marafano, checking the fuselage and "Christian", a French mercenary side-gunner, to his rear waiting to board. (Photo: Author)

Group – had over the diggings. In theory, after independence, these were to have been open to all, but it was not to be and soon it was Lebanese interests that dominated all.

Even traditional paramount chiefs were in their pocket. If somebody got in the way, he was dealt with. Killings then, as now, were all part of the business, which was hardly difficult when your enforcers were gang-lords who had been blooded in the Lebanese Civil War.

London has been consistently blamed for much of this post-uhuru mayhem. Some Sierra Leonian politicians maintain that it was the British that had originally allowed the Lebanese a free hand in what was then regarded as an emerging country. And while this may have been a valid argument with regard to mining, farming and exploration interests among wealthier members of the Commonwealth such as Kenya and South Africa, it didn't apply to the west coast. Westminster never allowed permanent white settlements in any of the West African states, though obviously, this didn't apply to Arabs who, during colonial times, were snootily regarded by some members of the Imperial administration as an almost subhuman species.

In contrast, there were – and still are – large Lebanese communities

The United Nations spent hundreds of millions of dollars supporting its failed military initiative in Sierra Leone, including the deployment of these giant Mi-26 transports that are capable of carrying 100 troops or almost 70 civilians. (Photo: Author)

Chapter 26
Freetown: Diamonds, a civil war and amputees

in other former British possessions such as Ghana and Nigeria. Many of these people, like the Leventis family, have always been a positive force for the good. There are also those individual Lebanese who have done much to help the country, even marrying into local families. The difference with Sierra Leone though, was diamonds, coupled to a manifest lack of control by the state.

It's no secret either, that apart from Lebanese diamond concession holders, together with an army of locals (who in the past sold most of their stones to these Arabs anyway) very few foreign companies were able to maintain an effective presence east of the Rokel River. By the mid-1980s – when I visited that region for the third or fourth time – the Lebanese were nominally in control of just about everything there as well.

Even then, there was a set fee for government ministers "doing something". And as more Lebanese refugees began to arrive on the west coast from their own civil war, conditions for other expatriates became desperate. By then, there were few foreigners doing business in the capital who were not from the eastern Mediterranean.

For instance, the country's only casino was in Lebanese hands. So were many of the country's banks. They had their own clubs and social institutions to which only Lebanese were admitted as members. Also, the huge Lebanese school in the centre of town – with more than 1,000 enrolled scholars – admitted no ethnic Sierra Leonian students unless they were related to or were the actual children of Lebanese families. Unusually, this form of apartheid was not only tolerated, but actually sanctioned by government.

Being interested in what was clearly a very unusual social phenomenon on an almost black continent, I managed to gain entry to this school in the mid-1980s, and, camera crew in tow we filmed the lot. In spite of a few objections, I got what I wanted and that film exists today in the SABC archives as a record of West African racial excesses.

On my return to the west coast more recently, I found that Freetown had totally transmogrified. Indeed, the only reason why this capital city isn't today the largest slum on the African continent is because as cities go, Lagos, Kinshasa, Conakry and Luanda are bigger.

From the quaint post-colonial, prosperous little settlement that was Freetown of the 1960s and 1970s, the malaise that follows in the wake of a Lebanese "takeover" means that – war or no war – the people of Sierra Leone continue to lead ghastly lives. More to the point, nothing is going to change any time soon.

During that visit, parts of Freetown stank like a Delhi *nullah*. The violence, obviously, had a lot to do with it. The capital of the Republic of Sierra Leone had become a city of palms, all outstretched and waiting to be greased. So it was that over the years, the Sierra Leone Army has overthrown a succession of governments and it is inevitable that one bunch of thugs should replace another.

Enter the mercenaries. Executive Outcomes was one of a dozen organisations that tried to gain a toehold in Sierra Leone's misfortunes. Before that crowd, there had been several European companies, as well as groups of Russians and Ukrainians.

At the root of it all was diamonds, a hundred Rajahs' ransoms worth of precious stones. Diamonds also caused the civil war, with Foday Sankoh's friend and confidante, Charles Taylor demanding a piece of the action, for which, more recently, he has been answerable at the International Court of Justice at The Hague.

CHAPTER TWENTY SEVEN

INTO THE BUSH WAR WITH THE RHODESIAN SAS

Although modest in terms of numbers when compared to other units involved in Rhodesia's seven-year bush war, the Rhodesian SAS played a significant role in countering insurgency, especially in neighbouring countries like Mozambique and Zambia, and on several occasions, as far north as Tanzania. Lieutenant Colonel Brian Robinson remained in command of the unit longer than any of his contemporaries. He tells us about some of it:

It was at the start of the Malayan Emergency (1951–1953) that British Army Brigadier Michael Calvert, the wartime Chindit commander, flew to Rhodesia and asked the government to help with the provision of a Special Air Service squadron to be called C (Rhodesia) Squadron. It surprised nobody that Salisbury responded enthusiastically, especially since this young nation had provided so many volunteers during two world wars: a future prime minister, Ian Smith and some of his associates had flown Spitfires against the Huns.

Consequently, when a group of men from Southern Rhodesia volunteered to go to Malaya, they were warmly received and initially known as The Far East Volunteer Group, later to become the Malayan Scouts. While in Asia, this was the unit to become C Squadron (Malayan Scouts) of the already-formed A and B Squadrons of the British Special Air Service.

The formation of the Rhodesian SAS goes back to November 1959, when it was decided in the Rhodesian Federal Assembly to form a Parachute Evaluation Detachment (PED) to examine the practicalities of military parachuting and parachute training in the Federation of Rhodesia and Nyasaland. Initially, the idea was the possible formation of an airborne unit. This was announced by the then Federal Minister of Defence, but it was the Prime Minister, Sir

The Rhodesian SAS took part in numerous cross-border raids into both Zambia and Mozambique. This was the column that struck at the rebel base in Operation Miracle. (Photo: Author's collection)

Roy Welensky who was the driving force behind the reforming of what was to ultimately become Rhodesia's SAS.

In 1960 a Royal Air Force detachment arrived in the country under Squadron Leader Errol Minter to conduct PED's training and three months later, the unit was complete and those on the course presented with their wings. The "experiment" – for that is what it was, was a success and the government decided to form a regular European Special Air Service Squadron. Late in 1960, No. 1 Training Unit was formed, and once assembled and trained, it would form the nucleus of what was jointly to become 1 Rhodesian Light Infantry, or more commonly, the RLI and C Squadron SAS.

Chapter 27
Into the bush war with the Rhodesian SAS

By early 1961, six volunteers from the Air Force were sent to RAF Abingdon in Britain for parachute instructor training and a further group of volunteer officers and NCOs departed to complete a selection course with the SAS in Britain. On their return, they called for volunteers from No. 1 Training Unit and in August 1961 the first of many selection courses was run in the Matopo Hills outside Bulawayo.

Late 1961, the SAS was moved to the copper mining town of Ndola in Northern Rhodesia, along with the Selous Scouts Armoured Car Regiment.

By July the following year, No. 9 basic course received their wings from the Federal Prime Minister. A month later, the unit – to be known as C Squadron (Rhodesian) Special Air Service – had sufficient men to go fully operational.

With the break-up of the Federation at the end of 1963, the squadron was virtually made redundant by so many of its troops taking a "golden handshake". Some were enticed to stay in what was then still Northern Rhodesia, among them, many of the officers as well as its officer commanding. Only 38 NCOs and men opted to serve in Southern Rhodesia and the unit was relocated to Cranborne Barracks in Salisbury.

The initial years after the break-up found the unit having difficulty in attracting recruits. This was largely due to the high standards required of an SAS soldier and also due to some real or imagined rancour between the SAS and the RLI (from where most of the recruits would have been selected). In fact, as former SAS veteran Tony de Bruin points out, "the SAS was tapping into all the better members of all the regiments and a lot of the old 'salts' were unhappy about our receiving the best equipment available and the fact that we came under direct command of Army Headquarters and not brigade structures."

Nevertheless, both the SAS and the RLI were soon to play crucial roles in the domestic counter-insurgency effort during the Rhodesian Bush War. They, and the equally clandestine Selous Scouts were the principal Special Forces units used in external operations, and in terms of some of the most important of the external operations, Operation Dingo, which took place in November 1977 the SAS and RLI were both involved in what was one of the most successful preemptive operations conducted during the course of the war.

Operation Dingo, also known as the Chimoio massacre (and covered in detail in Hannes Wessels's Chapter 22) was arguably the single most daring and damaging raid of the period. Targeted were the ZANLA headquarters of Robert Mugabe at Chimoio as well as a smaller camp at Tembue in Mozambique. More than 3,000 ZANLA fighters were reported killed and 5,000 wounded, while government losses amounted to two soldiers killed and six wounded.

Meanwhile, SAS strength went up to approximately 250 when, in June 1978, C Squadron (Rhodesian) Special Air Service became 1 (Rhodesian) Special Air Service Regiment. The unit moved to Kibrit, their new barracks, in 1979 and continued to serve with success and distinction until it was disbanded with the transition to black majority rule on 31 December 1980 when the Rhodesian flag was struck and the young country renamed Zimbabwe.

The 250 soldiers who wore SAS colours would include ERE (Extra Regimentally Employed) members: members who had served in the unit and could be called upon for a maximum-effort operation. The regiment was formed to give the unit the flexibility to hold additional ranks over and above the establishment.

At that stage, I was a major and commanding officer in the Rhodesian Army and my second-in-charge was also a major. That would not have been acceptable to the ministry for accounting

Ron Reid-Daly's Selous Scouts often collaborated with the SAS in striking at external targets. (Photo: Author's collection)

purposes, so the establishment was changed from squadron to regiment. This was not done because they had hundreds of potential SAS soldiers, but put into effect to "crook" the books and allow us an increase in rank structure which a squadron would not allow.

Also relevant here is that there has been talk in the past of an SAS "D" Squadron. The D Squadron (South African) story – formed during the Rhodesian war years – followed, a 1967 request from Colonel Jan Breytenbach of No.1 Reconnaissance (Recce) Regiment, that some of his boys go north to Rhodesia and assist us in operations in which C Squadron was then involved. There would be a good exchange of both information and experience since South Africa was gradually dealing into its own insurgencies in South West Africa and along the Angolan and Zambian borders.

With time, Breytenbach and I became good friends, and obviously, I grasped his offer with both hands…it was then approved at the highest levels in both Salisbury and Pretoria since any South African presence in Rhodesia would obviously have been classified. Because of this new development, I put forward a deception plan which put them into SAS uniforms and we called them D Squadron. Of course they were South Africans operating under a different guise.

At the break-up of the Federation in 1963, there was very little encouragement from the politicians or the Federal Army hierarchy for the officers and men of C Squadron SAS to move to Southern Rhodesia. Officers were offered short-term contracts at inflated ranks to remain in Northern Rhodesia. The British Army came forward with offers of their own or "golden handshakes". In fact, there were no career prospects in Southern Rhodesia, guaranteed or otherwise.

The immediate consequence of this "man management" disaster was the loss of many top-rate SAS officers and other ranks to "Civvy Street" and other British units. Many of these disillusioned officers who elected to leave had excelled at Sandhurst and the School of Infantry, Gwelo, and would have been a credit to any military establishment in the world.

As a result of this debacle, Major Dudley Coventry and Captain Peter Rich were sent to Northern Rhodesia in December 1963 to collect the 31 other ranks who were the disheartened survivors of a well-trained over-strength unit of some 180 officers and men. So began the reformation of the new C Squadron, Rhodesian SAS in Southern Rhodesia.

Major Dudley Coventry was my first company commander. He had served with the British Parachute Regiment and the Royal

Marine Commandos during World War II and, I believe, R Squadron SAS in Malaya. He had also held a commission in the French Foreign Legion.

A huge, charismatic man with a large handlebar moustache, Dudley was a natural English gentleman with great charm. He kept his subalterns enthralled with his stories of partying with David Niven on his yacht and dating the actress Ava Gardner. Because Dudley was the most senior officer who had seen previous service with the SAS, he was the obvious choice as its new commanding officer. For his part, Captain Peter Rich was recruited directly from the UK, having seen active service in Korea and Malaya with 22 SAS Regiment where he held the post of training troop commander. He was consequently an ideal second-in-command to Dudley.

Like Dudley, Peter was his own sort of man, a highly intelligent officer with a cutting sense of humour. And although much older than most of us, he was full of courage and made every effort to conform to all the physical requirements of the SAS. He eventually made brigadier and had the satisfaction of flying into action in the same stick as his son, Lieutenant Michael Rich, who at the time was a serving SAS officer. Having emerged unscathed from action in Malaya, Korea and Rhodesia, Brigadier Peter Rich was tragically killed in a freak motor vehicle accident in Britain after Mugabe had assumed power.

Recruiting soon became a top priority for Dudley. An agreement had been reached to allow Captain John Donaldson-Selby, the former selection troop commander to run the first Southern Rhodesian selection course for entry into the SAS. This attracted some 14 potential officers and about 60 other ranks.

Donaldson-Selby was assisted by some of the senior NCOs who had made the journey south from Zambia and at the end of that cycle, five officers and about three other ranks passed the first selection course. I had elected to follow my company commander to the squadron and was also fortunate to be one of the five who successfully got through.

There was a fair amount of resentment felt by the 31 SAS survivors toward newcomers, with the result that the new recruits were hardly given a rousing welcome.

Warrant Officer Bouch was one of the senior NCOs assisting with that first selection course, but he had very little time for officers, sharing the belief of many of his British Army counterparts that most officers were a "waste of time". Hence the derogatory term "Ruperts",

used to describe their officers.

I believe that Dudley secretly held the same sentiments with regard to young and inexperienced subalterns: he far preferred the experienced old NCO who knew the form and never gave trouble. Boards of Inquiry, bureaucracy and lengthy paper work resulting from lost or damaged equipment did not please him.

He never ever said as much, but he certainly shared the opinion of some of the senior men that an unwarranted air of arrogance pervaded the remainder of the SAS old boys' club. It was not unusual to see a squadron member roaring around Salisbury in his own Sabre Land Rover glancing at his reflection in the rear-view mirror to ensure that the fit of the coveted beige beret was to his satisfaction.

To be fair, there were also some outstanding young NCOs who came south. They were the heart and soul of the squadron and made every effort to pass on their SAS skills and knowledge to the new arrivals.

Britain also played a role during this time. 22 SAS offered C Squadron an officer attachment to join the regiment based in Hereford in the UK in 1965 and once again I was fortunate enough to be selected to take up this attachment. Looking back, I believe this was the most important opportunity of my military career.

These were interesting times, especially in South Asia. In 1964, 22 SAS was heavily involved in counter-insurgency operations in Borneo. Once I was able to prove that we colonials were thoroughly house-trained and knew how to use a knife and fork (and did not live in mud huts), the British facade of superiority disappeared and I was able to extract valuable information about the hands-on-tactics employed by the SAS in a contemporary guerrilla warfare. This was a huge step-up when compared to the role played by Colonel David Stirling dashing around the Sahara Desert in a Jeep.

I was soon to learn more about the current SAS modus operandi in such areas as:

- Methods of infiltration
- Four-man "stick" deep-penetration tactics
- Shoot-and-scoot operations
- Troop skills
- Hearts-and-minds operations
- Hot extraction
- Command and control of SAS troops

I was also able to observe and take part in aspects of their selection course. I was even on the flight manifest to go to Borneo when our Prime Minister Ian Smith decided to issue his Unilateral Declaration of Independence (UDI) on 11 November 1965.

A rather embarrassed commanding officer, Colonel Mike Wingate-Grey did not quite know what to do with me and I expect his options were somewhat circumscribed. He could offer me a selection course, lock me up in the coal cellar or send me back to Rhodesia. For me,

Chapter 27
Into the bush war with the Rhodesian SAS

the choice was simple: I could not wait to get back into a potential punch-up back in Rhodesia. Moreover, the period spent in the UK had provided me with the background and knowledge I would call upon throughout my Special Forces tour of duty.

From 1964 to March 1968, Major Dudley Coventry commanded C Squadron but WO2 Bob Bouch actually ran the unit with his hand-picked NCO cronies. Early in 1965, Jack Berry of the Rhodesian Central Intelligence Organisation (CIO) approached Dudley to carry out clandestine operations on their behalf. As this was the original reason for creating the squadron, Dudley jumped at the opportunity and Bob Bouch and his team of fellow NCOs – they were dubbed the "Secret Seven" – were duly summoned and briefed on the first-ever external operation.

The exclusive use of the "Secret Seven" for the "funnies" (otherwise referred to as Special Classified Operations) most certainly created a lot of resentment among members who had just won their SAS wings but had been excluded from this rather exclusive group. But this was of little concern to SAS management, who pressed on regardless.

In October 1966, an operation was planned to be mounted from below the Chirundu Bridge near Kariba. The idea was for the team to be transported across the Zambezi River into Zambia by Klepper canoes, where explosive charges were to be placed on a selected terrorist target. During the final stages of preparation, an accidental detonation took place which ended with five of the "Secret Seven" being killed. It was the biggest single catastrophe to date.

The only survivor was Dudley, while the life of Jannie Boltman had been spared because he had gone on leave shortly before the group were due to go out. Dudley only lived because even though he was close to the blast, he was bent double, doing up his shoelaces when the explosion happened. He was also in what is known in the lingo as "dead ground". Though knocked out cold by the blast, he regained consciousness a short while later with all his hair singed.

At the time of the accident, an RLI detachment was deployed on border-control duties at the Chirundu Bridge. Their members were totally unaware of the prospective SAS operation or even of their presence in the area. Warrant Officer Tourle came rushing down to the river to establish what was going on and was greeted by a much-dishevelled Major Coventry who, in his cultivated manner of speech, said: "Hello, Sergeant Major … how are you?"

Sadly, it was a terrible disaster, with body parts everywhere. An immediate casualty evacuation was arranged for Dudley and arrangements made to cart the dead away. An Alouette helicopter landed shortly afterwards, picked up Dudley and set course for Kariba. At about 100 feet off the ground the chopper's engine malfunctioned and Mark Smithdorff, the pilot, was forced to make an emergency landing.

The event was marked down as a failure as well as the first of the SAS deaths. As an operational unit, the "Secret Seven" was no more and the squadron had lost its most experienced NCOs. Morale plummeted as the SAS set about reorganising itself. This was also a desperately cruel lesson about, as the saying goes, never putting all one's eggs in one basket. What the tragedy did allow was for me to become part of a team to be involved in the first incursions into Zambia.

The planning for that first venture was elaborate. For security reasons we were not permitted to wear or carry any Rhodesian military equipment. In the event of being captured, we were to claim to be a dissident group acting on our own initiative. Although we carried AK-47 weapons, we were not allowed to use Rhodesian radios, and for all of us, the prospect of operating in hostile territory without communications was problematic.

Operating in two-man teams, we crossed the Zambezi River at night in Klepper canoes, most times paying scant attention to a very large hippo and crocodile population in the river or afterwards, on land, to the many lion, elephant and buffalo that roamed the bush. Our task was both basic and dangerous: we were looking for terrorist base camps.

I am aware today that we made numerous mistakes in those early

A pair of South African Air Force Super Frelon "troopers" are framed by a Soviet 12.7 mm DshKa heavy machine gun at a bush airstrip inside Mozambique during an external strike. (Photo: Author's collection)

days: like using two-man teams when we should have employed a standard four-man call sign (team), and possibly crossing the river at the same place once too often. Nor did it help that we operated with no communications and having no proper air support or backup. Clearly, we were lucky not to have suffered serious losses in those early days.

Although our initial efforts achieved little tangible operational success, we were starting to become more sophisticated in our planning and execution of some very ambitious operations. Operation Sculpture involved SAS operators flying into Zambia at night in a privately-owned Cessna 206, a rather ambitious adventure on its own. It involved Peter Scales, a Rhodesian Police Reserve Air Wing pilot who navigated his way at night, deep into Zambia to an unlit airfield. He achieved this without any of today's electronic navigational aids. In fact, in those days we hadn't even heard of GPS navigation.

Our recovery took place from Lusaka's main international airport where Peter screened his approach from radar by tucking his plane in neatly behind a commercial BAC 1-11 passenger aircraft on final approach. Suddenly we were starting to think like true SAS operatives.

There were other developments. We were soon to learn that it was almost impossible to engage the enemy without trackers.

Initially the Rhodesian Army was totally dependent on Game Department trackers who were mainly black. All went well until the terrorists started to kill these specialists. Consequently, to avoid becoming involved in a contact, we found that tracks were frequently lost when a contact became imminent. That was when we realised that it was essential to train trackers within the ranks of the squadron.

Thanks to the initiative of Allan Savory, a series of tracking and bushcraft courses were run for the unit and it wasn't long before SAS tracker combat teams, temporarily attached to other units were in much demand throughout the Rhodesian military. It is worth noting that it was the SAS that originally pioneered the use of white soldiers as trackers.

These early courses also contributed to the formation of mixed black and white Special Branch (BSAP) and Army tracker teams which would customarily operate together. It was this concept that led to the formation of the Selous Scouts, founded and commanded by Colonel Ron Reid-Daly, who himself had previously served with

C Squadron, SAS in Malaya. It is also on record that both André Rabie and "Stretch" Franklin originally served in the SAS and were both subsequently to become founder-members of the Selous Scouts.

As hostilities intensified, SAS tracker combat teams were involved in operations as distant as Mozambique and Angola. In 1970 the School of Infantry Tracking Wing was established for the Army at Kariba, staffed mainly by SAS instructors under my command. Hundreds of Rhodesian Army soldiers were subsequently trained at Tracking Wing.

The formation of the Selous Scouts took place in 1973. Their recruiting drive was given top priority throughout the army and the newly appointed Lt Col Ron Reid-Daly was brought out of retirement and appointed CO by the commander of the army, General G.P. (Peter) Walls.

It was an excellent choice and for several reasons; the most important being that Ron was a natural leader with great charisma coupled to exceptional man-management skills.

By 1973/1974 the Selous Scouts recruiting programme also started to take its toll on the C Squadron establishment. At one stage we were reduced to about 21 operational soldiers because we refused to lower our selection standards and some of the men had moved across to Reid-Daly's Scouts. We were now critically short of trained personnel and hardly operational and, as the saying goes, the boot was firmly on the other foot because for years, we had recruited from whom we liked: now, for the first time, we were getting a taste of our own medicine and we did not like it.

Squadron officers formed up and requested a meeting with the CO. They believed that General Walls was deliberately sabotaging the squadron in favour of the Selous Scouts. Their argument that we were losing our best men, that the Scouts were now becoming parachute trained, going external and taking over our role, was valid. Further, they suggested that it was only a matter of time before we were disbanded.

To illustrate that point, I was told that one of our highly rated NCOs was about to join the Scouts and should he do so, he would take with him many of his mates, all SAS. Were that to happen, we could expect to lose most of our own people who would follow him across. It was then that I decided to stick my pride in my pocket and contact Ron Reid-Daly. In measured terms I explained my predicament and to give him his due, out of loyalty to his former unit, the Special Air Service, he agreed to a temporary moratorium on poaching from us.

We both agreed that we could not prevent movement between the units, but at that moment, the SAS needed some breathing space and time to regroup. Reid-Daly was certainly under no obligation to agree to my proposal since his mandate was to recruit from where he desired in a bid to get the Scouts up to strength.

At the same time, the formation of the Scouts had a profound impact on the squadron. Within a comparatively short time, there were other troops who could do the things that we excelled at, like following tracks, parachute and go external. Almost overnight, we were faced with some serious opposition. We also had to accept that we no longer had friends in "high places" that would look after our interests or give us effective help or support. Indeed, we could no longer consider ourselves as a privileged or elite unit. The message that came down to the line was clear: we had to perform or else take the consequences. And, as expected, our troops did exactly that, as did the entire Rhodesian military structure.

An instructive analysis of the Rhodesian war effort appeared in America in 1983. Titled *Rhodesia: Tactical Victory, Strategic Defeat*, it was written by United States Marine Corps' Majors Charles M. Lohman and Robert I. MacPherson. The two officers maintained that although the Rhodesian security forces were small and its air force supported by well-worn equipment, "it was one of the finest counter-insurgency units in the world".

They went on: "Its lack of sophisticated weaponry and equipment was the basis for its success. It was an army, which dealt with the insurgent at his own level. It lacked extensive lines of logistics support, and the air force was incapable of dropping tremendous quantities of bombs. Yet, it was very adept at small-scale operations throughout a broken and ragged countryside.

"In order to compensate for its small numbers, the Rhodesian combatants had to rely upon the basic ingredients of victory – professionalism, training and an intimate knowledge of the terrain. It operated in small units, and relied upon mobility, surprise, flexibility, and tactical dispersion for success. The army tended to confront the insurgent on his own ground in a man-to-man fashion of combat.

"The security forces also reflected the spirit of the Rhodesian culture. It was a highly efficient organisation. The tight bonds within the Rhodesian society reduced the elements of traditional friction between soldiers, civil servants and politicians. The army and police forces were not plagued by a sense of social isolation [while the] European population was willing to endure the necessary taxation, and the required conscription of its children in order to achieve a gradual and moderate transition of power to a black majority that would tolerate a privileged European minority[1]."

As in any modern war, helicopters were always in great demand and 7 Squadron of the Royal Rhodesian Air Force – it became the Rhodesian Air Force in 1970 – could never hope to cope with all the army's needs.

Whereas the SAS initially regarded parachuting as just a means of "getting there", under certain circumstances it now became the only way of going anywhere. Within a comparatively short time, guerrilla landmines had made obsolete the Sabre Land Rover – an SAS favourite – so movement was by mine-protected vehicles (both one- and three-ton transports) or, alternatively, we had to be dropped into the target area by air.

From a security point of view, infiltration on foot was preferred. However, using this method involved several imponderables. First, the Zambian and Mocambican local population lived near the border and would instantly report any movement. These were rural people who were conscious of signs and there were many individuals within their numbers who had well-honed tracking and bushcraft skills. A foreign footprint would immediately be reported to the military or to the guerrillas, who would commence an immediate follow-up.

Second, the Zambezi River was a major obstacle to infiltration. Boat engines were noisy and Klepper canoes only carried two operators at a time. The other option was helicopters, but Alouettes were noisy and could only haul three fully equipped SAS men aloft. Also, these rotor-craft could be seen and heard for miles by day and did not have night capability: there were no night-vision goggles in those days, or if there were, the Rhodesian Exchequer couldn't afford them.

In later days, the Bell Huey 205 helicopters – solid and reliable veterans of the Vietnam War – improved the load-carrying capacity substantially and also added a new weapon to our infiltration armoury. The eastern border was protected by the *cordon sanitaire* minefield and that required a breach before infiltration.

This situation was obviously untenable and obliged us to begin using HALO (High Altitude-Low Opening) and static-line parachute deployments at night. This combination was an unmitigated success and we routinely surprised the enemy in our attacks, sometimes inflicting heavy casualties.

However, there was also a need in such operations to almost completely disregard parachuting safety regulations. Night drops would take place at 700 feet and drops by day as low as 500 feet.

Chapter 27
Into the bush war with the Rhodesian SAS

RLI "troopies" would often go into action in strikes that might have involved the SAS. It was a war in which the Rhodesians tended to use all available assets. (Photo: Argus Africa News Service)

Trees and other obstacles were mainly ignored. HALO "Pathfinders" controlled the drops from the ground, giving Dakota pilots the red- and green-light command from the ground. This, too, was an SAS first.

Because of the shortage of helicopters, we also pioneered tactical air-assault tactics using vertical envelopment at squadron strength. The deployment of a "Box" of SAS men around an enemy position provided instant stop lines, with the result that this system was to be used on future operations with great success and also adopted by other Rhodesian Army airborne units acting in the Fire Force role.

In March 1968, Dudley Coventry handed over command to Peter Rich, and I was chosen to become adjutant and second-in-command. The immediate effect was that command and control of the squadron reverted to the officers. The drawback was that while the majority of the squadron new boys had gained experience, its operational performance could best be described as "shaky". In short, we had hardly distinguished ourselves. In one case, the "tactical withdrawal" by a troop commander from a large terrorist contact, resulted in the instant return-to-unit (RTU) of the officer deemed responsible.

Peter Rich immediately set about trying to put things right and it wasn't long before the squadron's performance started to improve. It took a little longer to develop a reputation for professionalism which, in turn, started attracting the right sort of officers and other ranks.

Garth Barrett, Mike Graham and Martin Pearse were some of the officers who followed Peter from the Rhodesian Light Infantry, all of them outstanding leaders. Barrett went on to command the unit with distinction. Mike Graham was that rare mix of operational soldier and staff officer, who, as my second-in-command when I eventually took over, became my most valuable asset as my second-in-command. So was Martin Pearse, a highly professional SAS officer who was killed in action a week before he was to be presented with the Silver Cross of Rhodesia.

The "guru" of the modern-day SAS, Colonel John Woodhouse, visited us during the war and described an intelligence briefing by Mike Graham as one of the best he had ever heard. This was praise indeed from someone who had a reputation for being a man of few words. Mike would surely have commanded the Rhodesian Army had he not decided to leave the force.

As the quality of the SAS improved, so did its operational performance. The tempo of operations had by now increased to such an extent as to be virtually continuous.

The much-celebrated Major Grahame Wilson (GCV, SCR, BCR) was a serving officer with the Rhodesian African Rifles when he decided to try for selection with the SAS. A rather chubby, pear-shaped individual in those early days, he wore spectacles, which he frequently adjusted on the bridge of his nose. On the face of it, he could hardly have been described as the epitome of an SAS officer. Once in our ranks though, his portly appearance did not last long.

Interesting, I was not overly impressed when he only just made the selection. I ended up making several telephone calls and eventually accepted him, both grudgingly and against my better judgement. How wrong my initial impressions were, because Grahame Wilson went on to become the most highly decorated soldier and one of the most professional Special Forces operators in the Rhodesian Army. During this period he planned and led a number of successful high-risk SAS operations and later went on to command the unit and received a number of decorations for bravery. It goes to prove – never judge a book by its cover.

Other than a temporary posting as Staff Captain HQ 2 Brigade and Officer Commanding Tracking Wing, most of my Army career was spent with C Squadron. This was probably because I was unemployable as a staff officer rather than indispensable as an SAS officer.

It goes without saying that to command an elite SAS unit, in whatever army, is the dream of every soldier who has ever served in such a unit. When I took over command in December 1972 from fellow officer and friend Barney Bentley, I could hardly believe my luck. My first task was to educate the Army hierarchy on the role of the SAS.

Other than General Walls, Bruce Campling and Peter Rich, the majority of senior army officers knew very little about what we actually did, or the actual purpose for which the unit was established in the first place. I took the line of stressing that the squadron was a strategic force and that command and control had to be at the highest level. This hardly went over well with many brigade commanders, who wanted everything to go through the correct channels, essentially to maintain their own involvement.

Filled with confidence, I was once tasked to carry out an internal operation in support of operations being conducted by Colonel Dave Parker who commanded the Rhodesian Light Infantry and who was known to his men as "The King". He asked me to take on several tasks, to which I produced the standard reply: "That's not really an SAS job, Sir." Exasperated, Dave eventually exclaimed, "Brian, I don't know what is or isn't an SAS job, but why don't you take yourself and your squadron and fuck off back to Salisbury."

I'll never forget those words of advice. The SAS was a very expensive toy and it was fast becoming, what some observers termed "too precious". Had we gone on like that, our antics could easily have called into question the need to have an SAS unit at all.

Appropriately chastened by one of the best officers in the Rhodesian Army, I saluted, did a smart about-turn and got on with the job.

At that time, I continued to study all aspects of insurgency. It was then that I believed the solution to the terrorist infiltration problems to be quite simple:

- Destroy the shipping that was carrying the terrorist arms and equipment in the Mozambique harbours
- Blow all the bridges along major lines of communication
- Mine the roads and make the terrorists walk: basically prevent them from driving to the border and coming across into Rhodesia in droves
- Destroy their fuel depots.

The answer from Army HQ was that all of this was politically unacceptable. I never did understand this rationale and nor did many others: we were fighting a war, dammit! It was also ironic that when we eventually did get the green light, most of the terrorists we sought were already safely inside the country and it was too late.

It wasn't long before I was surrounded by some outstanding

officers and men. The majority had become very experienced and professional and had achieved remarkable results. I also realised that involving these officers with actual operational planning in a bid to get them to contribute was far better than simply issuing sets of orders.

By now the squadron had also developed its own unique methods of operation, which were best suited to Rhodesian conditions within a guerrilla war scenario. Sanctions and limited finances forced us to make do with what we had, so we adapted classical British SAS doctrine to suit our own situation and conditions.

The British set certain standards, the first being that 22 SAS would not even look at a potential SAS aspirant unless he had at least three years' of military service. We, in Rhodesia, would take recruits directly from school, provided they managed to pass our extremely rigorous selection course, though generally we preferred the men to be 25 years or older, even if we never considered age to be a limitation.

The British SAS only allowed an officer a tour of duty that lasted three years. We believed that an officer only began to understand SAS tradecraft and tactics after that many years, so why get rid of him when he was just starting to make his contribution and become profitable.

22 SAS never kept ex-regiment personnel on their call-up books. We, in contrast, tried to keep all ex-squadron members current. We ran continuation courses to achieve this aim and frequently called up these volunteers for major operations, regardless of rank. In Rhodesia we also recruited, trained and called up National Service volunteers, which was contrary to what the parent regiment did.

Our standing operational procedures consequently revolved around the following set-piece operations:

- Conventional parachute vertical envelopment operations
- Deep-penetration long-term reconnaissance missions (four-man call-sign)
- Classical SAS deep-penetration strategic demolition tasks
- Tracker combat team support operations
- Enemy base camp close reconnaissance missions
- Deep-penetration waterborne operations
- Deep-penetration ambush, shoot and scoot operations

And then the selection process: The agony of the SAS selection course has been written about since 1942 and it will continue to feature for the remainder of my lifetime. Selection procedures were specifically designed to weed out the unsuitable and enlist only those with the right qualities.

First, a unit member had to be compatible. Living with a four-man call-sign for six weeks in enemy territory requires team members to be able to get along with one another. Moreover, they needed to be able to do this on a better-than-average basis.

Second, an SAS soldier had to be both mentally and physically tough, as well as self-reliant. He needed to have the kind of intelligence that would enable him to think through an extremely difficult situation, regardless of conditions or circumstances. Hauling a 40-kilo Bergen rucksack that contained two weeks' rations, together with enough ammunition to last for the duration, required an exceptional level of fitness. A failed operation could easily lead to consequences that might not only be embarrassing but could put lives at risk.

The transformation from parachute-trained infantry to Special Force soldier took place in December 1972 when for the first time four-man call-signs were deployed for the requisite six weeks in a classical "reconnaissance-only" role. Reporting on the enemy without being detected or firing a shot called for extremely demanding disciplines, usually only achieved by the selection course. In effect, the SAS role was to become the "eyes and ears" of the army and, with them in place, the army commander and staff could now consider deploying conventional infantry forces based on our intelligence reports on enemy movement and lines of communication.

The operational role of the SAS was intimately linked with the air force. Air assets provided all parachute training at the Parachute Training School (IPTS New Sarum). That included Dakota DC-3 transport aircraft for parachute deployment and recovery as well as logistical re-supply tasks often hundreds of kilometres into hostile territory. The aviators also deployed and recovered our troops by helicopter and fixed wing aircraft and provided a casualty evacuation facility anywhere and at any time. Casualty evacuation under fire was never refused.

The Rhodesian Air Force conducted deep-range photographic sorties for us as far afield as Tanzania, much of it to pinpoint enemy base camps. Recovery on foot by these crews would have been impossible had they gone down. Additionally, they provided close-air-support on pre-emptive attacks on enemy base camps as well as to operational call-signs when needed.

More important, we were all dependent on our aircraft coming in

Rhodesian soldiers stand down after an external raid. (Photo: Author's collection)

– sometimes under heavy fire and in the most extreme conditions – to "hot extract" members of the unit when they got into trouble.

The Rhodesian Air Force set the highest possible professional standards which would be difficult to surpass in any modern-day air force. A map-reading error was almost unheard of and "blue-on-blue contact" unknown. In those days map reading was by the Mark One "eyeball" with no GPS or any other electronic navigational aids to assist the pilot. HALO infiltrations were within a square-kilometre after flying for three hours at 20,000 feet and in the dark.

We were indeed fortunate to have had the services of some outstanding "Blues" in our planning team. In this regard, Group Captain Norman Walsh was one of the best.

He had flown both strike jets and helicopters before joining the air staff, and with his hands-on practical experience and unconventional mindset, he was able to play a sterling role in Special Forces operational planning. He remained current as a helicopter pilot and commanded numerous air operations leading from the front. Norman, who died peacefully in Australia late 2010, went on to command the Rhodesian Air Force.

I believe that this feeling of mutual respect and trust came as a direct result of conducting army forward air control courses in the early days. Army officers flew with pilots on ground-attack sorties and were quickly made aware of the problems that faced pilots,

Chapter 27
Into the bush war with the Rhodesian SAS

Rhodesian twin-barrel provides the SAS and RLI with support during an operation. (Photo: Author's collection)

including that of target identification. The two arms of the military eventually developed a remarkable esprit de corps.

Being familiar with the first name of the Hawker Hunter pilot who was providing you with air support against an enemy barely 100 metres away, was always a great comfort.

A statement made by Rudolph Giuliani, former mayor of New York in his book *Giuliani Leadership,* was simply put: "Surround yourself with outstanding people."

Whether it be a nation's president, the CEO of a company or the commanding officer of the SAS, the rationale is the same: get the selection of the officers and the men right and the remainder just follows.

Commanding C Squadron remains the highlight of my life, but to be honest and without false modesty, if an officer cannot command a unit where he has free and unrestricted access to the finest officers and men that Rhodesia could produce, he has to be pretty useless. Popularity was unfortunately never my forté. In fact, after I was involved in a near-fatal aircraft accident, it was rumoured that I had visibly raised the morale of the men ... until they realised I had survived!

In June 1978, I finally handed over command of the Unit to Major Garth Barrett who had been my second-in-command. Until then, I had had the privilege of command for five-and-a-half years at the height of the Bush War. These were extremely stressful years and when it was over, I needed a change and so did the guys.

Barrett and the squadron, which had now become a regiment, would continue to achieve outstanding success over the next two years until the end of the Rhodesian era.

1 Major Charles M. Lohman, USMC, Major Robert I. MacPherson, USMC: *Rhodesia: Tactical Victory, Strategic Defeat*: Marine Corps Command and Staff College Marine Corps Development and Education Command Quantico, Virginia, June 7, 1983.

CHAPTER TWENTY EIGHT

AIR WING IN AFRICA'S MOUNTAIN KINGDOM

Lesotho is a tough, resilient little nation that more than a century-and-a-half ago stood firm in the face of encroaching Boer settlers moving up from the Cape. Until independence, it was listed on the charts as the British Protectorate of Basutoland.

South Africa found that out to its cost when it sent an expeditionary armoured force into Maseru in 1998. Unplanned and uninvited, the South African Army thought it would be a walkover. It was anything but.

The tiny mountain kingdom waited until the South African armoured column was across its frontier and struck hard. The invading force was handed a tough and unambiguous lesson in retaliatory tactics that came from nowhere. Within hours the South Africans called for a ceasefire and arrangements were made to pull back their forces.

What had begun as a limited military campaign to counter a political coup d'etat, ended days later with a debacle that would probably have done better justice to something out of the pages of Evelyn Waugh. The South African National Defence Force (SANDF) got a bloody nose for its efforts, never mind the casualties, in part, because nobody had bothered with planning, the single most essential ingredient in any kind of military action. Naturally, hubris had much to do with it all.

The Lesotho Defence Force – founded after independence from Britain in 1966 – again reacted with gusto once soon afterwards. This time it sent its army after a group of South African stock thieves that had entered the mountain kingdom from KwaZulu-Natal's Winterton-Bergville area. Armed with modern weapons – including

One of Lesotho's BK-105 helicopters, routinely used in civilian or paramilitary roles in this mountainous southern African country. When the South African Army invaded Lesotho in September 1998, all aircraft stationed at Maseru Airport – including the Air Wing – "took refuge" across the border at Ladybrand Airport in the Free State. (Photo: Dave Atkinson)

Kalashnikovs – the robbers grabbed several hundred head of cattle before heading home.

It was a bad mistake. A Lesotho Army stopper-group was put in place by one of the Air Wing's three all-purpose Bell Textron-412 helicopters and ended up cornering the gang well inside South Africa, about 10 miles from the Lesotho frontier. In the shootout that followed, three of the thieves were killed with the Lesotho Army taking no casualties. At the end of it, all the cattle were driven back across the mountains and home again.

Why didn't the SANDF react? The attack wasn't at all unexpected, especially since the entire area adjacent to South Africa's majestic Drakensberg mountains had seen a spate of stock thefts in recent years. There had also been numerous attacks on local farmers in the area. A reliable police source in Pietermaritzburg, two or three hours by car from where all this went down, replied rather unconvincingly that the SANDF presence in the region was apparently unable (or unwilling) to react "because of other commitments".

Nor was that the end of it. A welter of controversial diplomatic exchanges followed, almost all of it obscurantist. Maseru accused Pretoria of not properly policing its border and, going by the record, they weren't out of line. Curiously, the matter still rests there. It is worth observing that the South African Police Services (SAPS) has

Chapter 28
Air Wing in Africa's mountain kingdom

since upped its helicopter patrols out of Durban in all areas adjacent to the Lesotho border. These days barely a week goes by without SAPS Air Wing Squirrels and BO-105s patrolling the region.

Lesotho is a difficult country in which to move about and the mountains are just part of it. No African country has winters as harsh as the tiny Kingdom of Lesotho, which is one of the reasons why it maintains one of the most efficient helicopter-oriented air wings on the continent. For many of Lesotho's residents – a country with barely 1,000 kilometres of paved roads (it has 29 airports, four with surfaced runways) – winter routinely brings both ice and isolation.

Matters are also not helped by a country that is dreadfully impoverished. Its two million inhabitants rely almost entirely on South Africa to bolster its resources. According to a UN report, about 55 per cent of its people are without work and most of those live below the poverty line.

For much of the year, Maseru depends on its air wing to bring relief. Missions include ferrying supplies to villages cut off by snow, as well as the rescue of travellers in a few of the isolated mountain stretches of road in this Belgium-sized enclave.

Other tasks normally handled by the Air Wing, include the repair and maintenance of communications, radio and TV antennae – many of which are damaged in storms each year – as well as the movement

During the southern hemisphere winter months, temperatures plummet and snow is commonplace. Choppers come into their own in some of the remoter areas, mountain passes especially, where some communities can be isolated for weeks. (Photo: Dave Atkinson).

Dave Atkinson flew helicopter gunships for Robert Mugabe's Zimbabwe Air Force in the Congo. He has since taken over as training officer for the Lesotho Air Wing. (Photo: Author)

of relief crews to areas associated with construction in the US $2 billion Highland Water Project. The Air Wing is also on call for the transport of government ministers and staff around the country's ten administrative districts. In some respects, quite a few of these interior regions would otherwise be inaccessible.

Many of the projects handled for the water project involve heavy-lift items, the crews often resorting to slings strung beneath the choppers. While engineers are still constructing dams – and planners envisage that more will follow – this work goes on. Ultimately the dams will provide South Africa with more than half its water needs.

One of the biggest single projects completed by this tiny band of aviators in the past year was the delivery of several tons of books to just about every school in the country, some of them on the edge of beyond.

According to former South African Air Force pilot Dave Atkinson – the same pilot that piloted French-built Alouette and 412 helicopter gunships for Zimbabwe's President Mugabe in the Congo more than a decade ago – the Lesotho Air Wing used its Bells to airlift roughly a ton of books on each mission. Each flight involved more than 50 landings a day.

By the time it was over, more than 280 Lesotho schools scored handsomely, the entire operation sponsored by UNICEF.

While the 412 helicopter is capable of lifting much heavier cargoes than the Alouette III, altitude limitations at some destinations precluded heavier lifts.

Atkinson's role with the Lesotho Air Wing is on a contract basis as a flying civilian advisor. His job, he stressed, involved nothing military or security related which, he admitted, was a welcome change from what he did before. For years he flew helicopters in

Chapter 28
Air Wing in Africa's mountain kingdom

Isolated village in the mountains cut off by icy weather. (Photo: Author's collection)

South Africa's border wars and in Angola.

Another ongoing project involved the building of a succession of radio relay towers, the idea being to bring Lesotho Radio into every valley in the country. Basically, it involved moving 40 tons of building materials – including steel girders, pylons, cement and the rest – to almost a dozen high points in mountains throughout the country. And when that is all done, there will be another task at hand.

One of the Air Wing's regular jobs is to ferry Lesotho's King Letsie III to gatherings in remote corners of his kingdom. Though the genial, always-smiling monarch prefers to drive his own car, usually a four-by-four sedan, that isn't always possible in some of the more distant outposts, all of which he likes to regularly visit.

The Lesotho Air Wing – commanded during my visit by Brigadier Edward Motanyana – is a compact force with about a dozen rotor and fixed wing machines. These include the three Bells, a pair of Canadian-built 105-LS Superlifters, two Casa 212s (one each Series 300 and 400), a Cessna 182 for training, a Bell 47 and one or two more. The unit has a complement of just over a hundred, of which about a score are pilots, the majority trained by Atkinson and his pilots.

Of all the craft, the most versatile – with its three-hour flying time at a maximum of 120 knots – is the Bell Textron. Since Lesotho is a little more than 300 kilometres across at its broadest, there is no part of the country that cannot be reached during a single mission.

Apart from its transient labour force, the helicopters are obviously the country's most valuable asset. During the 1998 South African armoured invasion, the entire Air Wing was evacuated across the border to Ladybrand Airport. There, in a curious state of affairs that could only take place in Africa, they sat out the duration of ongoing hostilities, never hampered by the South African authorities who were very much aware of their presence or any of the aircraft seized. The "invasion" over, they all returned safely to Maseru.

Interestingly Lesotho's other major attribute, its labour resources, remain problematic. Total remittances from Lesotho nationals working on South African mines in 1990 totalled 67 per cent of the country's GDP. A decade later, this plummeted to a third of the original figure and since then, has diminished still further.

According to Colonel Sam Makoro, a 50-something year-old veteran pilot who was originally trained in Germany in 1979–1980, it is the weather, not politics, that is the Lesotho Air Wing's most formidable adversary. It is also the most unpredictable, he reckons.

"There are times when flying in these mountains can be tough," he told me during one of the flips into the interior where he was at the controls.

He explained that there were two critical periods to watch out for: from July to September – when the wind whips up to a fury up to 80 knots or more and when the turbulence can be bone-cracking – and the southern hemisphere summer months from November to April. In a combination of muggy heat and heavy cloud that routinely bundles across the mountains from the Indian Ocean, Lesotho becomes what some aviators like to term "a thunderstorm factory".

Another of the helicopters used by the Lesotho Air Wing. (Photo: Author's collection)

Chapter 28
Air Wing in Africa's mountain kingdom

Cold weather too, can make things impossible, especially if crews are called out in an emergency and they have to fly blind in snow.

"That's not something we try to avoid," he said, adding that it was not that easy to predict. "Snow is fine if it's not blowing too hard, but sometimes conditions don't allow us to see wind direction: it obscures the grass and bush that we normally use for that purpose," he stated. He intimated that while the government did provide wind socks in the past, these were often stolen by the locals. Still, he and his crews had their own ways of getting past that hurdle, he intimated.

Colonel Makoro is arguably one of the most experienced helicopter pilots in Africa.

A village boy from the remote mountainside village of Mohale's Hoek in the extreme south of the country, he spent a while working as a labourer in several of South African gold mines. Then, having gone back home again, he was chosen for pilot training during his first year in the Lesotho Defence Force, from where he progressed to Russian-built Mi-2s in Libya in 1983. That was followed by a similar stint in Marxist Mozambique. The youthful colonel finally achieved his commercial ratings in Dallas in 1988 and worked in Florida in the US for a time. Further instrumentation training was completed in Texas in 1998.

Lesotho first acquired helicopters in 1979. It is notable that over the years, the Air Wing has had comparatively few mishaps. One of the more serious accidents occurred at Mohale Dam in 1993. Explaining circumstances, Colonel Makoro said that the crew was working with a heavy lift near the dam wall that proved more difficult than first thought.

"It was a project that we'd had in the planning stages for a while and which allowed barely a metre clearance from the adjacent cliff face. But a sudden draft swept the chopper sideways about 15 metres and straight into the wall: the helicopter's boom snapped and she went down."

Having lost it rotors, the 412 rolled down the hill and came to a halt just inches short of a precipice. The crew were lucky to get out of it in the end, in part because the Bell is designed to take serious shock, "just as long as you're strapped in, as the instructors kept telling us throughout our training," he quipped.

The second time the Air Wing lost a chopper was when high winds forced one of the helicopters down while on a return flight from the interior to Maseru during a particularly nasty storm in January 1998. There have been others since, most involving work on dam construction.

At the time of Al Venter's visit to Lesotho, he was hosted by the then head of the Lesotho Air Wing, Colonel Sam Makoro. Originally chosen for pilot training in the Lesotho Defence Force, he progressed to Mi-2s in Libya in 1983, followed by a similar stint in Mozambique and finally Germany. Today he sits at the head the country's miniscule Air Wing. (Photo: Author's collection)

Atkinson has also had to cope with a new set of conditions after flying for decades in the more passive tropics of Central Africa. That is essential, he says, because so much of the terrain in which he operates lies at altitudes in excess of 10,000 feet. In weather that can turn nasty in a moment, it didn't take Atkinson long to learn that in Lesotho, there is nothing that is taken for granted.

"It's certainly one of the best flying jobs anywhere, but it needs a measure of skill not encountered in a hellova lot of other places." By comparison, he reckons, Angola, the Congo and Zimbabwe were a breeze. "Here, in the mountains," he added, "you're always on the edge." But it helps to be involved with a bunch of professionals, he said confidently.

"The work is tough, it can sometimes be difficult, it is *always* demanding and invigorating, but then that's what I'm here for."

Does he enjoy his posting? "Double-Dave" Atkinson's reaction was unequivocal. For a start, he and his wife Jenny slotted easily into life in Maseru, though she increasingly needs to make time for the family in Johannesburg. On arrival, the Air Wing provided them with a comfortable house in Maseru and it's been that way for the duration.

An old hand at flying around Africa, the old warhorse believes he might finally have found a permanent home.

LIST OF ABBREVIATIONS USED IN THIS BOOK

AFO: Early African liberation group
AGL: Above ground level
ANC: African National Congress also National Congolese Army
AO: Area of Operations
AP mines: Anti-personnel landmines
APC: Armoured personnel carrier
BDF: Botswana Defence Force
BIAP: Baghdad International Airport
BMP: Soviet/Russian armoured personnel carrier – BMP-2 or BMP-3
BMPs or BTRs: Eastern Bloc armoured personnel carriers
CAR: Central African Republic
CIA: Central Intelligence Agency
CIDEV: Mine clearing operation
CIO: Central Intelligence Office
CMAO: Central Mine Action Office
CNN: United States-based international news service
CP: Command Post
CRS: Congressional Research Service
CSI: Chief of Staff Intelligence, an SADF appointment
CSM: Company sergeant major
CUF: *Companhia Uniao Fabril:* Colonial Portuguese firm
DRA officers: Afghan officers during the Soviet occupation
DshKa: 12.7 mm Soviet anti-aircraft machine gun
EOD: Explosive ordnance disposal
ERE: Extra regimentally employed
EU: European Union
FAC: Forward Air Control
FAPA: Angolan Air Force
FAPLA: *Forcas Armadas Popular de Libertação de Angola:* People's Armed Forces for Liberation of Angola
FLING: *Frente de Luta pela Independência Nacional da Guiné:* Front for the National Independence of Guinea

FLN: *Front de Libération Nationale:* Algerian National Liberation Front

FN: Belgium's Fabrique Nationale 7.62 mm rifle, standard issue in the SADF until replaced by the R-4, a variation of the Israeli Galil in .223 calibre

FOB: Forward Operating Bases

FOB to the PRT: Forward Operating Base to the Provincial Reconstruction Team: (Afghanistan)

FPLN: *Frente Patriotica de Libertação Nacionale:* Portuguese resistance group

FRELIMO: *Frente de Libertação de Moçambique:* Mozambique Liberation Front

GSS: General Security Service (Israel)

HALO: High Altitude Low Opening (parachute jump)

IAEA: International Atomic Energy Agency

IDF: Israeli Defense Force

IEDs: Improvised Explosive Devices

IMC: Instrument Meteorological Conditions

INAROE: Removal of Obstacles and Explosives

IPTS: Parachute Training School

ISIS: Washington-based Institute for Science and International Security

KIA: Killed in action

LMG: Light machine gun

LZ: Landing zone

MAGs: Acronymn for GPMG or automatic rifle magazines

Manpads: Shoulder-fired, anti-aircraft missile – Stinger, SAM 7(Strela), SAM-14 etc

MBE: Member of the Order of the British Empire

MBRL: Multi-barrelled rocket launcher

MBT: Main battle tank

MEDDS: Mechem Explosive and Drug Detection System

MiG: Soviet/Russian Mikoyan fighter aircraft – i.e. MiG-23 or MiG-29

MINARS: Ministry for Social Reintegration and Assistance

MPLA: *Movimento Popular de Libertação de Angola:* Popular Movement for the Liberation of Angola

NATO: National Atlantic Treaty Organisation

NCA: National Congolese Army

NCO: Non-commissioned officer

NKVD: The [Soviet] People's Commissariat for Internal Affairs: Early communist secret police

NOTAMs: Notice to Airmen

NVGs: Night vision goggles
NYPD: New York Police Department
OC: Officer commanding
OGL: Observer Group Lebanon – A United Nations military entity
OIC: Officer in charge (US Military)
OP: Observation post
PAIGC: *Partido Africano de Independencia da Guiné e Cabo Verde:* Liberation group in Guiné-Bissau
PATU: Police Anti-Terrorist Unit (Rhodesian security forces)
PBS: Public Broadcasting System (United States)
PED: Parachute Evaluation Detachment
PKM: Russian equivalent to NATO's GPMG (general purpose machine gun)
PMA-2: Anti-personnel landmine
PPT: *Partie Progressiste Tchadien*
PROM-1: Yugoslav anti-personnel mine (bouncing)
PRT: Provincial Reconstruction Team – Afghanistan
PSC: Private Security Company
RAAC: Royal Australian Armoured Corps
RAR: Rhodesian African Rifles
RENAMO: The Mozambican National Resistance Movement
Rhodesian SAS: Rhodesian Special Air Service
RLI: Rhodesian Light Infantry
RONCO: American company involved in mine and UXO clearing
RPD: Soviet/Russian general-purpose machine gun
RPG: Rocket-propelled grenade, usually RPG-7
RPK: Heavy-barrelled AK-47
RPV: Remote-piloted vehicles
RSM: Regimental sergeant major
RTU: Return to unit
RUF: Revolutionary United Front (rebel group in Sierra Leone)
RV: Contact point, or rendezvous
SADF: South African Defence Force (apartheid era)
SAM: Supersonic anti-aircraft missile
SAM-7s: Name for first-generation hand-held SAM missile (Soviet)
SANDF: South African National Defence Force (post-apartheid)
SAP: South African Police (apartheid era police force)

SAPS: South African Police Services (post-apartheid)
SF: Special Forces
SIPRI: Stockholm International Peace Research Institute
SLA: South Lebanese Army
SOP: Standard operating procedure
SP: Security Police
SWAPO: South West Africa People's Organisation
TCN: Transport Control Number; Tactical Component Network
UCAH: UN Humanitarian Assistance Coordination Unit (Angola)
UN: United Nations
UNAVEM: United Nations Angolan Verification Mission
UNICEF: United Nations International Children's Emergency Fund
UNIFIL: United Nations Interim Force in Lebanon
UNITA: *União Nacional para a Independência Total de Angola:* National Union for the Total Independence of Angola (Dr Jonas Savimbi)
UNMIK: United Nations Interim Administration Mission in Kosovo
UNTAG: United Nations Transitional Assistance Group
UNTSO: United Nations Truce Supervision Organisation (Middle East)
USAID: United States Agency for International Development
UXO: Unexploded Ordnance
VFR: Visual Flight Rules
VHF: Very high frequency
WHO: World Health Organisation
ZANLA: Zimbabwe African National Liberation Army
ZANU: Zimbabwe African National Union – Rhodesian guerrilla group
ZAPU-ZANU: Zimbabwe political and guerrilla alliance
ZIPRA: Zimbabwe People's Revolutionary Army

ACKNOWLEDGEMENTS

Having covered what us hacks like to call the "Africa Beat" for almost half a century, the effort of putting together another military title should have been a breeze. It was anything but. There have been a lot of changes in Africa and the Middle East in the past quarter-century and, as we go to press, a lot more ructions are taking place.

In the interim, apartheid was relegated to the history books, as were some of the old tyrants who always made for good copy; forever, one would hope. That iniquitous bunch included tyrants like "Emperor" Jean-Bedel Bokassa who would punish children for "disobeying instructions" by cutting off their ears. There was also his good friend, the pompous Ugandan buffoon who called himself Idi Amin Dada. This was the same person who showed Robert Mugabe how to destroy a proud and economically viable African nation.

Others included "Field Marshal" John Okello, who disappeared almost without a trace after fomenting a bloody revolt on beautiful Zanzibar Island. That little episode was eventually put down by a Royal Navy and Royal Marine task force, but not before 5,000 people of Arab origin were slaughtered. Peter Younghusband covered that peasant revolt for the London *Daily Mail* and he tells us a bit about it in Chapter 6. What he doesn't disclose is that Okello was last spotted selling fish in the vicinity of the Dar es Salaam harbour. There are a host of other miscreants who had their 15 minutes of ignominy, almost always with disastrous consequences. Looking at recent developments, the carnage is not yet over.

In order to get all those happenstances between these covers, I needed an awful lot of help, much of it from fellow contributors already named. The additional list, below, is as detailed as I am able to recall, and if I have left out anybody, apologies are warranted and appropriate corrections will be made in future editions.

Among those who were involved with the book from the start was Madelon Venter, who was called in at very short notice to edit the book in a record 11 days. My old pal and diving buddy Jerry Buirski gave the manuscript a final once-over and, as with Madelon, his contribution was invaluable. Not many people are aware that by the time Jerry had left school – and here we are going back a few years – he had read more than a thousand books. These days he is into scripting screenplays, and pretty good they are too.

Also to be commended is Durban's Bruce Gonneau who, as a

graphic artist of note, put this whole caboodle together; no easy task for a volume of 530 pages. What you have in your hands is totally his creation, and a good job he has done of it.

I am also grateful for the efforts of Manie Troskie, a young troopie when we first met 30 years ago in the rear of a SAAF Puma about to drop us into battle when we hit the big FAPLA military base at Cuamato in southern Angola. That episode forms Chapter 1, arguably the best bit of action in the book. Manie – then a section leader in Charlie Company – was right alongside when things started to happen, as was Theo Kluyts, presently in Malawi, another member of that Parabat unit.

These days Manie is the moving force behind keeping many of the *ou manne* in touch and providing succour to those members of the unit in distress. Additionally, he organised Charlie Company's recent 30th Anniversary commemoration of the battle.

Walter Volker deserves a page of his own. His timely services over a period of several years have been invaluable, especially since he was in the process of completing his own three-volume opus on wartime signals units in South Africa. So, too, with Hannes Wessels, who provided a bunch of photos for his chapter on the Rhodesian Light Infantry, as well as illustrating my own tribute to old friend Ron Reid-Daly, whose survival book I produced while I was still at the helm at Ashanti Publishing. Richard Wood was the source of some of Ron's earlier comments on the RLI Fire Force.

James Mitchell, formerly the books editor on the Johannesburg *Star*, regularly came up trumps with info when I needed it most, often at very short notice.

A word of appreciation is also extended to Sally and Ken Howard, the latter currently holding the elevated position of mayor of Woking. A lovely couple, they took a batch of photo material from Britain to South Africa. Also my old pal Jerome Conley, who provided photos of the American rescue effort in Somalia immediately prior to the First Gulf War (Chapter 7). Jerry has moved on from flying helicopters for the US Marines to become a figure of note at the prestigious Johns Hopkins University. Interestingly, his peregrinations have since taken him into many African states, Eritrea and Somalia included.

Thanks also go to Graham Linscott for giving valuable assistance in several of the chapters, including Aubrey Brooks' Seychelles misadventures with a crazy bunch of mercenaries commanded by Colonel Mike Hoare.

I cannot conclude without a vote of thanks to Nicol Stassen, the man who made this book possible. An adventurous (and successful) publisher, Nicol spotted a gap and, without hesitation, went for it. He has taken a similar approach with two other unrelated titles that deal with the magnificent realm of the underwater, my other "passion".

Finally, there is my lovely Caroline. Much of the work involving this book was done at her delightful 600-year-old home in the Surrey Hills. Her patience and understanding, many times when I was almost totally preoccupied with nothing but my own and other peoples' scribblings – sometimes for days on end – was remarkable. Thank you, darling, even if I have tried to deprive you of your 1,000cc Triumph Bonneville.

Al J. Venter
Surrey Hills,
May, 2011.

INDEX

1 Parachute Battalion 29, 31, 34, 44
2 Commando 361, 362, 365, 370, 372, 377, 379
3 Commando 373, 374, 378
7 Medical Battalion Group 342
22 Special Air Service Regiment 364
27th October Square 149
31 Batalion 32
32 Battalion 32, 34, 36, 42, 43, 44, 76, 79, 161, 163, 165, 168, 171, 249
44 Parachute Brigade 31

A Company 364
Abass, Ali (Captain) 411
Abidjan airport 391
Act, Affected Organisations 354
Act, Armaments Development and Production 354
Act, Atomic Energy 354
Act, Criminal Law Amendment 354
Act, Defence 354
Act, Gatherings and Demonstrations 354
Act, General Law Amendment 354
Act, National Key Point 354
Act, National Supplies Procurement 354
Act, Official Secrets 354
Act, Riotous Assemblies 354
Act, Terrorism 354
Act, Unlawful Organisations 354
Adams, Mark (Lieutenant) 378
Addis Ababa 147, 289
Afghanistan – conflicts in 157; war in 22
Africa – 34, 54; 180, 184, 196, 203, 205, 217, 225, 226, 228, 253, 258, 259, 274; al-Qaeda training bases 152; arms brokers in 111; coups 1, 92, 104, 256, 258, 345; elephant population 105, 114; ethnic rioting 118, 249; hunting in 92–105; illicit trade in small arms 29, 106, 110, 112–114, 153, 449; liberation wars 259, 266; Portuguese involvement 202, 260, 261, 268, 280, 293; uhuru 225; wildlife in 93, 194
Africa's killing fields 389, 401

African leaders – Amin, Idi 8, 344, 453; Bokassa, Emperor 344; Khama, Seretse (Sir) 344; Nkrumah "Osajyefo" Kwame (President) 14, 229, 273, 285, 294, 344; Sese Seko, Mobutu 256, 249, 344, 388, 389
African National Congress (ANC) 32, 107, 186, 228, 340, 344–345, 348, 350
African Sunsets 92, 99, 105
African Union Mission in Somalia (AMISON) 150
Afrikanerdom 228
Agric-Alert alarm system 102
Aideed, Farrah (General) 137
Aideed, Mohammed 149
Aids 396–397
Ain Zalah 137
Air India Boeing 707 73–74
Air Wing, Lesotho's 479–487
aircraft – Rugby 142; Thunder 142
AK-47 1, 58, 107, 110, 125, 224, 366, 393, 425, 466,
Al Manaar, Hizbollah broadcast station 411
al-Shabaab 145, 156–158
Aldeamentos 202, 203, 317, 322
Aldo, Guaccio (Colonel) 418
Ali, Tariq 448
Aliwal Shoal 390
Allah
Almal 145, 209, 278, 308
Alouette gunship helicopter 33, 35, 48, 51–54, 192, 193, 222, 235, 237, 239, 272, 338, 362, 367, 377, 466, 470, 482
Alpha Bouncing-Bomb 376
Alphonse (Lieutenant) 304, 305, 311
al-Qaeda 19, 145, 147, 150–153, 156–158, 428
al-Shabaab militants 158
Alshadax 112
Alves, Vitor (Captain) 268
Al-Zahawiri, Ayman 151
American Embassy (US Embassy) – in Baghdad 427; – in Freetown 397; – in Somalia 17, 138, 139, 140; – in Tanzania 147

494

American forces 181, 262
American Peace Corps volunteers 283, 400
American Silver Star 235
Amin, Idi *see* African leaders
Amman 432
Amphibious Group Two 137
Ancient Order of Froth Blowers, the 66, 68, 70
Anderson, Rob 37
Angola – African soldiers in 290; after independence 261; anti-Portuguese rebellions 259; conflict in 32, 33, 326, 328; helicopter formations 330, 334; Luanda 80, 162, 260, 265, 267, 327, 329, 332, 333, 396, 455; Marxist-oriented MPLA 261; Nova Lisboa 267; Sá da Bandeira 267; Silva Porto 267; South Africa's cross-border operations in 326; trade and exports 287; United Nations peacekeeping troops 420; war in 20, 29, 80, 269, 292, 356, 381; withdrawal of forces (1976) 357
Angolan Air Force 16, 28, 168, 326, 327, 329–331, 333, 334
Angolan Army 34, 35, 42, 80, 159, 327
Angolan captives 46
Angolan civil war (1975) 356
Aning, Emmanuel Kwesi 112
anti-personnel mines 205, 241, 275, 288, 294
anti-tank mines 20, 381, 383
Apapa 387, 400
apartheid 77, 186, 228, 249, 269, 328, 339, 342, 343, 344, 455
Arab – leaders 402; terrorist attack 18; hostilities 426
Arabian Peninsula 153, 155
Argus Africa News Service 1, 3, 8, 387
arms markets – Arjantin 156; Balaara Market 156; Elasha 156; Huriwa 156; Karaan 156; Medina 156; Suuq Ba'ad 156
Arms Sales Monitoring Project 110
arms shipments – Aden, Omar Hashi 155; La Spezia 154; Leghorn 154; Ravenna 154;
arms trafficking – Karaan 154, 156; Somalia 110, 111
Asia 266, 269, 340, 364, 393, 457, 464

Associated Press 135, 339
Atkinson, Dave *also* "Double-Dave" (pilot) 482–483, 486
Atlantic Ocean 166, 266, 285, 295, 323, 397, 445
Aviatrend 115, 116

Bacar, João (Captain) 273–281, 289, 296, 298, 300–310, 313, 315–320, 324
Bagamoyo 120–123, 135
Baganda tribe 9
Baghdad International Airport 423
Balanta – ceremonies 321; tribe 320
Baledogle 143, 146
Balewa, Alhaji Sir Aboubakar Tafewa 385
Balkans – mine-clearing specialists 241, 242, 245; minefields 241, 243–244, 246–247; Todd, Richard (Colonel) 242–244
Banana Sunday 16
Barrel of a Gun 22, 54, 104, 247, 285
Barrell, Sarah 364
Barret, Garth (Major) 471, 478
Basutoland 266, 479
Battle of Como Island, The 271
Battle of Mengo Hill, The 8
BBC 16, 119, 279, 357, 396, 449
Bcau Vallon Bay Hotel 67
Beeston, Richard 135
Beijing 61, 325
Beirut – American University in 211; civil war 206–220; Crusader Castle 219; Lebanon 18, 149, 154, 208–211, 213–214, 217–220, 364, 402–404, 407–421, 451; Sidon 214, 219; Tyre 218, 219, 403, 406, 416
Beirut Airport 206
Beit Bridge 97, 103, 357
Beka'a Valley 214, 408
Belgian Congo 1, 2, 259
Belgium 3, 405, 451
Bell, Bill 433–434
Bell Textron helicopter 480, 483
Ben Taleb, Gazi 444
Berlin Wall 33
Biafra 1, 294, 298, 387, 388

Biafra – civil war 385
Biddle, Keith 449
Bierman, John (editor) 128, 130, 133
Bigene 311
Bin Laden, Osama 150, 151, 152
Bint Jubayl 404, 412, 413
Birao 104
Bishop, James (US Ambassador) 138, 139, 143
Bissalanca Airport 280, 296, 318
Bissassema 296, 300, 305
Blaauw, Jan (Colonel) 235, 239, 240
Blaauw, Johan (Captain) 41–43, 48, 53
Black Hawk Down 146, 150
Black units – *Comandos Africanos* 263, 311, 317; *Fuzileiros Especiais Africanos* 263
Black, Andrew 154, 158
BlackWater 423, 426
Blood Diamond 21
"Bokkie" 255, 446
Boltman, Jannie 465
Border War 32, 43, 49, 97, 150, 221, 318, 339–359, 483
Botha, Helena 227
Botha, P.W. 357
Botha, Pik 227, 228
Botswana 14, 78, 81–82, 85–91, 93, 266, 328, 344
"Bouncing Betty" 275
Bout, Viktor (Russian) 111, 154
Bowan, Mark (author) 146
Boy Scouts 146
Brand, Richard 373, 375
Breytenbach, Cloete 269
Breytenbach, Jan (Colonel) 31, 159, 237, 239, 267, 461
Bridgland, Fred 348
Brigade of Guards 363
Brink, Danie (Sergeant) 30
Britain's Consolidated African Selection Trust 454
Britain's Jane's Information Group 99
British Ministry of Defence 185
British Special Air Service 31, 161, 457

British VSO 400
Bronze Cross of Rhodesia 166
Buba 289, 303, 323
Buganda Kingdom 8
Bukavu 5
Burkina Faso 111
Bush War in Rhodesia 166
Bush, George (President) 138
Bushmen 32, 34

C (Rhodesian) Squadron SAS 457–461, 464–465, 468, 472
Cabral, Amilcar 262, 286, 287, 289, 302, 306
Cabral, Luis 283, 287
Caetano, Marcelo (Prime Minister) 289
Cagnoni, Romano 388
Cahama 171, 173
Cahora Bassa hydroelectric dam 270
Calvert, Michael (Brigadier) 457
Cameroons 92, 391, 393
Camp Victory 437
Canada 19, 262, 405
Cann, John (Captain) 264
Cape Canaveral 285
Cape, the 311, 479
Cape Times 348, 350, 352, 354
Cape Town 15, 38, 75, 117, 206, 227, 347, 348, 349, 350, 351, 352, 354
Caprivi 231, 233, 328, 329, 331
Caprivi African National Union 228
Caprivi Strip 327, 355
Cardoza, Oscar 203
Carey, Barney 60, 61, 72
Carlson, Paul (Dr) 3, 4
Casamance Province 394
Cassinga 31
Cassinga – assault on 164
Casspir 150
Catholic Church 171
cattle – in Kosovo 246; in Lesotho 480; in Rhodesia 94; Pokot rustlers 114
Central Africa 2, 110, 114, 291, 394, 486
Central African Republic (CAR) 14, 93, 104, 105, 266, 344

Central Intelligence Agency (CIA) 22, 404, 409, 135
Centre Nationale de Documentation (CND) 388
Centrex (Polish company) 154
Cessna 14, 123, 234, 467, 483
Chad 258, 266, 365, 393
Charlie Company – in Angola 29–55, 383; parabats 383
Chechnya 153, 158, 252
Chianti 92
Chimoio massacre *see* Operation Dingo
Chimoio or Vila de Manica 369–371, 378, 379, 460
Chinese communist guerrillas 187
Chiredzi 382
Chirundu Bridge 465
Churchill, Winston (Prime Minister) 283
Coalition Forces – in Iraq 137, 407
Cock, Chris (author) 362
Cockerill Barracks 250
Coelho, João Paulo Borges 296
Coey, John 365
Cold War 143, 163, 261, 343, 345, 346
Coloured: A Profile of Two Million South Africans 240
Comandos Africanos 311, 317, 363
Commander Superhero 250
Commonwealth 164, 454
communism – fighting 233, 364; fall of 32
Community Hunting Zones 104
Como Island 271, 282, 285
Comores Archipelago 187
Conakry (Republic of Guinea) 280, 283, 285, 286, 290, 315, 381, 455
Congo 1, 3, 5, 6, 62, 72, 104, 123, 170, 249, 250, 258, 259, 260, 267, 287, 304, 307, 327, 388, 391, 482, 486
Congo Mercenary 57, 63
Congo River 256
Congo-Brazzaville 14, 226
Congolese prison 396
Conley, Bob 135
Coom, Tony 378

Cops: Cheating Death 20, 383, 425
Coral Strand 67
Côte d'Azur 417
Coutinho, António Alva Rosa (Admiral) *see* "Red Admiral, the"
Coventry, Dudley (Major) 461, 465, 471
Cranborne Barracks 459
Creoles 65
Croatia 20, 154, 241–245, 247, 382; army 243
Croukamp, Dennis (company sergeant major) 166, 170, 173, 178
Cuamato 29–35, 39, 42–46, 383; attack 36, 48–52, 54; debacle 35; Portuguese colonial structures in 44
Cuba – 61, 262, 274, 288; advisers 263; expeditiary force 356; "made in" 178; training in 162; troops 80, 168, 249, 326
Cuito Cuanavale 80, 327, 329, 334, 335
Cumming, Arthur 97–100, 103
Cumming, Sandy 100, 102, 103
Cuzombo Panhandle 327
Cyprus 18, 154, 214, 364; conflict 79

D Squadron 461
Da Gama, Vasco 311
Daily Mail 15, 16, 117, 121, 123, 128, 130, 133, 348
Daily Mirror 16
Daily Express 122, 123
Dakar 226, 280, 283, 286, 395, 443
Dalglish, Ken 63
Dar es Salaam 118–122, 145, 229, 231, 234, 262, 345
Davidson, Basil 263, 292
Davis, Richard 20, 382
Dawson's Field 19
D'Eath, George 349
De Beer, Jan (Corporal) 365, 367
De Bruin, Tony 459
De Carvalho, Otelo Saraiva (Captain) 268, 292, 294, 295
De Klerk, F.W. (President) 344
De Spínola, Antonio (General) 268, 282, 284, 292, 293

497

Debray, Regis 263
Democratic Republic of Congo (DRC) 113
Denard, Bob 187
Dennison, André 295, 364, 380
Detroit 19, 383
Diego Garcia 285
Dillon, P.J. (Brigadier) 235, 236
Directorate for Covert Collection 342
Directorate for Special Tasks 342
Directorate of Military Intelligence's Civil Cooperation Bureau 342
Directorate of Public Relations 342
Dolinchek, Martin 69
Donaldson-Selby, John (Captain) 462
Donovan, John 97, 101, 357
Doran, Johan (New Zealand reserve officer) 406
Doss, Robert 137
Drakensberg Mountains 107, 480
Druze – leader 209; people 211; soldiers 211
DshKA anti-aircraft gun 23, 58, 59, 360, 466
Du Plessis, J.C. (Lieutenant) 36
Dukes, Charlie 67
"Dum-Dum" bullet 110
"Dum-Dum" Dumisane 110
Duncan, Elizabeth Murial 446
Durban – 61, 72, 73, 102, 110, 443, 481; Press Club 63; Riviera Hotel 63

Eastern Bloc nations 221
"Echo Road" 416
Economist 447
Egypt 3, 110, 158, 231, 265, 274, 402
Egypt – government 409; military training 228; president 147
El Aabboudiye 218
El Maamariye 218
El Salvador 391
El Wak 8, 152
Elizabethville *see* Lubumbashi
Ellis, Neall 181, 248–257, 381, 384, 442, 443, 446, 453
Els, Paul 221, 223, 240

Emofauna 104
encephalitis 396, 447
England, Roger 59, 67
Entebbe – 25; international airport 401
Eritrean militaries 154
Estado Novo 267
Europe 1, 8, 9, 10, 104, 205, 219, 225, 226, 229, 261, 262, 264, 265, 266, 272, 277, 287, 293, 295, 364, 391, 393, 400, 451
Europe – Eastern 80, 224, 244, 262; Western 157, 183, 260
European – clients 93; colonial power 282; companies 456; network 154, 396; parliament 268; population 105, 469, 470; soldiers 4; Special Air Service Squadron 458; Union 399
Everson, Chris (cameraman) 23
Executive Outcomes 16, 21, 75, 79, 249, 253, 254, 331, 440, 449, 452, 456
explorers – Burton 118; Speke 118; Stanley 118

Far East Volunteer Group, The *see* Malayan Scouts
farangi (foreigners) 146
Federation of American Scientists in Washington 110
Ferreira, Deon (Commandant) 31, 34, 38, 42, 43, 45, 49, 51
Ferreira, Manuel 281
Ferreira, Piet (Warrant Officer) 236
Fire Force 188, 195, 197–201, 361, 365, 371, 471
Fireforce 362
First World – 251; military force 51; nations 255
Fisk, Robert (author) 209
Fleet Street 5, 8, 123, 136
FLING – 286, 287; attacks 289
foreign correspondents 14, 117, 123, 135, 280, 348
Forsyth, Freddie 388
Fort Roçadas 169
Four One Alpha 409
francophonie 395
Freetown – 180, 181, 182, 183, 249, 250,

254, 255, 257, 395, 396, 397, 399; airports (Lungi 255, 446, 450; Hastings 450); Annie Walsh Girls School 445; Creole 318; diamonds 439–456; Foulah Town 443; Fourah Bay College 445; harbour 248; Harford School for Girls 445; health problems 447; Kenema Centre 447; Paddy's Bar 248; Paddy's Pig 442; Pirate Bay 248; Revolutionary United Front in 440; suburbs 254, 441; Tower Hill 446
FRELIMO 202, 204, 205, 270, 370
French Foreign Legion 104, 362, 462
French Indo-China – French troops in 318
Fritz, Johan 72
Fulacunda 289, 303, 323
Futa-Fula – officer 279, 307, 317, 318, 320; tribe 275

Gabon 226, 266, 391
Gambia 226, 393
Gandhi, Mahatma 273
Gates, The 190–193
Gaz ammunition trucks 48
G-Car (Gun-Car) 362
Geba River 321
Gedo region 7
Geldenhuys, Jannie (General) 42, 43, 49
Gellhorn, Martha 26
Gemayel, Bashir (President) 209
 Geneva Convention 110, 383
German Army 198
Geyser, Henrie 348
Ghana 14, 21, 112, 113, 229, 231, 266, 285, 344, 391, 455
Giap (General) 306
Gilmore, Graham 159
Giuliani Leadership 477
Giuliani, Rudolph 477
Goksell, Timur 417, 419
Gold Coast 266
Gold Order of the Tower and the Sword 279
Graham, Mike 471
Grasselli, Giorgio 92–94, 103, 105
Grasselli, Liliana 103, 105

Green Line 207, 212
Green Zone 424, 430
Greene, Graham 395
Grey Scouts 161
Griffiths, Harold 374
Grootfontein 165, 224, 226, 231, 233
guerrillas 24 – in Chinese communist 187, Hizbollah 410, 411; in Angola 20, 23; in Freetown 250, 263; Mozambique 202, 203, 205; in Rhodesia 57, 99, 188, 470; PAIGC movement 275, 276, 280, 283–290, 302–304, 310, 315, 322, 323; SWAPO 56, 223, 224, 225; warfare 201, 216, 260, 273, 292, 302, 464
Guevara, Che 223, 258
Guinea-Bissau 273, 275, 277, 279, 280, 286, 288, 293, 295, 296, 303, 306, 307, 310, 319, 322
Gulf of Aden 112, 153, 155, 158
Gulf War I 137, 138, 185, 423
Gulu 389
Gwelo 373, 461

Hague, The 111, 227, 456
Haigh, Phil 377
Hainjeko, Tobias 231
Halliburton 426, 436
Hamitic nomads 7
Hamowayo, James 231
Hariri, Rafiq (Prime Minister) 209
Harper's Bazaar 9
Hawker Hunters 372
Hawthorne, Peter 348
Heaney Junction 360
Heard, Tony 350, 353
Heidemann, Gerd 290
Heitman, Helmoed-Romer 348
Hemingway, Ernest (author) 1, 26, 348
Hennig, George "Org" (Rifleman) 39
Higgins, William R (Colonel) 401
Highland Water Project 482
"Highway to Hell, The" 270
Hitchcock, Bob 348
Hizbollah – 208, 214, 215, 218, 220, 402–421; air attacks on 408; ambushes – Bani

Hayyan 407; – Houele 407; – Markabe 407; radio station in Beirut 213, 411; headquarters in Beirut (Harek Horeik) 213; training grounds 218; Party of God 402, 403; prisoners 403; suicide bombers 407
"Hizbollah Highway" see Wadi Salaq 407
HMS Owen 133, 134
Hoagland, Jim 290, 321
Hoare, Mike (Colonel) 57–74
Hobbesian anarchy 153
Holliday, Tony 348
Holy Land 402, 417
"homelands" 343
Hong Kong 78, 393
Honoris Crux decoration 49, 54
Horn of Africa 7, 112, 145, 147
Hotel Victoria 3
Huisgenoot 387
Human Rights Watch 253
Hussein, Hamama Ashad 411
Hussein, Saddam 144, 137, 411
Huyser, "Bossie" Piet Bosman (Brigadier) 49

Ibn Khaldoon 137
Ikeja Airport 385, 387
Ikorodu Road (Lagos) 385
illegal diamond dealings – by Nigerian troops 155, 255; in Freetown 444, 450, 451
illicit small arms 106, 110, 112–114, 153, 449
Imams 145, 213
Impala jet 43, 331, 333, 334, 338
"Incredibles, The" 369
India – 150, 258, 311, 428; expats 211; Air India jet – 73, 74
Indian Ocean 61, 64, 65, 117, 139, 153, 157, 256, 285, 485
Indians 65
Indonesia (West Irian) 265, 266, 325
influx control 343
Injun country 160
Inkatha 107
Institute for Security Studies 110

Institute of Chartered Shipbrokers (Baltic Exhange, London) 225
International Court of Justice 111, 227, 456
International Herald Tribune 349
international sanctions 346
International Security Assistance Force 181
Ipangelwa, Agape 222
Iran – 157, 438; London Embassy in 250; mullahs 145; Pasdaran 403; weapons 56, 215, 312, 410
Iraq – 39, 79, 91, 137, 157, 341; Greg Lovett in 422–438; Kurds 151; minefields 185; Operation Desert Storm 137; Police 436; security companies in 423–429; vessels 137; withdrawal from Kuwait 138
Iron Curtain 229, 263; war in 141, 145, 151, 407
Islamic – faith 211; Group, The 147
Israeli Defence Force (IDF) 163, 211, 405
Israeli General Security Service (GSS) 409
Israeli – invasion – Operation Grapes of Wrath 405, 407, 416; passenger aircraft 17; Special Forces group 218
Italian – campaign 371; Mafia 154
Ivory Coast, the – 21, 76, 226, 258, 266, 287, 391, 393, 395; rebel group 113; shipment of small-arms ammunition 115

Ja-Toivo, Herman 234
Jamba 326, 327, 330, 331, 347
Jamestown Foundation 153, 158
Jane's Defence Weekly 180
Jane's International Defence Review 99
Jensen, Holger 339
JFK (airport) 400
Jihad 214
Jimenez (Lieutenant) 296, 298–300, 303, 305, 308, 311, 317–319
Johannesburg 3, 18, 32, 66, 93, 104, 110, 119, 184, 186, 249, 265, 317, 348, 351, 352, 387, 393, 394, 399, 443, 487
Jordan 19
Joubert, Elsa (author) 387
Jounieh 214–217

Jumblat, Kamal 209
Juwad, Muhammed Talar 411

Kabakas 8
Kabbah, Ahmed Tejan 182
Kabul 22, 148
Kailahun 451
Kalashnikov 18, 54, 57, 58, 70, 104, 106, 153, 156, 393, 480
Kampala 8, 25, 389
Kamurasi, George (King) 9
Kandeya Tribal Trust Land 365
Kanyemba – 190; base 191, 193; police 190
Karume, Abeid 136
Katanga – 3,5; soldiers 104; copper mine 388
Katatura township 229
Katima Mulilo 355
Katzke, Heinz (Captain) 35, 39, 50, 51, 53, 54
Kavango River 328, 350
Kazungula 327
Kenealy, Henry 397, 399
Kenya – 67, 114, 139, 145, 147, 152, 260, 265, 307, 393, 454; Islamic community 150; Lake Naivasha 26; Mau Mau insurrection 197, 259, 273; Northern Frontier District 4, 6, 7; troops 68
Kenyatta, Jomo "Mzee" (President) 6, 7, 8
Kevlar 21, 241, 383
Khartoum 259
Khomeini, Ayatollah 213, 403
Kibrit 460
Kiganda 9
Kilimanjaro 298
King Freddie 8, 9
Kingdom of Lesotho *see* Lesotho
Kinshasa – 389, 399, 455; British Embassy in 388
Kintu, Kato (King) 9
Kisangani *see* Stanleyville
Kismayu, port of 152, 155
Kissi penny 451
Kissinger, Henry 356, 358

Kitwe 397
Kivu, Lake 5
Kivu Province 5
Klepper canoes 465, 466, 470
Klomp, Colonel (doctor) 239
Klootwyk, Ares 388
Kluyts, Theo 29, 43, 44
knobkieries 149, 229
Koevoet 240, 249
Kolwezi 104
Kosovo – 241, 422, 430, 432, 434; Base Defence Operations Centre 432; Camp Bondsteele 431; Liberation Army 243; minefields 241–242, 244, 245, 247; police 432
Koundara – 283, 284; to Kantika 285
Kunene River 32, 159, 169, 171, 221
Kuwait 138, 144, 185
KwaZulu-Natal 106, 107, 479

Ladybrand Airport 480, 484
Lake Alexander 372, 374
Lake Kariba 196
Lake Tanganyika 25, 123
Lake Victoria 8, 401
Lamb, Guy 110, 113
Lambon, Tim 24
Lamouline, Robert (Colonel) 4
Land at the End of the Earth or *Terras do Fim do Mundo* 327
landmines, anti-tank 42
Larnaca Airport 18
Las Anod 152
Lassa fever 447
Latvia 154
Le Grange, Louis 345
League of Nations 33, 229, 338
Lebanese – Army 206, 207, 214, 217, 218, 405, 410, 412; diamond consortiums 453
Lebanon – 18, 208, 210, 213–219, 364, 452, 481; arms trafficking 154; Israeli invasion of 149; South 402–421; Syrian presence 209; travel ban 214; war in 19, 149, 208, 451;
Lehmann, Peter Hannes 290

Lesotho – 266, 479, 483, 485, 486; Air Wing 482–486; Defence Force 479, 480, 485, 486; King Letsie III 483; labour resources 484; radio 483
Lewis, Roy (British historian) 447, 451
Liberia 14, 104, 111, 113, 115, 116, 155, 183, 226, 304, 391, 392, 393, 394, 441
Libya 14, 154, 162, 228, 274, 485
Life 9
Limpopo 63, 97, 400, 428
Lisbon – 184, 282, 283, 286, 289, 292, 293, 295, 310, 324; in Africa 273–274; in Angola 226, 260, 261–272; *aldeamentos* programme 202, 203, 290, 317, 322; exit from Africa 260, 310; fighters 304; "replenishing posts" 272
Litani River 413, 416
Little, Allan 182, 183
Llewellyn Barracks 360
Lomba River 335
London – 9, 24, 61, 109, 128, 129, 183, 184, 186, 215, 225, 257, 266, 295, 309, 351, 353, 383, 391, 442, 448; Guinea embassy in 381; influence in Sierra Leone 447, 451, 454
Long Bar at Meikles 185
Lopes, Baptista (Colonel) 316, 317, 320
Lords Resistance Army 389
Lovett, Greg 422–438
Luanda 80, 162, 164, 170, 260, 265, 267, 279, 327, 329, 332, 333, 396, 399, 455
Lubumbashi 3, 388

MacDougal, Steven 38, 39
MacKenzie, Robert (Colonel) 38, 39
Madagascar 62, 157
Mahé, island 57, 65, 66, 73
Majdal Zun 412
Makeni 448
Makoro, Sam 484–486
Malawi (Nyasaland) 92, 188, 205, 270
Malawi Rifles 364
Malaya – 102, 196, 201, 202, 265, 288, 293, 345; British in 318; Ron Reid-Daly in 187, 196; SAS Regiment 462, 468
Malayan Emergency 259, 456
Malayan Scouts 457

Mali – 393; small-arms smugglers 112, 113
Malloch, Jack 371, 375
Malaysian Rangers 364
Mancham, James (Jimmy) 61, 67
Mandela, Nelson 32, 145, 216
"Man-Pak" transmitter 303
Manpads 51, 52, 56, 157, 330
Manuel (*Alfares*) 304
Mao dictum 202, 301
Mao Tse-tung 223, 290, 306, 365
Marafano, Fred (Fijian Fred) 248, 453
Margate Airport 109, 112
Marine Medium Helicopter Squadrons (HMM) 137
Marj'Ayoun 11, 208, 412
Marocchino, Giancarlo 154
Marshall, Don 348
Marxism 163, 375
Marxist Republic of Guinea 283
Marxist revolutionaries 64
Maseru 475, 480, 481, 484, 485, 487
Matabele tribe 94
Matetsi (town) 93, 99
Matetsi River 98
Matopo Hills 95, 459
Matusadona Range 192
Mau Mau 197; emergency 201; insurrection in Kenya 259, 273
Mauretania 393
Mauritius 65
Mavinga 327, 331
McAleese, Peter (British mercenary) 30, 31, 37, 45, 47, 48, 76, 164, 166, 383,
McCarthy, Peter (Australian captain) 413, 417
McColl, René 348
McDermid, Angus 16, 17
McGee, Mike (Captain) 35, 49, 50, 51, 54
Mechem 245, 247, 383
"Medevac Missions" 329
Menongue *see* Serpa Pinto
"Merchants of Death" 111
Mexico 112
Michigan 383

Middle East – 99, 206, 214, 219, 258, 262, 382, 391, 393, 402, 413, 415, 421, 433; Airlines 18; culture and customs 432, 452; St Valentine's Day massacre 210; UN presence 137, 138, 406, 420

Midwest Bible Belt 397

military training – Colonel Jan Breytenbach 237; Egypt 228; Nanking Military Academy 228; SWAPO 228, 229, 231

Miller, Robert (*Toronto Globe Mail*) 135

minefields – Angola 20, 172, 382; Balkans 20, 241, 244, 245, 246, 383; Kuwait 185; Mozambique 270; Rhodesia 470

Minter, Errol 458

Minter, William 260

Mirage strike fighters 168

Missionaries – Finns 225

Mitchell, James 32, 51

Mitterrand, Francois (French premier) 389

mobile warfare 292

modern-day slave trade 106

Mogadishu – 7, 17, 137, 401, 138–143, 145–155; International Airport 138, 146, 148, 154, 155

Mohale Dam 485

Mohale's Hoek 485

Mohammad al-Amin Mosque 208

Mombasa 150, 225, 390

Monde, Le 388

Monks, John "Piggy" 122, 123–135, 348

Monks, Noel 122, 348

Monrovia 393

Moorcraft, Paul 21

mopani tree 2, 29, 41

Morocco 21, 262

Moroni Airport 71

Moscow 22, 61, 80, 111, 115, 168, 229, 231, 273, 274, 268, 325, 326, 330

Motanyana, Edward (Brigadier) 483

Movement for the Resistance 66

Mozambique – 24, 147, 184, 188, 189, 201, 202, 203, 263, 264, 265, 267, 269, 271, 283, 288, 298, 304, 346, 366, 369, 485; Air Force 373; guerilla units in 361; hunting in 92–104; illegal arms 107, 110; liberation wars in 259, 260, 261, 266,267, 269; mine-clearing teams in 244, 245; Portuguese army patrols in 203, 205, 292; PAIGC 325; SAS role 78, 457–473; Soviet bases 261; Tite regional headquarters 316, 320; Tete Region 270; trade and exports 287

Mpata Gorge 190

Mpumalanga 107

Mubarak, Hosni (President) 147

Mueda area 205

Mugabe, Robert 76, 77, 78, 91, 163, 200, 328, 371, 372, 380, 396, 453, 460, 462, 482

mujahideen 23, 25

mullahs, the 17, 145

Mungo's 245

Munnion, Chris 16, 17, 348

Musa, Mansa (General) 274

Museveni, Yoweri (President) 9

Muslim groups 145, 421

Nahariya 402, 414, 419

Nairobi 1, 3–7, 15, 119, 128, 133, 145, 146, 147, 150, 152, 157, 265, 396, 399

Namibia 17, 24, 31, 162, 221, 229, 240, 261, 262, 327, 388, 346, 355

Nankudhu, Johannes Otto 223, 224, 234, 237, 239

Napoleonic Wars 65

Naqoura 218, 402, 404, 405, 412, 413, 417, 418, 419

Nasr, Olivia 210

Nasrallah, Hassan "Sayyed" 213

Natal Supreme Court 73

National Congolese Army (ANC) 3, 5

National Intelligence Service (NIS) 342

National Party 227, 228, 341, 344

NATO allies 261

Ndola 459

Neeld, Dennis 135

News Check 387

Newsweek 15, 16, 117, 135, 339, 348

Ngwenya, John 372

Nhongo, Rex 371, 379

Nhongo, Mrs Teuri (Spillblood), 379

Niger Delta 304
Niger River 112
Nigeria 15, 170, 259, 315, 351, 384, 385, 387, 391, 393, 396, 400, 448, 455
Nigeria – Army 155, 385, 388, 443, 447; Calabar area 322
Nimba Mountains 393
"Ninjas" 259
Nivala, Gregg 427
Nkrumah, "Osajyefo" Kwame (President) 14, 229, 285, 294, 344
No. 1 Hunter Squadron 373
No. 1 Military Hospital 31
No. 1 Parachute Battalion 29, 31, 34, 44
No Mean Soldier 76, 383
NorBatt 419
Northern Ireland 78, 79, 106, 364
Northern Rhodesian Copperbelt 3
Norwegian Army 419
Nugent, Jack 135
Nujoma, Sam 162, 221, 229, 231
Nussey, Wilf 351, 387

Oba (chief) 304
Obote, Apollo Milton (President) 8
Observer Group Lebanon 402, 404, 407, 411, 413, 414
Odimbo 233
Okello, Field Marshal 124, 125, 130, 131, 133, 136, 507
Olympia Hotel 146
Olympio, Sylvanus (President) 14
Omani – Arabs 265; soldiers 149, 150
Ombalantu 35, 51, 54
Ongulumbashe 221, 223, 224, 229, 232, 234–236, 238, 239
Ondangua 41, 232
Ondangua Air Force Base 34, 43, 165, 176
Oom Willie se Pad (Uncle Willy's road) 328
Oosterbroek, Ken 349
Op Mar 405, 407, 409
Operation Blouwildebees 221, 240
Operation Daisy 20, 381
Operation Desert Storm 137, 144

Operation Dingo 459
Operation Eastern Exit 137, 139, 144
Operation Grapes of Wrath 405–407, 416
Operation Miracle 458
Operation Protea 161, 162, 165, 382
Operation Restore Hope 11, 144, 145, 151
Operation Savannah 322, 328, 355, 356, 358
Operation Second Congress 326, 327, 338
Operation *Tridente* 271
Operation Vastrap 5 35
Order Group, the 34, 43
Organisation for African Unity 289
Oshakati 34, 48, 49, 159, 172, 232
Oshikango 226, 233
Ouagadougou 396
Ovambo – 33, 162, 223, 225, 226, 227, 228, 232, 233, 235, 236; Commissioner General 232; People's Congress 228
Oxfam 170

Paetzold, W.H.J.F. (Major) 235
PAIGC (*Partido Africano para a Independência da Guiné e Cabo Verde*) – 262, 263, 271, 272, 275, 283, 285, 286–290, 292, 293, 295, 301, 302, 321, 322, 323, 325; guerrillas 275, 279, 303, 306, 309, 310, 315, 316, 324; policy 306, 325
Pakistani has dealers 211; troops 149
"Panzer Group" 198
Parabats 29, 31, 34, 39, 52, 249, 383
Parachute Evaluation Detachment (PED) 457
Parachute Regiment 78, 237, 363, 461
Parachute Training School 475
"Paradak" 201
paratroopers – Belgium 3
paratroopers – British 79, 182, 255
Parker, Dave (Colonel) 473
Pasdaran 403
Pathfinders 31, 159–178, 471
Pearse, Martin 471, 472
Pearson, Mike 36
"penny dreadful" 2

Pentagon 264, 397
Penthouse 391
People's Armed Forces for the Liberation of Angola, the 35
People's Liberation Army of Namibia (PLAN) 33, 161, 221, 229
Persian Gulf 137, 139, 144
Pidjiguiti Docks 286
Pires, Lemos (Lieutenant Colonel) 319
Places des Martyrs 208
Plough, Conway 390
Point Laurie 72
Pokot nomadic cattle herders 114
Police Anti-Terrorist Unit (PATU) 95
Popular Movement for the Liberation of Angola (MPLA) 228, 261, 268, 356
Porch, Douglas (American academic) 264, 274
Portugal – 184, 264, 265, 273, 294; casualties 184; colonies in Africa 167, 260, 261, 264, 278, 280, 282, 286, 287, 316, 324, 451; in Angola 80, 261, 265, 289
Portuguese – Air Force pilots 303; allies 226
Portuguese Armed Forces Movement 282
Portuguese Army 92, 107, 201, 202, 203, 263, 268, 272, 274, 276, 282, 285, 290, 295, 303, 309, 320, 321
Portuguese Communist Party 268
Portuguese Guinea – 184, 201, 267, 268, 269, 273, 278, 299, 303, 304, 318, 325; conflicts in 259, 260, 262, 265, 266, 267, 271, 282–295; counter-attacks 285, 291; guerilla strategy 280, 325; political and economic reforms 293; socialist programme 293
Powell, Graham 390
Pretoria 31, 32, 33, 35, 77, 78, 88, 90, 161, 168, 216, 221, 225, 226, 229, 231, 232, 234, 235, 249, 331, 332, 333, 338, 345, 358, 359, 362, 461, 480
Pretoria Central 239
Prince Henry's navigators 265
Private Eye (British satirical magazine) 10, 136
private military/security companies 249, 425

Pseudo journalists 347, 348
Pseudo Operations 197
Pseudo Operators 197
Public Broadcasting Service 389
Puma helicopters – 30, 31, 33, 35, 38, 45, 46, 48, 49, 51, 332, 333; pilots: Port, Billy 51, 52; Ras, Willem 51; Reynolds, Kevin "Klip" 51
Puren, Jerry 72, 73
Pyongyang 61

Qu'ran 306
Quartel 170
Quesunde festival 322

Rabie, André (Sergeant) 197, 468
Radio Conakry 280
Radio Tanzania 236
Radmore, Des (Colonel) 17
Ramrakha, Priya 1
Rand, Peter (*New York Herald Tribune*) 135
Ras Kamboni island 152
Ratel 20, 161, 171, 172, 381
Rebel movements 110, 157
Recces 32, 42, 79, 164, 172, 223, 237, 269
Reconnaissance Commandos *see* Recces
Reconnaissance Regiments *see* Recces
"Red Admiral, the" 268
Red Sea 112, 152, 384
Rees, Mervyn 348
Reid-Daly, Ron (Uncle Ron) 270, 399, 468, 469; – tribute to 179–205
Republic of Guinea (Conakry) 280, 283, 285, 293
Reuters 119
Revolutionary United Front 111, 181, 248, 440
Reynolds, Kevin "Klip" 51
Rhodesia – 25, 57, 59, 62, 63, 78, 79, 93, 95, 96, 97, 103, 179, 185, 188, 189, 190, 228, 261, 271, 283, 346, 364, 366, 372, 374, 378, 380, 382, 457, 461, 464, 465, 474; Bronze Cross 166; counterinsurgency pattern 201, 473; C Squadron 457–461, 464, 468, 472, 477; Northern Rhodesia 188, 459, 461; Silver

Cross 472; Southern Rhodesia 188, 457, 459, 461
Rhodesia: Tactical Victory, Strategic Defeat 469, 478
Rhodesian African Rifles 201, 364, 472
Rhodesian Air Force 52, 192, 199, 370, 372, 470, 475, 476
Rhodesian Army–bushcraft 194, 365, 467; veterans 24, 63, 72, 164
Rhodesian insurgency war 190
Rhodesian Light Infantry (RLI) 163, 165, 360–380
Rhoodie, Eschel (Dr) 345
Rich, Michael 462
Rich, Peter (Captain) 377, 461, 462, 471, 473
Richards, David (Sir) 179–184, 447
Richards, Ishun 431
Rio Pungue 375
Robinson, Brian 370–375, 379, 457
Rodrigues, Amália 313
Rodrigues, Bethencourt (General) 183–184, 292
Rokel River 455
Rolls-Royce 138, 219
Roosevelt, Eleanor 26
Rosh Haniqra 414, 415, 417
Royal Marines 75, 363
Royal Rhodesian Air Force *see* Rhodesian Air Force
Ruacana 221, 222, 235, 236, 238
Rundu 233, 327, 328, 331, 333, 334, 335
"Ruperts" 462–463
Rushoek, farm 93, 94, 97, 103
Russia 162, 211, 222, 231, 245, 262
Russian – advisers 168, 263, 338; arms dealer 111, 154; helicopter 18, 250, 255, 290, 326–337, 384, 388, 392, 443, 485; Warsaw Pact Allies 274; weapons 18, 173, 174, 315
Russians 68, 111, 169
Rwanda 5, 14, 25; Kagera National Park in 25
Rykaardt, Duncan 401

SABC 20, 352, 389, 455

Sabre fighters 272
Sahara Desert 464
Salazar, Antonio De Oliveira 267, 289, 294
Salisbury *see* Harare
San Franscisco Chronicle 381
Sandline International 254
Sanger, Clyde 135
Sankoh, Foday (Sergeant) 181, 183, 456
"Saturday Night Special" 106
Saudi Arabia 158, 262
Saurimo 16, 21, 452
Savimbi, Jonas 326, 327, 329, 330, 331, 332, 378
Savory, Allan 467
School of Infantry 188, 200, 461; Tracking Wing 468
Schramme, "Black Jack" Jeanne 5
Schroeder, Matt 110, 113
Schulenburg, Chris 195
Schulz, Arnaldo (General) 292, 293
Schweitzer, Albert (Dr) 391
"Secret Seven" 465–466
Sector One Zero 34, 42
Security Police 222
Seso Seko, Mobutu (President) 265, 269, 344, 388, 389
Selous Scouts – 57, 64, 78, 79, 161, 166, 181, 183, 184, 188, 194, 195, 196, 197, 199, 200, 367, 371, 459, 460, 467, 468
Senegal 280, 283, 286, 289, 317, 391, 393, 394, 395
September 11 (9/11) 151
Serpa Pinto 327
Seychelles 256; Archipelago 62, 157; mercenary invasion of 57–74; Reef Hotel 60, 61, 67, 69, 73
Seychelles Affair, The 71, 74
Seychellois Resistance Movement 67
Shangugu 5
Shaqraq 411
Sheikh Mohamed Gelle Kahiye (General) 157
Sheikh Mukhtar Robow Abu Mansur 156
Shi'ite 208, 211, 215, 218, 220, 407, 413

Shifta 4, 6, 7, 8
Shihin 404
Shimon (Israeli captain) 406
Shuuya, Leonard "Castroli" (Major) 222, 233, 234, 235, 236, 237, 239
Siegel, Adam 142
Sierra Leone – 14, 104, 179, 181, 182, 183, 227, 258, 318, 393, 394, 395; Air Wing 181; Army 181, 456; civil war 155, 182, 392, 397; corruption 442; diamond fields 249, 253, 255; economic potential 448; Freetown 439–456; gemstone smuggling 449; illegal diamond dealings by Nigerian troops 155, 255; mines 217; Neall Ellis in 248–257, 381, 384; president 182; UN troops in 393
Sierra Leone's Revolutionary United Front (RUF) 111, 248
Silver Cross of Rhodesia 472
Simba rebels 3, 4
Simms, Bobby 65, 69, 70, 72
Sinoia area 231
Small Arms Survey 112, 113, 116
Smith, Bill 135
Smith, Charles (New Zealander) 411, 412, 414
Smith, Cyrus (Brigadier) 354, 357
Smith, Ian 97, 228, 363, 371, 457, 464
Smithdorff, Mark (pilot) 466
Smuts, Jan (General) 342
socialism 61, 245, 263, 293
Somali – 7, 112, 141, 143, 144, 145, 147; al-Qaeda fighters 145, 152, 157; arms market 155, 156; capital 8, 17, 147; government-backed NFD Liberation Movement 7; piracy 153, 156, 157; Shifta 6, 7, 8; warlords 111, 112, 151, 154
Somalia, French (Djibouti) 7, 384
South Africa – 58, 63, 69, 73, 77, 78, 89, 90, 186, 216, 225, 227, 239, 245, 255, 261, 273, 283, 294, 316, 393, 454, 461, 480, 481; apartheid era 339, 344, 345, 247; Army 479; Border Wars 339–349; crime 107, 109, 113; farm killings 107, minerals in 345; nuclear energy programme 354; reporters in 339, 346, 347, 348, 350, 354, 358, 394; trade union movement 340, 341; white-ruled 33, 273; withdrawal of forces in Angola 357

South African Air Force 31, 33, 159, 165, 168, 169, 221, 326, 327, 329, 381, 482
South African Communist Party 340
South African Defence Force 77, 91, 150, 225, 341
South African Navy 341
South African Police Services (SAPS) 107, 480
South Angola 20, 33, 203, 331, 358
South Lebanese Army (SLA) – prison at El Khiam
South West Africa *see* Namibia
Southeast Asia 184, 187, 258, 267, 282, 302, 322, 325
southern Africa – hunting camps in 93
southern Congo 3, 104
Soviet Union – 8, 285, 345; allies 176, 273, 326; bases in Angola 80, 261; helicopters 22, 315, 326, 329; missiles 290; Navy 315; threat 33; weapons 17, 20, 29, 31, 51, 56, 58, 99, 164, 205, 290, 382
Spectator 148
Ssese Island 9
Staley, Tom 392
Stanleyville (Kisangani) 2, 3
Stanleyville – airport 3; radio 4
"Stalin's Organs" 178
Steenkamp, Willem 339–359, 386
Stirling, David 161
Stern 290
Stevenson, Adlai 27
Steytler, Klaas 387
Stingers 56, 330, 332, 338
Stirling, David (Colonel) 464
Stockholm International Peace Research Institute (SIPIRI) 155
sub-machine guns 96, 236
sub-Saharan Africa 2, 106, 397, 448
Sudan, the 14, 105, 110, 144, 147, 152, 170, 259
Suez 79, 90, 186, 399
Sukhoi fighter-bombers 168
Sullivan, Joseph 207
Sunday Express 15
Sunni 211, 220, 428

Susana 289
Swahili 6, 9, 121, 124, 125, 126, 128, 130
Swan, Jimmy (Corporal) 370, 374, 375, 376, 379
Swanepoel, Theunis (Major) 236, 370, 374, 375, 376, 379
SWAPO – 30, 32, 33, 34, 161, 167, 229, 262, 381, 382; base Ongulumbashe 221, 232, 237; camps 162, double agent Shuuya 239; in South West Africa 233, 234; leadership 221, 223, 229, 235; military training 228, 229, 231; propaganda 171; support of Angolan government 162; veterans 222
Swaziland 66, 69
Syria 18, 214, 218, 403; army 209; secret police 209

Tabancas 305, 322
Tambo, Oliver 350
Tanganyika King's African Rifles 133
Tanzania –14, 61, 118, 145, 147, 204, 224, 262, 266, 372; al-Queda attack 147, 152; Army 57, 67; guerillas 325; president 136; radio 236; Rhodesian SAS 457, 475; SWAPO 162, 228, 231
Target Yankee 159
Task Force Alpha 159, 161
Taylor, Charles 111, 456
Team Victor 404
Team X-ray 404, 405
Team Zulu 404
Tel Aviv 18, 209, 215, 216, 218, 415, 419
Tembue 370, 460
Templer, Gerald (Sir) 293–294
Tete – 92, 204, 205, 269; military hospital in 270; Province 203, 270, 271
The Dogs Of War 248, 388
The Last Domino 20
The Star 32
Theron, Nigel (Lieutenant) 365
Third World – Africa 57, 62, 395, 425, 427; buyers 244, conflict 248, 261, 325
Thornhill Air Base 373
Tickey, tracker 98–99, 103
Time 9, 135, 348

Tite – 275, 279, 280, 289, 296, 298, 303, 309, 310, 313, 319, 320, 322, 324 ; attack by PAIGC 289, 315, 316, 323, 324; Balanta community 322; operational area 296
Togo 14, 307
Tomaz, (*Alfares*) 299, 304, 305, 308, 311, 318–319
Tommasi, Pepe (Corporal) 36, 37
Tonga tribe 98
Toro, Princess Elizabeth of 9; kingdom of 9
Toto 9
Troskie, Manie 38, 47
Truter, "Chunky" 38
Truth and Reconciliation Commission 342
Tsafendas, Dimitri 352, 353
Tugela River 107
Turkish troops 208
Tutu, Desmond (Archbishop) 106
"Twelvers" 211

Uganda – 9, 14, 25, 114, 389, 401; King Kabaka of Buganda 9; Mountains of the Moon 25
uhuru 104, 266, 454
uitlanders (foreigners) 159
Ukrainian – arms dealer Minin, Leonid 115, 116; small-arms ammunition 115, 116
umfaan 107
United Nations (UN) – 79, 111, 148, 255, 310, 322, 402, 404, 415, 421; arms embargo 28, 111, 115, 254; headquarters, Naqoura 218, 402, 404, 417, 419; Israeli relations 406; Mine Action Team 243; mine clearing teams 244, 247; Observor Group Lebanon 411, 413, 414, 415; Operation Restore Hope 144, 145, 151, 154; reports on illegal arms trading 155, 156; sanctions 138; soldiers 154, 255, 257, 393, 395, 406, 407, 416, 420, 421; UNTSO 405, 413
Unilateral Declaration of Independence (UDI) 464
UNITA – 330, 332; command structure 332; guerrilla movement 110, 178, 326, 329, 330; rebel forces 10
United Kingdom Parliamentary Office on Science and Technology

United Nations Truce Supervision Organisation (UNTSO) 405, 413
United Party (Smuts) 342
United Press International 352, 387
United States Marine Corps 402, 469
United States Homeland Security 19
Upper Volta 266, 393
US Naval Institute 143
USS Cole 147
USS Guam 137
USS Manley 133
USS Trenton 137, 144

Valente, Art (Major) 323, 324
Vampire jet 377
Van den Bergh, Hendrik (Lieutenant General) 342
Van der Merwe, "Fingers" 15
Van der Waals, Willem "Kaas" (Brigadier General) 260, 272
Veldhuizen, Captain 159, 174, 175, 176
Verela 289
Verwoerd, Hendrik (Prime Minister) 352
Victoria Island 400
Viet Cong 306
Victoria Cross 49, 275
Victoria Falls 83, 95, 96
Vietnam 16, 33, 44, 184, 204, 230, 242, 258, 260, 264, 267, 274, 280, 288, 339, 359; veterans 76, 163, 362, 364, 365, 430, 434, 470
Viljoen, Hennie (Corporal) 36, 37
Villagio Quattro Chilometri 149
Voortrekkerhoogte Military Hospital 239

Wafa Wafa, camp 196, 197
Walker, Arthur (Lieutenant) 35–54
Walker, Walter (General) 364
Walls, Peter (General) 187, 363, 468, 473
Walsh, Norman (Group Captain) 373, 375, 378, 379, 476
Walters, Major 135
Wankie Game Park 93
War Dog 5, 181

Warren, Charlie 374, 376
Washington 3, 19, 61, 110, 137, 145, 147, 152, 157, 214, 265, 272, 358, 397, 429, 330
Washington Post 290, 321
Welensky, Roy (Sir) 458
Wessels, Hannes "Min Dae" (Sergeant) 36, 37, 360
West Africa 3, 14, 27, 179, 182, 183, 248, 285, 391–395, 399; 442; coastal tribes 304, 305; conflict in 283; disease 442, 447; Ikeja airport 385; peacekeeping debacle 255; small arms 110
West, J.B. 49
Whitehall 182, 254, 255, 257, 260, 453
Wild Geese Club 206, 215
Willemse, Dawid (Lieutenant) 53
Wilson, Grahame (Major) 472
"Winds of Change" 266
Wingate-Grey, Mike (Colonel) 464
Winning, Dough 37
Wise, Don 16
Wood, Richard 197, 205, 364, 380
Woodhouse, John (Colonel) 472
World Bank 244, 246, 254
World Health Organisation (WHO) 447
World War I 225, 265, 338
World War II 3, 10, 25, 178, 179, 181, 183, 204, 242, 261, 265, 270, 316, 338, 371, 375, 462
Wor-Wor boy 250, 253, 255, 257
Wozniak, Stanislav (Major General) 419

Xangongo 32, 34, 35, 49, 159, 162, 168, 169, 171, 178

Yemen 112, 150, 154, 155, 157, 158
Yemeni port of Aden 147
Younghusband, Peter 15, 117, 348
YouTube.com 20

Zagreb 243, 246, 247, 383
Zambezi River 81, 83, 99, 104, 189, 191, 193, 194, 327, 355, 465, 466, 467
Zambezi Valley 94, 191, 270, 318

Zambia 3, 33, 78, 84, 86, 95, 99, 188–191, 224, 231, 233, 234, 240, 270, 327, 328, 361, 388, 397, 399, 457, 462, 465, 466, 467

Zanzibar – 117–136; airport 119; Arab rule 118, 266; British presence in 119, 132, 133, 134, 135; English Club 132–134; revolution (1964) 117; Sultan of 118, 134

ZAPU-ZANU insurgents 318

Zimbabwe – 81, 82, 85, 89, 90, 91, 110, 163, 258, 261, 327, 328, 340, 372, 380, 453, 460, 482, 486; security forces 76, 78

Zimbabwe People's Revolutionary Army (ZIPRA) 99

Zipvel 327

Zulus 107, 149

Zululand 307